Working with People

Second Canadian Edition

Working with People

Interviewing and Assessment Skills for Human Service and Social Work Practice

Louise Harms and Joanna Pierce

OXFORD
UNIVERSITY PRESS

OXFORD
UNIVERSITY PRESS

Oxford University Press is a department of the University of Oxford.
It furthers the University's objective of excellence in research, scholarship,
and education by publishing worldwide. Oxford is a registered trade mark of
Oxford University Press in the UK and in certain other countries.

Published in Canada by Oxford University Press
8 Sampson Mews, Suite 204, Don Mills, Ontario M3C 0H5 Canada

www.oupcanada.com

First Edition published in 2011

Original edition published by Oxford University Press,
253 Normanby Road, South Melbourne, Victoria, 3205 Australia

Library and Archives Canada Cataloguing in Publication

Title: Working with people : interviewing and assessment skills for human service and social work practice /
Louise Harms & Joanna Pierce.
Names: Harms, Louise, author. | Pierce, Joanna, author.
Description: Second Canadian edition. | Includes bibliographical references and index.
Identifiers: Canadiana (print) 20190097493 | Canadiana (ebook) 20190097507 | ISBN 9780199029860
(softcover) | ISBN 9780199029907 (EPUB)
Subjects: LCSH: Communication in human services—Textbooks. | LCSH: Interpersonal communication—
Textbooks. | LCSH: Human services personnel. | LCGFT: Textbooks.
Classification: LCC HV29.7 .H37 2019 | DDC 361/.06—dc23

Cover image: Martin Barraud/OJO Images/Getty Images
Interior and Cover design: Laurie McGregor

Oxford University Press is committed to our environment.
Wherever possible, our books are printed on paper which comes from
responsible sources.

Printed and bound in the United States of America

6 7 8 — 24 23 22

Contents

Contributors

Carolyn Aston is a social worker, educational consultant, and child/adolescent psychotherapist, in private practice, with a background in teaching, community health, and child psychiatry. She was founder of the Connect-a-Kid Mentoring Program in 2002 for at-risk middle-school students. A former tutor in the Bachelor of Social Work Program, University of Melbourne, and Lecturer in Education, Deakin, she has lectured in counselling techniques for the Graduate Diploma of Mental Health for Teaching Professionals, Monash University, and as a clinical supervisor in the Master of Child Psychoanalytic Psychotherapy program.

Heather Carmichael has experience in the disability field, quality assurance accreditation consultancy, and has been practicing in the alcohol and other drugs field for years in a range of areas including prison, withdrawal, counselling, and supported accommodation. She has co-ordinated several projects at UnitingCare Moreland Hall, including the Intensive Playgroup, Student Unit, Intensive Support Program, and several youth programs. Her academic background is in social work and psychology and she has a diploma in AOD work.

Louise Harms is a social worker who worked for nine years in hospital and educational settings before moving into social work teaching and research. She has worked full-time in the School of Social Work at the University of Melbourne since 2001, where she is senior lecturer and co-ordinator of the entry-to-practice social work program.

Suzie Hudson has worked in the social work field in various Australian states and overseas. While her main passion has been clinical work with adolescents and adults in the areas of substance abuse, offending behaviour, and group work, she has also had the opportunity to teach at both Edith Cowan and Melbourne Universities. She has a PhD in public health and community medicine.

Rebecca Parsons has a bachelor of arts (psychology) and a bachelor of social work. She works in Alice Springs, Australia, with children and young people.

Joanna Pierce is an associate professor in the School of Social Work at the University of Northern British Columbia. Prior to her academic appointment, Joanna spent several years practicing social work in remote northern communities in British Columbia, Canada. Currently, Joanna teaches remote northern social work practice at the undergraduate and graduate levels and continues her research in the area of social work and place.

Melissa Petrakis holds concurrent appointments as a senior lecturer with Monash University, Department of Social Work, and as the senior research fellow (Early Psychosis and Mental Health) with the Mental Health Service, St Vincent's Hospital (Melbourne).

David Rose worked as a social worker for over 20 years in direct practice and in management roles in the alcohol and drug treatment, offender support, and forensic mental health areas before taking up his currently position as senior lecturer in social work at the University of Melbourne.

Jane Sullivan is a senior social worker at a pediatric hospital. Her areas of practice include disability, chronic and life-shortening illness, palliative care, and bereavement support. She has qualifications in adolescent and child psychology and theology and an MSW. Jane believes that developing communication skills is a life-long process.

Nicole Tokatlian is a senior social worker and team leader in a pediatric hospital. She has a particular interest in the impact of trauma on children, adolescents, and families as well as in management and leadership in social work.

Karen White has worked as a social work practitioner in the areas of child and family welfare and community and mental health. She has taught a range of social work subjects at the University of Melbourne, and with the support of an Australian Research Council scholarship, she studied children's perspectives and participation within the family welfare sector, the subject of her doctoral dissertation. Karen is an active member of the Australian Association of Social Workers with regard to ethical issues and promotes children's rights in practice and policy.

John Douglass Whyte was a social worker who earned his MSW at Michigan State University before completing a PhD at the School of Social Work at the University of Melbourne. He is currently an associate professor and the deputy dean of the Policy Practice and Social Innovation discipline in the School of Global, Urban and Social Studies at RMIT University as well as the deputy dean of the University's Indigenous Studies Unit.

Preface

Who Is This Text For?

Human service work is about working with people. Government and non-governmental organizations provide services to enhance people's lives and the communities in which they live. These services aim to help people cope better with daily stressors and demands. The profession of human service work includes work with individuals, group work, social policy, management, leadership, and administration; work with families and partnerships; community work; research and evaluation; and education and training (Chenowith & McAuliffe, 2005). Human service workers are committed to making a difference at individual and structural levels.

Workers listen to and respond to the unique stories of each person, family, group, or community. Good assessment and communication skills are fundamental to engaging and working with others about their needs and rights. This book explores the importance of interviewing and assessment skills within the context of human service practice.

Some Emphases within This Book

This book focuses particularly on

- *Applying a multi-dimensional approach.* A multi-dimensional approach interprets human experience as arising from inner- and outer-world influences. A multi-dimensional approach not only acknowledges all these dimensions of an individual's experience (referred to as the biopsychosocial-spiritual dimensions), but it also suggests that any responses by human service workers also need to be multi-dimensional, addressing both cause and consequence, for example, of human adversity and difficulty. A multi-dimensional approach emphasizes the importance of understanding experiences of both vulnerability and resilience, and therefore of understanding both risk and protective factors.
- *Drawing on practitioner experiences and the unpredictable nature of the work.* Much of what is considered to be human service work happens "on the run" and in diverse and uncontrollable settings, and in single contacts or one-time interventions. This book, therefore, looks at all these dimensions as expected components of practice, rather than as the surprises that interrupt a more controlled counselling approach.

Contributions from experienced practitioners in the field ensure that the examples are grounded firmly in the realities of everyday practice.

- *Thinking beyond the first point of contact.* Communication and interviewing skills often are introduced in relation to only the early phases of working with people. While you gain a sense of the skills to begin and (sometimes) end the work, no real sense emerges as to what the actual work "in the middle" might be. This book identifies skills across a range of human service work encounters so that you can move beyond the first interview or the first point of contact.
- *Reflecting on how you make decisions.* Many of the frequently utilized microskills of interpersonal communication and interviewing are introduced. Greater emphasis is placed, however, on the critical decisions we make in using these skills in any given situation. It is not just "what" these skills are but "why," "how," and "when" we use them. Working creatively, critically, and consciously with other people is our focus. The book will not provide you with a "prescription" for practice, but will instead raise lots of possibilities for you to consider and to practice throughout your career.
- *Paying attention to a multiplicity of factors continuously.* In human service work, we bring together our theoretical knowledge of human beings and the social environment, of adversity and oppression, and of coping and adaptation. At the same time, we bring our practice knowledge and self-awareness to each situation. Given each situation's uniqueness, no "right" way to communicate exists.
- *Practicing in a critical, reflective way.* You will be encouraged to think about your own communication style: how it has developed over your life course, the ways in which communication impacts and influences with the lives of others.

Chapter Overviews

This book is divided into five parts, each dealing with a specific aspect of the communication process in human service work.

PART ONE Framing the Relationship

This first part of the book considers the ways in which human service workers conceptualize key practice issues.

- Chapter 1 explores why human services are provided and what key values and ethical considerations are at the forefront in any professional client–worker relationship. In the final part of this chapter, some ways in which change is thought about are introduced—change through methods of practice, through various stages or phases, and through the use of particular microskills.
- Chapter 2 examines current conceptualizations of communication processes. What are the micro-processes that take place within human communication processes and how can they be used to communicate more effectively? This chapter focuses on how change occurs through communication processes, at verbal and non-verbal levels, and from the individual through to collective levels. The chapter also explores subjective perceptions of good communication and why effective communication matters.

- Chapter 3 presents theoretical perspectives as ways of informing practice. It looks at the influence of three dominant paradigms—the positivist, constructivist, and critical. Then, the chapter explores anti-oppressive practice, cultural considerations, and practice with newcomers.

PART TWO Forming the Relationship

The second part of the book focuses on understanding oneself in the role of worker—your context and the very specific microskills used in communication and the interviewing processes. While they are described individually, they are part of an overall communication process. Therefore, the decisions we make in using these skills at different times for different purposes are vital.

Chapter 4 explores why we need to reflect critically on our personal communication style and experiences. In human service work, the worker is the key "tool" in the process. Conversation is the means by which most of the work is conducted and we need to understand our role in that process. The focus here is on understanding the client and building empathy. Identifying the purpose and context of work with individuals, families, or communities and a "use of self" are central to the discussion.

Chapter 5 focuses on the essential preparatory work in relation to your self-care and professional development. This preparatory work is as much about your self-care as your skill development. Supervision, debriefing, and critical self-reflection are important maintenance strategies in the ongoing challenges of human service work.

Chapter 6 examines how engagement and rapport with clients can be built. The focus is on preparing to meet, making initial contact, and engaging with people. We also consider issues of confidentiality and your use of self-disclosure.

PART THREE Focusing the Communication

The third part of the book explores how communication can be focused more specifically to explore a person's key concerns and how we might work with them to formulate an assessment of their circumstances and areas for work.

Chapter 7 presents the processes of interpersonal contact through asking questions and various forms of questioning (opening, exploring, clarifying). Chapter 8 provides an overview of paraphrasing and summarizing skills. These skills are important for clarifying and challenging what you have heard in order to establish what is important to the client. The importance of empathy will be revisited in this chapter.

The final chapters in Part Three focus on forming an assessment of the work to be undertaken. Chapter 9 examines the skills involved in setting specific goals for the work, goals that are mutually agreed to. Chapter 10 then focuses on assessing, and responding to, particular situations of risk.

PART FOUR Focusing the Intervention

Part Four looks more closely at the ways in which our practice is informed by theory.

Chapter 11 examines the skills of task-centred and crisis intervention approaches. Chapter 12 presents the skills of psychodynamic and cognitive behavioural approaches. Chapter 13 addresses narrative and solution-focused skills. Chapter 14 explores feminist and critical approaches, and their key skills.

PART FIVE Finishing the Work

The final chapter of the book explores how endings are understood. Chapter 15 focuses on the skills of finishing, including dealing with endings that are both anticipated and unanticipated, contracting for further work, and referral. An emphasis is placed on evaluating practice, through evaluations with clients and other stakeholders and through critical self-reflection.

A Map for Your Practice

This book proposes that you use the following task map to think about your practice:

PART ONE—Framing the Relationship

- the purpose of human service work
- your value base, professional ethics, and regulatory guidelines in Canada
- your theoretical and factual knowledge
- the purpose of human service work
- your value base, professional ethics, and regulatory guidelines in Canada
- your theoretical and factual knowledge.

PART TWO—Forming the Relationship

- your use of self
- your organizational context
- your ongoing support and professional development needs
- meeting the people involved
- opening the communication
- active listening and working with silence
- listening empathically
- using self-disclosure.

PART THREE—Focusing the Communication

- establishing the story
- forming an assessment
- goal setting.

PART FOUR—Focusing the Intervention

- drawing on theoretical perspectives
- doing the work.

PART FIVE—Finishing the Work

- ending well
- evaluating the work.

Acknowledgements to the Australian Edition

My deepest gratitude goes to

- the students of the School of Social Work at the University of Melbourne who continue to teach me so much
- Melissa Petrakis, Karen White, and Chris Daicos, the Communication Skills teaching team
- my colleagues and friends who have so generously contributed stories from their practice and helped to bring this book to life
- the publishing team from Oxford University Press—particularly Debra James, my publisher, and Pete Cruttenden, my editor
- my ever-supportive and loving parents, Glenys and Peter
- Jane Sullivan, who listens, lives, and talks in excellent measure.

Louise Harms

Acknowledgements to the Second Canadian Edition

I would like to express my sincere appreciation to everyone who encouraged me through this process: to Louise Harms, for all her work; the students of the School of Social Work at the University of Northern British Columbia, who continue to inspire me and make the learning process a true adventure; my colleagues who, without hesitation, continue to support me in my academic journey; the publishing team from Oxford University Press—particularly the developmental editors, Mariah Fleetham and Leah-Ann Lymer. Finally, I thank my family, who always support and encourage me unconditionally.

Dr. Joanna Pierce

How to Use this Book

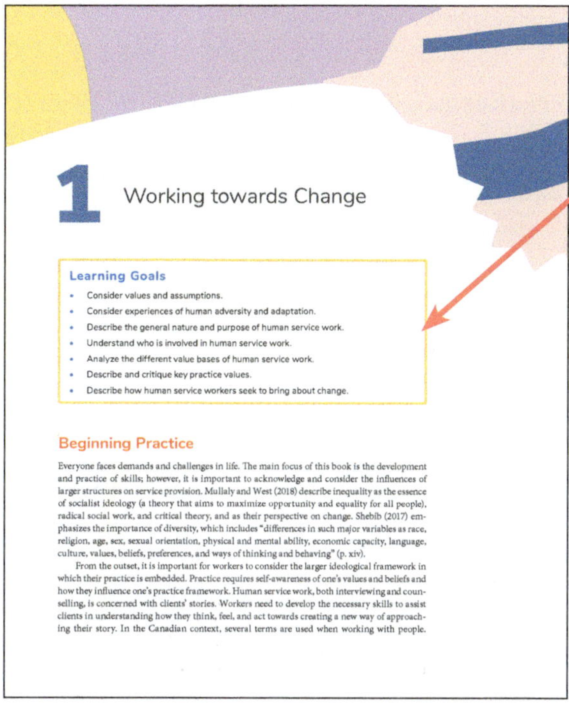
1 Working towards Change

Learning Goals

- Consider values and assumptions.
- Consider experiences of human adversity and adaptation.
- Describe the general nature and purpose of human service work.
- Understand who is involved in human service work.
- Analyze the different value bases of human service work.
- Describe and critique key practice values.
- Describe how human service workers seek to bring about change.

Beginning Practice

Everyone faces demands and challenges in life. The main focus of this book is the development and practice of skills; however, it is important to acknowledge and consider the influences of larger structures on service provision. Mullaly and West (2018) describe inequality as the essence of socialist ideology (a theory that aims to maximize opportunity and equality for all people), radical social work, and critical theory, and as their perspective on change. Shebib (2017) emphasizes the importance of diversity, which includes "differences in such major variables as race, religion, age, sex, sexual orientation, physical and mental ability, economic capacity, language, culture, values, beliefs, preferences, and ways of thinking and behaving" (p. xiv).

From the outset, it is important for workers to consider the larger ideological framework in which their practice is embedded. Practice requires self-awareness of one's values and beliefs and how they influence one's practice framework. Human service work, both interviewing and counselling, is concerned with clients' stories. Workers need to develop the necessary skills to assist clients in understanding how they think, feel, and act towards creating a new way of approaching their story. In the Canadian context, several terms are used when working with people.

Learning Goals at the start of each chapter encourage identification of the skills required to communicate effectively in any given situation or scenario..

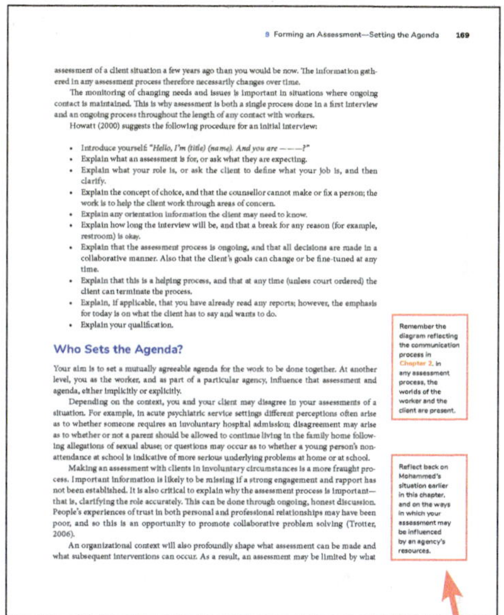
9 Forming an Assessment—Setting the Agenda 169

assessment of a client situation a few years ago than you would be now. The information gathered in any assessment process therefore necessarily changes over time.

The monitoring of changing needs and issues is important in situations where ongoing contact is maintained. This is why assessment is both a single process done in a first interview and an ongoing process throughout the length of any contact with workers.

Howatt (2000) suggests the following procedure for an initial interview:

- Introduce yourself: *"Hello, I'm (title) (name). And you are ———?"*
- Explain what an assessment is for, or ask what they are expecting.
- Explain what your role is, or ask the client to define what your job is, and then clarify.
- Explain the concept of choice, and that the counsellor cannot make or fix a person; the work is to help the client work through areas of concern.
- Explain any orientation information the client may need to know.
- Explain how long the interview will be, and that a break for any reason (for example, restroom) is okay.
- Explain that the assessment process is ongoing, and that all decisions are made in a collaborative manner. Also that the client's goals can change or be fine-tuned at any time.
- Explain that this is a helping process, and that at any time (unless court ordered) the client can terminate the process.
- Explain, if applicable, that you have already read any reports; however, the emphasis for today is on what the client has to say and wants to do.
- Explain your qualification.

Who Sets the Agenda?

Your aim is to set a mutually agreeable agenda for the work to be done together. At another level, you as the worker, and as part of a particular agency, influence that assessment and agenda, either implicitly or explicitly.

Depending on the context, you and your client may disagree in your assessments of a situation. For example, in acute psychiatric service settings different perceptions often arise as to whether someone requires an involuntary hospital admission; disagreement may arise as to whether or not a parent should be allowed to continue living in the family home following allegations of sexual abuse; or questions may occur as to whether a young person's non-attendance at school is indicative of more serious underlying problems at home or at school.

Making an assessment with clients in involuntary circumstances is a more fraught process. Important information is likely to be missing if a strong engagement and rapport has not been established. It is also critical to explain why the assessment process is important—that is, clarifying the role accurately. This can be done through ongoing, honest discussion. People's experiences of trust in both personal and professional relationships may have been poor, and so this is an opportunity to promote collaborative problem solving (Trotter, 2006).

An organizational context will also profoundly shape what assessment can be made and what subsequent interventions can occur. As a result, an assessment may be limited by what

Remember the diagram reflecting the communication process in Chapter 2. In any assessment process, the worlds of the worker and the client are present.

Reflect back on Mohammed's situation earlier in this chapter, and on the ways in which your assessment may be influenced by an agency's resources.

Notes in the margins highlight key points and refer to other chapters in order to facilitate understanding of more challenging concepts.

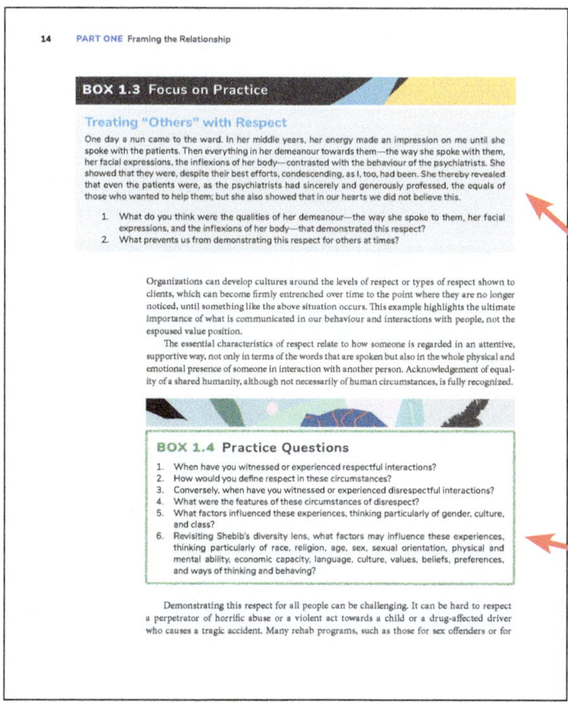
14 PART ONE Framing the Relationship

BOX 1.3 Focus on Practice

Treating "Others" with Respect

One day a nun came to the ward. In her middle years, her energy made an impression on me until she spoke with the patients. Then everything in her demeanour towards them—the way she spoke with them, her facial expressions, the inflexions of her body—contrasted with the behaviour of the psychiatrists. She showed that they were, despite their best efforts, condescending, as I, too, had been. She thereby revealed that even the patients were, as the psychiatrists had sincerely and generously professed, the equals of those who wanted to help them; but she also showed that in our hearts we did not believe this.

1. What do you think were the qualities of her demeanour—the way she spoke to them, her facial expressions, and the inflexions of her body—that demonstrated this respect?
2. What prevents us from demonstrating this respect for others at times?

Organizations can develop cultures around the levels of respect or types of respect shown to clients, which can become firmly entrenched over time to the point where they are no longer noticed, until something like the above situation occurs. This example highlights the ultimate importance of what is communicated in our behaviour and interactions with people, not the espoused value position.

The essential characteristics of respect relate to how someone is regarded in an attentive, supportive way, not only in terms of the words that are spoken but also in the whole physical and emotional presence of someone in interaction with another person. Acknowledgement of equality of a shared humanity, although not necessarily of human circumstances, is fully recognized.

BOX 1.4 Practice Questions

1. When have you witnessed or experienced respectful interactions?
2. How would you define respect in these circumstances?
3. Conversely, when have you witnessed or experienced disrespectful interactions?
4. What were the features of these circumstances of disrespect?
5. What factors influenced these experiences, thinking particularly of gender, culture, and class?
6. Revisiting Shebib's diversity lens, what factors may influence these experiences, thinking particularly of race, religion, age, sex, sexual orientation, physical and mental ability, economic capacity, language, culture, values, beliefs, preferences, and ways of thinking and behaving?

Demonstrating this respect for all people can be challenging. It can be hard to respect a perpetrator of horrific abuse or a violent act towards a child or a drug-affected driver who causes a tragic accident. Many rehab programs, such as those for sex offenders or for

Focus on Practice boxes throughout the book draw on practitioner experience to reveal and examine the multidimensional approach of human service work.

Practice questions encourage critical reflection about many of the frequently utilized microskills of interpersonal communication and interviewing.

PART ONE

Framing the Relationship

In this first part of the book, we explore ways in which the relationship between you, as the worker, and your client can be understood. We look at some of the ways in which human service work can be conceptualized, which enables you to think about the ways in which your core understandings, communication processes, and practice theories influence what you will do.

Chapter 1 explores why human services are provided in the first place, and what values and ethics are at the forefront in any professional client–worker relationship. We continue with examining change processes and social justice.

Chapter 2 examines current conceptualizations of communication processes. We look at how change occurs through communication processes, at verbal and non-verbal levels, as well as the individual through to collective levels.

Chapter 3 presents theoretical perspectives as ways of informing practice. It looks at the influence of three dominant paradigms—the positivist, constructivist, and critical. A multi-dimensional approach is introduced as a way of understanding human adaptation, as well as providing a broad perspective on intervention.

PART ONE Framing the Relationship

- the purpose of human service work
- your value base, professional ethics, and regulatory guidelines in Canada
- your theoretical and factual knowledge.

1 Working towards Change

Learning Goals

- Consider values and assumptions.
- Consider experiences of human adversity and adaptation.
- Describe the general nature and purpose of human service work.
- Understand who is involved in human service work.
- Analyze the different value bases of human service work.
- Describe and critique key practice values.
- Describe how human service workers seek to bring about change.

Beginning Practice

Everyone faces demands and challenges in life. The main focus of this book is the development and practice of skills; however, it is important to acknowledge and consider the influences of larger structures on service provision. Mullaly and West (2018) describe inequality as the essence of socialist ideology (a theory that aims to maximize opportunity and equality for all people), radical social work, and critical theory, and as their perspective on change. Shebib (2017) emphasizes the importance of diversity, which includes "differences in such major variables as race, religion, age, sex, sexual orientation, physical and mental ability, economic capacity, language, culture, values, beliefs, preferences, and ways of thinking and behaving" (p. xiv).

From the outset, it is important for workers to consider the larger ideological framework in which their practice is embedded. Practice requires self-awareness of one's values and beliefs and how they influence one's practice framework. Human service work, both interviewing and counselling, is concerned with clients' stories. Workers need to develop the necessary skills to assist clients in understanding how they think, feel, and act towards creating a new way of approaching their story. In the Canadian context, several terms are used when working with people.

For example, human service workers, also called social service workers, are generally people who have obtained a certificate or diploma and who typically work in various agency settings. Social workers usually have a university degree at the bachelor's or master's level (BSW, MSW).

For the purposes of this book, and to capture the importance of communication skills at all levels, the term "human service worker" will be applied. Broadly defined, a **human service worker** is someone who provides targeted services, typically within a government, non-profit agency, or community setting, to alleviate human adversity and bring about constructive social and individual change.

The next section provides examples of individual adversity. As you read the case scenarios, consider the larger societal influences that underpin each event.

Experiences of Adversity

People experience **adversity** as a result of many different circumstances. Some adversities are short term and crisis-driven, while others present long-term concerns and difficulties. Demands on the individual arise from the social, structural, and cultural contexts in which he or she lives, as well as from relational and inner-world experiences. Human services aim to alleviate adversity and to promote well-being and health in all of these circumstances. Consider the following four scenarios.

BOX 1.1 Focus on Practice

Alleviating Adversity

Scenario 1

A child protection worker is going to meet with a parent, against whom allegations of abuse have been made. The worker, on arrival at the family home, notices that the parent is drug-affected and not happy at all about the notification to protective services.

Scenario 2

A housing worker is meeting with a group of concerned tenants to consider writing a letter of protest about the reopening of a road through a quiet neighbourhood where children have been playing. The group includes people from many culturally and linguistically diverse backgrounds. Other actions may be developed after a community consultation.

Scenario 3

An intake worker on a telephone crisis line receives a call from a 24-year-old distressed woman who has been assaulted by her partner, Ann. She asks the intake worker to tell her what she should do—whether to leave or stay.

Scenario 4

You are a social worker in an agency that provides services to homeless youth. Services are provided for young women and young men but in different locations so as to allow separation by gender. An 18-year-old who identifies herself as a transgender person has been kicked out of her home and comes to your agency for services as she has been sleeping on the street for the last two weeks. Your agency, after initial assessment, decides to refer the client to an agency in another city. An agency supervisor mentions, "They know how to handle these kind of people; we don't." The client is provided a bus ticket, called a cab, and sent on their way. How would you respond to this situation?

These scenarios demonstrate how different the life stressors and traumas are for people and how varied the human service workers' responses need to be. In Scenario 4 the worker is unable to establish a relationship, whereas in Scenario 3 the worker has had no face-to-face relationship at all. In Scenario 1, the worker receives a hostile reaction as compared with a more sought-after and sustained relationship in Scenario 2. In working with people across such a broad spectrum of experience, human service workers need to develop an adaptable repertoire of **skills** to engage, assess, and intervene appropriately with people. It is important for human service workers to examine the social context in which the above scenarios are embedded.

These four scenarios raise questions as to how you would respond as a worker. In particular, they raise questions about the agenda for change and who is driving that agenda. This chapter is structured around four core questions. First, why are human services provided as a response to these experiences? Second, how do we think about who is involved? Third, what are some of the core **values** that underpin human services? Finally, how is change thought about within the human services, from the perspective of different values, **methods**, and stages?

Why Do We Provide Human Services?

Human services are provided in the belief that resources should be provided in situations of adversity to support and enhance the well-being of individuals, families, and communities. The benefit of people supporting each other through times of adversity is well documented, whether through practical and instrumental support (Harms, 2005, pp. 38–9; Hobfoll, Ennis, & Kay, 2000; Ife & Tesoriero, 2006) or with emotional support through talking with someone or assisting someone writing about her or his experiences (Howe, 2008; Knott & Scragg, 2016; Shebib, 2017).

Studies of individual and community experiences of grief, trauma, and stress have consistently identified the availability of resources, social support, secure attachment relationships, and affirmation as key protective factors. All of these factors can be translated into practical, instrumental, and emotional interventions. Human services are based on beliefs about intervention at two levels. Supportive relationships are a protective factor in their own right, and are also effective vehicles for change in other circumstances—for example, providing resources such as education, skills, information, and other practical resources. A relationship base, therefore, is at the core of human service work. This is reflected within the social work profession's *Code of Ethics* and *Guidelines for Ethical Practice* (CASW, 2005).

The Canadian Association of Social Workers (CASW) describes its core values and principles on its website as follows:

> Social work is a profession concerned with helping individuals, families, groups and communities to enhance their individual and collective well-being. It aims to help people develop their skills and their ability to use their own resources and those of the community to resolve problems. Social work is concerned with individual and personal problems but also with broader social issues such as poverty, unemployment and domestic violence.

The outcome of direct social work practice is that needs of clients are met, their potential is developed, and their control over their lives is fostered.

The four scenarios above raise some of these key questions about well-being. For example, how does a society decide what constitutes risk for children within the context of family life? How does a society determine access to resources such as playgrounds in housing estates? How does a society provide the necessary resources for women and children who are separating from family violence? How does a community respond to a family whose child has died? How are these questions translated into relevant and effective human service policies, programs, and practices?

Human services are based on notions of well-being, but these notions can become the source of not only of support but of risk. One person's notion of well-being can lead to culturally inappropriate solutions for others and result in generations of damage and harm (Haebich, 2006). The balance between human service workers being agents of social care, change, or control (Howe, 1994) is a delicate one and depends on a continuous review of the values underpinning our work.

Who Is Involved in Human Service Work?

Many people seek support voluntarily as a result of particular experiences of upheaval and crisis in life—experiences of poverty, unemployment, and migration; of violence and abuse; of illness, disability, and death; or of family stress and breakdown, mental health, low self-esteem or bullying. Other people are involuntary users of services, mandated as a result of court orders or legal regulations relating to child protection, juvenile justice, or community treatment orders, for example. They are involuntary **clients** in that they are required to have contact with workers as a result of behaviour deemed to be risky by others. In these instances, human service workers can be an unwanted intrusion into their lives. Other people are somewhere in between the experience of being a voluntary or involuntary client—they experience violence in the context of an abusive relationship or they are admitted to hospital following a fall and consequently have to access human services for support during recovery. Many people are forced by circumstances to become human service clients rather than their choosing freely to access those services.

As illustrated in the above scenarios, language is a crucial influence on how clients are perceived by workers who interact with them. A parent, a group of concerned citizens, a person at the end of the telephone, or a family come to be termed clients, **consumers**, customers, or service users—depending on the agency with which they come in contact. From a client perspective, these labels can be experienced as negative and depersonalizing. From the worker's perspective, these terms raise fundamental questions about your perception of the identities of the individuals who are accessing services and how you frame and understand their experience.

The term "client" is defined by the *Code of Ethics* of the Canadian Association of Social Workers:

> A person, family, group of persons, incorporated body, association or community on whose behalf a social worker provides or agrees to provide a service or to whom the social worker is legally obligated to provide a service.

The term "client" will be used throughout this book, consistent with this professional base.

The term "service user" is reflective of many of these assumptions—that is, that they are people accessing services because of neglect, vulnerability, disadvantage, or needs. This term differs, however, in the assumption that they are active users of a service, possibly denoting a voluntary access of the organization or service. In some specific contexts, such as the Canadian Association of Sexual Assault Centres, where a feminist philosophy underlies all

© Loganban – Dreamstime.com

Why are the distinctions between terms for human service workers important? Which term best fits the designation that you are working towards through your human service program? What kinds of training, focuses, and values distinguish that role from others listed in this chapter?

dimensions of service delivery, the term "victim/survivor" is used to demonstrate the status of the person independent of an agency involvement. This emphasizes both the person's risk and strength status.

The use of the word "client" or "service user" self-referentially is rare. These terms tend to be used by workers to identify the people they work with, and are not necessarily used by the person herself or himself. Each of these terms has particular connotations about the nature of the relationship between the service, the worker, and the person accessing the service. Throughout this book, the term "worker" will be used for "human service worker." Many other terms are frequently used, including "helping professional," "social worker," "community worker," "child protection worker," "counsellor," "practitioner," and "therapist." All of these terms reflect different training, emphases, and values in human service work.

Values in the Relationship

Values are central to human service work. As a worker, you rely on processes of personal, professional, and wider cultural beliefs and values to form an assessment that will lead to interventions. According to Banks (2012),

> "values" can be regarded as particular types of belief that people hold about what is regarded as worthy or valuable. In the context of professional practice, the use of the term "belief" reflects the status that values have as stronger than mere opinions or preferences. (p. 7)

These strongly held beliefs about what is "worthy or valuable" also have other qualities: they are recognized as being "generalized, emotionally charged conceptions of what is desirable, historically created and derived from experience, and shared by a population or a group within it" (Weber, 2006, p. 18). This definition captures some essential components of our value bases: they can be emotionally charged and, therefore, sometimes fiercely protected; they are developed within a specific historical and experiential context, and may not always be readily transferable; and they are upheld by a group of people as a way of bringing a shared focus and understanding. Values-based practice is complex when uncertainty and unpredictability are prevailing factors in your work. While there are ethical guidelines for practice, even referring to these in times of crisis will not always lead you to a straightforward solution or strategy. One such example might be working with a client who has perpetrated an act of violence challenging the workers' personal and professional values. You need to revisit and reflect on your value base in an ongoing way.

Professional Value Bases

Extensive and useful discussions in relation to values can be followed in texts by Payne (2006) and Banks (2012). Social values do differ across professions and it is important to be familiar with your professional value base. Social workers generally have university training at the bachelor of social work (BSW) or master of social work (MSW) level. Organizations such as the CASW provide information on the provincial associations' and colleges' regulatory guidelines specific to each Canadian province (see www.casw-acts.ca). For example, when you graduate from a social service worker program in Ontario, you are eligible for admission to the Ontario College of Social Workers and Social Service Workers. As a member of this body, you can use the title "Registered Social Service Worker" (see www.ocswssw.org). (See Appendix 1, "Further Resources," for provincial and national governing associations.)

Focus on Values

Core Values of Social Work

In carrying out their professional tasks and duties, social workers strive to act in ways that give equal priority to **respect** for *human dignity and worth* and the pursuit of *social justice*. This commitment is demonstrated through *service to humanity, integrity*, and *competence*, which characterize professional social work practice. Social work principles are derived from the values; together, they underpin ethical social work practice.

Value 1: Respect for the Inherent Dignity and Worth of Persons

The social work profession holds that:

- Social workers respect the unique worth and inherent dignity of all people and uphold human rights.
- Social workers uphold each person's right to self-determination, consistent with that person's capacity and with the rights of others.
- Social workers respect the diversity among individuals in Canadian society and the right of individuals to their unique beliefs consistent with the rights of others.
- Social workers respect the client's right to make choices based on voluntary, informed consent.
- Social workers who have children as clients determine the child's ability to consent and, where appropriate, explain to the child and to the child's parents/guardians the nature of the social worker's relationship to the child.
- Social workers uphold the right of society to impose limitations on the self-determination of individuals, when such limitations protect individuals from self-harm and from harming others.
- Social workers uphold the right of every person to be free from violence and threat of violence.

Value 2: Pursuit of Social Justice

The social work profession holds that each society has an obligation to pursue social justice, to provide maximum benefit for all its members, and to afford them protection from harm.

The profession understands social justice to encompass:

- Social workers uphold the right of people to have access to resources to meet basic human needs.
- Social workers advocate for fair and equitable access to public services and benefits.
- Social workers advocate for equal treatment and protection under the law and challenge injustices, especially injustices that affect the vulnerable and disadvantaged.
- Social workers promote social development and environmental management in the interests of all people.

Continued

Value 3: Service to Humanity

The social work profession holds service in the interests of human well-being and social justice as a primary objective. The fundamental goals of social work service are as follows:

- Social workers place the needs of others above self-interest when acting in a professional capacity.
- Social workers strive to use the power and authority vested in them as professionals in responsible ways that serve the needs of clients and the promotion of social justice.
- Social workers promote individual development and pursuit of individual goals, as well as the development of a just society.
- Social workers use their knowledge and skills in bringing about fair resolutions to conflict and in assisting those affected by conflict.

Value 4: Integrity in Professional Practice

The social work profession values honesty, reliability, and impartiality in social work practice.

- Social workers demonstrate and promote the qualities of honesty, reliability, impartiality, and diligence in their professional practice.
- Social workers demonstrate adherence to the values and ethical principles of the profession and promote respect for the profession's values and principles in organizations where they work or with which they have a professional affiliation.
- Social workers establish appropriate boundaries in relationships with clients and ensure that the relationship serves the needs of clients.
- Social workers value openness and transparency in professional practice and avoid relationships where their integrity or impartiality may be compromised, ensuring that should a conflict of interest be unavoidable, the nature of the conflict is fully disclosed.

Value 5: Confidentiality in Professional Practice

The social work profession values confidentiality in professional social work practice.

- Social workers respect the importance of the trust and confidence placed in the professional relationship by clients and members of the public.
- Social workers respect the client's right to confidentiality of information shared in a professional context.
- Social workers only disclose confidential information with the informed consent of the client or permission of client's legal representative.
- Social workers may break confidentiality and communicate client information without permission when required or permitted by relevant laws, court order, or this Code.
- Social workers demonstrate transparency with respect to limits to confidentiality that apply to their professional practice by clearly communicating these limitations to clients early in their relationship.

Value 6: Competence in Professional Practice

The social work profession values proficiency in social work practice.

- Social workers uphold the right of clients to be offered the highest quality service possible.

- Social workers strive to maintain and increase their professional knowledge and skill.
- Social workers demonstrate due care for client's interests and safety by limiting professional practice to areas of demonstrated competence.
- Social workers contribute to the ongoing development of the profession and its ability to serve humanity, where possible, by participating in the development of current and future social workers and the development of new professional knowledge.
- Social workers who engage in research minimize risks to participants, ensure informed consent, maintain confidentiality, and accurately report the results of their studies.

Source: Canadian Association of Social Workers, Code of Ethics (2005, pp. 4–10). Focus on Values box, page 8: The Social Work Code of Ethics, adopted by the Board of Directors of the Canadian Association of Social Workers (CASW) is effective March, 2005, and replaces the CASW Code of Ethics (1994). The Code is reprinted here with the permission of the CASW. The copyright in the document has been registered with Canadian Intellectual Property office, registration No. 1030330.

The fundamental values of social work practice are "driven by a mission of **social justice** and change to balance inequities and to create a more enabling society" (Fook, 2000, p. 129). Within the CASW *Code of Ethics* (2005, pp. 4–10) six core values are outlined, relating both to views of the client and to the working relationship.

The CASW's six values, as outlined in its *Code of Ethics*, points to particular practice directions. For example, the practice frameworks cannot just be about inner-world change. They must include a focus on outer-world dimensions.

Personal Value Bases

While many practice standards and codes of ethical conduct highlight values that are essential to a particular profession, workers within each of these professions will vary considerably. Your view of social justice may differ from those of your colleagues as a result of different experiences and expectations. While people work under the assumption of a common value base, individual workers will have their own experiences of culture, religion, gender, and class that vary. Personal awareness and self-reflection about these values are important.

Balancing our personal and professional beliefs is important. O'Hagan (2001) describes the ways in which workers may be publicly respectful of a client's religious values, for example, even though they privately disagree. Therefore, we can differ not only along a spectrum of professional values about a particular issue, but also along a spectrum of personal and professional inconsistencies.

Cultural Value Bases

The above discussion has focused on the professional and personal location of values in practice. Our values also are historically and socially situated. These broader social and cultural attitudes profoundly influence our beliefs, for example, about well-being. The political and cultural values held by a nation or a state influence which services are provided and how they subsequently are delivered. Mullaly (2007) describes a cultural sensitivity model, which "enables white social workers to better establish a 'helping relationship' with members of other races and cultures to make services more accessible and to advocate for the enactment of equal rights legislation" (p. 281). A major consequence of globalization is that assumptions of a universal value base no longer hold. Mullaly notes that the dominant theory of multicultural social work in Canada, the United States, and Australia is aimed at a cultural sensitivity and focuses on the importance of increasing workers' sensitivity to cultural norms and institutional racism. Different value bases are acknowledged as existing in Indigenous (Coates & Hetherington, 2016; Connolly, 2001; Lynn, 1999) and non-Western communities (Esteva & Prakash, 1998). For example, Dwairy (2006) provides an overview of how the individual is regarded from an Islamic perspective, which presents some major discontinuities with, if not contradictions to, Western values:

1. The self is not autonomous but is connected to an extended family or tribe. It directs its energy towards achieving group rather than personal goals.
2. The behaviour of the individual is more situational and contextual than dispositional. It is controlled by external factors such as roles and norms rather than internal factors such as personal attributions of behaviour.
3. Priority is given to interpersonal responsibilities rather than to justice and individual rights.
4. More other-focused emotions (for example, sympathy and shame) are experienced rather than ego-focused ones (for example, anxiety). (p. 61)

He argues that, contrary to Western cultures, the main source of suppression of behaviours is external rather than internal. This can lead to major incompatibilities with many of the practice perspectives widely used in the Western context, which focus more on the individual and on liberal understandings of well-being, such as psychodynamic, cognitive, behavioural, and feminist perspectives. Dwairy (2006) suggests a continuum for understanding work with Arabic or Islamic clients, from individualism to collectivism and from liberalism to authoritarianism, the two main dimensions on which cultures are spread in his paradigm.

Authors such as Hall (1976), Fisher (1991), and Hick and Stokes (2017) discuss the importance of understanding cross-cultural communications dynamics. The authors describe the importance of examining theories of cultural screening, collectivism, and constructivism, and how these theories underpin successful communication cross culturally. **Cultural screening** is described by Hall as the process by which information is taken in by an individual and translated to fit the context of the individual's cultural group. If information becomes overwhelming or threatens the individual's cultural identity, a cultural screen can interrupt the process as a personal safety mechanism. "The authors explore the notion of understanding a 'person's place of knowing.' To interact with a client or group on any other level will not be successful" (Pierce, 2007, p. 20). Further, this cultural connection to communication is significant if the practitioner is attempting to facilitate individual, community, or social shifts.

Diversity issues raise some fundamental questions for you as a worker in a Canadian human service delivery context in relation to shared beliefs about well-being, the nature of relationships, expectations about communication and intervention, and who is the identified client. The following example raises some of these cultural differences.

BOX 1.2 Focus on Practice

Addressing Aggressive Behaviour

A local school is experiencing difficulties with two young boys who are displaying aggressive behaviour, particularly towards girls. These boys have recently moved from a northern and remote Indigenous village with a population under 1,000. The teachers have sought assistance because they are concerned about the increase in the levels of aggression and the possible trauma these young boys may be experiencing. The teachers are uncertain if or how the behaviour is connected to their recent move. In consultation with the boys' families, however, a shared concern about this behaviour cannot be found.

1. What would you see as some of the important issues to be addressing in this situation? What is your initial reaction to it?
2. What would you find most challenging in this situation if you were the worker called in to develop a response with the teachers and the parents?
3. What cultural considerations require careful consideration?
4. What education may need to occur for the teachers in this scenario?
5. What education may need to occur for the parents in this scenario?
6. What education may need to occur for the boys in this scenario?

As a worker, you will need to find a common language of rights and responsibilities that can be developed respectfully out of diverse experiences. Discussion and dialogue are critical steps in this process (Furlong & Ata, 2006; Martin & Nakayama, 2012).

Five Core Practice Values

We will now consider five specific practice values. They are (1) respecting the human person; (2) promoting social justice and people's right to a good life; (3) privileging the right to self-determination, empowerment, and autonomy; (4) valuing people's strengths and resilience; and (5) being authentic.

Respecting the Human Person

The value of "respect for persons" is regarded as central to human service work. How this actually may be achieved is less frequently articulated.

The philosopher Gaita (1999) reflects on how this fundamental respect for another human being was shown when he worked in a psychiatric hospital in the 1960s, where "the patients were judged to be incurable and they appeared to have irretrievably lost everything which gives meaning to our lives" (p. 17). He relates the experience in Box 1.3.

Respect for another human being, and the importance of an authentic engagement, is described in this brief encounter. The scenario highlights that we can make all sorts of assumptions about our conduct until we witness truly respectful moments and interactions.

BOX 1.3 Focus on Practice

Treating "Others" with Respect

One day a nun came to the ward. In her middle years, her energy made an impression on me until she spoke with the patients. Then everything in her demeanour towards them—the way she spoke with them, her facial expressions, the inflexions of her body—contrasted with the behaviour of the psychiatrists. She showed that they were, despite their best efforts, condescending, as I, too, had been. She thereby revealed that even the patients were, as the psychiatrists had sincerely and generously professed, the equals of those who wanted to help them; but she also showed that in our hearts we did not believe this.

1. What do you think were the qualities of her demeanour—the way she spoke to them, her facial expressions, and the inflexions of her body—that demonstrated this respect?
2. What prevents us from demonstrating this respect for others at times?

Organizations can develop cultures around the levels of respect or types of respect shown to clients, which can become firmly entrenched over time to the point where they are no longer noticed, until something like the above situation occurs. This example highlights the ultimate importance of what is communicated in our behaviour and interactions with people, not the espoused value position.

The essential characteristics of respect relate to how someone is regarded in an attentive, supportive way, not only in terms of the words that are spoken but also in the whole physical and emotional presence of someone in interaction with another person. Acknowledgement of equality of a shared humanity, although not necessarily of human circumstances, is fully recognized.

BOX 1.4 Practice Questions

1. When have you witnessed or experienced respectful interactions?
2. How would you define respect in these circumstances?
3. Conversely, when have you witnessed or experienced disrespectful interactions?
4. What were the features of these circumstances of disrespect?
5. What factors influenced these experiences, thinking particularly of gender, culture, and class?
6. Revisiting Shebib's diversity lens, what factors may influence these experiences, thinking particularly of race, religion, age, sex, sexual orientation, physical and mental ability, economic capacity, language, culture, values, beliefs, preferences, and ways of thinking and behaving?

Demonstrating this respect for all people can be challenging. It can be hard to respect a perpetrator of horrific abuse or a violent act towards a child or a drug-affected driver who causes a tragic accident. Many rehab programs, such as those for sex offenders or for perpetrators of gendered violence (Laming, 2005; Allen, 2013), are based on a fundamental respect for the person and work successfully towards addressing the causes of violence (John Howard Society of Canada, 2019). The programs are based on respecting the person, not on any implication of approval of the behaviour in which he or she may have engaged.

One student shared her experiences of working in Juvenile Justice for her student placement and the ways in which her view of these young people changed throughout her placement. The placement experience assisted the student in understanding the various social issues that resulted in youth facing involvement with the Youth Justice system (homelessness, family violence, addiction, mental illness, for example). Respect for them as individuals was a critical dimension of that work.

Using an anti-oppressive practice framework (Mullaly & West, 2018) as a basis for practice can sometimes seem quite contradictory to work in involuntary settings, where workers can be perceived to be agents of social control rather than of social care. As the examples above highlight, however, the value of respect can be demonstrated in the most difficult or constrained settings.

Mullaly (2007) views **oppression** through a structural lens: "Oppression exists and persists because of the number of positive functions it carries out for the dominant group at the expense of the subordinate groups" (p. 285).

BOX 1.5 Focus on Practice

Respect for Involuntary Clients

Working with involuntary clients is a challenge in itself. As workers we are given tools and skills to equip ourselves in working with all sorts of people, but when clients are being forced to report to you and they refuse to engage in the process, practice can seem futile. I was working in an area with young men who had sexually offended, who were involuntary clients. Young male adolescents can be difficult to engage in therapy for developmental reasons, but coupled with a history of sexual offending, counselling can seem a difficult road to navigate.

However, given that adolescence is considered a transitional phase, it would follow that their behavioural patterns of offending do not necessarily reflect clients' lasting personal beliefs or attitudes. When working with involuntary clients it is important to separate their offending behaviour from who they are. Unfortunately, many young men begin to identify themselves as defined by their offence, and believe that others will do the same. Just by giving involuntary clients an emotionally safe space to share their side of the story, without judgement, can unlock many doors.

BOX 1.6 Focus on Practice

Seeking to Understand the Oppressed and Subordinated

Mulan has recently lost her husband and is struggling in many areas to parent her four children on her own. Her Asian credentials are not recognized by employers as she tries to gain employment. Mulan faces derogatory remarks because English is her second language. She feels professionals (teachers, doctors,

Continued

bank employees, etc.) perceive her as less intelligent when the reality is language barriers. Currently, Mulan fears losing her family's housing due to being unable to gain employment. What underpins the demeaning treatment faced by Mulan? Practitioners should be aware of the characteristics that make them part of the dominant group. How do these characteristics influence communication and the practice framework in work with clients?

Promoting Social Justice and People's Right to a Good Life

In 1948, in the context of the post–Second World War international environment and the atrocities that had taken place, the Universal Declaration of Human Rights was developed. While it has undergone extensive criticism for both its gendered (Division for the Advancement of Women, 2007) and Western (Esteva & Prakash, 1998) biases, it reveals that people were striving for justice and equality of opportunity at a global and universal level. The first article of the declaration, for example, reads: "All human beings are born free and equal in dignity and rights. They are endowed with reason and conscience and should act towards one another in a spirit of brotherhood" (United Nations General Assembly, 1948).

Many other national and international treaties and conventions have similarly sought to establish ground rules or visions for basic human rights and needs in order to overcome inequalities and oppression. The constitution of the World Health Organization (WHO), established by the United Nations, makes a strong statement about the principles that are "basic to the happiness, harmonious relations and security of all peoples" (WHO, 2018). These principles are fundamental to how we think about well-being and resilience both locally and globally.

In Canada, the Canadian Charter of Rights and Freedoms describes as fundamental the following freedoms:

- freedom of conscience and religion
- freedom of thought, belief, opinion and expression, including freedom of the press and other media of communication
- freedom of peaceful assembly
- freedom of association.

If the aim of such interventions is the improvement of lives for individuals, families, and communities, then what is valued in this is some view of what constitutes a good, happy, or healthy way of living.

Human service work often occurs at the interface of rights violations, so rights dilemmas are part of the worker's territory. As Banks (2012) points out, an ethical dilemma involves "a choice between two equally unwelcome alternatives relating to human welfare" (p. 20). Recall the earlier scenario, where a child protection worker is making her way to meet with a parent about abuse allegations. In this situation, removing the child from the violent parent may fulfill the child's right to safety but violate the parent's right to parent as he or she wishes.

Two workers with the UNHCR, the United Nations Refugee Agency, take a picture with a person seeking asylum at the border between Serbia and Croatia. As a human service worker, when might you find yourself responsible for acting in accordance with the human rights established by international and political bodies like the United Nations? (See www.unhcr.ca for more information on the Canadian branch of this organization.)

Focus on Rights

Some Basic Rights

1. Health is a state of complete physical, mental, and social well-being and not merely the absence of disease or infirmity.
2. The enjoyment of the highest attainable standard of health is one of the fundamental rights of every human being without distinction of race, religion, political belief, economic, or social condition.
3. The health of all peoples is fundamental to the attainment of peace and security and is dependent upon the fullest co-operation of individuals' states.
4. The achievement of any state in the promotion and protection of health is of value to all.
5. Unequal development in different countries in the promotion of health and control of disease, especially communicable disease, is a common danger.

6. Healthy development of the child is of basic importance; the ability to live harmoniously in a changing total environment is essential to such development.
7. The extension to all peoples of the benefits of medical, psychological, and related knowledge is essential to the fullest attainment of health.
8. Informed opinion and active co-operation on the part of the public are of the utmost importance in the improvement of the health of the people.
9. Governments have a responsibility for the health of their peoples, which can be fulfilled only by the provision of adequate health and social measures.

Privileging Self-Determination, Empowerment, and Autonomy

Self-determination and autonomy are long-held core values in human service work.

Valuing self-determination acknowledges that people have the capacity to make choices (Dowrick, 1983) about their lives, if they are given the opportunity. What makes it possible for people to influence their environments is an important question for workers to address. In supporting the notion of self-determination, the usual assumption is that self-determination is positively oriented. Workers can support the notion of self-determination only so far as legal and ethical limits apply. In some cases, for example, people express a wish to harm themselves and/or others. At these times, you need to take steps to ensure human safety, over and above a client's right to be self-determining.

Other dilemmas arise in relation to views about how much a person experiencing illness should know about the diagnosis or illness. Again, different cultures regard this information exchange in different ways, with some cultures firmly of the belief that clients should be protected from such knowledge at all times (Duffy et al., 2006). Their right to be fully informed—and therefore potentially self-determining—is overridden by a belief that the patients' health may be negatively impacted by distress if too much information about their health circumstances is revealed. In addition, in some cultures the decision regarding whether or not a client will receive care is made by the family, and not medical professionals or the client themselves.

In other situations, the capacity to realize the value of self-determination is compromised by the person's capacity to participate in decision-making processes or to give informed consent—for example, in situations where a person is living with a severe intellectual or psychiatric disability or is too young to be able to verbalize an opinion. If your underlying value is the promotion of self-determination, empowerment, and autonomy, steps can always be taken to ensure that actions are oriented to the greatest possible extent in the best interests of the person concerned.

A tension arises in practice in emphasizing autonomy. Some authors argue for the client's right to experience a transitional dependence at times, rather than a continuous independence and self-determination (Trevithick, 2005). An example of this tension occurs when a person is in the middle of a major crisis and the usual coping capacity is overwhelmed. Within this circumstance, though, the emphasis is still on clients being self-determining within the limits of their capacities at such a time.

Valuing People's Strengths and Resilience

If we are to have a positive impact as workers, a core belief needs to be that a client has strengths and a capacity and motivation towards change for the better (Brun & Rapp, 2001; Banks, 2012). Coggins (2016) provides a useful explanation of a strengths-based practice:

> A strengths perspective in social work involves identifying the strengths found in individuals, families, groups, and communities; however, it also includes an acknowledgement of the ability of client systems to endure and overcome difficult events or circumstances, even in situations where problem solving may have resulted in only partial success. (p. 151)

Other strengths-oriented beliefs include the notion that unlimited strengths can be found in every individual, group, family and community; that adversities can be both sources of loss and opportunity; and that collaboration works best.

Being Authentic

Authenticity on the part of the worker has been consistently named as critical to the success of forming a client–worker relationship and being able to facilitate change (Hepworth, Rooney, Dewberry-Rooney, Gottfried, & Larsen, 2017). Authenticity, like respect, emerges in the totality of verbal and non-verbal dimensions of your relationships.

Authenticity is about openness to, empathy with, and the understanding of another's situation. We can be authentic in many other ways when working with people. Authenticity is not necessarily about self-disclosure—an assumption that is often made. It can be about recognizing and articulating the limits of our knowledge, our understanding, or our skills. It can be about expressing our deep concern for someone. It can be about articulating our time limits and our capacity to be present in an interaction with someone. It is fundamentally about our willingness to share our humanness in the context of our professional integrity and our ability to act within the capacities and limitations of what we bring to an encounter.

This value raises many questions in relation to how authentic the relationship can be that is established with a client. The expectations of a professional relationship are different from those of a personal relationship, yet many qualities are similar. Even in a professional context we genuinely like some persons more than others. Some people we genuinely fear. The way we express authenticity emerges in the boundaries we metaphorically and practically create in our work with another person.

How Do Human Service Workers Influence Change?

As a human service worker, you aim to bring about change through your use of skills at both individual and social levels (Payne, 2014). In this section, the ways in which change is thought to occur as a result of methods, phases, and skills will be discussed.

Change is something that is deliberately fostered and worked towards through specific interventions in human service work. Change can occur in our inner worlds, in relation to how we feel and how we think. Change can also occur in our outer worlds, in relation to how we behave and how others behave towards us. In our outer worlds, change can occur in relation to particular circumstances or conditions such as the alleviation of poverty, violence, or unemployment.

BOX 1.7 Practice Questions

Four client scenarios were presented earlier in this chapter.

1. Revisit each of these scenarios and reflect on what you see as the change agenda you would bring to each of them.
2. How similar or different do you think they would be compared with the clients' perception of the change agenda?
3. What structural influences are present?

The precipitants of change are similarly multiple. Some people change because they have to, as a result of rock-bottom experiences. Sometimes people engage in change processes because either they are mandated to or because of some other circumstance; for example, to get their children back from being placed in foster care. Many other people engage in change processes because they want to, recognizing that they need to change to satisfy their own values. Motivations for seeking help with change are often unique and complex.

What influences people's attitudes to change? Change for some people is a terrifying prospect, full of uncertainties and unfamiliar territory. For other people, change is exciting and energizing. Some of the variables that influence our attitudes to change include the perceptions and realities of available supports and resources, the availability of role models, the internal and external encouragement received, and, sometimes, the negative motivational encouragers; for example, seeing someone experience major problems with drug and alcohol abuse and determining never to go down that path. For many people, internal change is possible and motivation can be extremely high, but social circumstances make it extremely difficult to maintain any gains. The change process can be conceptualized as involving various methods, stages, and skills.

Change through Methods of Practice

Working with individuals primarily involves interviewing and counselling skills in one-to-one (and typically face-to-face) focused conversation with individuals, couples, or families.

A wide range of terms is used to differentiate this work—interviewing, counselling, or therapy being three common ones. Some practitioners regard these terms as interchangeable, whereas others see them as distinct forms of individual practice. Sommers-Flanagan and Sommers-Flanagan (2004) argue that the key differences between counsellors and psychotherapists is not that they engage in different behaviours but rather that they engage in the behaviours of "listening, questioning, interpreting, explaining, advising, and so on . . . in different proportions" (p. 8).

In all work with people, interpersonal skills are critical. Group work, community development, and research methods similarly rely on gathering information through communicating with others, forming an assessment, and undertaking some form of further intervention.

We will look at how different theoretical approaches influence the use of these responding skills in **Chapters 11 through 14**.

Change throughout Various Stages or Phases

Change is often seen as occurring in stages or phases. For example, Prochaska and DiClemente's (1983) **stages of change** model continues to be the most widely used in Western contexts. Developed from research in relation to addictions, the model proposes people move from

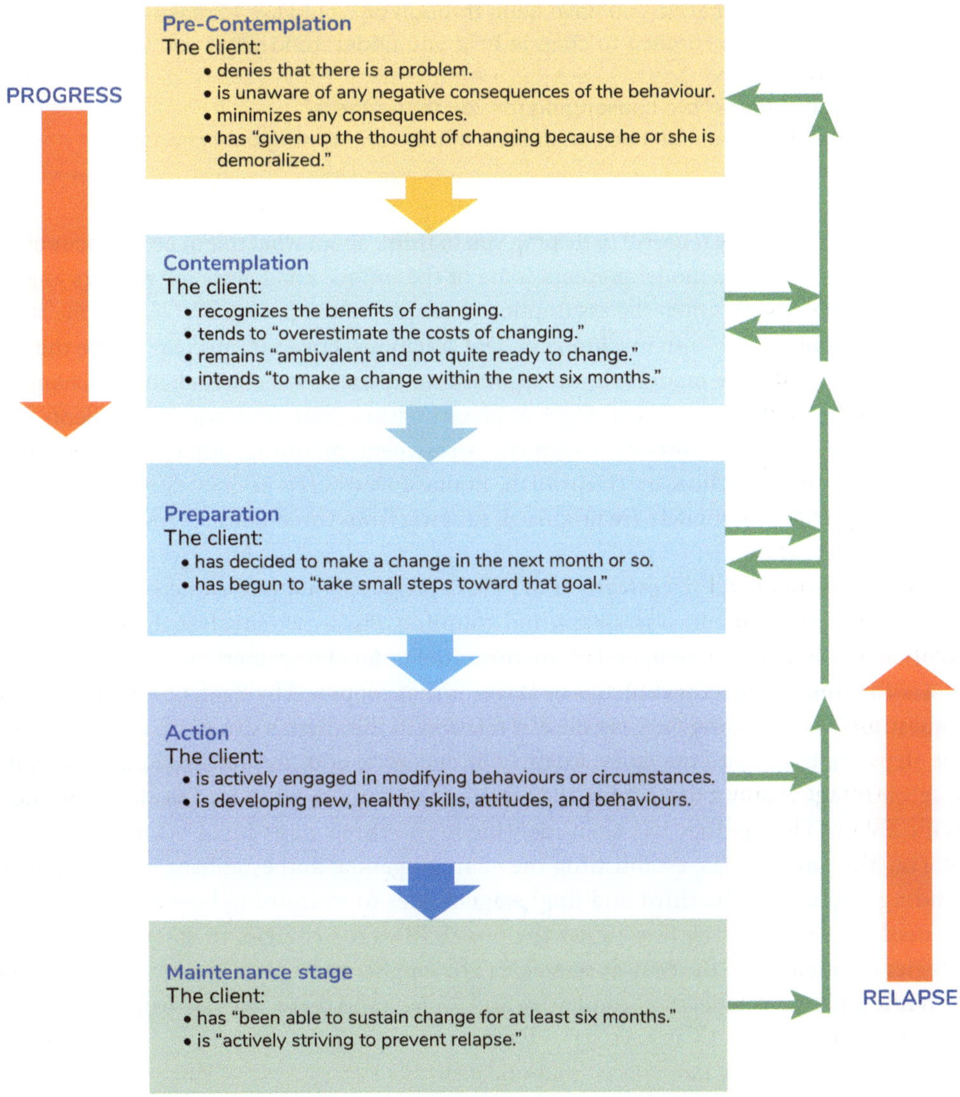

FIGURE 1.1 The Stages of Change Model

Source: Adapted from Levesque, Cummins, Prochaska, and Prochaska (2006, p. 1373). Focus on Change box, p. 22. Stage of Change for making an informed decision about Medicare health plans. *Health Services Research, 41*(4), 1372–92.

a pre-contemplation to a contemplation stage, then to preparation, and on to action. When change is achieved, a maintenance phase begins. Throughout all of these phases, relapse is possible to an earlier phase of change. People can move, therefore, in and out of these phases of commitment to change, depending upon a number of factors. The model does not imply that change occurs in a linear manner. Rather, change is cyclical. The cycle is as follows.

BOX 1.8 Practice Questions

Think about a major change you have been through or would like to make.

1. Does this stage approach to change help you understand what you went through/would go through?
2. Are some stages more challenging for you than others?
3. What habits do you fall back on in each of the various stages of change?

This model of change is useful in helping you to think about what might be the focus of work at a particular point. The model presents some of the unique challenges for workers engaging with involuntary clients. Often the assumption is made that the person is at least at the stage of "contemplation of change"—in involuntary client situations, however, this may not be the case.

The stages of change model is a way of thinking about how a client changes. Change can also be thought about as a series of stages or phases within your work with your clients. These specific tasks include the tasks of engagement, assessment, planning, implementation, evaluation, termination, and follow-up (Hepworth, Rooney, Dewberry-Rooney, Strom-Gottfried, & Larsen, 2017). Different models are proposed, ranging from three-phase through to five-phase models of intervention.

A three-phase model (Hepworth et al., 2017) proposes that phase one involves the tasks of exploration, engagement, assessment, and planning. Phase two involves the tasks of implementation and goal attainment, and phase three, the tasks of termination.

Another model with three phases or stages is that proposed by Egan (2007). In stage one, the question "What's going on?" is asked in relation to the client's situation. In this stage, the three steps are to explore the story, identify blind spots, and find leverage on the problem. The second stage is about examining the solutions that make sense for the client around the specific area of change that has been identified. The three steps involved in this stage are exploring the possibilities, establishing the change agenda, and establishing a commitment to finding a solution. The third and final stage relates to examining how a client gets what they need or want. Having fine-tuned the possibilities for change, in stage three, possible strategies are identified, the best-fit strategies are sought, and a plan of action is put in place.

While different perspectives emphasize and understand these tasks slightly differently, the common tasks are

- establishing availability and a contract of work with the client;
- engaging with the client in a working relationship;
- expressing empathy;

- exploring the problem or issue through an assessment;
- undertaking work together to resolve or address the problem or issue; and
- finishing the work together, often with a process of review.

Many approaches, therefore, recognize that across human service settings these phases are important steps through which the work is conducted. Greatest emphasis tends to be placed on the initial phases, with less emphasis on the last phase—how to ensure safety and belonging, for example, or how to finish the work.

Below, these phases of work are summarized in Table 1.1. The ways in which these phases will be understood throughout this book are presented in the top row: framing and forming the relationship, focusing the communication, focusing the intervention, and finishing the work.

TABLE 1.1 Phases of Social Work Practice

Author(s)	Framing and Forming the Relationship	Focusing the Communication	Focusing the Intervention	Finding Solutions	Finishing
Connolly		Engagement and assessment	Seeking solutions	Securing safety and belonging	
Corey & Corey	Establishing a working relationship	Identifying client problems	Creating goals	Encouraging client exploration and taking action	Termination
Egan		Establishing what's going on	Examining solutions and possibilities	Finding best-fit strategies	
Hepworth, Rooney, & Larsen		Exploration, engagement, assessment and planning	Implementation and goal attainment		Termination
Shulman	Preliminary or preparatory	Beginning or contracting	Middle or work		Ending or transition

Such a table makes a complex, circular, or unshaped process seem logical and linear. In some agencies, you may be able to function in that way. Most workers, however, are in much less predictable environments and relationships, and therefore find that these phases do not typically represent the ways in which the work is undertaken. They do provide a useful map, however, of the tasks involved in change-oriented work.

Change through the Use of Skills

As we explored earlier in the chapter, human services are provided because of the belief that change can occur when workers provide support, in all its forms. You need a skill base to be able to provide appropriate support to others.

The word "skills" is used throughout human service practice, and for that reason it is important to consider its multiple meanings. Skills can mean, first, knowledge; second, "the ability to do something well: proficiency; expertness, dexterity"; third, "an ability to do something, acquired through practice or learning"; and fourth, "an art, a science" (Brown, 1993, p. 2882). Each of these dimensions is relevant to developing a base for human service practice.

In relation to *knowledge*, understandings of people and conditions of adversity are essential, as are understandings of human behaviour and development in context. In addition to these forms of knowledge, theoretical perspectives on practice are also important, along with the practice wisdom you will develop over the course of a career. Other forms of knowledge emerge from research understandings—for example, gaining an understanding of what works with whom in what context is crucial, and research provides a useful basis of understanding.

The second dimension refers to the *ability to do something well*; that is, it is not enough to know about the skills of active listening. To use a skill means that the barriers to good communication are removed or that a capacity to apply specific skills at a particular time is developed.

The third dimension, *an ability acquired through practice and learning*, emphasizes that learning to communicate effectively in a professional capacity takes practice and application, throughout a career.

The final dimension of the definition—that skills refer to both *an art and a science*—highlights another level of complexity (Connolly, 2001). To contribute effectively to human service work, a sound evidence base for what works is important. But it is also an art to communicate well with others, to support others, and to respond empathically and effectively to those experiencing difficulty and adversity. Connecting with other people and establishing a creative process of working together to resolve situations are skills of a high order.

These four dimensions are all critical in bringing about change. You will need to develop the total package to be effective while making decisions about how to act and what to say in various situations.

Later, we will focus on the **microskills** of communication that are used to direct change. The microskills that we will look at in later chapters help us

- establish and maintain empathy;
- communicate non-verbally;
- establish the context and purpose of the work;
- open an interview;
- actively listen;
- establish the story or the nature of the problem;
- ask purposeful and intentional questions; and
- intervene and respond appropriately.

Microskills are the building blocks of human communication. They are transferable skills (O'Hara, 2006); that is, they can be used in many contexts and adapted according to the setting in which the worker and client meet. You influence that process through theoretical perspectives. As Howard (2006) states,

> From the most fundamental aspects of the relationship, such as how we greet a client, to the use of advanced therapeutic skills like making interpretations, our whole way of relating to and thinking about our client is driven by the theoretical model we subscribe to. (p. 8)

In the next chapter, we review these microskills before moving in Chapter 3 to how practitioners come to theorize and apply these skills.

Chapter Summary

In this first chapter, we have explored the role of human services in responding to people's experiences of adversity and need. The ways in which your professional, personal, and cultural value bases will influence your perceptions of human service work were also identified. Five core practice values were presented: (1) respecting the human person; (2) promoting social justice and people's right to a good life; (3) privileging the right to self-determination, empowerment, and autonomy; (4) valuing people's strengths and resilience; and (5) being authentic.

We looked at how change can be understood—through using different practice methods; through understanding individual change processes and understanding change in the phases of work you will undertake with your client; and through using particular communication skills.

Questions for Analysis

1. What have you learned about
   - the value base you bring to your practice?
   - the understandings of change you bring to your practice?
   - the methods of change human service workers use?
   - the phases of change within a client–worker relationship?
2. Going back to the earlier client scenarios, has your view of them changed since reading this chapter?
3. What would you see as the purpose of your work?
4. What do you see as the most important values underpinning your practice?
5. What do you see are some of the tensions in those values?
6. How would you go about resolving some of those tensions?
7. What have been some of the major influences on the development of these values?

Recommended Readings

Allen, M. (2013). *Social work and intimate partner violence*. New York, NY: Routledge Publishing.

Banks, S. (2012). *Ethics and values in social work* (4th ed.). Basingstoke: Palgrave Macmillan.

Bodor, R., Green, R., Lonne, B., & Zapf, M.K. (2004). 40 degrees above or 40 degrees below zero: Rural social work and context in Australia and Canada. *Rural Social Work*, 9, 49–59.

Brooker, P. (2001). *A concise glossary of cultural theory.* New York, NY: Oxford University Press.

Coggins, K. (2016). *The practice of social work in North America: Culture, context, and competency development.* New York, NY: Oxford University Press.

DuPraw, M.E., & Axner, M. (1997). *Working on common cross-cultural communication challenges.* Retrieved from http://www.pbs.org/ampu/crosscult.html

Fook, J. (2016). *Social work: A critical approach to practice.* Thousand Oaks, CA: Sage Publications.

Graham, J.R., Brownlee, K., Shier, M., & Doucette, E. (2008). Localization of social work knowledge through practitioner adaptations in Northern Ontario and the Northwest Territories, Canada. *Arctic, 61*(4), 399–406.

Graham, J.R., Fukuda, E., Shier, M.L., Kline, T.J.B., Brownlee, K., & Novik, N. (2011). Demographic work-related, and life satisfaction predictors of northern social workers' satisfaction with work and profession. *International Social Work, 56*(5), 588–607.

Hall, E. (1976). *Beyond culture.* New York, NY: Anchor Press.

Hepworth, D., Rooney, R., Dewberry-Rooney, G., Strom-Gottfried, K., & Larsen, J. (2017). *Direct social work practice: Theory and skills* (9th ed.). Boston, MA: Brooks/Cole.

Hick, S. (2005). *Social work in Canada.* Toronto, ON: Thompson.

Hick, S., & Stokes, J. (2017). *Social work in Canada: An introduction* (4th ed.). Toronto, ON: Thompson.

Mullaly, B. (2007). *The new structural social work.* Toronto, ON: Oxford University Press.

Mullaly, B., & West, J. (2018). *Challenging oppression and confronting privilege: A critical approach to anti-oppressive and anti-privilege theory and practice* (3rd ed.). Toronto, ON: Oxford University Press.

Internet Resources

Canadian Association of Sexual Assault Centres
www.casac.ca

Canadian Association of Social Workers (CASW)
www.casw-acts.ca

Canadian Charter of Rights and Freedoms
www.canada.ca/en/canadian-heritage/services/how-rights-protected/guide-canadian-charter-rights-freedoms.html

Canadian Medical Association
www.cma.ca

Canadian Psychological Association
www.cpa.ca

Center for Social Justice
www.socialjustice.org/index.php?page=fact-sheets

Government of Canada
www.canada.gc.ca/home.html

Social Care Institute for Excellence
www.scie.org.uk

United Nations, Universal Declaration of Human Rights
www.un.org/en/universal-declaration-human-rights/index.html

World Health Organization
www.who.int

2 Understanding Communication and Change

Learning Goals

- Identify the different ways of understanding communication.
- Understand some of the core verbal and non-verbal skills for human service practice.
- Consider the dimensions of individual and collective communication.
- Understand why communication is so linked with survival, healing, and well-being.
- Reflect on the ways in which communication expresses power.

Understanding Communication

Communication can be understood in many different ways by many different disciplines. Psychology, linguistics, sociology, and anthropology all have contributed enormously to how we think about communication in practice. In relation to human service work, we can understand communication first as a process (involving **verbal** and **non-verbal skills** at individual and collective levels), and second, as a means of survival, a means of healing and therapy, or as the basis of **power**.

Recall the four scenarios from Chapter 1. Each situation would require different communication skills. You need skills to communicate with clients in altered (drug-affected) states of consciousness; with involuntary clients; with groups of people rather than individuals; through face-to-face communication; through telephone communication where non-verbal cues cannot be experienced; across language barriers; and over a long period of time, where there is an established relationship. In this chapter, the dimensions of communication in all of these scenarios and others will be explored.

Communication is so fundamental to our survival and our well-being that we tend not to think about it as a complex skill that we have acquired across our lifespan.

BOX 2.1 Practice Questions

Think of the many skills you might draw on to raise a difficult relationship issue with a particular close friend or partner.

1. How would you approach such a discussion?
2. What do you anticipate could happen during that discussion?
3. Share your response with someone else and discuss the points of similarity and difference in your reactions.

In the moment of speaking with another person, however, we also constantly monitor the other person and adapt verbal and non-verbal responses all the time in that exchange. This focus on process is important, particularly when it is recognized that communication is a simultaneous, continuous, and nuanced process.

Some expansion of understanding beyond what is **encoded** and **decoded** in language is increasingly recognized. Acknowledged in this process is that the "receiving system consists of the five senses, the receptors" (Kadushin, 1972, p. 25). More recent understandings of Indigenous world views (Coates & Hetherington, 2016) and chaos and complexity theories (Hudson, 2000) would include a sixth sense or receptor: a sense of intuition or "knowing" at other levels of sensory awareness.

In processing the verbal and non-verbal messages we receive from an external source, we conduct an internal monologue simultaneously. That is, we cognitively process the information we are receiving through our past and our present structures of understandings. This process produces the meaning of the message (Heath & Bryant, 2000). Sometimes a shared intent can be established easily. At other times it needs to be explicitly addressed; for example, in involuntary client settings or where significant cultural or communication diversities exist.

We will explore understandings of these biological, psychological, social, and spiritual dimensions further in Chapter 3 and as a form of assessment in Chapter 9.

What earlier models perhaps overlooked most was the significance of context (Heath & Bryant, 2000), with context referring both to the individual's particular biopsychosocial-spiritual context and the broader socio-cultural context. Social and cultural influences determine whether certain issues are taboo, important, or valid for conversation.

Current communication models emphasize interaction rather than transmission and reception. We hold that communication is a simultaneous, reciprocal process, involving interactions between at least two people and their context. The degree of commonality of contexts becomes an important area of focus within the communication, in recognition of how profoundly the wider physical, social, structural, and cultural contexts influence interactions. Integrating this perspective, the figure shown earlier might now look more Figure 2.1.

These models may seem to be stating the obvious. However, they are useful reminders of the depth of analysis that can be undertaken when reflecting on interactions, particularly when they have not gone so well. When we think about these skills in a professional context, the focus is on a more deliberate selection of particular skills at a particular time. For example, when we receive a critical message in a personal context, we might react emotionally and impulsively to it. We decode it in a particular way. When we receive a similar message in

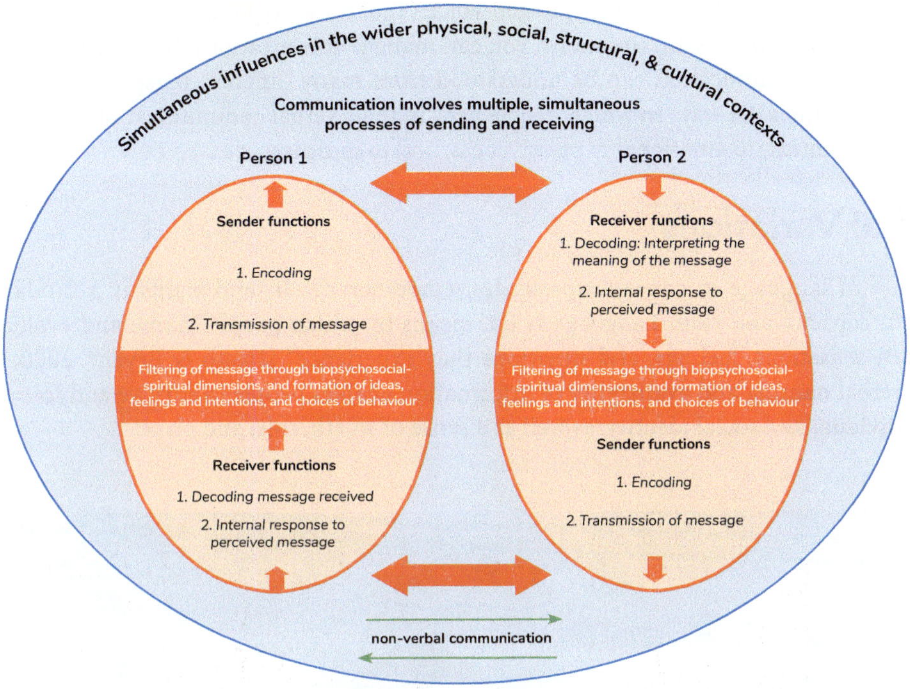

FIGURE 2.1 Communication as a Multi-Dimensional Process

a professional context, we may be more acutely aware of the sender than of ourselves in the interaction, and we will filter the information differently.

In your practice, you will make decisions constantly as to how you will interact with your clients. In many situations, this will involve communicating in empathic and supportive ways. At other times, this will involve being assertive with people, setting limits, or taking decisive and directive action. On other occasions, it will involve dealing with angry, aggressive, and oppressive clients and colleagues.

Building communication skills, therefore, is not about a one-person approach (that is, what the worker should do) but about an interactive approach (in this situation, this is the right thing to do) (Koprowska, 2005). The model also helps us to think about different means of communication, and the strengths and limitations they present in relation to effective communication.

This discussion of communication relates to the concept of "use of self," which we will explore in Chapter 4.

Verbal Communication Processes

Verbal communication processes include everything that is spoken or uttered in a conversation and refer primarily to the content or message that is exchanged. Language expressed through conversation enables the communication of needs, wants, and experiences. As discussed later in this chapter, communication is essential for participating actively and influentially in daily relationships and the wider social environment, and is integral to human well-being and survival. In later chapters, we explore in detail how to use these verbal skills in the context of specific interviewing and interventions.

These specific verbal skills of active listening are considered in Chapters 6 through 8.

Changes in the quality of voice production can communicate all sorts of information relevant to an assessment. For example, when under stress, people tend to speak both faster and louder, and sometimes in a higher pitched voice (Tao, Kang, & Li, 2006). If you are aware of these tendencies in stressful situations, you can manage conversations differently if needed.

Verbal communication can be understood from many different perspectives. This next section examines the ways in which people vary in their verbal communications according to the social context, to emotional expressiveness, and to meaning.

Social Variations

The use of language to convey experiences, emotions, needs, and wants is a fundamental human capacity and skill. Language is the means by which people "name and evaluate the objects, sensations, feelings, and situations they experience" (Heath & Bryant, 2000, p. 91). This verbal naming and availability of information enables people to survive and to establish an individual and social identity, as well as a sense of worth, role, and place.

© PaylessImages/123RF

Reflect on your own conversational style. What cultural influences do you think shaped your conversational style? What are some specific personal traits that you can identify in the way that you speak with others? Do you find that you speak differently to different people—for example, your university or college instructor as opposed to a close friend? If so, what are some specific differences between these different conversational styles in terms of vocal style, word choice, body language, and emotional expression?

Throughout infancy and early childhood, children rapidly acquire the capacity to apply names in their world and to interact verbally with others (Harris, 1995). What is increasingly recognized is that, from childhood, we learn a particular **conversational style** (or styles), in particular social groupings, with particular "ethnic, regional, and class distinctions that have so many reverberations in society" (Tannen, 2000, p. 393). In addition to the ethnic, regional, and class distinctions children also learn gender and age differences.

Emotional Variation

Other variations in verbal styles relate to the degree to which individuals and families articulate their emotional experiences. The quality emphasized here is "emotional expressiveness" (Yoo, Matsumoto, & LeRoux, 2006; Vogel Wester, Heesacker, Boysen, and Seeman, 2006), and it has been a feature of many studies in the mental health area—for example, where both extreme emotional expression and repression have been studied.

These variations become important in client-worker relationships. A conversation that one person may perceive to be reflective may be seen by another as deeply introspective, too emotional, and, overall, inappropriate. These relative depths of experience and expression of experience become important points of congruity or incongruity in the context of conversations.

Language as Signifier: Language Variation

The process of communication is a translation process, which often relies on assumptions—that is, we can think we know what people mean, more or less, by what they are telling us, and by their non-verbal communication (discussed later). Words carry many different meanings, however, and both individual and contextual interpretations are relied on in practice.

In a recent research study at a major trauma hospital, social workers stepped into the role of research assistants, asking people about their perceptions of trauma and about their resources when a member of their family had been admitted to the intensive care unit. In their role as research assistants, the social workers were surprised by some of the information they were told by the family members when they compared it with some of the information they had received in their role as social workers. The "research assistants" heard some new or quite different dimensions of the "same" stories. What this example revealed to the research team was that the family members told different dimensions of their story according to differences in what they presumed their roles were at different times. Many people report that one of the difficulties following trauma or grief is finding a vocabulary with which to talk about their experiences—that is, finding a way of using words that will accurately convey what has been seen, experienced, and felt (Walter & McCoyd, 2009). As later chapters on narrative approaches will emphasize, finding the appropriate words to use is an important part of adaptation and recovery.

This notion of narrative variation is explored in Chapter 13.

In the scenario, in Box 2.2 Jane, a senior hospital social worker, shows how specific choices of language can be. Words have personal meanings and "loading" for particular individuals and their experiences in a particular context.

Language variation perhaps occurs most fundamentally across cultures. Throughout Canada's history, people have migrated from all over the world, bringing a diversity of

BOX 2.2 Focus on Practice

Finding the "Right" Words

Once a year our department holds an afternoon for brothers and sisters who are bereaved through the death of a sibling. As we talk with the children, we feel it is important to use *correct factual* language and not euphemisms. One year, after an introduction to an activity in which I used the terms "dead" and "died," a little girl who was seven years old took me to one side and whispered, "You should say passed away, it's much nicer." A little taken aback, I asked her if this is what she said. "Of course it is," she replied. I asked her who else said "passed away" and she replied, "My mother." Her point was well made. She knew very well that her sister was dead and didn't need to have this stated bluntly. An alternative response to the little girl might have been to ask her if she could tell me what "passed away" meant, but I think we both already knew.

languages. **Cross-cultural communication** not only differs linguistically, but also "involve[s] diverse experiences, worldviews and differential social power and privilege" (Miller, Donner, & Fraser, 2004, p. 377; Bishop, 2015).

For human service practice, you need to be culturally educated and aware. Debates about cross-cultural competence are complex. The First Nations Health Authority (n.d.) applies the term "cultural humility" as "a process of self-reflection to understand personal and systemic biases and to develop and maintain respectful processes and relationships based on mutual trust. Cultural humility involves humbly acknowledging oneself as a learner when it comes to understanding another's experience." However, some authors suggest it is actually impossible to be a culturally competent practitioner outside of one's own culture (Dean, 2001; Coates & Hetherington, 2016). They argue it is more important to maintain an awareness of this impossibility, which leads to far greater communication sensitivity or focus on building cultural safety.

BOX 2.3 Practice Questions

欢迎光临 Kanata

You may or may not be able to read either of these words.

1. What do you notice happens if you cannot understand a word?
2. How do you go about trying to understand it?
3. What would you do if you were confronted with one of these words and you were required to respond, even if you do not understand it?

BOX 2.4 Focus on Practice

Working with Interpreters

Working with interpreters is a vital skill in working with people from culturally and linguistically diverse backgrounds. "Canada" is derived from *Kanata*, the Huron word meaning "settlement" or "village." The Victorian Interpreting and Translating Service (VITS, 2017, pp. 19-20) proposes the following strategies.

- Introduce yourself and the interpreter to your client.
- Explain what the interview is about and what you hope to achieve.
- Explain to the interviewee the interpreter's role within the interview. Inform the person that the interpreter's role is to assist communication by interpreting everything that is being said, by all parties.
- Maintain control of the interview. You must ask the questions and hear the replies fully. The interpreter's task is to assist in communication, not to conduct the interview.
- Position yourself in a way that permits you to speak directly with the client and allows you to have maximum eye contact with her or him.
- Use the first person when speaking to your client; that is, say "I" instead of "Ask him/her" etc. Doing so will encourage both you and your client to talk to each other and use eye contact and body language, which assists in effective communication.
- Keep your questions, statements, and comments short and deliver them in segments, allowing the interpreter to interpret everything you say in stages. Take note of the interpreter's method of signalling to you that your comments or questions are too long and allow the interpreter to do the same with the client.
- Never assume that interpreting is a simple mechanical task of matching the non-English word or expression with an English equivalent.
- It is unreasonable to expect an interpreter to be a walking dictionary.
- Do not assume that because a person appears to have a basic understanding of English, he or she will be able to comprehend specific terms and difficult expressions or jargon, particularly when under stress.
- Do not isolate the client by engaging the interpreter in discussion. If you need to clarify or discuss something with the interpreter, request that this be explained to the client first.
- Allow the client to raise any questions or issues of concern.
- Before the end of the interview, summarize key points for the client.

The Use of Silence

The use of silence—that is, the *absence* of verbal communication—is an important skill. Silence can be regarded as a verbal skill in that it is a deliberate refraining from the use of words to communicate different messages.

Silences can provide extremely powerful spaces in which to reflect and simply "be" in that moment with another person. On the other hand, silences can be agonizingly long and awkward moments. Human service workers uncomfortable with silence may rush to fill this space to address their own feelings of uncertainty. Thompson and Ladany (2003) suggest the use of silence is "primarily to facilitate reflection, encourage responsibility, facilitate expression of feelings, not interrupt session flow, and convey empathy" (p. 513). It is important to consider if silence is present because the client is processing and deciding how to respond, or if he or she is unclear and confused. A client's silence can also represent his or her feeling vulnerable and uncertain about client–worker trust, or it can reflect the difficulty of discussing a painful subject. Regardless of the situation, it is important for the worker to be patient with silence and support the client in working through this process.

Assumptions about the appropriateness of silence and pausing are both culturally and individually based. As Tannen (2000) notes about differing assumptions:

> The one who is waiting for a longer pause finds it harder to get a turn, because before that length of pause occurs, the other person begins to perceive an uncomfortable silence and rushes to fill it, to save the conversation. (p. 393)

John, a social worker who has researched differences between Indigenous and non-Indigenous communication assumptions, spoke with Margaret, a respected Indigenous Elder, about the use of silence. The following is an excerpt from that interview, reprinted with permission.

Margaret:	Nah, they have to fill in every minute with talk, with words. They don't know how to just listen, to just hear silence.
John:	*[after a pause]* How do you mean?
Margaret:	It's like they can't stand it when nobody is saying nothing. Silence is important to us. But they don't get that, don't respect that. . . . If you don't answer right away they say you're angry or not interested or something. . . . After a while, you just say stuff you know they want to hear.

Finding the commonalities and congruities in the content of your conversations is important. You should learn about and consider the use of silence as it is defined by the culture you are working with. Here are some questions to consider when working with silence cross-culturally:

1. How is silence defined within the culture you are working with?
2. Is silence defined as a sign of respect and therefore important to maintain in your working relationship?
3. Is silence part of processing language translation?
4. Is silence a sign of miscommunication?
5. Is silence a reflection of the overuse of professional language or jargon creating difficulties with language translation?

Silence can be defined in many different ways. When working cross-culturally, the worker should consider the cultural context in which silence is defined. Working with silence is summarized by Jaworski (1993): "On the one hand, silence is useful when one wants to be indirect or to be polite by 'leaving options'" (p. 25). Jaworski continues by noting that silence provides time for understanding and to think of a response, which may avoid conflict. "On the other hand, one's failure to say something that is expected in a given moment by the other party can be interpreted as a sign of hostility or dumbness. This negative aspect of the use of silence becomes especially apparent in cross-cultural communication" (Jaworski, 1993, p. 25).

Non-verbal Communication Processes

Equally important is the use of non-verbal communication. The term "non-verbal" refers to the process of sending a message to another person without speaking. Non-verbal messages can be relayed by the way people look, dress, move their body, facial expressions, or even a lack of expression during a single interaction. It can refer as well to communication through touch or smell, through various kinds of artifacts such as masks and clothes, or through formalized

©Mark Bowden/123RF

If this were your client, how would you interpret his emotions based on his facial expressions and body language? How might you change the way you spoke with him based on these interpretations? Ask someone else to do the same exercise and compare your answers.

communications such as semaphore. Thus, non-verbal cues relate to both the voluntary and involuntary physical reactions and responses we have in the context of a conversation, as well as the messages we transmit physically about our social identity. We rely on these non-verbal cues to indicate that we are listening and being listened to in a conversation.

Each person has a unique repertoire of non-verbal reactions and skills. This understanding is important as many communication texts suggest that up to 85 per cent of communication is conveyed in our non-verbal language. Understanding the context of non-verbal behaviour is vital for a number of reasons. First, non-verbal behaviour conveys information for our survival. Research has found that we process some information emotionally in the first instance, and then at a cognitive level as a secondary process (Schacter, 1996). These understandings have emerged from studying how people process traumatic situations. They contradict some earlier assumptions that a cognitive process occurred first, followed by a physiological response. At a basic survival level, we rely on non-verbal cues to read safety in situations, reacting to stress and trauma with fight or flight or freeze reactions (Selye, 1987). Our non-verbal reactions, therefore, convey our immediate physiological responses to situations. In less stressful situations, it is easier to monitor and influence non-verbal reactions.

Second, given that "negative impressions often result from differences in conversational style" (Tannen, 2000, p. 394), it is important to think analytically about what we hope is being conveyed and why.

BOX 2.5 Practice Questions

1. What non-verbal cues would you rely on to know that someone
   - is agreeing with you?
   - is disagreeing with you?
   - is confused by you?
   - understands you?
   - is offended by something you said?
2. What non-verbal cues stood out or were focused on in your interpretation?
3. Why did you emphasize these cues and not others?

Increasingly, non-verbal cues are recognized as being highly cultural and gender-specific, as well as context- and age-specific. You can find texts that identify all sorts of cross-cultural differences in eye contact, body language, and personal space (e.g., Evans, Tulsky, Back, & Arnold, 2006, cited in Morris, 2006). The problem with identifying differences on the basis of group membership is that the differences become oversimplified and stereotyped, and group membership is assumed, often wrongly. On the other hand, these important differences can be neglected when they are profound influences. It is important to listen to what these gestures or styles of communication indicate—for example, eye contact can be either about respect or indifference, which are two fundamentally different messages.

The following exercise encourages you to play with some of your non-verbal comfort levels by testing out different physical proximities.

BOX 2.6 Focus on Practice

Your Physical Comfort Zones

In a class or small-group situation, try to keep a conversation going while working from a number of different physical **postures**. For example, maintain your conversation while you are

- sitting or standing
- back to back
- shoulder to shoulder
- three metres apart
- ten centimetres apart or toe to toe.

Then, find a comfortable distance and maintain the conversation in that position for a few minutes, noticing the features of this position.

1. What changes do you make in trying to find a comfortable position in which to maintain a conversation?
2. Reflecting on the comfortable position you moved to, how similar or different is that position from your colleagues' positions?
3. What cultural factors or assumptions do you think have influenced your position?

Over many years, the acronym SOLER (Egan, 2007) has been used to promote the optimal non-verbal positioning in an interviewing situation. SOLER stands for sitting **s**quare on (that is, facing the client), with an **o**pen posture (no crossed legs or arms), **l**eaning forward towards the client to express interest, maintaining **e**ye contact, and being **r**elaxed. Egan later changed the acronym to SOLER, following feedback from a woman who had been working with blind students and found that the **aim** of eye contact, not necessarily eye contact itself in this instance, was of greatest importance. This positioning was thought to reflect a genuine and respectful non-verbal orientation to the client. However, as a reflection of cultural changes and particularly shifts in gender relations, this acronym is now heavily critiqued. We will think about these issues of body language more broadly under separate subheadings of facial expression, body posture, and physical proximity.

Facial Expression

Over the past decades, a continuing effort has been made to establish whether non-verbal behaviours, particularly facial expressions, are common to all people, regardless of context. Cultures vary enormously, however, in the so-called display rules that are developed around the expression of these emotions. Major differences have been found between the extensive use of direct eye contact in Western contexts and more avoidant and hierarchical rules relating to eye contact in Asian and Indigenous contexts (Kinloch & Metge, 2014; Sciarra, 1999).

Your understanding of cultural influences, therefore, is critical. At the same time, it is difficult to develop such understandings outside of a particular situation. On the one hand, there may be generalizations that can be drawn about specific cultural groups regarding all sorts of dimensions of communication, such as the use of eye contact, touch, proximity, and emotional expressiveness. Generalizations can also become stereotyped. On the other hand, glossing over cultural differences can lead to misinterpretation of behaviour because of assumptions that do not adequately acknowledge cultural difference.

BOX 2.7 Practice Questions

Watch a number of conversations taking place in different contexts—in a workplace, in public, or on television, for example. Observe how people use their non-verbal skills to communicate their message and to respond to other persons.

1. What do you see working effectively and ineffectively in these encounters?
2. What communication differences would you attribute to gender, class, or cultural differences?

This modification of your emotional responses relates to your "use of self," which we explore in Chapter 4.

In previous decades of counselling training, the emphasis was on the worker maintaining a very neutral facial reaction to the client and the client's story. This neutrality was assumed so the worker was not reacting to the emotional experience of the client but providing a neutral sounding board. Rather than working towards some artificial neutral response, a quality of intersubjectivity—shared meaning(s) constructed by people in their interactions with one another—is now valued.

One of the opportunities, therefore, throughout any skills class is to learn the skills of monitoring and/or modifying emotional reactions. Four processes of modification have been noted (Bull, 2002, pp. 30–1), including (1) attenuation, whereby an emotional reaction is weakened in its intensity; (2) amplification, whereby it is exaggerated; (3) concealment, whereby it is hidden by adopting a neutral facial expression; and (4) substitution, whereby a different expression of the emotion being experienced is reflected. For example, it is not uncommon for people to smile while they are telling you about how sad they are feeling. If you have the opportunity to record your use of these skills, you will be able to witness your own reactions to clients and their stories, even if in a role-playing situation.

BOX 2.8 Focus on Practice

Analyzing Non-Verbal Behaviour

If you have the opportunity, use a recording device (tablet or phone) or an observer to map your non-verbal behaviour throughout a role-play interview. A recording, in particular, can provide the opportunity for you to see yourself as others experience you. Often the person on-screen feels a sense of shock when seeing the video for the first time. This sort of viewing links our usually entirely subjective experience with an objective experience of ourselves.

From a British study (Cartney, 2006) of the usefulness of viewing recordings in developing communication skills in social work training, students had these comments:

> During the recording you can see your practical skills and then you can analyze yourself and base this in theory and in reading from different books. So you get all parts.
>
> You see things that you do yourself but you never realized. . . . You watch and re-watch and all the time you see new things. (p. 839)

Body Posture

Many different postures have been proposed as the most suitable posture for workers, such as SOLER mentioned earlier. While the absence of clear guidelines about physical **posture** may seem to make the task of interpreting these cues impossible, the quality of the physical alignment between communicators does seem to be the most important factor. Egan (2002) states, "The point is that your bodily orientation should convey the message that you are involved with the client" (p. 69). This means a general orientation of your body towards the person is important, but further "rules" may not be helpful.

Perhaps the most important quality of any physical posture is that it conveys respect to the other person. That is, you are available to listen and respond, finding a sustainable posture and one free of distractions. You may need to consider how sustainable your posture is. While it may initially seem a good idea to kneel down beside a child to talk, for example, it can become an awkward position beyond a few moments of conversation and distracting to then shift.

Physical Proximity and Location

Issues of physical space and proximity are similarly important considerations. A conversation too close to another person can seem violating of private or personal space. A conversation that is conducted too remotely can seem impersonal. Again, individual interpretation is influential here. At a recent cross-cultural seminar, two workers had fundamentally different reactions to a photo of two people in conversation. One worker considered them to be very awkward in their posture and disengaged, whereas another worker thought they were two people relaxed in conversation with each other. The only way to know whether or not it was a difficult encounter would have been by asking the participants themselves about their experience.

Another non-verbal dimension in human service work to consider is the use of physical contact with clients. This has been, and remains, a contentious area of practice. On the one hand, a rule of "no contact" is maintained, primarily to safeguard the client from unwanted touch and intimacy. On the other hand, there are times when physical contact, such as a handshake, becomes an important marker of respect and engagement in work together (Trevithick, 2005). The use of touch raises questions of personal safety, for both your client and yourself.

These non-verbal cues can become the inhibitors rather than the enhancers of good communication interactions. Rather than there being one correct way to physically interact, interactional synchrony, congruence, or alignment within a conversation have been identified as core components of an effective communication. Underutilized physical cues tend to leave the talker uncertain as to how the conversation is going. If you receive no response from someone in terms of facial expression, for example, it can be difficult to continue talking. Overused physical cues can similarly leave the client feeling unheard; an overreaction is perceived instead. One person recounted seeing a counsellor whose eyes welled up with tears every time she spoke of her parent who had died some time earlier. The person was seeking help with other matters and felt that the counsellor was involved in her own grief rather than with the difficulties she was expected to address.

Other overbearing physical cues can emerge in relation to eye contact that is too intense or a physical presence that is too close or too overbearing, thus overstepping a client's sense of personal space that many consider important. Fidgeting or doodling with a pen and paper can similarly indicate stress or boredom and disengagement. Sometimes we are unaware of our habits—of flicking hair, clicking pens, or playing with jewellery or fingernails, for example. In any of these situations, if you are distracted, the client will be left feeling unattended to in the conversation.

Non-verbal cues also are presented through a bodily discourse. Our physical presence tells a story to the client. For example, how you dress and how you present in relation to confidence are interpreted by your clients. In this sense, the "body can be inscribed with societal norms, values and mores (customs in a particular group) . . . and . . . our actions and behaviours . . . illuminate personal values and ideas" (Osmond, 2005, p. 892). These worker dimensions can alienate a client or provide reassurance, depending on how congruent they are with the client's world.

Your physical proximity can sometimes be beyond your control. Human service work frequently is done in physical locations other than private rooms where people are sitting together in comfortable chairs. Many significant conversations can be made in corridors standing together, over a patient's bed, or in public places where someone's response to the interview may have as much to do with the overall physicality of the environment as with the immediate conversation. Your awareness of the possible impact of all of these non-verbal dimensions on your capacity to talk together is vital.

Individual and Collective Communication Processes

So far, we have considered communication in relation to at least two people in some form of direct verbal and non-verbal communication contact with each other. Other dimensions of communication complexity in this process include thinking beyond the one-to-one context of communication and beyond a "five senses" understanding.

Communication Involving More Than One Person

As people are added to the conversation, so the complexity of the communication web grows. As noted in Chapter 1, Western approaches to human services, and interviewing and counselling in particular, have been criticized for failing to recognize communication processes beyond individual interactions. The site of intervention remains primarily the individual, even though family, community, and the broader social context that have such profound influences on well-being are acknowledged. This was illustrated in John's research with a non-Indigenous social worker talking about her experiences with Indigenous clients.

On the one hand, pragmatic realities such as limited agency resources can justify this individual focus. On the other hand, the lack of integration into practice of recent theoretical understandings around communication and interaction leads to a considerable outdatedness of practice assumptions (Whyte, 2005). Seeing the client as an individual rather than as part of a family or community means that the context of the problems, and therefore often the solutions, are overlooked. This has been particularly noted by Indigenous researchers and practitioners, who emphasize that because ways of living and thinking are collective and communal, problems should be addressed in collective and communal ways (Coggins, 2016; Schmidt, 2017; Zapf, 2001).

BOX 2.9 Focus on Practice

On Communication Skills

Susan: There are two things I wish I'd been taught in school. The first, about how to keep boundaries, how much to reveal—both with clients and co-workers. . . . The second, particularly about working with [Indigenous] clients, is how hard it is to ensure successful communication. In many cases, work is done at the community level or the client attends with extended family. I definitely prefer individual work. I fear missing cross-cultural communication issues and possibly offending the client or sending the wrong message.

Morrissette, McKenzie, and Morrissette (1993) write,

> Aboriginal people do not embrace a single philosophy, there are fundamental differences between the dominant Euro-Canadian and traditional Aboriginal societies, and these have their roots in differing perceptions of one's relationship with the universe and the Creator. . . . Decision making was based primarily on sharing, understanding, and the building of consensus. (p. 93)

Such a philosophy requires the worker to consider cross-cultural values, such as a collective, interdependent ways of relating. This standpoint will require the worker to gain skill in working with both individual clients and, when requested, client groups.

Communication beyond the Five Senses

The individualized approach is privileged further within Western discourses in regard only to verbal and non-verbal interactions within the physical realms, thus acknowledging five, not six, basic human senses. Various theorists have tried to articulate understandings of other ways of knowing. Jung (1963) termed one dimension of this extra-verbal communication the "collective unconscious" (p. 160), referring to the inherited, transpersonal dimensions of communication. Dreams and intuitions are thought to be the ways in which these shared dimensions of communication are transmitted.

Indigenous cultures have always respected the reality of other levels of communication, recognizing conscious and unconscious, individual and collective, physical and metaphysical, and transpersonal ways of knowing (Smith, 2001).

The capacity for human consciousness to effect change, even when people are not physically present together, has been proven in many studies (Hudson, 2000). This research is relatively new and contentious, but it highlights that there are different levels of influence in any communication process. Rogers (cited in Moore & Purton, 2006) identified this when he noted it was not so much the qualities of genuineness or empathy that influenced the process of engagement with another person, but the subsequent transcendent state of being that was experienced as a result of these qualities.

BOX 2.10 Practice Questions

"I was in London in 2005 in the week following the terrorist attacks in the Underground. On the Thursday after the bombs, at midday, a minute's silence was held. Thousands of people across London stopped to respect this silence.

"During that time, for about 30 seconds, I felt an incredible tingling sensation through my arms and neck. On talking with several other people afterwards, it seems that we had shared this experience."

1. What is your immediate reaction to this description?
2. Have you had similar experiences?
3. What would you be thinking if a client told you this story?
4. How might you respond to a client who told you this story?

We look now at three major ways in which communication is critical in the change process. Communication influences survival, promotes healing, and expresses power.

Communication for Survival

Communication connects people and facilitates the formation of social bonds and attachments (Koprowska, 2005), which in turn facilitate our very survival. The infant learns to cry when hungry to elicit a response from a caregiver. Over time, young children acquire specific words to communicate specific needs. Across the lifespan, we communicate not only our basic physical needs and wants but also our most complex intimate and psychological needs.

We rely also on non-verbal communication for our survival. For example, we experience parataxic distortions (Sullivan, 1953) when we first meet someone, whereby we try to identify whether this person reminds us of anyone else. We scan our memories to see if there is any corresponding cue that reminds us of this person from our experience to date. This is the typification process indicated earlier in Chapter 1, whereby we very quickly group people, determining, for instance, as to whether this person looks safe or threatening.

Communication impacts our survival in other ways. The impact of health professionals' communication styles on patients has been studied, looking at compliance with medication and rehabilitation programs, and reduction of stress and anxiety (Glintborg, Andersen, & Dalhoff, 2007; Yedidia, 2007). Effective communication strategies enhance health outcomes, although, in regard to neuroleptic medications, evidence suggests that compliance with doctors' and workers' promotion of these medications has greatly increased the incidence and degree of mental illness (see, e.g., Whitaker, 2010; Cech, 2010).

This link is emphasized across a wide range of professional guidelines. Rider and Keefer (2006), for example, report on the competencies required of doctors in the US context. They include the capacity to

> create and sustain a therapeutic and ethically sound relationship with patients; use effective listening skills and elicit and provide information using effective non-verbal, explanatory, questioning and writing skills; work effectively with others as a member or leader of a health care team or other professional group. (p. 626)

Communication generally has been found to profoundly impact mood states and self-esteem, which, in turn, are known to impact physical health states (Goleman, 2006). Positive communications lead to positive outcomes. Thus, communication plays a key role in enhancing or inhibiting well-being.

Communication as Healing or Therapeutic

As a worker, you will be using communication to bring about positive change for individuals and their communities. Thus, communication is both a means and an end in itself. The telling of and listening to human stories is a well-known protective factor for well-being. The **therapeutic** quality seems to be related both to what is said and that someone has listened. Conversations can be healing, therapeutic, relieving, and normalizing.

For example, one Australian Indigenous man reflects on how sharing stories is healing: "My medicine is listening to other people, too. The first time I was listening to others talking, I thought they were talking about my life. "I am not alone" is powerful medicine for people who have felt completely isolated, unheard, unacknowledged in their pain" (Atkinson, 2002, p. 198).

When working with clients, it is important to identify individual strengths early in the first meeting. It might be acknowledging the initial courage it took to make the appointment and then show up. The strength may appear through the desire to improve parenting skills or the trust in the practitioner to disclose "a long kept secret," for the first time. Early identification of the client's strengths enhances the engagement process and brings awareness to the client's existing available resources.

The orientation of human service communication, therefore, is towards the promotion of the values discussed in Chapter 1. It is intentional communication towards evoking strengths, positive emotions, and resilience. This can come about in many ways—through the deep listening to the story of the client and through breaking down a sense of isolation.

Communication as Power

Verbal and non-verbal communication is, therefore, the major means of the human service worker's influence. One further way of understanding and analyzing communication is in relation to the power relations inherent in any communication process.

Power is exerted by individuals for many reasons: as a result of unconscious motivations, as attempts to manage uncertainty, or to maintain the social order. Power is exerted through assumptions about ways of being, through hierarchies of interaction, and through language. These forms of power play out whether or not words for particular experiences exist within a particular culture, whether or not recognition is granted to individual constructions of meaning, and whether or not knowledge bases are the privileged ones for power.

Power is exercised by workers in relation to the subsequent flow of information following a conversation with clients. For example, client confidentiality is in many ways protected by privacy legislation and codes of ethical practice. At times (and for family members in particular), the power of workers to withhold certain information from families—even out of respect for the client and consistent with privacy laws—can lead to tensions and frustrations (Deveson, 1991). Not communicating information—the withholding of information from colleagues and clients, because of legislation requirements and/or personal style—can also be an extremely powerful act. Not communicating verbally leaves people unclear, powerless, and unable to ascertain limits and boundaries.

The power dynamics of any relationship, therefore, are important to attend to in the context of professional practice. Often, power dynamics are talked about as if they are something that can and should be removed from a relationship. It seems paradoxical that you become a human service worker to effect change, yet would deny there is any influence or power in that role. For example, if you are the social worker working in child protection, you have the capacity under the legislation to remove a child to safer circumstances. As a worker, you have the power to breach confidentiality in situations where there are major concerns about the safety of an individual. Another way to think about it is that power dynamics are always functioning in any relationship, along with shifting experiences of influence, interdependence, dependence, and independence.

Legislation and the responsibilities vested in the worker raise all sorts of questions about the degree to which client–worker relationships are "equal." Some authors and practitioners emphatically state that client–worker relationships are equal or that the worker should strive to make them equal. One strategy for ensuring that power inequality is not a destructive inequality is to develop a consciousness and an articulation of the dilemmas and decisions we encounter throughout a relationship. That is, one needs to recognize the distinction between having power and managing the inequality respectfully and openly. There are ways of minimizing the inequality and the use of power within any relationship.

Another practice skill to ensure power equity is addressed by negotiation. "Negotiation" can be defined as the process of the worker's developing an agreement with the client that clearly defines the working relationship. Deryl's work with Chris, a 17-year-old who has not been attending school, offers a practice example of negotiation.

BOX 2.11 Focus on Practice

Negotiating the Relationship

Deryl: Hi, Chris. What brings you in today?
Chris: My parents are making me come.
Deryl: Why do you think your parents want you to come?
Chris: They are angry because I have been missing lots of school; but it is too much, and I am not going to go back!
Deryl: Tell me about school. What are you taking?
Chris: Well, I have five classes and it's not like I hate school but . . .

Chris explains to Deryl that he has been cutting school because he feels his class schedule is too difficult for him to manage. Chris is dealing with the pressure by not attending.

1. Where might some of the power inequities be in this example?
2. How would you negotiate with Chris to increase his attendance?
3. In negotiating the working relationship, what might be some of the initial steps?

This chapter ends with an example, provided by John, of some Indigenous clients talking about their non-Indigenous social worker. It draws together some of the themes that have run through this chapter—the use of verbal and non-verbal skills, the degree to which conversations are therapeutic or not, and the degree to which power is exerted or not in client–worker interactions.

BOX 2.12 Focus on Practice

Communication and Power

Lee: We'd meet at the hall and she'd have us sitting in a row and she would sit facing us. . . . We'd just sit there and she would talk.
Rita: Yeah, she'd tell us what we were there to talk about and stuff. But it's like she wasn't really listening, she just kept on talking even when we didn't answer.
Lee: Yeah, and then she'd talk even more. Once, after [several such meetings] we just sat there, didn't say a word. After a few minutes she just got up and left.
Rita: We broke up laughing, damn near rolled on the floor!

1. What is your reaction to this interaction?
2. Identify the dimensions that you think were problematic in the client–worker relationship.

Chapter Summary

Remember the five core practice values, including respect, that were explored in Chapter 1.

In this chapter, we have explored the many microskills involved in the key dimensions of communication. While communication is regarded as a verbal process, the critical role of non-verbal communication in conveying the emotional and physical components of messages that are important in work with clients. We looked at the dimensions of verbal and non-verbal communication processes that enhance or inhibit effective communication.

As a practitioner, you will bring to communication with clients a specialized understanding of the significance of that communication, which constitutes a form of power. We have looked at the impact of communication on health and well-being; the role of communication in healing; and communication as sustaining, reinforcing, or changing power dynamics in individual and social relationships.

Questions for Analysis

1. What have you learned about
    - the verbal skills of communication?
    - the non-verbal skills of communication?
    - the ways in which communication is integral to culture, survival, health, and power?
    - the communication challenges within a client–worker relationship?
2. Which points in question 1 do you feel confident applying?
3. Which specific skills do you require more practice with and why?
4. What have you learned about your own communication style from reading this chapter—in relation to both your verbal and non-verbal skills?
5. What are some of the strengths and challenges you experience in your communication style with other people?

Recommended Readings

Coates, J., & Hetherington, T. (2016). *Decolonizing social work: Contemporary social work studies*. New York, NY: Routledge.

Hargie, O. (2011). *Skilled interpersonal interaction: Research, theory, and practice* (5th ed.). London: Routledge.

Jaworski, A. (1993). *The power of silence: Social and pragmatic perspectives*. London: Sage.

Jeffrey, D. (2015). Meeting here and now: Reflections on racial and cultural differences in social work encounters. In J. Carrier, & S. Strega (Eds.), *Walking this path together: Anti-Racist and anti-oppressive child welfare practice* (pp. 45–60). Halifax, NS: Fernwood Publishing.

Kinloch, P., & Metge, J. (2014). *Talking past each other: Problems of cross cultural communication*. Wellington, New Zealand: Victoria University Press.

Koprowska, J. (2005). *Communication and interpersonal skills in social work*. Exeter, UK: Learning Matters.

Newhouse, D., Voyageur, C., & Beavon, D. (2005). *Hidden in plain sight: Contributions of Aboriginal Peoples to Canadian identity and culture*. Toronto, ON: University of Toronto Press.

Trevithick, P. (2005). *Social work skills: A practice handbook* (2nd ed.). Maidenhead, UK: Open University Press.

Spencer, E., Massing, D., & Gough, J. (Eds.). (2017). *Social work ethics: Progressive, practical, and relational approaches*. Toronto, ON: Oxford University Press.

Sinha, V., & Kozlowski, A. (2013). The structure of Aboriginal child welfare in Canada. *International Indigenous Policy Journal*, *4*(2), 1–21.

Truth and Reconciliation Commission of Canada. (2015a). *Canada's Residential Schools: Missing Children and Unmarked Burials. Vol. 4 of The Final Report of the Truth and Reconciliation Commission of Canada*. Montreal and Kingston: McGill-Queen's University Press.

Truth and Reconciliation Commission of Canada. (2015b). *Honouring the Truth, Reconciling for the Future: Summary of the Final Report of the Truth and Reconciliation Commission of Canada.* Winnipeg, MB: Truth and Reconciliation Commission of Canada.

Weaver, H. (1999). Indigenous people and the social work profession: Defining culturally competent services. *Social Work*, 44(3), 217–25.

Internet Resources

Crown–Indigenous Relations and Northern Affairs Canada, *First Nations in Canada*
www.aadnc-aandc.gc.ca/eng/1307460755710/1307460872523

First Nations Child and Family Caring Society of Canada
https://fncaringsociety.com

First Nations Health Authority
www.fnha.ca

500 Nations
http://500nations.com/Canada_First_Nations.asp

Missing the Mark in Cross-Cultural Communication: A Case Study of a Stoney Nakoda Sioux Community, by John W. Friesen and John D. Snow
http://elacata.ca/uploads/files/Alberta%20Voices/Alberta_Voices_Vol13_No1_November_2016.pdf#page=23

The New Social Worker
www.socialworker.com/extras/creative-work/the-power-of-social-work

Social Media Use in Social Work Practice
www.casw-acts.ca/sites/default/files/policy_statements/social_media_use_and_social_work_practice.pdf

3 Diversity in Communication

Learning Goals

- Analyze the influences on our listening.
- Consider the paradigms that influence listening.
- Describe the influence of theory on listening.
- Understand how different practice perspectives influence our practice.
- Apply a multi-dimensional approach to listening.

The Influences on Our Listening

In Chapter 2, we looked at the communication process in some detail, breaking it down into the verbal and non-verbal skills that influence a conversation. As Thompson (2002) notes, "skill development does not occur in a vacuum—there are also knowledge and values to be taken into consideration" (p. xviii). This chapter focuses on how we can bring together these skills with a theoretical understanding of clients, their particular circumstances, and the events or conditions that require change.

Developing an understanding of the knowledge bases we bring to our practice is essential. Two knowledge bases, in particular, inform human service work—an evidence-based perspective and a reflective practice perspective (Chui & Wilson, 2006; Lewis, 2002). That is, our practice is based on the observed result of the application of knowledge and theory, as well as on the use of an understanding of ourselves as workers.

We can think about knowledge, theories, and skills in a number of different ways. These differences often lead to confusion because a sharp distinction is not made between the level or type of **theory** or knowledge that is being presented (Walsh, 2006). In this chapter, **paradigms**—dominant views held by groups of people at a certain point in time that determine and explain human society or a particular field of knowledge—are described. The chapter concludes with a presentation of a multi-dimensional approach, an overarching framework used within this book.

To focus the discussion, Jahzara's story will be used to show the different ways we might go about thinking about our work.

BOX 3.1 Focus on Practice

Seeking Help

Jahzara has called your organization and spoken with the duty worker about her concerns that she's going to harm her four children. She's exhausted and depressed following the birth of her baby seven weeks ago. The other three children are all under six years of age, and over the school holidays she has found it increasingly difficult to manage with them at home every day. Her partner, Davu, is working part time in the local car factory, but it has been threatened with closure. The financial stress is the worst it has ever been, with the rent in arrears and the bills piling up. If Davu loses his job, she does not know what they will do.

This morning, her eldest son dropped his breakfast all over the floor. His stepfather hit him and he has bruises on his face. He has been withdrawn in his room all morning and she is now feeling so angry and frustrated with him, she thinks she may lash out at him as well. She realizes this and picks up the phone, calling your family service instead. She realizes she needs help before things are more out of control.

1. What is your reaction to this situation and why?
2. Why do you think this situation has arisen?
3. Who would you view as your client(s) in this situation and why?
4. What would you see as your main purposes in working with this situation and whomever you have identified as the client(s)?
5. What would you want to do in this situation to achieve your purpose?
6. What would be your first step?

Jahzara's story raises a lot of questions for your practice: Where would you begin in your response to Jahzara and the others in her family? What would be the purpose of your involvement and intervention, along with the other questions raised in the box above?

Theoretical Knowledge

While we may be able to agree on what is verbalized in a conversation and demonstrated at a non-verbal level, many interpretations can be made of what the meaning or intention of that communication may be. Theoretical perspectives provide a language and a structure for interpreting information. Theoretical perspectives inform what we ask about in the first interview (Sommers-Flanagan & Sommers-Flanagan, 2004), what we talk about with the client, how we interpret what we hear, and how we respond.

For ideas to be called a theory or to provide a conceptual framework for therapeutic work, four main dimensions must be present (Nelson-Jones, 2006):

1. a statement of the basic . . . assumptions underlying the theory
2. an explanation of the acquisition of helpful and unhelpful behaviour
3. an explanation of the maintenance of helpful and unhelpful behaviour
4. an explanation of how to help clients change their behaviour and consolidate their gains. (p. 6)

> Remember that in Chapter 2 we looked at how meaning and intent is a major filter on what we hear in a conversation (non-verbal expressions, active listening, or diversity considerations, for example).

TABLE 3.1 Three Dominant Paradigms

	Positivism	Interpretive or Social Constructivism	Critical Theory
Reason for research	To discover natural laws so people can predict and control events	To understand and describe meaningful social action	To smash myths and empower people to change society radically
Nature of social reality	Stable pre-existing patterns or order that can be discovered	Fluid definitions of a changing situation created by human interaction	Conflict-filled and governed by hidden underlying structures
Nature of human beings	Self-interested and rational individuals who are shaped by external forces	Social beings who create meaning and who constantly make sense of their worlds	Creative, adaptive people with unrealized potential, trapped by illusion and exploitation
Role of common sense	Clearly distinct from and less valid than science	Powerful everyday theories used by ordinary people	False beliefs that hide power and objective conditions
Theory looks like	A logical, deductive system of interconnected definitions, axioms, and laws	A description of how a group's meaning system is generated and sustained	A critique that reveals true conditions and helps people see the way to a better world
An explanation that is true	Is logically connected to laws and based on facts	Resonates or feels right to those who are being studied	Supplies people with tools needed to change the world
Good evidence	Is based on precise observations that others can repeat	Is embedded in the context of fluid social interactions	Is informed by a theory that unveils illusions
Place for values	Science is value-free, and values have no place except when choosing a topic of study	Values are an integral part of social life; no groups' values are wrong, only different	All science must begin with a value position: some positions are right, some are wrong

Source: Neuman, W. 2006. Social Research Methods: Qualitative and Quantitative Approaches, 6th edn. Needham Heights, Mass.: Pearson Education.

The paradigms described above provide a theory or a grand narrative about behaviour and social interactions. They are theories that provide an explanation for human experience and behaviour. Theories also provide specific explanations for why social events occur and provide broad prescriptions or bases for interventions. To illustrate this point, one theory of human experience is that people need to find meaning or a sense of coherence to maintain well-being and function optimally. This observation is based on the understanding that from birth we develop cognitive and emotional sets of internal working models and assumptive paradigms. That is, from infancy, we develop ways of making sense of what goes on in our own internal and external worlds and, increasingly, in the worlds of others. A sense of coherence and predictability emerges, for most people, through the development of a story of how the world works and how we are positioned within it, which is integral to our mental health and to our capacity to relate to other people and to function effectively in our daily lives. We develop a sense of meaning, order, and security through these stories.

In the above paragraph, a theory of behaviour and experience has been outlined, drawn from attachment and narrative theories. It provides an explanation of a phenomenon—thus satisfying our need for theory—that has come about following the *observation* of the phenomenon by numerous authors. From that brief *description*, an *explanation* can be given as to how human beings might go about building an assumptive world, and a worker can consider how *predictions* and even *interventions* in a situation with a particular client can be undertaken. These five dimensions are identified by Howe (2002) as ways in which a theory is useful for practice.

If we are working with Jahzara as our client, we need to move from the general issues in her situation first outlined to very specific questions, such as why have these problems occurred? What can be done about them? How should change be brought about and with whom? We will need to make sense of particular dimensions or priorities in her family situation. Theoretical frameworks provide distinctive maps for the priorities in practice and the directions of any intervention.

Theories have different strengths and limitations. They vary in the degree to which they focus on change in the inner worlds of individuals and families or focus on change in the outer worlds that individuals and families occupy. To illustrate, the "conservation of resources" theory (Hobfoll, Ennis, & Kay, 2000) contributes to our understanding of grief, stress, and trauma experiences. This theory proposes that there are four domains of resources—condition, energy, personal, and time—and that experiences of grief, stress, and trauma emerge when one or more of these resource domains is affected negatively. Thus, resource losses—that is, impoverishment, the threat of income loss, the physical/emotional stress of recent childbirth—could explain Jahzara's distress reaction. This theory provides a strong and useful explanation for why people may be experiencing stress, grief, or trauma. It provides no explanation, however, of the possible trajectories of reactions experienced by an individual. No theory of intervention at an interpersonal level emerges from this, other than that financial resources are the critical need.

One of the challenges students face when they turn from theories of change to actual practice is that theories of change do not necessarily lead to the details of theories of intervention, or to the particular microskills needed to work in alignment with the theory. For example, while anti-oppressive approaches focus on change beyond the individual—a more equitable society—they do not prescribe practice at the micro level of interaction with another person. The theoretical focus for change is academic and policy-making groups of people and is not explanatory at the interpersonal level. The problem remains that the interpersonal level is where much of the work actually begins and, indeed, most often is done. Theories of relationship and of communication from a structural perspective do not supply a paradigm of practice at this micro level. Similarly, theories relating to intrapsychic work do not offer models for practice that relate the worker's interaction with the social realities to the structural dimensions of the theoretical paradigm.

See section titled "Anti-Oppressive Practice" later in this chapter.

Another challenge of theory is that it is often presented as if in practice we function in a "pure" way, adhering strictly to all the fundamentals of a particular theoretical perspective. In practice, we tend to work eclectically, relying on a range of knowledge bases at any one time and integrating them into our practice.

A further difficulty is the extent to which what is espoused as the theoretical perspective is consistently practiced by each worker. That is, someone may declare that they are a feminist or a cognitive behavioural practitioner, but how would someone else know that their practice is actually consistent with that perspective? Banks (2012) observes this kind of gap between theory and practice when she highlights that "the focus in social work generally is on the individual service user or family and therefore inevitably the stress is on personal change, even if the broader societal context is acknowledged" (p. 116).

An extreme challenge in relation to the use of theories is that they can be contextually inappropriate or wrong. For example, the practice of removing Indigenous children from their families was based on theories of well-being current at that time. These theories are now considered ethnocentric and racist for having failed to take into account sufficient appreciation for Indigenous ways of living, and the importance of attachment in child and family well-being. Dominant, colonizing theories have been imposed on many other Indigenous populations around the world with similarly devastating impacts on well-being (Smith, 2001).

Having considered some of the limitations of theory, we acknowledge that theories play an important role, nonetheless, in guiding our practice. The ways in which a number of theoretical perspectives explain some important dimensions of human behaviour and experience illustrate their points of compatibility and points of difference. These theoretical perspectives are examined in greater detail and as they may be applied in practice in later chapters in this book. The key elements for comparison are as follows:

- What dimensions of the human person are considered core?
- What should be the focus of change?
- What is the reason for the human service intervention?
- What are the major or dominant skills used by the worker?
- What are the core beliefs about the helping relationship?
- What are the assumptions about the length of relationship?

Factual Knowledge

To work with Jahzara we will need further information to help us understand her circumstances: what she is dealing with and, therefore, how we might respond. Jahzara and her family are coping with many contemporary psychosocial issues. You might identify postpartum (following birth) depression, emotional stress (interior) and duress (imposed by others), impoverishment and financial stress (such as rental arrears), employment uncertainty, poor public housing options for low-income earners, inadequate parenting skills or children with special challenges, the consequences of physical and emotional abuse in at least one of the children, and extreme social disadvantage and disempowerment due to immigration.

Your intervention will vary depending on whether you understand postpartum depression to be a mental illness—in which case you might encourage contact with a general practitioner as a first step—or an outcome of the stress, exhaustion, and loneliness of becoming a mother—in Jahzara's case, for the fourth time. If the latter, you might link her with a mother's group for peer support. Or you might understand her depression to be related to her extreme financial stress, and connect her with a financial counsellor and emergency relief resources.

TABLE 3.2 Paradigms and Theoretical Perspectives Informing Practice

	Paradigm				
	Positivist	Positivist	Solution-Focused	Critical	Social Constructivist
	Theoretical Perspective				
	Psychodynamic	Cognitive behavioural	Task-centred and crisis intervention	Feminist and critical	Narrative and solution-focused
Dimension of human person considered locus of change	Bringing unconscious thoughts, behaviours under conscious thought and control	Primarily establishing healthy thought patterns, although also feelings and behaviours	Emotional state; restoration of emotional control	Personal functioning and sociopolitical context	Stories we live by, particularly stories that disempower and oppress
Focus of change	Thoughts, desires, impulses: brought from unconscious to conscious	Established patterns of thoughts challenged to produce healthier ways of thinking about self	The immediate tasks associated with the problem as well as the emotional response	Gender and power relations; patriarchal social structures that oppress women and other minority groups	Stories that are empowering and strengths-based, often externalizing the problem
Goal of intervention	Interpretation on behalf of therapist and self-reflection and insight on behalf of client; anxiety reduction	Behavioural and cognitive change	Return to functioning to be able to begin to cope and deal practically with crisis	Externalizing of gender and power problems rather than internalizing	Narrative stories of self and circumstances that lead to healthy, strengths-based ways of living
Dominant skills	Listening, interpreting relationship	Showing the client how thoughts, feelings, and behaviours are connected; challenging patterns of thinking and behaving	Education; resourcing; emotional release	Listening to the story; empowering; externalizing the issue as a political rather than a personal issue; advocacy and social change	Acknowledging problem stories; externalizing the problem; deconstructing negative stories; reconstructing positive ones; living out (enacting) the new stories
Beliefs about helping relationship	Previously seen as "blank screen"; now intersubjective	Listening for faulty, unhelpful beliefs; not much emphasis on relationship as an essential process	Initially directive and assertive; gradually shifting responsibility to client after initial crisis	Equal, empowering relationship; explicit focus on gender relations and power in client–worker relationship	Helps in constructing a story and in listening to gaps/ silences

Source: Harms, Louise. (2007).

Working with People: Communication Skills for Reflective Practice. South Melbourne: Oxford University Press.

The information you need comes in many forms—in the form of statistical data, an evaluation, or stories provided by individuals or families. You need a foundational base of factual knowledge about the phenomena to which you are responding. Issues of child abuse and neglect, disability and chronic illness, poverty, mental and physical illness, and substance use and abuse are issues with which workers need to be familiar. Research knowledge helps you to understand the context in which the lived experience of one person is taking place and the possible effects on that person and on others of such conditions or experiences.

Some disciplines refer to this broad knowledge as a "social epidemiological" approach, whereby the medical terminology of epidemiology is adapted to understanding social issues. Epidemiology refers to "the study of how often and for what reasons a health problem occurs in specific groups of people" (Butchart & Kahane, 2006, p. 17). In an epidemiological approach, issues of etiology (cause), incidence and prevalence, and the effects and/or outcomes (on the individuals both directly and indirectly affected) are taken into account.

Another important dimension of work with Jahzara is a consideration of the broader legal context of practice (Swain, 2002), which influences or controls the decisions we make in practice. Randomized controlled trials have some place in human service work, but these cannot be the only ways in which human behaviour, rights, and needs are understood. Many people argue strongly that in human service work it is neither possible nor desirable to apply the rigour of laboratory science because the uniqueness of each person and circumstance must be considered, and it is not possible to research the outcomes of each unique intervention (see Duncan & Miller, 2005). Therefore, in the absence of statistical and observational bases for much human service work, some have called for use of the best available evidence (Kessler, Gira, & Poertner, 2005, p. 247) and others refer to evidence-informed practice (Evans & Benefield, 2001).

You will face all kinds of contradictions, tensions, and complexities in your daily practice. Due to the current risk management environment, never before within the literature, research, and organizations has there been such a push to have practice that adheres to certain standards (Webb, 2006). The emphasis is on workers having a strong, established evidence base for the work undertaken, and clear, accountable boundaries around time and practice with people. In short, a paradigm of **positivism** governs much practice. On the other hand, never before has there been such an extensive "evidence base" for the importance and influence of critical reflective practice; an emphasis on practice wisdom; an appreciation for the uniqueness of individual experience and the importance of cultural sensitivity and spirituality; and an emphasis on an authentic, open relationship between client and worker. That is, constructivism also governs much practice.

See Chapter 1 for websites for the Canadian Association of Social Workers practice standards.

Jahzara's circumstances, and the possible courses of action in working with her and her family, highlight how complex human service work is. You are being called on to mediate the unique circumstances of each person, family, or community with your knowledge and skill as a worker.

Client Perspectives

The question as to what works for whom and why in human service work is only one part of the practice. Increasingly, client perspectives are being incorporated into solutions. What would Jahzara want from her human service worker and intervention? It is striking that this perspective is often ignored both by researchers and by organizations. As workers, we need to keep in mind the research that suggests lay interventions are just as effective as professional ones or therapeutic ones.

Clients have identified other factors in the relationship in mandated situations (Ribner & Knei-Paz, 2002):

- feelings of closeness
- a working style that creates an enabling atmosphere and an equal stance
- working together on issues
- flexibility in contact—accessibility
- keeping in touch.

Another small-scale study in the field of child welfare (de Boer & Coady, 2007) focused on matched client and worker perspectives and identified similar qualities. These qualities came under two major themes: (1) a soft, mindful, and judicious use of power; and (2) a humanistic attitude and style that stretches traditional professional ways of being.

BOX 3.2 Focus on Practice

Attitudes and Actions That Build Good Relationships with Clients

A soft, mindful, and judicious use of power:

- being aware of one's power and of the client's fear, defensiveness, and anger as normal
- responding to client negativity with understanding and support instead of counter-hostility and coercion
- conveying a respectful and non-judgemental attitude
- providing clear and honest explanations about reasons for involvement
- addressing fears of child removal and allaying unrealistic fears
- not assuming the veracity of intake, referral, or file information
- listening to and empathizing with the client's story
- pointing out strengths and conveying respect
- constantly clarifying information to ensure mutual understanding
- exploring and discussing concerns before jumping to conclusions
- responding in a supportive manner to new disclosures, relapses, and new problems
- following through on one's responsibilities and promises.

A humanistic attitude and style that stretches traditional professional ways of being:

- using an honest and direct, person-to-person, down-to-earth manner (versus donning the professional mask)
- engaging in small talk to establish comfort and rapport; getting to know the client as a whole person—in social and life-history contexts
- seeing and relating to the client as a person with understandable problems
- recognizing and valuing the client's strengths and successes in coping

Continued

- being realistic about goals and patient about progress
- having a genuinely hopeful and optimistic outlook on possibilities for change
- using judicious self-disclosure towards developing personal connection
- being real in terms of feeling the client's pain and displaying emotions
- going the extra mile in fulfilling mandated responsibilities, and stretching professional mandates and boundaries.

Source: de Boer, C. & Coady, N. (2007). Good helping relationships in child welfare: Learning from stories of success. *Child and Family Social Work*, 12, 32–42.

Practice Knowledge or Wisdom

A further source of knowledge is the unique store of subjective experience that develops from practice as a worker. Over time, and through various encounters, we come to understand situations through the lens of experience. We can draw on that experience to think about what we did then and what happened as a result, and change our current behaviour as a consequence. This knowledge is referred to as **practice wisdom** (Scott, 1990). As Kessler, Gira, and Poertner (2005) observe, "Practitioners are expected to be pragmatic, self-reflective, and to learn from their work with clients. The result is practice wisdom, or experientially and inductively derived knowledge" (p. 245).

Practice wisdom has been defined as "the accumulation of information, assumptions, ideologies, and judgements that have seemed practically useful in fulfilling the expectations of the job" (De Roos, 1990, p. 282, cited in Osmond, 2005, p. 891). An understanding of practice wisdom is critical because of the widespread recognition that workers draw more explicitly on their practice wisdom, as well as values and legal parameters, than on theory or research (Chui & Wilson, 2006). Gambrill (1999), however, cautions against the assumption that practice wisdom is necessarily a good thing: "Experience does not necessarily result in improved performance. In fact, it may have the opposite effect. Experience does not offer systematic data about what works with what clients and what problems" (p. 348). The crucial distinction to make is between practice wisdom, as distinct from practice experience. One of the challenges in beginning practice is, of course, that one has relatively little practice base from which to draw. At first, every encounter is a major learning experience.

The development of practice wisdom is explored further in Chapter 4.

How do we bring together these various knowledge bases and integrate them into a perspective or approach for practice? One of the ways is to think about a multi-dimensional approach (Harms, 2005; Hutchison, 2003), which has emerged from an ecological or ecosystemic perspective (Germain & Bloom, 1999).

For more on the multi-dimensional approach, see Chapter 9.

Thompson (2003) and others (e.g., Mullaly & West, 2018) use the "PCS" model—***p***ersonal, ***c***ultural, and ***s***tructural—to take into consideration all dimensions of any given situation. However, one of the limitations of the PCS model is its tendency to underemphasize the relational and social dimensions of any given situation. Giving unique character to Jahzara's experiences are individual, family, and group forces shaping identity (Miller, Donner, & Fraser, 2004). That is, the unique influences of gender, class, culture, and sexual orientation are understood to influence identity, and to influence the experience of problems of social identity. The multi-dimensional assessment and intervention process is mirrored in the Canadian Association of Social Workers' *Guidelines for Ethical Practice* (2005), reproduced in the box below.

BOX 3.3 Focus on Practice

Assessment and Intervention

The social work assessment and the intervention taken are appropriate to the client's situation, in keeping with ethical and legislative requirements and directed towards appropriate outcomes reached in agreement with the client wherever possible.

1.0 Ethical Responsibilities to Clients

1.2 Demonstrate Cultural Awareness and Sensitivity

- 1.2.1 Social workers strive to understand culture and its function in human behaviour and society, recognizing the strengths that exist in all cultures.
- 1.2.2 Social workers acknowledge the diversity within and among individuals, communities, and cultures.
- 1.2.3 Social workers acknowledge and respect the impact that their own heritage, values, beliefs, and preferences can have on their practice and on clients whose background and values may be different from their own.
- 1.2.4 Social workers seek a working knowledge and understanding of clients' racial and cultural affiliations, identities, values, beliefs, and customs.
- 1.2.5 Where possible, social workers provide or secure social work services in the language chosen by the client. If using an interpreter, when possible, social workers preferentially secure an independent and qualified professional interpreter.

1.3 Promote Client Self-Determination and Informed Consent

- 1.3.1 Social workers promote the self-determination and autonomy of clients, actively encouraging them to make informed decisions on their own behalf.
- 1.3.2 Social workers evaluate a client's capacity to give informed consent as early in the relationship as possible.
- 1.3.3 Social workers who have children as clients determine the child's capacity to consent and explain to the child (where appropriate), and to the child's parents/guardians (where appropriate), the nature of the social worker's relationship to the child and others involved in the child's care (see section 1.5.5 regarding confidentiality).
- 1.3.4 Social workers, at the earliest opportunity, discuss with clients their rights and Indicators responsibilities and provide them with honest and accurate information regarding the following:
  - the nature of the social work service being offered;
  - the recording of information and who will have access to such information;
  - the purpose, nature, extent, and known implications of the options open to them;
  - the potential risks and benefits of proposed social work interventions;
  - their right to obtain a second opinion or to refuse or cease service (recognizing the limitations that apply when working with involuntary clients);
  - the client's right to view professional records and to seek avenues of complaint; and
  - the limitations on professional confidentiality (see section 1.5 regarding confidentiality).

Source: *The Social Work Code of Ethics*, adopted by the Board of Directors of the Canadian Association of Social Workers (CASW) is effective March 2005, and replaces the CASW Code of Ethics (1994). The code is reprinted here with the permission of the CASW. The copyright in the document has been registered with Canadian Intellectual Property office, registration no. 1030330.

The other dimension that has more recently been included in understanding a client's situation is the dimension of the worker. The client's story is constructed in the context of the worker's story—what the worker brings to the relationship. When you tell a story, your audience influences how you tell it—what you tell and what you emphasize or omit in that co-creation. Thus, your inner- and outer-world dimensions are important considerations in any client–worker interaction. A worker's ability to self-locate is critical to anti-oppressive practice.

Anti-Oppressive Practice

An anti-oppressive perspective recognizes the intersectionality (refers to the intersection of identities that shapes a person's experiences throughout society) of the numerous oppressive forces in society (Coggins, 2016, p. 38). Anti-oppressive practice focuses on the analysis of structural oppression that reinforces the barriers clients face. An anti-oppressive practice model analyzes and advocates against macro and micro levels of oppression and emphasizes social justice and social change. In social work, an anti-oppressive approach seeks to promote the principles of social justice, which are also upheld in social work values, by acknowledging diversity within oppression and considering intersectionality. Therefore, intersectionality is a valuable way of thinking in practice. It supports critical reflection and captures dynamic power relations and oppression in a way that creates awareness of differences and oppression both within and among groups (Mattsson, 2013).

An aspect of understanding diversity or difference is being aware of our location in society (Mullaly & West, 2018). This process is often termed "self-location" or "locating oneself." Self-location is the process of acknowledging privilege that exists in a person's gender, age, sexual orientation, religious beliefs, or class, and the many other categories of difference. The process of self-locating can be complex; individuals often have multiple identities that can include aspects of being oppressed in one space and being the oppressor in another (Bishop, 2015). Hick (2010) reminds social workers to maintain an awareness of these multiple identities and the potential of disempowering clients.

BOX 3.4 Focus on Practice

Salina is a 30-year-old mom of two children, ages 2 and 4. Salina recently moved to Canada from Mexico where she was a practicing nurse. Salina was very proud of her accomplishments, as she lost her parents very young and grew up in several different homes until she was able to get work and save to pay for school. Upon her arrival in her new country, Salina learns that her nursing credentials will not be recognized. She finds herself suddenly unemployed and fears losing her children.

Apply an anti-oppressive lens to Salina's story.

Anti-oppressive practice is a complex topic that is only briefly touched on here, but it is an important foundational piece of effective communication in social work practice. Many authors have written on this topic (Baskin, 2016; Bishop, 2015; Mullaly & West, 2018). Coggins (2016) summarizes the importance of understanding anti-oppressive theory for new social workers noting,

> more privileged members of professional organizations need to realize that expecting all social workers to be tireless advocates for social change can become itself an oppressive stance. Instead, social work students should be helped to see the importance of balancing the realities of the contemporary workplace environment with professional ethical values and principles that shape our interaction with those we serve at the individual, family, group, organizational, community, and societal level. Social workers who can see the current realities of clients' lives through the lens of an ongoing struggle to ensure social and economic justice will be better prepared to be truly anti-oppressive practitioners. (p. 59)

Diversity in Practice

As the Canadian Association of Social Workers (2005) reminds workers, "social workers recognize and respect the diversity of Canadian society, taking into account the breadth of differences that exist among individuals, families, groups and communities" (p. 4). The CASW's focus on diversity as an ethical standard in social work practice emphasizes the importance for workers to maintain cultural awareness in their practice. It reminds workers to reflect on how world views, values, and belief systems can influence how a person understands the world around them.

Canada has an international reputation for celebrating diversity, and its embrace of multiculturalism is most visible at the various cultural events that take place across the country, which honour the cultural heritages of Canadian citizens. However, this has not always been the case. While Canada has long been home to a diverse population, the Canadian government has not always treated different groups equally; Canadian history is rife with examples of racism, bigotry, and other forms of discrimination. In particular, Canada has an extensive history of perpetrating systematic violence against Indigenous Peoples, perhaps most insidiously through policies targeting children and families (Baskin, 2016; Macdonald, 2007; Benvenuto & Woolford, 2015). From the 1870s to the 1990s, more than 150,000 First Nations, Métis, and Inuit children were removed from their homes and placed in government-funded, church-run schools, with the stated goal of "eliminat[ing] the Indian in the child" (Truth and Reconciliation Commission of Canada, 2015b; Baskin, 2016). The number of child deaths due to forced attendance in Indian residential schools was disproportionately higher than the general child population (Truth and Reconciliation Commission of Canada, 2015a). Social work child welfare practices were also used to perpetuate attacks on Indigenous Peoples in Canada. Beginning in the late 1950s and continuing into the 1980s, Indigenous children were removed from the guardianship of their parents at exceedingly high rates, a practice now commonly referred to as the "Sixties Scoop." During this period, upwards of one third of Indigenous children were removed from their homes and adopted, in many cases into non-Indigenous families (Sinclair, 2007). This act of colonization is still being addressed today; as recently as 2016, the Canadian Human Rights Tribunal ruled that child welfare services on reserve are underfunded and racially discriminatory. Moving forward, as we continue to call attention to these acts of colonization, and intergenerational trauma (the transmission of historical oppression and its negative consequences across generations), Blackstock (2011) calls for a paradigm shift, stating that child welfare institutions

Young Inuit throat singers perform at a vigil honouring missing and murdered Indigenous women at Parliament Hill. The ongoing crisis of Indigenous women and girls being targeted for murder and sexualized violence at much higher rates than the non-Indigenous population has been connected to the systemic violence of the residential school system and the Sixties Scoop.

require structural changes to address equitable funding of services on reserve. Building on anti-oppressive theory, Blackstock (2011) believes this approach must be enacted through a bi-cultural paradigm, or an "ethical space where western and First Nations knowledge can coexist to inform solutions" (p. 1).

Presently, there are several terms workers can bear in mind as they work to maintain a cultural awareness in their practice framework. Terms such as "cultural competence," "cultural sensitivity," "cultural awareness," and "diversity training" all refer to practices that attempt to provide social workers with contextual knowledge regarding working cross-culturally. The theory of "cultural safety" draws together these terms and refocuses conversations on power relationships and acts of racism, which result in barriers to meaningful and safe cross-cultural engagement (Baskin, 2016; Jeffrey, 2015; Nelson & Wilson, 2017). Culturally safer practice is a commitment to the process of lifelong learning and an engagement in self-reflexivity, which considers how our own culture and the colonial values that surround us exist in our practice.

© iStock/stacey_newman

Canadians wait at Toronto's Pearson Airport to welcome the first plane of Syrian refugees arriving in Canada on 11 December 2015. What factors might a human service worker have to consider when working with a newcomer who arrived in Canada under the Canadian Immigration and Refugee Protection Act?

Working with Newcomers

Drawing from concepts of anti-oppressive practice and reflective culturally safer practice, it is important when working with newcomers to Canada to take the time to understand the process and circumstances of how they came to be in Canada. Some newcomers, for example, come to Canada under the Canadian Immigration and Refugee Protection Act. In these cases, refugees are often fleeing from violence or life-threatening circumstances, while at the same time leaving their known home and culture. In these cases, service workers must devote time and attention to issues of trauma, culture shock, and language barriers before engaging in any type of service planning. Overlooking these aspects of a client's experiences due to time constraints or a lack of awareness can further oppress and traumatize newcomers who require support.

Language is a very important aspect to consider when working cross-culturally. For example, even if a newcomer has basic English language skills, words can take on different meanings depending on the context in which they are used. Unchecked, this can result in miscommunications.

BOX 3.5 Focus on Practice

Examples of Cross-Cultural Language Barriers

Early on in my practice, I [Joanna] attended a women's group as an opportunity to engage with women cross-culturally, exchange ideas, and provide support at the request of the group. I learned a lot from the women by listening to their cultural beliefs regarding their roles and wishes for their families. One day, at the end of our time together, I stood up to leave and said, "Thank you, everyone, for sharing with me today, but I have to jet." The women in the group burst into laughter as I walked out the door. They were laughing so loudly that I had to go back in and ask what I had said that was so funny. No one wanted to tell me, but everyone continued to laugh uncontrollably. After some convincing, I managed to persuade them to explain the joke. The women informed me that when I said that I had to "jet," I had basically just announced to the women in the group that I had diarrhea. After I got over my embarrassment, I got to experience some of my best cross-cultural practice learning. We spent the afternoon talking about the struggles of language and context. The women shared their fears about hearing words that they knew, but which held a different meaning for them than for the people with whom they were speaking. They told me that this challenge is compounded in conversations with professionals, as the women stated that they feel reluctant to tell a professional when word is unfamiliar or used outside of its known context.

This idea came up again later in my career. I was speaking with one of my former students, a male newcomer to Canada, who was then working in child welfare. He shared with me that in his country, the word they used to describe spanking is directly translated to "beat" in English. This difference in translation made it more difficult for him to assess risk in his role as a child protection worker.

In addition to language barriers, issues of unemployment bring significant challenges for newcomers. Many newcomers find that the credentials they held in their home country are not recognized in Canada. Someone who is a registered nurse, teacher, or a medical doctor in their home country might find themselves facing unexpected unemployment, the loss of their career, and, over time, issues of poverty. The additional stressors of culture shock and new social norms can make job interviews more challenging, and the overall process of trying to seek new employment can easily become very overwhelming.

Gender and family roles also require careful consideration. Practitioners need to be open to learning what role gender plays in the newcomer's culture. Traditional cultural roles may impact families over time. Children who are more frequently exposed to the Canadian culture through school systems can begin to challenge family cultural norms. As children grow older and their exposure to the outside culture increases, the challenge of maintaining traditional cultural practices can place stress on the larger family system.

Human service workers should also strive to learn more about how their clients view themselves as an individual in relation to their families and communities. Many cultures, including some from China, Korea, and Japan, function from a collectivist framework, in which the overall health of an individual is closely connected to the health of the family system. Decision making often involves the whole family unit and can even include extended family members. Sheafor and Horejsi (2008), note that misinterpreting or "overlooking client strengths, misreading nonverbal communication, and misunderstanding family dynamics are among the most common errors made in cross-cultural helping" (p. 177).

In working with people, knowledge of diversity and cultural contexts are learned skills that become supplementary practice tools. Effective practice with diverse populations from an anti-oppressive and culturally safe position requires workers to begin their work with cultural awareness embedded in their approach to practice. To avoid miscommunication and harm, workers should remain open to learning from clients regarding the origins of their culture and how this may guide their understanding of the current context. In addition to cultivating their openness to learning a client's cultural origins, workers must also be aware of their own origins to ensure that they are not imposing their own world view on the client.

Chapter Summary

In this chapter, we have explored the ways in which paradigms, theories, factual knowledge, and practice wisdom integrate to form a coherent practice base. We looked at three broad paradigms before looking at the various forms of theoretical and factual knowledge required for practice. We then considered a multi-dimensional approach as one way in which these many aspects of your client's world and your own could be more comprehensively understood.

Questions for Analysis

1. What have you learned about
   - the importance of understanding paradigms or world views that inform practice?
   - the knowledge bases of practice?
   - the importance of practice wisdom?
   - the strengths and limitations of the theoretical approaches that were presented?
2. Within which paradigm would you locate yourself as a practitioner?
3. What is it about this paradigm that attracts you to it?
4. Which of the five theoretical approaches appeals to you most and why?

Recommended Readings

Al-Krenawi, A., Graham, J., & Habibov, N. (Eds.) (2016). *Diversity and social work in Canada*. Toronto, ON: Oxford University Press.

Baskin, C. (2016). *Strong helpers' teachings: The value of Indigenous knowledges in the helping professions* (Vol. 2). Toronto, ON: Canadian Scholars' Press.

Dumbrill, G., & Yee, J. (2019). *Anti-oppressive social work: Ways of knowing, talking, and doing*. Toronto, ON: Oxford University Press.

Bishop, A. (2015). *Becoming an ally: Breaking the cycle of oppression*. Halifax, NS: Fernwood Publishing.

Germain, C., & Bloom, M. (1999). *Human behavior in the social environment: An ecological view*. New York, NY: Columbia University Press.

Harms, L. (2005). *Understanding human development: A multidimensional approach*. South Melbourne: Oxford University Press.

Healy, K. (2005). *Social work theories in context: Creating frameworks for practice*. Basingstoke: Palgrave Macmillan.

McIntosh, P. (1988). White privilege: Unpacking the invisible knapsack. Retrieved from http://hd.ingham.org/Portals/HD/White%20Priviledge%20Unpacking%20the%20Invisible%20Knapsack.pdf

Mullaly, B., & Dupre, M. (2019). *The new structural social work: Ideology, theory, and practice* (4th ed.). Toronto, ON: Oxford University Press.

Mullaly, B., & West, J. (2018). *Challenging oppression and confronting privilege: A critical approach to anti-oppressive and anti-privilege theory and practice* (3rd ed.). Toronto, ON: Oxford University Press.

Yan, M., & Anucha, U. (Eds.). (2017). *Working with immigrants and refugees: Issues, theories, and approaches for social work and human service practice*. Toronto, ON: Oxford University Press.

Internet Resources

Aboriginal Community Social Work: Committing to Anti-Oppressive Practice
www.casw-acts.ca/sites/casw-acts.ca/files/attachements/angel_compton-osmond_sep_26.pdf

Campbell Collaboration
www.campbellcollaboration.org

Canadian Association of Social Workers (CASW) Code of Ethics
www.casw-acts.ca/en/Code-of-Ethics

Canadian Centre for Policy Alternatives
www.policyalternatives.ca

Institute of Health Services and Policy Research
www.cihr-irsc.gc.ca/e/13733.html

Healing Families, Helping Systems: A Trauma-Informed Practice Guide for Working with Children, Youth and Families, 2016
www2.gov.bc.ca/assets/gov/health/child-teen-mental-health/trauma-informed_practice_guide.pdf

pflag Canada: Family for all
https://pflagcanada.ca

Pride at Work Canada
https://prideatwork.ca

Standards for Cultural Competence in Social Work Practice
www.nlasw.ca/sites/default/files/inline-files/cultural_competency_standards.pdf

Statistics Canada
www.statcan.gc.ca

PART TWO

Basic Skills: Forming the Relationship

In this second part of the book, we focus on understanding yourself in the role of worker, your context, and the very specific microskills used in communication and interviewing processes.

Chapter 4 explores why we need to reflect critically on our own communication styles and experiences. In human service work, the worker is the essential "tool" in the process. Thus, your insightful awareness of your "use of self" and your identification of the purpose and context of your work with individuals, families, or communities are of paramount importance.

Chapter 5 focuses on the essential preparatory work you do before entering into the client relationship and on the differences between your personal self-care and on your professional self-care and development. Supervision, debriefing, and critical self-reflection are introduced as important maintenance strategies for meeting the ongoing challenges of human service work. We approach this examination of self as part of your thinking about *forming* the relationship, rather than considering it in the contexts of problems that could develop later in the client relationship. This precaution is because both personal self-care and professional self-care are necessary parts of your practice that should be part of your skill development from the outset—not an afterthought when you have already experienced burnout or have come to some harm.

Chapter 6 establishes skills for the early stage of forming the relationship with a client. We examine the importance of good engagement skills and rapport building when beginning work with clients. We also consider issues of confidentiality and your use of self-disclosure as important influences on this formation stage.

PART ONE Framing the Relationship

- the purpose of human service work
- your value base, professional ethics, and regulatory guidelines in Canada
- your theoretical and factual knowledge.

PART TWO Forming the Relationship

- your use of self
- your organizational context
- your ongoing support and professional development needs
- meeting the people involved
- opening the communication
- active listening and working with silence
- listening empathically
- using self-disclosure.

4 Preparing for Practice

Learning Goals

- Understand why the "use of self" is an important concept.
- Understand the concept of empathy.
- Review the dimensions of your workplace that influence practice.
- Analyze how your practice links with your organizational context.

Why the "Use of Self" Is an Important Concept for Workers

In earlier chapters we have looked at values and theoretical and factual knowledge bases as key determinants of your practice. This chapter focuses on another critical factor: you. With many other jobs the worker may be one important part of the matrix, but other technical or mechanical interventions are also involved. The ways you apply yourself in your practice will fundamentally affect what happens.

A discriminating use of self is central to all relationships. Think of how you interact differently with each of your friends. Compare how you interact with your friends as distinct from someone you have just met. You might be wary and self-censoring with the unfamiliar person until you have established a stronger connection. This is "use of self" in action.

Reflect on the various interactions in your past that have been with individuals unfamiliar to you, such as speaking with a new doctor, being introduced to a new supervisor or instructor, or meeting a friend of a friend. What are your first thoughts or reactions to the new person? Do potential power differences shape your response? Reflect on your internal process in becoming more open in new relationships and what steps occur to increase your comfort level. Is there social diversity or cultural implications in the new relationship that may impact language communication or mutual understanding of what is being communicated?

Another way of speaking about "use of self" is to think about your spiritual and physical use of self. Egan and Schroeder (2009, p. 11) suggest that perhaps "social-emotional intelligence" is a better term. Egan and Schroeder (2009) define maturity—social-emotional intelligence—as containing the following key concepts:

1. *Mature people are self-managers. They know themselves, are in control of themselves, and get things done.* Self-managers are noted as being aware (self-awareness) of their strengths and limitations, aware of their emotional expressions, and having an awareness of self-worth. Self-managers possess self-control through demonstrating honesty, integrity, and decency. Self-control includes keeping impulses in check and managing stress levels in a constructive manner. It also includes being open to new information and ways of doing things and the ability to take responsibility for personal actions. Self-managers have a bias towards action, are assertive not aggressive, strive for excellence, develop opportunities, and overcome obstacles.

2. *Mature people handle relationships well. They know how to move creatively beyond themselves.* Mature people understand empathy, communication, interpersonal relationships, and the wider world. They are aware of people's feelings, listen and communicate clearly, anticipate concerns, are able to establish solid working relationships, have a sense of the world in which they live and a sense of social responsibility. (pp. 13–14)

Given that good relationships are core to effective practice, we need to think about what social rules come into play. Social rules exist in all communication interactions, varying according to the context in which we are functioning.

In a professional relationship, your **purpose**, boundaries, and behaviour are very different from your personal relationships. The shift to a sense of a professional use of self can be challenging. Furthermore, it is a contentious issue within the human service field. For many students, it feels like giving up important personal traits to become someone else. However, loss of self-identity is not at all the aim of adopting a professional use of self.

The notion of the "use of self" emphasizes a decision-making process—choices about conduct, about priorities, and about responses. The term "use of self" can therefore refer to the direct use of our own personal "material" in terms of feelings, views, and experiences, as the content in the conversation. Or it can refer to our more global understanding of how we are central in the client–worker conversation and can make conscious decisions as to how to act in each context. The "use of self" concept acknowledges that the worker is a critical influence in both the process and content of any interaction. We make choices about how we will be in this particular interaction with this particular person at this particular time. We make the shifts in our interactions and communication skills as a result.

How you relate to someone varies. Like personal relationships, we have expectations and experiences of interactions in the professional context. Your use of self changes over time. The change in self may be about getting to know a person and moving into a more established, trusting way of relating. As a relationship develops, different strategies are used to continue the work of change and support.

BOX 4.1 Focus on Practice

An Example of Learning to Use "Self" Differently

In the early weeks of communication skills classes, students often express feeling overwhelmed by the client's story. How do you listen to it and remember all the details? What do you do to make some sense of it? How do I form the right question? What do I do with silence?

The worker may also have "solved" the situation he or she is hearing about, as if in a role-play situation, three to five minutes into the discussion. Engaging with the person in a role-play to "solve" the situation short-circuits the deeper engaging with the person to listen to more of the story. For some students, this hasty response stems partly from feeling uncomfortable with managing silence, and the student's internal focus on what to ask next, instead of realizing questions arise through listening to the client's story. Finding solutions together is a collaborative work and the goal of the intervention.

Your use of self can be thought about as a biopsychosocial-spiritual process. In this sense, you reflect on your practice, taking into account the **biopsychosocial-spiritual dimensions**—how you use yourself psychologically or emotionally, socially, spiritually, and physically in an encounter. You apply yourself differently, according to the purpose of the communication. Each of these dimensions is now briefly considered.

Your Emotional Use of Self

What are the differences between the client's and the worker's emotional reactions to the circumstances and what should be the differences? How does your emotional self engage in the work you are doing? Consider the following example. In one of my (Louise's) hospital student placement experiences, another student on placement and her supervisor witnessed the severe physical wounds of a patient's very recent surgery. The student screamed when she saw the wounds, not having witnessed anything like them before. It was her natural reaction to what she saw.

The student's initial reaction was an authentic human reaction to the patient's injury. The injury, however, was not the focus of her intervention. The client was the focus of the intervention and her reaction was certainly not helpful to that person in this situation. Instead, she reinforced the patient's own horror and distress over his physical predicament.

This example is, perhaps, extreme; but it highlights the dilemma as to how we emotionally respond in interactions, particularly when we have an overwhelmingly strong response. Not until we are faced with a very stressful situation do we realize what our authentic reaction will be. Where the boundaries lie in practice around an *appropriate* and authentic response is not always clear. Learning to manage any immediate responses and yet to remain client-focused is a critical component in your professional development. This kind of self-control is not about being distant or unauthentic; it is about remaining focused on the client's experience rather than your own.

In Chapter 12, we explore the skills for challenging unhelpful beliefs. In these instances, your engagement needs to be high so that you can present other ways of thinking or behaving within the context of a supportive relationship.

Emotional engagement is an important aspect of building rapport. Coggins (2016) refers to empathy as the process of reflecting on how you might feel if you had experienced another person's circumstance (p. 129). The purpose of empathic skills is for the worker to engage the client in a reflective process—applying open-ended questions, paraphrasing, and clarification skills—that results in the worker coming as close as possible to understanding the client's story (Coggins, 2016). It sends the message that you are present with the client. A grieving mother talks from a consumer perspective about what kind of understanding she wants from those around her (Wolterstorff, 1987, cited in Elkhuizen, Kelleher, Gibson, & Attoe, 2006): "What I need to hear from you is that you recognize how painful it is. I need to hear from you that you are with me in my desperation. To comfort me, you have to come close. Come sit beside me on my mourning bench" (pp. 281–2).

Empathy

Empathy has many dimensions. It can be seen as a skill, a value, or even as an outcome of an encounter. It is considered by many to be the "glue" of client–worker relationships: the quality that enables advanced insight in hearing the story behind the story and in sharing social empathy. Empathy is the sympathetic connection within a relationship, rather than mere reflecting of feeling: "'Reflection of feeling' can be taught as a cognitive skill. . . . Genuine sensitive empathy, with all its intensity and personal involvement, cannot be so taught" (Rogers, 1987, p. 39).

Empathy can be conveyed through an attentive presence and attunement with the client. The client needs to hear that you have listening fully to the situation—your empathy must be conveyed verbally as well as non-verbally. This kind of listening is what Egan (2007, p. 102) refers to as **empathic highlights**. The "formula" for this active response is:

Worker: You feel . . . [insert emotion] because . . . [insert event, behaviour, or condition].

Using the formula, an empathic statement may be:

Worker: You feel confused because what you thought was going on actually turned out to be quite different.

Or:

Worker: You feel overwhelmed because no one told you how to prepare for work in a small, remote northern community.

> Remember the discussion of respect in Chapter 2.

> This use of paraphrasing to convey empathy is discussed further in Chapter 8.

A lot of "bad press" for workers comes from the formulaic use of these statements. We rarely use such formulaic statements in practice. What the formula helps us to do is to think objectively, which is different from how we chat with friends. Whereas with friends we are likely to agree or join with them in some way, this formula keeps us focused on a progressive or directed way of listening and responding to the client. A purpose is maintained while listening to the thoughts, feelings, and behaviours of the client, and while thinking of the connections between these personal factors and the structural and cultural environment of the client. "Advanced empathy" (Egan, 2007) refers to the skill of being able to hear and convey the underlying or unspoken meanings of a client's story. Karen offers an example from one of her classes, in which the issue of empathy became a focus.

BOX 4.2 Focus on Practice

What Does the Client Want You to Hear?

If students are required to present and re-present "real but not current" issues for discussion in a classroom, counselling skills can be developed for emergency situations before such crises are faced during professional work. The opportunity afforded by the "client" experiencing varieties of styles of questioning, and in giving feedback, can be very informative. One such student had witnessed an injured, possibly stabbed, person while waiting at a bus stop. Her description of the situation provided a classroom scenario that encompassed a range of elements and strong emotions:

- shock at the unexpected and traumatic event
- fear in not knowing what had happened or of the whereabouts of a perpetrator
- anger and frustration about the lack of consideration by the many bystanders
- guilt at not being able to treat the injured person
- worry that her being immobilized in some ways by the event would happen in an even more serious situation at some other time
- fear of accountability around her becoming involved or assisting with the situation
- self-doubt, questioning if she had enough skill to know how to be helpful and not injurious
- feelings of distress around the need to know what she should have done and how.

A number of the student counsellors concentrated on the traumatic event and became engrossed in the detail of the event. The student whose impact was greatest made a point of listening to the meaning of the issue for the "client," recognizing her sense of helplessness and guilt over her role in the situation. Furthermore, by exploring this situation in detail, the other students were able to challenge the client's view (a blind spot) that she had been completely ineffectual by drawing out more of her story that included other actions she had taken, which included calling an ambulance and staying with the injured person to reassure him until help arrived. Subsequent feedback from the student revealed her frustration at the efforts by some to explore the sensational details, and how valuable it had been when the worker listened to the part that mattered most to her. Of course, it should be noted that for some others the "sensational details" would be the context they would need to have in order to assess what their own reactions would be in a similar situation. Also, values connected to gender and diversity influences need to be considered.

Empathy is about striking the right balance of focus between the worker and client. As the above example shows, focusing too much on the detail in this instance led the "client" to feel her experience had not been understood. Similarly, focusing too sympathetically hijacks the client's need to understand his/her emotions and to find emotional release, and can create distance.

Sympathy sometimes is contrasted with empathy. Egan (2007) states, "Sympathy denotes agreement, whereas empathy denotes understanding" (p. 118). Sympathy is a joining with or colluding with the client, as distinct from being able to understand their world and feelings without necessarily agreeing, condoning, or participating in that world. Although these are fully human traits, they are not particularly useful in counselling (Egan, 2007). Two arguments for not using sympathy are that, first, your response could be misplaced and therefore unhelpful. For example:

Client:	I've just left my partner of five years.
Worker:	I'm so sorry to hear that.
Client:	Oh, no, no, it's such a good thing. It's not that I'm worried about.

In this instance, the sympathetic response has not helped, primarily because an assumption was made about the experience rather than an exploration of it. The above scenario highlights some of the **differential use of self**—what you might say to family and friends in such a circumstance may be different from your response with your clients, because your role has a different purpose.

BOX 4.3 Practice Exercise

1. Reflect on a conversation or encounter with another person, not necessarily in a formal interview situation, where you have experienced what you consider empathic communication.
2. What occurred during the conversation that made you feel understood?
3. What are the qualities, attitudes, and skills that you think were essential in this experience?
4. What words or phrases defined the expression of empathy for you?
5. What specific empathic skills can you identify from the experience?
6. What are your personal skills in which you feel confident in working with empathy and where do you want to improve?

Empathy is predominantly perceived to be a positive skill and is distinct from intimacy or sympathy. It is about understanding and supporting someone emotionally, but not being immersed in the same feelings and reactions. In a community health centre context, Karen identifies how she came to manage her own empathy in her work with Mark.

BOX 4.4 Focus on Practice

Dealing with the Unbearable

Sometimes a person's pain is so extreme that you will be affected. A man in his thirties with suicidal concerns attended a first interview. His story related to the recent traumatic event of watching as his small daughter ran across the road, was hit by a car, and dragged a long distance. She had suffered multiple injuries including some brain damage, and he was wracked with guilt as well as with the trauma of witnessing the terrible event. He had left his family and the province, feeling numb and hopeless.

The telling of his story, in all its graphic detail, together with his projection of his own feelings, was a moving and deeply sad experience, and my way of coping was to ask myself, "What does Mark need from me in telling me this today?" At such a time, what he needed from me was to be able to bear to hear his pain, in all its detail, without providing either blame or reassurance. By asking myself the question, I was able to contain my own feelings, not without a tear, but to the extent that he could feel supported to move away from believing that he had no other choice than suicide.

This reflection on practice is an important consideration in professional development. In some cases, when the worker becomes over-engaged in a client's story, the client may shut down out of concern for the worker's emotional well-being. The client should always feel safe to express all the details of the story and confident that the practitioner can listen and be present.

1. What is your immediate reaction to this story and why?
2. What do you think could emerge as issues for you personally in working with someone in Mark's situation?
3. How will you manage any issues that arise for you?
4. What skills do you feel you need to develop further so that you could remain present in the situation in this example?

Your Social and Practical Use of Self

Workers also vary in the degree to which they are involved practically in situations—with and for clients. Sometimes attending to the practical needs, either directly or indirectly, can make an enormous difference—for example, making phone calls on behalf of someone or providing transport. These actions can bring about sheer relief when such basic human needs are not being met otherwise. Maslow's hierarchy of needs (Table 4.1) is a useful reminder of the importance of meeting basic human survival needs, before other growth needs such as self-actualization and self-transcendence can be realized.

Social support, whether emotional, instrumental, or practical, is consistently identified as a key protective factor (Harms, 2005).

Your response as a worker will be determined in part by your views of empowerment and the place of independence, interdependence, and dependence. Some workers view practical needs as critical opportunities to provide support when a client may not have the resources, either practically or emotionally, to attend to such issues. Trotter (2006) maintains that a much clearer basis for action emerges when human rights, rather than needs, form the basis of action.

TABLE 4.1 An Adapted Version of Maslow's Hierarchy of Needs

Motivational need	A person at this level
Self-transcendence	Seeks to further a cause beyond the self
Self-actualization	Seeks fulfillment of personal potential
Esteem needs	Seeks esteem through achievement
Belongingness and love needs	Seeks group affiliation
Safety needs	Seeks security through law and order
Physiological (survival) needs	Seeks the basic necessities of life

Source: Koltko-Rivera, M.E. (2006) Rediscovering the Later Version of Maslow's Hierarchy of Needs: Self-Transcendence and Opportunities for Theory, Research, and Unification. Review of General Psychology, 10, 302–317.

Your Spiritual Use of Self

The spiritual dimension is less frequently discussed as a way in which the worker interacts with their clients, in part because of the diverse ways in which spirituality is experienced and defined.

Coates, Graham, Swartzentruber, and Ouellette (2007) credit four major Canadian social work scholars for their work in capturing spirituality in social work during the twentieth century. E.J. Erwick, Charles Hendry, Reverend Shaun Govenlock, and Reverend Frank Swithun Bowers "each was a director of a major school for over a decade; each was well published and well regarded; and together they represented a period in social work's history from the 1930s to the early 1970s" (Coates et al., 2007, p. 29).

Since the 1970s many authors have contributed to spirituality in social work practice (far more than can be summarized in this brief overview). After a decline in the literature during the 1970s and 1980s, spirituality and social work saw an emergence in Canadian publications by such authors as Graham, Ouellette, Al-Krenawi, Coates, Swartzentruber, Moffatt, and McKay. This re-emergence included a cultural perspective with Canadian authors Dei, de Mello, Mandamin, Morrissette, McKenzie, and Tester, all of whom recognize that "cultures are strongly linked with spiritual and religious world views, and this has consistently been a rationale for the inclusion of spirituality in social work" (Coates et al., 2007, p. 30).

Recently, Canadian texts have included sections or chapters on spirituality, including Indigenous theory, holistic practice, meditation, and transpersonal theories. Currently, a major contributor to the topic of spirituality in Canadian social work is the Canadian Society for Spirituality and Social Work (www.spiritualityandsocialwork.ca).

What would your response be to the following situation, and how would you answer the questions?

BOX 4.5 Focus on Practice

Considering the Spiritual Dimension

A client is telling you about his strong connection with spirituality, and the ways in which he knows this connection has helped him overcome so many difficulties. As a way of tapping into your beliefs about the spiritual dimension in practice, consider the following questions:

1. What is your reaction to this very brief scenario?
2. Would you feel comfortable continuing with the client?
3. What do you think you would want to know more about?
4. Do you think you would ask more questions? If so, what would your questions be and why?
5. How would you manage a client's spirituality if it is in direct conflict with your beliefs?
6. In what ways do you think your reaction would influence your client's experience?
7. How might you address cultural perspectives or theories, such as meditation, in your discussion?

Your Physical Use of Self

Many dimensions of your non-verbal skills and, therefore, of your physical use of self, were explored in Chapter 2. This discussion raises two further issues: touch and availability. Ethical guidelines across all professions prohibit sexual contact with clients, because of the inherent inequalities in power and control within client–worker relationships. In this respect, professional standards have never been as clearly articulated as they currently are in relation to physical boundaries. Yet a challenge emerges in that, theoretically, the emphasis on authentic human intersubjectivity has never been as strongly proposed, which leaves a worker wondering about some of the more subtle forms of physical interaction that commonly typify human relationships. For example, physical contact occurs at points of greeting or separation, through handshakes or hugs. Workers find themselves in situations where someone may spontaneously embrace them. To reject this embrace could be personally and culturally inappropriate.

Take some time to consider the use of touch in a human service worker–client relationship. Is it ever appropriate? As a human service worker, what tools or strategies will you use to maintain appropriate boundaries?

Your physical use of self also relates to your physical presence and availability. Punctuality and availability have been identified by clients in many studies as important issues of respect and relationship. If it is not possible to be punctual and available because of other work demands, conveying this to the client is a way of relating respectfully and genuinely. It is important for practitioners to ensure they are aware of how physical use of self and physical presence are defined in an urban agency, in institutional settings, and in the community. The expectations and dynamics likely will be different between urban and rural locations and in work with different cultures.

As discussed in Chapter 2, the question of whether touch should ever be used in practice is a complex one.

Your Use of Self in Context

Your agency will set the agenda for much of the work you do. Agencies reflect the wider policy context in which they are established, and the subsequent resources that are provided for service delivery. Agencies make decisions about service delivery models. They develop a workplace culture based on its employees and the work that is undertaken. These are dimensions of your **organizational context**.

At an everyday level, the physical and the service system environmental dimensions of an agency will influence the experience for both you and your clients. These dimensions give strong messages about the underlying values of the work and of the client–worker relationship.

An agency may have unique safety issues relating to health, violence, or location. In 2009, Canada faced the H1N1 influenza, also referred to as swine flu. This worldwide health concern saw institutions developing "pandemic preparedness policies" to increase awareness of how to manage exposure to the H1N1 virus. For some schools of social work, this involved specific policy development in the areas of student practicum aimed at addressing the potential risk for students in placements.

In organizations that provide refuge from domestic violence, threats of violence can be common, requiring different levels of security and confidentiality. Workers in international services in zones of war or disaster face unique physical and interpersonal risks. These environments will influence the precautions you need to take in your practice.

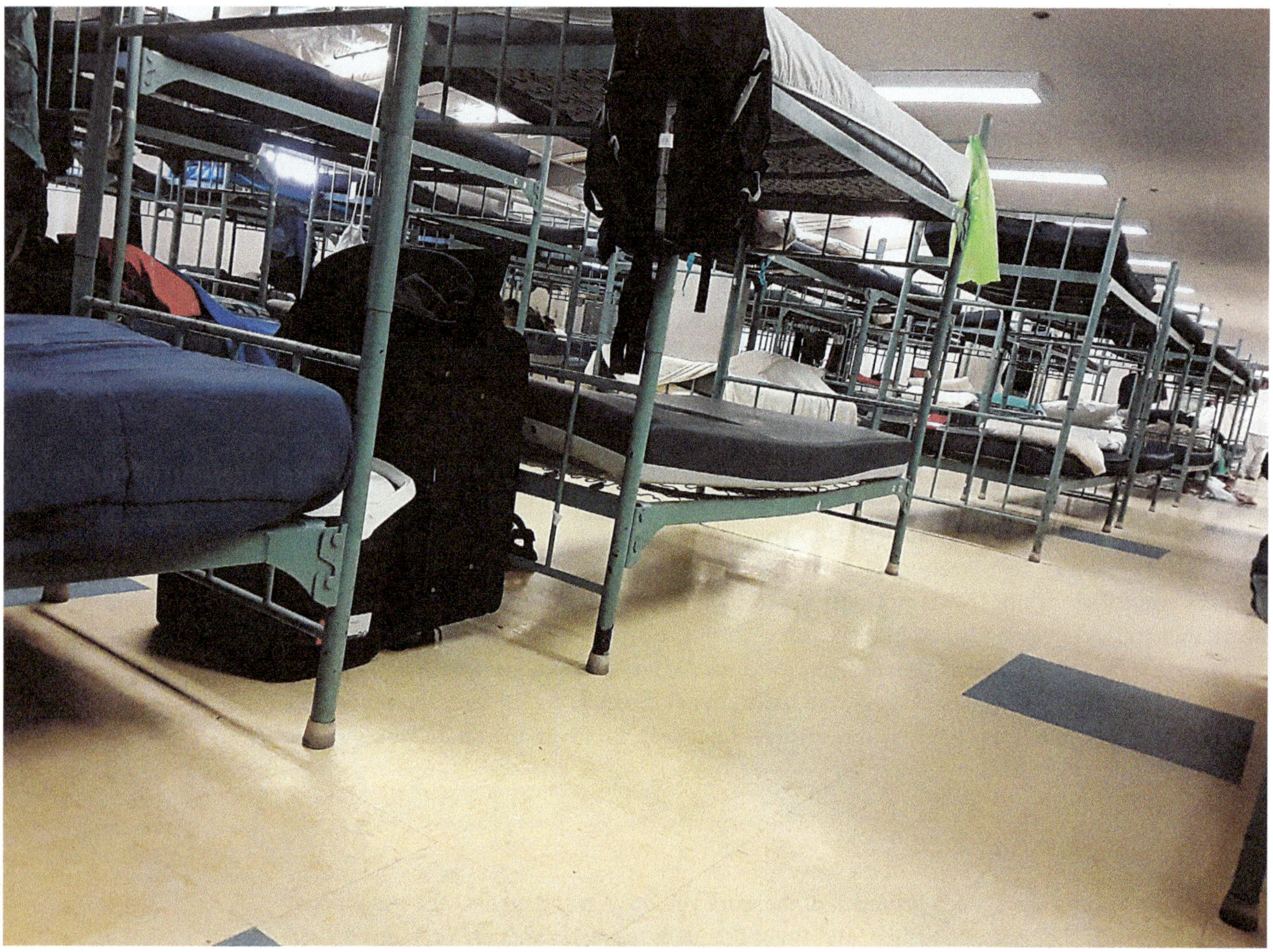

What steps could you as a human service worker take to maintain your client's privacy and anonymity in a crowded environment, such as a shelter?

The geographical location of the organization, whether rural, remote, or urban, can present other challenges in the provision of accessible services for clients. Not only is transport accessibility an issue, but accessibility also may be influenced by the visibility of individuals accessing a service. In rural communities, these difficulties can be amplified by the denser communication networks and reduced opportunity for anonymity (Green, 2003; Taylor, 2004, Schmidt, 2017; Zapf, 2001). The internet is a newer form of service delivery for the provision of information and online support through group and individual connections that do not involve the same levels of stigma as observable physical access. You may work in a structured setting, with interviews taking place in interview rooms, where privacy and comfort can be assured. Or you may be talking in corridors, at the bedside, outdoors, or in people's homes or at some place in their community. In all of these situations, being mindful of who else can and should hear what is going on is important.

Service delivery issues are also major influences on the client–worker relationship. Some considerations are whether services are offered on a short-term or long-term basis, whether there are limitations on the number and nature of contacts with people, and whether services are focused on crisis intervention or on longer-term treatment. Here are some other considerations that will influence your relationship and client work:

- What client group does your agency aim to reach?
- How does the agency, as well as specific workers, understand its clients' issues—for example, are they seen to be family issues, psychological issues, or issues arising from the structural context?
- What is the workplace culture? That is, what are the written and unwritten rules in relation to worker practice?
- How culturally diverse and/or sensitive is the agency and its workers?
- Does the agency primarily work with individuals, families, or communities?
- What staffing levels are available within the agency to meet the demands?
- What are the expectations of client caseloads for each worker?
- What budgetary restrictions influence service provision?
- Are clients' voluntary or involuntary users of the agency's services?
- How does a client access or connect with your service—through a referral, a drop-in duty system, or a waiting list process?
- How available are you as a worker?
- How structured is your time with clients?
- How private and uninterrupted is your work with clients?
- How do you address issues for clients coming to access your services from a rural or remote community who have limited experience navigating services in urban settings?

Community-Based Practice

Considering concepts that will influence your relationship with clients in community practice can look quite different from urban practice. Early on, Zapf (1991) states, "local control and community empowerment have emerged as key issues in most northern regions in Canada, northern social workers will be expected to use collaborative approaches working with communities rather than simply working in communities" (p. 45). Schmidt (2017) suggests that it is critical for urban-based social workers to understand that rural or remote practice context differs greatly. As a method to understanding the rural or remote context, Schmidt suggests facilitating a community profile to gain the community history, geography, governance structure, demographics, economic status, and community systems and resources. This requirement means shifting away from familiar practices towards a more creative, flexible, non-traditional mode of practice.

- How does community practice look different (setting, case load, needs, individual practice, community level practice) from an urban practice?
- How would you redefine your role and expectations to be effective in community practice?
- How would you address issues of visibility?
- How would you address issues of isolation in practice?
- What system would you put in place to address possible lack of supervision?
- How would you address client confidentiality?
- How would you incorporate the community structure into your practice?
- How would you learn the community culture?
- How would you plan for challenges in geography—access to roads, water travel, severe weather, and emergency accessibility?

BOX 4.6 Focus on Practice

The Impact of Agency Context

Using the questions above, think about the impact of each of these agency contexts on your practice and how differently you would work if you were located in each of the following four settings.

- *Remote Mental Health Centre.* You work in a northern remote area providing mental health services. While you are part of a provincial health service, you work with a small multidisciplinary team to deliver assessment and treatment services to people in their own communities. This involves extensive travel to northern and remote communities, often for weeks at a time. In addition, due to the geographic locations you have limited access to technology and phone services.
- *Youth and Homelessness.* You work in an urban agency that works with homeless or street-involved youth. The purpose of your work is to assist youth in gaining safe affordable housing and health care services. Your work involves going out to locate youth on your case load, case planning, locating funding, and bringing community awareness of youth homelessness.
- *Rural.* You work in a rural shelter for victims of domestic violence. Your agency offers emergency or crisis care, counselling, and support for survivors leaving a violent relationship. You are also involved in research projects, resource development, and community education and training. You work with a small team of counsellors/advocates who are committed to feminist understandings of violence and recovery.
- *Senior Care and Hospital.* You work in a large, regional hospital that provides specialist assessment, rehabilitation, advisory, and psychiatric services to older and disabled adults. You are involved in assessments, discharge planning, and individual patient and family support throughout the time of an admission.

In the following two vignettes, Jane provides insight into how many of the agency issues described above influence work in a hospital parent bereavement group. The group Jane describes is a co-led group, enabling the two workers to support the many tasks and processes involved in such a program. Clients and workers alike can be inadequately protected from some of the agency activities and disruptions outlined above. For example, Jane recounts the impact of workplace interruptions on her work with one particular mother.

BOX 4.7 Focus on Practice

Coping with Interruptions

Despite the best preparations and intentions in our agency, the phone can interrupt times with parents. Some may say, "Don't answer it." Yet long ringing can be very disruptive; ignoring a call could give the message that we don't respond to calls here; and answering even very briefly can imply someone else is more important than you! In any response the worker makes, she has to preserve confidentiality. Additionally, if a call comes through, there is always the possibility (as has happened) that there is an emergency in the worker's own family.

During an interview with a mother who was grieving for her baby daughter—her only child who had died within days of her birth—the phone rang and rang. I apologized to the parent and took the call. I asked our administration worker if she could take a message, saying, "I'm with someone, a client" (not a term I usually say), then, looking directly at her, I said, "I'm with a mother." From the look on the mother's face these words were probably the most meaningful in the appointment. Our choice of language is so important, yet so loaded.

To resume a conversation after such a discussion is difficult; it is helpful to try to hold the last words in mind and then to do a brief summary of what had been said so far:

"You were telling me about . . ."

"You were saying that . . ."

Sometimes this can be hard, especially if the call brings its own issues or tasks to be done. To acknowledge this, "Sorry, it can be difficult to get back to where we were after being interrupted like that. Where should we pick up/continue?" can restart the conversation.

1. What do you think you would do and say under similar circumstances?
2. How would you reflect on your practice to ensure you are maintaining the key elements (non-verbals, sense of self, rapport) described in previous sections and chapters?

Client interactions impact the work as well the organizational issues. Jane talks about some of the challenges of beginning on time a session of a bereavement group, given the diversity of arrival times and the continuing organizational interruptions.

BOX 4.8 Focus on Practice

Managing Interruptions

It is supportive to begin on time, especially as some parents may have come early and may find it excruciating to wait for such a group to start. Before the formal commencement of the group, as refreshments are offered, we give a brief description of the group (some of this recaps what has been sent in the letter). We would also consider who is already in the room and then do a round of introductions.

Continued

Sometimes parents may arrive half an hour into the group when the discussion, presentation, or experiential process is well under way. This interruption may include those coming for the first time who may feel very unfamiliar with the group. A quick welcoming and accepting response is called for; one that does not distract too much from the group or draw undue attention to them or make them feel awkward. We stand up, move to them and quietly do introductions, write out name tags, and ensure there are seats in the circle. We say what has been happening or, if it hasn't been long, "We've just begun," or "We haven't been talking for long." The presenter may also recap what has been going on; however, this cannot be assumed.

Interruptions have come from a security guard opening the door and looking in at us (occasionally, then locking us in, giving new meaning to the expression "closed group"!), and rowdy staff or students in adjoining rooms or someone turning off the lights in the corridor. These are the realities of the situation. Parents have dealt with much more difficult matters, yet these situations can been distracting; once more a brief reference to this interruption can be helpful, sometimes even gentle humour. Sometimes such *outside world* distractions can symbolize what's being or has been said in the group:

"What were we saying about others not seeing you or your grief . . .?"

"Well, that's how others can be . . ."

"OK we're on our own now . . ."

"That's what they think . . ."

"As impossible as it seems, the outside world keeps going on . . ."

What do you think you would do and say in similar circumstances? It is important to make sure your response is appropriate to the group and all of the participants present. An inappropriate comment may impact participants' willingness to stay or to return. Remember the key components when practicing your response: non-verbal, expressions, and gestures, all of which are part of the message you are sending in your response.

The Purpose of Your Agency

Many communication skills texts focus on skills for work that is primarily oriented towards "social care." This type of work demands that you use different influencing skills. The overarching purpose of your agency and the work you undertake within it is important to articulate and critically review.

The purpose of your work can be thought about at even more micro levels; that is, within the context of individual conversations and interviews. Is the purpose to give bad news, to change difficult behaviour, or is it to challenge the breach of an order with a parent? You will draw on various skills, depending on the different purposes of your relationship and the specific communication situation you are working in at any one time. For example, within the medical interview literature, the tasks are mapped out in relation to the doctor's role in the interview, from being patient-centred at the beginning and shifting to a doctor-centredness by the conclusion whereby the assessment and information phase is guided more by the doctor than by the patient (Smith et al., 2000). In an educational or welfare setting, a student may need support and information about coping strategies, so there may be movement from a supportive listening role towards a more psycho-educational role within the communication.

Chapter Summary

In this chapter, we have looked at some of the core ways in which you make use of yourself in your practice. We have explored the ways in which you consciously learn to use this self in practice in different ways—including all your biopsychosocial and spiritual dimensions, depending upon the circumstances. Agency contexts have been identified as defining influences on this "use of self," both at the macro level of determining the nature of the work that is undertaken within a particular setting and at a micro level of the daily structure of interactions with people.

Questions for Analysis

1. What have you learned from this chapter about
   - your differential use of self? (empathy and social-emotional intelligence)
   - the importance and potential impact of agency context?
   - defining the purpose of your work?
   - northern and remote considerations?
   - variations in cultural contexts?
   - areas you want to learn more about to improve your practice skills?
   - what strengths you have in this area?
   - where you most want to improve?
2. What are some of the unique tensions and questions for you in relation to these issues? How will you address these issues?

Recommended Readings

Carriere, J., & Richardson, C. (2013). Relationship is everything: Holistic approaches to Aboriginal child and youth mental health. *First Peoples Child & Family Review*, *7*(2), 8–26.

Coates, J., Graham, J.R., Swartzentruber, B., & Ouellette, B. (2007). *Spirituality and social work: Selected Canadian readings*. Toronto, ON: Canadian Scholars' Press.

Freedberg, S. (2007). Re-examining empathy: A relational-feminist point of view. *Journal of Social Work*, *52*(3), 251–9.

Freeman, T., Edwards, T., Baum, F., Laless, A., Jolley, G., Javanparast, S., & Francis, T. (2014). Cultural respect strategies in Australian Aboriginal primary health care services: Beyond education and training of practitioners. *Australian and New Zealand Journal of Public Health*, *38*(4), 355–61.

Goleman, D. (2005). *Emotional intelligence*. New York, NY: Bantam Books.

Goleman, D. (2006). *Social intelligence: The new science of human relationships*. London: Hutchinson.

Green, R., Gregory, R., & Mason, R. (2006). Professional distance and social work: Stretching the elastic? *Australian Social Work*, *59*(4), 449–61.

Greene, A. (2017). The role of self-awareness and reflection in social care practice. *Journal of Social Care*, *1*(1), 1–13.

Kirmayer, L. (2013). Embracing uncertainty as a path to competence: Cultural safety, empathy, and alterity in clinical training. *Culture, Medicine & Psychiatry*, 37(2), 354–72.

Raheim, S., & Lu, J.J. (2014). Preparing MSW students for integrative Mind–Body-spirit practice. *Clinical Social Work Journal*, 42(3), 288–301. doi:10.1007/s10615-014-0484-3

Rogers, C. (1987). Comments on the issue of equality in psychotherapy. *Journal of Humanistic Psychology*, 27(1), 38–9.

Wong, P., & Lee, A. (2015). Dual roles of social work supervisors: Strain and strengths as managers and clinical supervisors. *China Journal of Social Work*, 8(2), 164–81.

Weisman, D., & Zornado, J. (2018). *Professional writing for social work practice* (2nd ed.). New York, NY: Springer Publishing Company.

William, D.J., & Prior, E.E. (2015). Contemporary polyamory: A call for awareness and sensitivity in social work. *Social Work*, 60(3), 268–70.

Internet Resources

Canadian Society for Spirituality and Social Work
www.spiritualityandsocialwork.ca

Conflict Resolution Network
www.crnhq.org

Daniel Goleman's website (social and emotional intelligence)
www.danielgoleman.info

International Federation of Social Workers
http://ifsw.org

Journal of Social Care
https://arrow.dit.ie/jsoc/vol1/iss1

Towards a New Relationship: Toolkit for Reconciliation/Decolonization of Social Work Practice at the Individual, Workplace, and Community Level
www.bcasw.org/wp-content/uploads/2016/07/Reconcilliation-Toolkit-June-16-Edit.pdf

What Is Self-Awareness and Why Is It Important in Counseling?
https://positivepsychologyprogram.com/self-awareness

5 Sustaining Your Self in Practice

Learning Goals

- Learn about your self-care and professional development strategies.
- Understand the nature of critical reflective practice.
- Review the purposes and tasks of supervision.
- Describe the processes of debriefing and when it is useful.

Self-Care and Professional Development

In human service work, you are working with people who are coping with some of life's most extreme difficulties, challenges, and opportunities. The impact on the worker will be significant—both across the accumulation of experiences and through single, complex incidents that confront who we are and what we are doing. This chapter explores some of the ways in which you can prepare and sustain yourself for this personally confronting and rewarding work.

BOX 5.1 Focus on Practice

Protectors Need Protecting, Too

Maria McNamara described her experiences of working within the child protection system:

Given the unique difficulties of the job, it is possible there is widespread undiagnosed and untreated post-traumatic stress disorder (PTSD) among current and former child protection workers. Researchers have theorized that when protection workers deal with violent families, they are not immune from the violence. Not only are they vulnerable to assaults and abuse, but they can also experience secondary trauma from witnessing the violence and abuse to which children are subjected.

Continued

I was abused [verbally] countless times over the phone and in person, and I was assaulted [physically] once during an after-hours call-out. This happened one summer evening while I was questioning a woman about her young children, who were on a protective court order.

Source: McNamara (2006, p. 9).

Good professional **self-care** skills are essential throughout your career. You need to be aware of the risk and protective factors in your work and your workplace. The risk factors or the "costs" of caring have been understood in a number of ways.

It is important for practitioners to reflect on the differences between "professional self-care," and "personal self-care." Professional self-care consists of the elements a practitioner puts in place to address workplace stressors. For example, scheduled supervision is a way to debrief and gain support around your role and needs in the workplace. Personal self-care may include participating in a group or sport that is independent from your work.

Some self-care tasks benefit both your professional and personal life. Attending the gym on a weekly basis is one example of a self-care activity that would clearly benefit both

Have you ever practiced a form of meditation? How do you feel it would impact your human service work as a form of self-care?

professional and personal wellness. Meditation practice is another example. Margolin, Pierce, and Wiley (2011) highlight,

> The objective [of meditation] is to experience an underlying deeper aspect of self that many individuals do not perceive in day-to-day life. To attain this level of meditation, one must divorce themselves from anxious thought. Consistent identification with anxiety and pain act as barriers to identification with peace and joy. Sen (2005) ascertains that yoga (a Sanskrit word meaning to add or unite) is not possible without beyoga (meaning to subtract or detach). Meditation begins with beyoga—the subtraction, or detachment, of all that interrupts an integrated and balanced mind-body-soul on the journey toward yoga. (p. 236).

Human service work can lead to what is termed compassion stress (or compassion fatigue) or burnout (Jenaro, Flores, & Arias, 2007, p. 80). Burnout arises in relation to chronic workplace stress. It is characterized by "negative attitudes and feelings toward co-workers and one's job role. These experiences can lead to a pervasive cynicism or a lack of enthusiasm and motivation that can be harmful to you and your clients" (Jenaro, Flores, & Arias, 2007, p. 80). Unlike burnout, **compassion fatigue** is the result of emotional exhaustion stemming from continuous exposure to traumatic client stories and can happen following a single incident. A useful checklist has been developed by Figley (1995) for screening your own levels of compassion fatigue and burnout.

BOX 5.2 Focus on Practice

Compassion Fatigue Self-Test

Rate yourself on each of the following questions, using the 1–5 rating scale, where

1 = rarely/never
2 = at times
3 = not sure
4 = often
5 = very often

	Question	Score
1	I force myself to avoid certain thoughts or feelings that remind me of a frightening experience.	
2	I find myself avoiding certain activities or situations because they remind me of a frightening experience.	
3	I have gaps in my memory about frightening events.	
4	I feel estranged from others.	
5	I have difficulty falling or staying asleep.	
6	I have outbursts of anger or irritability with little provocation.	

Continued

7	I startle easily.	
8	While working with a victim, I thought about violence against the perpetrator.	
9	I am a sensitive person.	
10	I have had flashbacks connected to my clients.	
11	I have had first-hand experience with traumatic events in my adult life.	
12	I have had first-hand experience with traumatic events in my childhood.	
13	I have thought that I need to "work through" a traumatic experience in my life.	
14	I have thought that I need more close friends.	
15	I have thought that there is no one to talk with about highly stressful experiences.	
16	I have concluded that I work too hard for my own good.	
17	I am frightened of things a client has said or done to me.	
18	I experience troubling dreams similar to those of a client of mine.	
19	I have experienced intrusive thoughts of sessions with especially difficult clients.	
20	I have suddenly and involuntarily recalled a frightening experience while working with a client.	
21	I am preoccupied with more than one client.	
22	I am losing sleep over a client's traumatic experiences.	
23	I have thought that I might have been "infected" by the traumatic stress of my clients.	
24	I remind myself to be less concerned about the well-being of my clients.	
25	I have felt trapped by my work as a social worker.	
26	I have felt a sense of hopelessness associated with working with clients.	
27	I have felt "on edge" about various things and I attribute this to working with certain clients.	
28	I have wished that I could avoid working with some clients.	
29	I have been in danger working with clients.	
30	I have felt that my clients dislike me personally.	
31	I have felt weak, tired, and run down as a result of my work as a social worker.	
32	I have felt depressed as a result of my work as a social worker.	
33	I am unsuccessful at separating work from personal life.	
34	I feel little compassion towards most of my co-workers.	
35	I feel I am working more for the money than for personal fulfillment.	
36	I find it difficult separating my personal life from my work life.	
37	I have a sense of worthlessness/disillusionment/resentment associated with my work.	

38	I have thoughts that I am a "failure" as a social worker.	
39	I have thoughts that I am not succeeding at achieving my life goals.	
40	I have to deal with bureaucratic, unimportant tasks in my work life.	

When you have completed the survey, you can work out your score by circling these 23 questions: 1–8, 10–13, 17–26, and 29. You then add up the numbers you wrote next to the items for a total compassion fatigue risk score, which is rated as follows:

- You are at extremely low risk if your total score is 26 or less.
- You are at moderate risk if your total score is 31–35.
- You are at high risk with a total score of 36–40 and extremely high risk with a total score of 41 or more.

You then add up the numbers you wrote next to the items not circled to estimate your risk of burnout.

- You are at extremely low risk if your total score is 17–36 or less.
- You are at low risk with a total score of 37–50.
- You are at high risk with a total score of 51–75 and extremely high risk with a score of 76–85.

Source: Figley, C., ed. 1995. Compassion Fatigue: Coping with Secondary Traumatic Stress Disorder in Those Who Treat the Traumatized. New York: Brunner/Mazel.

Other impacts of the work emerge from more acute experiences of distress and trauma, as distinct from the accumulation of stress over time. **Vicarious trauma** stems from the empathetic engagement with a client and is viewed as a serious concern for mental health professionals. Practitioners experiencing vicarious trauma may present with a change in their world view; a weakened sense of trust, safety, and control; and compromised psychological and interpersonal functioning (Canfield, 2016). As a practitioner, hearing or witnessing stories of assault or abuse on a daily basis may create vicarious trauma. This process is subtle as it accumulates over time and often passes undetected by the practitioner.

Other trauma reactions include "feelings of emptiness, desolation, and despair," or as White (2004) describes, it is about becoming "overwhelmed by a sense of hopelessness and paralysis, and [believing] that there's nothing whatsoever they can do to affect the shape of their life or the shape of events around them" (p. 47).

Your self-care skills and strategies are usually about maintenance and prevention tasks, but sometimes about intervention—in particular, instances of stress and trauma. Professional maintenance tasks relate to the ongoing development of knowledge and skills. Personal maintenance tasks focus on care of yourself as a person engaged in demanding interpersonal work. This enables you to continue to develop as a worker and be well supported in that work. Some key professional self-care strategies workers adopt in relation to this include

- supervision, which will be discussed extensively in the following section;
- formal peer support strategies, which include journal clubs, ongoing practice discussion groups, and professional development activities; and
- continued access to training and workshops that assist a worker in successful practice.

In addition, personal self-care strategies workers adopt can include

- personal maintenance strategies, such as humour, fitness, sleep, diet, maintaining a good psychological sense of well-being, and maintaining a good network of friends outside of the workplace; and
- informal peer support strategies, such as social clubs and activities.

Applying the above professional and personal self-care strategies can assist practitioners in maintaining overall wellness. Intervention strategies relate to the more immediate strategies used at key times of stress or crisis—that is, when something particularly stressful has happened. Some key strategies adopted at these times include supervision and debriefing.

Self-care strategies are relatively straightforward and typically relate to a biopsychosocial-spiritual balance within a worker's daily life. Making them happen regularly as a preventive strategy is typically the greater challenge. One of the ways in which we can bring about an understanding of these issues is to think through them in critically reflective or reflexive processes.

Critical Self-Reflection

> If we do not maintain an awareness of this possibility of altering the oppressive structures within society, we can perpetuate the very oppressions we are looking to eradicate. Chapter 14 looks at these issues in greater detail.

Reflecting on your practice is an important skill. Numerous terms are used for this activity—reflection, reflectivity, and **reflexivity or critical reflection**, to name a few. "Reflexivity" refers to more of "a bending back onto a self, [which] can encompass many diverse processes, depending on what manner of connection, or relationship, is accomplishing the bending back" (Steier, 1995, p. 63).

Reflection on and in all dimensions of our practice has a number of functions. First and foremost, ongoing critical reflection is one way of ensuring good practice outcomes for clients. Ongoing awareness of the effects of these interactions is an essential part of transforming the lived experiences of clients. Second, it enables the impact of the work to be addressed. Human service work often provokes strong physical and emotional responses, such as intense sadness and distress or anger and frustration. Some experiences can be overwhelming and evoke a sense of helplessness or powerlessness.

Your work can bring you into contact with violence or extreme poverty. For some workers this may be their first exposure; for others, it brings reminders of past and present experiences. This type of work will inevitably have an impact on you. Its positive impact is the accumulation of practice experience and practice wisdom. Its negative impact can lead to distress, stress, burnout, or cynicism. Through a reflective process, practitioners can maintain awareness of both positive (practice wisdom) and negative (distress, burnout) events that impact daily practice.

Critical reflection provides an opportunity to assess the effect of these experiences, to integrate them in some way, and to develop assessments and interventions that lead to further change. Reflective practice builds the bridge between theory and practice (Payne, 2006, 2014), but also maintains a focus on change.

Reflection alone can be an introspective process that may influence our own practice but not influence the outer world in any substantial way. That is, problems in the outer world that lead to inner- and outer-world distress or difficulty for others remain unaltered. Critical self-reflection takes this reflective process one step further:

> Critical reflection, when used specifically to improve professional practice, is reflective practice that focuses on the power dimensions of assumptive thinking, and therefore on how practice might change in order to bring about change in the social situations in which professionals work. In order to be able to critically reflect, a worker must be able to think reflectively. (Fook, 2016, pp. 441–2)

A number of strategies can be adopted to practice reflection and critical reflexive practice.

BOX 5.3 Focus on Practice

Social Self-Awareness Exercise

A multi-dimensional approach suggests that all dimensions of our experience interact to form a personal and social identity. Reviewing the dimensions of our own experience through a social, structural, and cultural analysis can help us to understand how various dimensions have shaped our life and our life choices.

Reflect on the impact on your life and ways of being of the following dimensions of your life. Fook (2002) has identified the following dimensions and you might add others:

- relationship status
- occupation
- social class (past and present)
- education
- family type and background
- ethnicity
- religion
- membership of groups or subcultures
- gender
- sexual orientation
- health
- age
- particular ideologies.

Source: Adapted from Fook (2002, pp. 156–7).

This exercise raises important questions about what experiences influence us. A further step is to ask yourself how we influence each of these dimensions of our social identity, so that their means of expression and understanding are perpetuated or changed in our wider contexts.

This self-understanding is the essential component of reflexive practice and it raises more questions about how we then respond. A study that explored working with couples in interfaith relationships, specifically Muslim and Christian relationships (Furlong & Ata, 2006), encountered dilemmas pertaining to this kind of self-knowledge. Workers were conscious of the importance of cultural sensitivity and of awareness of difference generally, but the study showed that verbalizing that stance may not be enough: "As practitioners, we are never neutral and we do not wish to be. Yet, it is naïve to believe that the simple declaration of one's position will always be received as courteous and engaging. Nor is it always the case that such declarations will facilitate the outcome that is desired" (Furlong & Ata, 2006, p. 259). Thus, the first step is recognizing your position, but other steps are involved.

BOX 5.4 Focus on Practice

Working in Triads

Use the earlier social awareness exercise to identify an issue for role-play. For example, it may be about how gender has impacted your choice of work or study.

One person is assigned the role of interviewer, one the role of client, and one the role of observer. The observer can participate in a number of ways:

- Watch the interview and provide comment at the end as to what was observed. This can lead to a critical discussion of what happened, what was intended to happen from both worker and client perspectives, and as a way of discussing the implications of the direction of the interview. For example, how was the problem constructed by each person: the client and the worker? Were there ways in which the interview perpetuated the social discourses for the client and reinforced the person's oppression rather than redressing it? If so, how?
- The observer can choose to intervene at points in the interview where the worker could have directed the interview differently. This action interrupts habits of thinking in the worker and can provide useful new insights. It encourages a process of thinking together by "freeze framing" the worker's choices for discussion.
- The worker can call on the observer when he or she feels stuck or realizes the interview is heading in an unhelpful direction. This step relies on the worker's recognition of those moments and leads to reflection on new possibilities for action.

The aim of the role of the external observer is to develop an awareness in the worker of thinking "outside" of practice. The goal is for the worker to internalize the observer role as a critical process so that the worker can have this sort of "dialogue" reflexively during practice. This skill is referred to as being a participant-observer in your practice; you are simultaneously participating in and observing the conversation during an interview with a client.

Another strategy for developing critical self-reflective practice is to undertake a process record. A "process record" is a systematic, written analysis of an interview, typically its content and process. Usually, it is written in columns so that the simultaneous moments of

TABLE 5.1 The Process Record

Content		What did you think was happening?	What would you do differently?
Worker:	"So you were not prepared for living and working in a northern and remote community. Have you looked for another job?"	I thought the client felt that living in a northern and remote community was too much and wanted out.	I asked two questions, and in the process assumed the client was looking to move and/or could not handle northern living.
Client:	"No, I just was not prepared for how different it is working in a small community. It is very different from what I expected."	I think the client is more overwhelmed than I'd originally thought. My questions suggested the solution was for the client to get another job, instead of talking more about what the client is experiencing.	I need to gain an understanding of where the client is living and what he finds overwhelming about his new environment.
Worker:	"Can you tell me a bit more about where you have moved to work?"	I invited the client to talk more about the original issue, which was the move to a northern remote community to work.	This was where I should have stayed with the story from the start rather than rushing to "fix" what I thought the issue was.
Client:	[tells more of his story]		

a conversation can be suggested graphically. It includes the transcribed (or approximated) content of the conversation, from both interviewer and client, and then varying amounts of comment or critique (Table 5.1). For example, many process records include a column for what the interviewer was thinking or feeling, or what could have done differently, as well as a column documenting the perceived reactions of the client. The opportunity for critical reflective practice takes another column in which the client–worker relationship can be analyzed as to whether it is reflecting, perpetuating, or challenging broader structural issues.

A process record gives insight into the interactions at the interface of a conversation and, in particular, where change can be identified. From this exercise, practitioners can reflect on their process when engaging with clients. In addition, it provides practitioners with the opportunity to self-evaluate and maintain a critical awareness of their skill levels relating to practice competencies. Practitioners may also want to consider keeping samples of their transcriptions to compare to future examples as part of an ongoing professional development strategy.

A more extensive analysis of a conversation or a particular incident can be done using a **critical incident** analysis framework (Cleak & Wilson, 2004). The practice exercise below shows how a formal analysis, written or verbal, can assist with this process of reflection.

BOX 5.5 Practice Exercise

Consider a critical incident that occurred in your practice or portrayed in the media, and reflect on what happened and why it was critical.

First, retrieve the memory.

1. What was the first image you recall?
2. Where were you in relation to your first image?
3. Who was closest to you?
4. What sounds, smells, and tactile sensations do you recall?
5. Which people, comments, or practices stand out in your mind?

Next, consider the affective domain—*reflect on how you felt.*

6. What was your first reaction?
7. What was the high or low part of the incident?
8. Were you surprised, delighted, angered, elated, curious, confused, frightened, or depressed by anything in the experience? Describe your mood and feelings.
9. What do you think others around you were feeling?

Now, *interpret the events.*

10. What have you learned from this incident?
11. From this experience, what can you conclude about your understanding of and skills in assessment or analysis? What are your strengths and what areas require practice?
12. What was your key insight or learning?
13. How does this relate to your framework for practice?

Finally, consider your decisions.

14. What skills and areas of understanding do you need to develop further as a result of your reflection?
15. What would this development entail?
16. What methods does this experience reinforce as valuable for future practice? Why?

Source: Cleak & Wilson (2004, p. 79).

Overall, processes of reflection and reflexivity are highly valued by workers as they enhance learning and insight, develop personal and professional skills (Coggins, 2016; Fook, 2016).

Supervision and Other Supports

One of the practice arenas where critical self-reflection most commonly occurs is within the context of **supervision**.

Supervision has different meanings in different professions. For human service workers, a supervisor is someone who takes responsibility, typically within the context of your agency, for you, your learning, and your practice. A supervisor assists you in developing your practice and practice wisdom through direct modelling, support, and intervention as an experienced worker.

Three key functions of supervision are administration, education, and support. In relation to other sections of administration, supervisors provide accountability to the organization and to clients by monitoring caseload issues and worker issues. The educational focus is on providing opportunities for learning and discussion, as well as exploring professional development needs.

© Mark Bowden/123RF

In your previous work or academic experience, have you had any experiences of supervision that have been particularly supportive? If a new supervisor asked you to describe a positive management experience, how would you explain what your former supervisor did to make that relationship so beneficial?

The support function relates to providing staff care, through the provision of an opportunity to reflect critically on practice and to receive support and encouragement. Supervision has preventive and supportive functions, which are important for the worker *and* the agency, and therefore ultimately to the benefit of clients.

Optimally, supervision can provide a safe learning environment—a place to test out new ideas and integrate them into practice. It can provide a place to integrate theory and practice, and the personal and the professional. Workers have someone who can help them to deal with the ongoing accumulation of work issues, as well as provide support around particular crises.

In many agencies, supervision and support are offered regularly in a structured format and are valued dimensions of the agency's functioning (Renzenbrink, 2005). In other agencies, supervision tends to be overlooked or undervalued. Some agencies structure individual supervision relationships according to management hierarchies within the organization. A senior worker provides support and mentoring to a junior one. Others run with peer models and/or group supervision models.

Heather works in a drug and alcohol treatment service, where a group model of supervision operates. She describes her experience.

BOX 5.6 Focus on Practice

Group Supervision

I was having a conversation in our supervision group with several clinicians about the difficulty of establishing a good rapport with a client who has been reluctant to engage due to past trust issues. Here is some of the feedback I received from the group:

- This can increase the difficulty when the clinician is in a situation where they are mandated to notify protective services about a client.
- This can amplify the conflict that this scenario can place a clinician in, and often the clinician is wishing to retain the hard-fought therapeutic alliance with the client, but is also well aware of risk issues requiring notification.

After, we highlighted the importance of consultation and debriefing when facing these dilemmas, especially in long-term therapeutic work.

1. What do you think Heather gained from this group supervision?
2. What are some of the key practice considerations for Heather?
3. What do you think would be different in individual supervision?
4. How do you have supervision organized in your work?

Practicum placements are a good opportunity for students to initiate active supervision. Consider the guidelines on the following page when developing your learning contract for a student practicum.

The usefulness of the supervisory experience depends on the agenda and the combined skill set of the supervisor and supervisee. As in any relationship, unrealistic or unclear expectations can inhibit a supervisory relationship (Bucknell, 2006; Reid & Westergaard, 2006), as can major differences in opinions about how practice should take place or, for example, what are the important skills to demonstrate. Sometimes, the expectations of either the supervisor or the worker can be unreasonable. Supervisors can be busy and stressed, working under similar agency demands as the supervisee, but often with higher management responsibilities. All of these dimensions can influence the availability, quality, and effectiveness of the relationship.

Like other professional relationships, having an initial discussion about the mutual expectations of supervision is important. Difficulties in the supervisory relationship occur when these expectations differ or when needs cannot be met within the context of the relationship. It is important to assess whether supervision can be an effective learning space or not.

BOX 5.7 Focus on Practice

Establishing a Supervisory Relationship

Here are some questions that workers have found useful to discuss with a prospective supervisor.

Questions relating to the structure of supervision:

1. When and where will you meet, including time, day, and length of time?
2. How frequently will you meet—weekly, twice per month, monthly?
3. What should happen in relation to phone calls, text messages, and other interruptions?
4. If so, who will document it? Will a record of supervision be kept?

Questions relating to the process and function of supervision:

1. What are the expectations and goals of each of you in supervision? For example,
   - How will the agenda be set and revised?
   - What should the worker bring to supervision (e.g., case material, workplace/team issues, and personal issues)?
2. What are the learning and communication styles of each of you?
3. Are there possible incompatibilities in the ways in which each of you works?
4. What measures, if any, can be in place should the supervisor be away for an extended period? For example, is there an alternate senior person who could be available to consult?
5. How should conflict or disagreement be managed?
6. What review processes will take place?

Other possibilities for ongoing professional development include using supervision that is external to the agency. A major benefit of this arrangement is the ability to step outside the politics of the workplace and to have someone as a more objective sounding board who is an independent support for you and your work. Outside of the forum of supervision, learning, reflection, and self-care can take place through numerous strategies:

- recording yourself in an interview (either audio or audio visually, and with the consent of the client) for review and critique
- undertaking joint work with a colleague, which provides the opportunity for critical feedback and discussion
- formalized mentoring with senior staff
- undertaking a process recording
- maintaining a personal journal, in which you critically reflect on your work
- maintaining reading of professional journals and texts.

Debriefing

Critical incident stress management (CISM) has been increasingly recognized as an important dimension of workplace support, in the aftermath of specific events or critical incidents. Recognition of critical incidents came from emergency services work, and in this context was defined as "any situation faced by emergency services personnel that causes them to experience unusually strong emotional reactions which have the potential to interfere with their ability to function either at the scene or later" (Mitchell, 1983, p. 36). This definition has also been applied to incidents involving a wider range of work contexts. It does raise the question as to whether it is the worker or the organization or the wider community that identifies the risk situation, an issue to which we will return later.

A formal **debriefing** is one process that can be used to address these factors. The aim is to reduce distress, to educate and provide support around reactions, and, in many instances, to review workforce strategies. Debriefing provides an opportunity to emotionally ventilate and psychologically process what has occurred. It can occur in dyads or in larger groups, and usually occurs between the first 24 hours following an incident, up to three days afterwards. It is used in many different practice contexts, such as schools, hospitals, and the community, particularly in the aftermath of distressing or traumatic incidents. In the context of human service practice, this could include a wide range of events such as natural disasters, deaths, accidents, and violent incidents.

Since its implementation, extensive debate has continued as to the effectiveness of debriefing and additional support interventions that make up CISM (Deahl et al., 2001; Dyregrov, 1997; McNally, Bryant, & Ehlers, 2003; Mitchell, 1983). The Mitchell Model, the debriefing model developed for firefighters in the United States, follows a facilitated six-stage group structure, moving from the incident details to issues of personal reactions and education around self-care strategies (Everly, Flannery, & Mitchell, 2000; Mitchell, 1983, 2004).

The introductory phase includes introductions of everyone in the group, an introduction of the purpose of the meeting, and the establishment of group rules, particularly in relation to confidentiality. The fact phase invites participants to give their account of what occurred, including their roles and responsibilities. This account includes "where they were [and] what they heard, saw, smelled and did as they worked in and around the incident" (Mitchell, 1983, p. 38). The intention is to re-create the incident from as many perspectives as possible.

The feeling phase involves asking questions relating to emotional reactions, such as

- How did you feel when that happened?
- How are you feeling now?
- Have you ever felt anything like that in your life before? (Mitchell, 1983, p. 38)

The emphasis is on hearing all emotional reactions and privileging no one over another. The symptom phase focuses on reactions through asking questions such as

- What unusual things did you experience at the time of the incident?
- What unusual things are you experiencing now?
- Has your life changed in any way since the incident? (Mitchell, 1983, p. 38)

This phase focuses on possible disruptions to functioning as a result of stress reactions. The teaching phase provides an opportunity for the facilitator to discuss normal stress and/or trauma reactions with the group and to educate around possible future reactions. The final phase of the debriefing session, the re-entry phase, draws the session to a close through review and careful planning about next steps, including what people might do immediately after the meeting, both individually and as a work group.

A follow-up debriefing is often included as a seventh stage. This provides an opportunity to review how people are coping and to implement other coping strategies as required.

Supporters of debriefing argue that a stress response is normal and usually follows a regular pattern among the majority of individuals and it is this pattern that debriefing addresses. The major criticism of debriefing efforts is that they are not effective in reducing the longer-term post-traumatic stress impacts of traumatic events. After years of offering debriefings, a more cautious approach is now being recommended. For example, Rose, Bisson, and Wessely (2003) recommend restricting "across the board" immediate psychological debriefings, but add that it is important to ensure early practical support and to notice those with possible acute stress disorder, an important predictor of PTSD. Mitchell's work, however controversial, has radically altered people's thinking about psychological first-aid responses, and has enabled a far greater awareness of the immediate and potentially devastating effects of critical incidents.

In negotiating complex workplace dynamics, adequate training of those who are to conduct a debriefing is essential. The status of the debriefer as either an insider or an outsider is an important consideration (Rose, Bisson, & Wessely, 2003). These dimensions are presented in Figure 5.1 and provide a useful checklist to think about as to whether a debriefing process is appropriate or whether a smaller-scale strategy is warranted. As discussed earlier in this section, the question of who decides whether an incident has had a significant impact and whether debriefing is required is important.

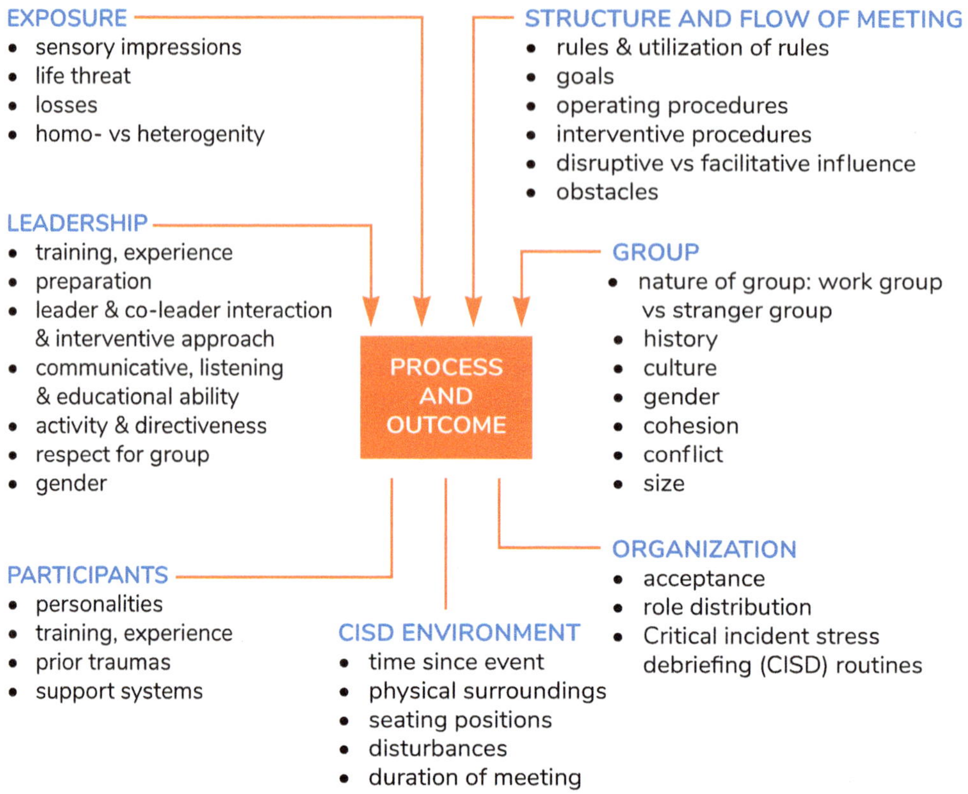

Many of the key dimensions of formal debriefing processes can be applied to more informal interactions, and even one-to-one interactions.

FIGURE 5.1 Workplace Conditions for Debriefing to Occur

Source: Dyregrov, A. 1997. 'The process in psychological debriefings', Journal of Traumatic Stress 10, 4: 589–605.

Chapter Summary

In this chapter, we have explored some aspects of your ongoing learning and support needs. These have been raised early in the text to emphasize that they are core preventative skills for your practice. Using supervision preventively, and debriefing when required, minimizes the impacts of stressful and traumatic events, often preventing vicarious traumatization and burnout. We also explored the processes of critical self-reflection, supervision, and debriefing as three ways in which you can be sustained in your practice.

Questions for Analysis

1. In thinking about your readiness for practice, what strategies do you have in place in for professional self-care?
   - What self-care strategies do you have in place aimed at your professional work?

- How are you prepared for critical self-reflection processes; in particular, what supervision or mentorship structures do you have in place and when do you use them?
- How would this differ in more northern and remote practice settings?

2. What strategies do you have in place for personal self-care?
   - What self-care strategies do you have in place aimed at your personal wellness outside of work?
   - How are you prepared for critical self-reflection processes; in particular, what personal support networks do you have outside work and when do you use them?
   - What would be the implications for personal wellness in rural or northern settings?
3. What have been your experiences of supervision or mentoring in other contexts, and how do you think they will influence your current expectations?
4. What do you see as some of the challenges of engaging in critical self-reflection?
5. What is your understanding of debriefing?
6. What are the arguments for and against formal debriefings?
7. What are your thoughts on debriefing the debriefers?
8. If you are working in isolation, what system do you have in place to address professional self-care?

Recommended Readings

Berzoff, J., & Drisko, J. (2015). What clinical social workers need to know: Bio-psycho-social knowledge and skills for the twenty first century. *Clinical Social Work Journal*, 43(3), 263–73. doi:10.1007/s10615-015-0544-3

Canfield, J. (2016). Secondary traumatization, burnout, and vicarious traumatization: A review of the literature as it relates to therapists who treat trauma. *Smith College Studies in Social Work*, 75(2), 81–101. doi.org/10.1300/J497v75n02_06

Dyregrov, A. (1997). The process in psychological debriefings. *Journal of Traumatic Stress*, 10(4), 589–605.

Eketone, A. (2012). The purposes of cultural supervision. *Aotearoa New Zealand Social Work*, 24(3/4), 20–30.

Figley, C. (Ed.). (1995). *Compassion fatigue: Coping with secondary traumatic stress disorder in those who treat the traumatized*. New York, NY: Brunner/Mazel.

Fook, J. (2012). *Critical reflection in context: Applications in health and social care*. Hoboken, NJ: Taylor and Francis.

Fook, J. (2016). *Social work: A critical approach to practice* (3rd ed.). London: Sage.

Golia, G., & McGovern, A. (2015). If you save me, I'll save you: The power of peer supervision in clinical training and professional development. *British Journal of Social Work*, 45(2), 634–50.

Lee, M.Y., Zaharlick, A., & Akers, D. (2017). Impact of meditation on mental health outcomes of female trauma survivors of interpersonal violence with co-occurring disorders: A randomized controlled trial. *Journal of Interpersonal Violence*, 32(14). doi:2139-2165. 10.1177/0886260515591277

O'Donoghue, K. (2003). *Restorying social work supervision*. Annandale: Federation Press.

Sullivan, P. (2016). Leadership in social work: Where are we? *Journal of Social Work Education*, 52(S1), S51–S61.

Tsui, M. (2005). *Social work supervision: Contexts and concepts*. Thousand Oaks, CA: Sage.

Yagil, D. (2006). The relationship of abusive and supportive workplace supervision to employee burnout and upward influence tactics. *Journal of Emotional Abuse*, 6(1), 49–65.

Internet Resources

American Academy of Experts in Traumatic Stress
www.aaets.org/index.htm

Canadian Centre for Emergency Preparedness
www.ceep.ca

Canadian Centre for Victims of Torture
www.ccvt.org/declaration.html

Canadian Mental Health Association
https://cmha.ca

Canadian Red Cross
www.redcross.ca

International Critical Incident Stress Foundation
www.icisf.org

North American Center for Threat Assessment and Trauma Response
www.nactatr.com

PsychOz Publications, Resources for Effective Psychotherapy and Counselling
www.psychotherapy.com.au/home

Trauma Informed Care Network
www.ticn.org

Trauma-Informed Practice Guide
http://bccewh.bc.ca/wp-content/uploads/2012/05/2013_TIP-Guide.pdf

Trauma Response in Canada
www.canada.ca/en/health-canada/services/environmental-workplace-health/occupational-health-safety/employee-assistance-services/trauma-response-services-employee-assistance-services-occupational-health-safety.html

6 Establishing a Good Working Relationship

Learning Goals

- Describe what you need to think about before meeting with someone.
- Know how to open the communication process.
- Understand the processes involved in engaging with and actively listening to your clients and their stories.
- Analyze the concept of confidentiality.
- Critique the notion of self-disclosure, understanding why it is such a controversial skill.

Preparing to Meet

Chapter 4 outlined many of the questions you could consider prior to your contact with any client in your organization, including questions about the physical environment and the type of service delivery. This discussion focuses more specifically on preparing for an initial contact with your client, and highlights three particular issues.

The first relates to who it is you will be seeing. The initial engagement process needs to be thought through. For example, in working with Indigenous clients, thinking about who you will meet with and whether Elders need to be approached before engaging in community practice. For survivors of torture and trauma, working with a support person present may be more appropriate (Victorian Foundation for Survivors of Torture, 2016). Working with children may require parental consent or the accompaniment of independent adult support. Work with some clients requires an interpreter, with whom the guidelines of the interface must be understood and agreed on beforehand.

The second issue is whether you are able to psychologically attend to this person or these people. An attitudinal readiness is vital. Many factors will impact your attitudinal readiness. For example, your contact with someone will be influenced by what has immediately preceded it, and what you might be anticipating afterwards. Being fully present in a conversation with another person is difficult if you are distracted by other issues. Part of being present with clients includes the verbal, non-verbal, and listening skills outlined in Chapters 2 and 3. Meeting people involves a biopsychosocial-spiritual attentiveness and, if for some reason it is not possible to be attentive, discussing the options with your supervisor is an important step.

The third issue relates to what you already know about this person, if anything. Someone in your organization may have been working with this client and an extensive case note history may be available to you. This history, or lack thereof, is important for you to be aware of prior to any contact. The history can convey important details, such as risks to be aware of that may affect your new involvement with the person. For example, if someone has a history of aggression when she perceives her needs not to be met, you may want to consider where you meet with her and, indeed, whether you meet alone or with a co-worker. On the other hand, a case history can maintain a particular story about a person that has never been verified and could lead to the perpetuation of incorrect labels being imposed on the person.

The issue of prior knowledge can be complicated in rural or remote practice. Often, the turnover rate of professionals is higher than in urban settings; therefore, case histories may not be available. In many such cases, the worker will be faced with clients who appear frustrated or aggressive, which may be due to fear or to a lack of trust that accompanies explaining their needs repeatedly to new workers.

Making Initial Contact

Whether in an involuntary client setting or a voluntary one, welcoming skills ensure that "the welcome people receive is warm and respectful" (Trevithick, 2005, p. 150). Introductions aim to help people feel at ease and to break down some of the initial anxiety or **anomie** that many people experience in unfamiliar relationships. Typically, people approach new relationships with some tentativeness, until trust and familiarity are established. Creating a mutually safe environment is a priority during the initial contact.

Suzie, a worker in a drug and alcohol treatment service, describes some of the steps she takes to create such an environment for her clients:

> One of the things I noticed early on that helped me and the client(s) to relax on the first session was to be very aware of the environment and how it might feel for them on their first visit. I would make sure they knew where the toilet was should they need it and offer to make them a tea/coffee or get them some water. Ask if they found the office location okay. This initial exchange enabled a type of "settling" time before anything more formal had commenced. I also find it useful to establish the amount of time you both have to avoid interruptions and, more importantly, to be able to create a safe place where there is some type of wrapping up or setting up of the next session before the time runs out. It is also important to leave time for the client to ask questions so you can be sure they understand the guidelines you have jointly created. This all helps to provide that safe environment for you and your client.

The "settling in" process may vary according to where the conversation is taking place. In some instances, this will not be in an organization but in the client's home or community.

Respecting the practices and space of another's world is critical. Suzie highlights the importance of a "settling" time before any formal work has commenced, as well as the importance of being clear about the boundaries of the contact. These are important steps in engaging with another person.

Another decision point relates to the role of "small talk" in engaging with people—the term even implies that there is "big," important talk and trivial talk. The beauty of small talk is that it puts us all at ease—and sometimes this aspect of the process is the most important in engaging with someone in a working relationship. It connects again with how we regard our role and what kind of relationship we want to establish with people.

Introductions are part of this process. We typically need to hear a new person's name a minimum of three times to connect it into our memory. The name is an important dimension of a person to remember. If we are not named properly, we can feel misunderstood or isolated. Getting to the end of an interview with someone and realizing that you cannot remember her or his name can be embarrassing. It is better to spend time at the start of any contact ensuring that names are remembered by both client and worker, and that other introductory issues are attended to, such as the worker's role and reason for contact.

Whoever is present should be engaged directly in the conversation, as individuals. In many family meetings in hospitals, for example, the person who is the patient can be referred to as "he" or "she," as if somehow not present in the room and not part of any decision-making process. To speak this way immediately disempowers and silences people.

Ways of opening an interview are considered in more depth in Chapter 7.

Some ways of getting started are suggested below:

BOX 6.1 Focus on Practice

Getting Started

Some ways of opening an interview include the following:

Worker: What's been happening, Tim? Are you still living at your dad's place?
Worker: Last week you planned to reconnect with your grandmother. How did that go? Or, is there something else you would like to talk about, Susan?
Worker: You did well to get through the holiday traffic, Jamal. How can I help you?
Worker: Are you comfortable, Andy? What would you like to discuss today?
Worker: You mentioned in your phone message that the storm kept you away Tuesday. What brings you here today, Joanna?
Worker: Now that you've changed your address, tell me about what's been going on, Dawn.

As discussed above, it is important to refer to a person by name, when appropriate, to model recognition of the person, as a person, not as a label or gender (he, she).

1. What do you see as the risks and benefits of each of these different questions or invitations?
2. How would you open a conversation with a person you have just met?
3. What do you feel you would avoid saying? Why?
4. Can you reflect on a time when you felt uncomfortable starting a conversation with someone? Why was it uncomfortable? Did things improve? How?

Engagement

"Engagement" refers to the process of entering into and establishing a positive working relationship or alliance with people. As explained in Chapter 1, the client–worker engagement or alliance is fundamental to good work being accomplished together. While engagement is acknowledged as fundamental to engagement in a therapeutic context, Davis (2006) claims practitioners must, to some extent, accept where the client "is at" for engagement to be successful.

Engagement varies in its intensity and also in how it can be negotiated between the worker and the client in tandem with external factors. Engagement begins with the practitioner's first contact with the client and evolves throughout the working relationship. Egan and Schroeder (2009) describe some of the key components of engagement, starting with the premise that clients can change if they choose and followed by: don't see clients as victims; don't be fooled by appearances; share the helping process with clients; help clients see counselling sessions as working sessions; use each helping interaction to promote client engagement in problem solving; and become a consultant to clients. Additionally, skills such as probing, **active listening**, and appropriate paraphrasing all assist a successful client engagement.

The concept of engagement should be considered from a community perspective, also. "Community" can be defined in many different ways. Al-Krenawi and Graham (2003) cite an early study that

> found ninety-four separate uses of the word. Yet, most definitions include four components: people, location in a geographic space, social interaction, and common ties . . . . Hence, the term "community" may be used to identify a First Nation of Plains Cree living in Saskatchewan, a group of Vietnamese refugees who settled in Halifax 20 years ago, or a group of Bosnian refugees dispersed across southern Ontario. (p. 50)

In a study conducted by Brownlee and Graham (2005) the authors quote a participant who explains, "comminutes cocoon themselves and become self-protective and wary of outside influences" (p. 7). In this context, a practitioner must view the process of engagement from a community perspective. It would be helpful for the practitioner to consider the following elements: the size of the community, geographic location, service limitations, community structure, current internal roles of community members, and what the appropriate method for engagement specific to the community would include.

Coggins (2016) reminds workers that we must also consider diversity as part of practice and that "practice can no longer consider diversity an 'add on' component of professional education in the preparation of practitioners" (p. 2). Bitter (2009) remarks that "before we can know the richness and diversity of other families, we must come to know our own heritage" (p. 40). Below, Jane talks about some of these dimensions in the parent bereavement support group discussed in Chapter 4.

BOX 6.2 Focus on Practice

Initial Engagement

Unexpected processes also happen when we hold our evening support group for parents who are bereaved. As it is an open group and no reply about attending is asked for, it is difficult to know how many people are coming. The room in which the group is held is located deep within a non-clinical area of the hospital, and lost visitors or parents or staff looking for other groups or meetings does happen from time to time.

From the outset it is critical to establish in a welcoming, respectful way that those coming are for the appropriate group. Signs along the way and on the door of the room are no guarantee of this, as we have found. Returning to the hospital and/or coming to the group for the first time may confront or overwhelm parents with powerful memories, images, or emotions. If couples are coming, one may have agreed to come for the sake of the other and bring their own reluctance. Some may find it hard to speak.

Jane then describes some of the ways in which she goes about the actual introduction and engagement processes with group members.

BOX 6.3 Focus on Practice

Meeting a Bereavement Group

Our greeting and the process of engaging takes place outside the door. "Hello, are you here for/looking for the parents' group? I'm Jane. Welcome."

We extend our hand for a handshake—there may be some instances when this is not appropriate, perhaps with some members of certain faith and cultural communities, and again a quick decision may need to be made, and assumptions about culturally and linguistically diverse citizens may be incorrect. Despite the context, a small smile may add to the sense of welcome, but sensitivity is needed.

Parents mostly volunteer their names, and the name of their child who has died. If, however, they are too distressed, it may be impossible for them in that moment to speak and we need to acknowledge this—a gentle nod and some brief words may help: "It can be very hard coming to the group for the first time." "Many parents who have come to the group have found it difficult, too." We may add, "See how you do tonight."

Depending on how the parent responds, it may be sensitive to ask the name of their child (if not already given) and how long it's been since the child died. There have been times when a parent is coming for the first time, several years after the child's death. At such times we would ask, "What brought you tonight?" or "Is there something about tonight's topic?" A fine line has to be trodden between introductions and moving too far into their story. Sometimes it may be appropriate to say, "Perhaps we'll be hearing more about [their child's name] or just more through the night." We then encourage the parents to write out a name tags and their names and their child's in the book (placed just inside the room) and offer refreshments and gesture to the seats.

The assumptions we make about who a person is, based on momentary contact and "first impressions," profoundly influences the initial engagement. Studies have demonstrated that information about another person's gender, sex, ethnicity, and age is processed within seconds of encounter. From a survival perspective, this makes sense. This instant survey enables us to make quick decisions as to whether this new person is "safe," based on our "typing" of them according to previous encounters with others like them. The drawback of this process is that typing can become stereotyping, and prohibits us from seeing individuals as individuals, outside of "labels" (Thompson, 2003, 2006).

Engaging or bonding with another person can happen very quickly under some conditions. Working intensively as a small group over a weekend, for example, can build a very strong sense of cohesion, particularly if contact with others outside of that group is discouraged and intense time is spent together talking about emotional issues. Some groups rely on this process to form rapid and seemingly strong bonds. The phenomenon of speed dating is based on this process of quick assessment and engagement with another person. Within a matter of minutes, people have decided whether they wish to continue to engage with a person.

These decisions, nevertheless, are complex processes, and different theoretical perspectives understand this complexity in very different ways.

BOX 6.4 Focus on Practice

Finding Commonalities

In a small group, form pairs and talk for one minute with that person before moving around to talk for one minute with other group members. Find as many points of commonality as possible.

1. How did you gather the information from the other person? For example, did you ask questions or did you talk with each other in a non-questioning way?
2. When did you realize that there were points of commonality—or not?
3. What did you notice about your style and other group members' styles of gathering information?
4. Did you incorporate any of the engagement techniques (listening, non-verbal, verbal) discussed in previous chapters?
5. What did you find most effective?

Gibney (2003) proposes that four levels of engagement occur in a therapeutic context. Level one refers to the negotiation around whether therapy "is required, wanted or needed or is even appropriate at this time, in this place, between these people in attendance" (pp. 81–2). Level two refers to a form of problem-solving or solution-focused therapy: "They perceive something is wrong that they want fixed, and they have no particular wish for understanding or insight" (p. 83). Level three refers to engagement when the therapeutic relationship is seen as the "nexus of change" by both the therapist and client. Level four refers to a deep engagement in the relationship that is regarded as transformative, and the therapist is "an implicated witness" (p. 86). While specific to psychotherapy, this typology reveals that, even in the most highly mandated of client–worker relationships, it may be possible to achieve level three or four engagement, returning to the arguments of Chapter 1 that the client–worker relationship can be positively influential in and of itself.

Nicole, a social worker at a children's hospital, wrote about her experience of engagement with Mrs B.

BOX 6.5 Focus on Practice

Initial Engagement with Mrs B.

Mrs B. is the mother of an eight-year-old son diagnosed with a treatable but life-threatening condition. I received the family's file at the point of her son's diagnosis and Mrs B. spent two formal sessions with me discussing the impact of the diagnosis on her, her son, and their family. Mrs B. did not attend a subsequent appointment, but was informed by me that she could have ongoing sessions with me and that I would also make contact with her during her son's subsequent outpatient appointments.

In the introduction, notice the process of establishing a relationship. Nicole was given the file to the family as their worker. This often occurs through weekly team meetings or daily intake reviews of clients. It raises important questions about the goodness of fit or the compatibility between the worker and the client. A poor fit can limit engagement, strain relationships, and influence both the worker's practice and the client's opinion about the value of the service provision. Nicole describes what happened next.

BOX 6.6 Focus on Practice

Working with Difficulties in Engagement

After two months of no contact from Mrs B., and little contact in outpatients due to my feeling that Mrs B. did not want to further engage with me, I heard via a colleague that Mrs B. was not happy because I had not spent enough time with her. I organized a session with Mrs B. to discuss her support needs. I began by inquiring about Mrs B. and her family's current situation. I then stated that I would like to discuss openly the concerns that Mrs B. discussed with her colleague. I said that the purpose of the discussion was to ensure that Mrs B. and her family received the support that was needed. I had discussed this strategy with my supervisor and attempted to ensure that I was not defensive of my actions during my sessions with Mrs B.

Mrs B. stated she felt that other parents saw their social workers on a more regular basis and that she would like another social worker who could spend more time with her. I said that it was very important that Mrs B. have access to the level of support that she felt was necessary. I commented that Mrs B. had given me the impression that she was not comfortable receiving support from social work and that she seemed reluctant to engage in anything more than discussion about practical issues. Mrs B. disclosed that she did find it difficult to trust people and that she felt that some of the material discussed with me in the first two sessions was "more than I've discussed with most people."

In this interaction, Nicole and Mrs B. have been able to discuss the situation openly. Nicole framed the discussion in terms of supporting Mrs B. She was open to critical feedback from Mrs B. about why the engagement process had gone the way it had. This enabled Mrs B. to talk about the difficulties both between them and in relation to the ongoing issues with which Mrs B. was grappling. In this example, despite the difficulties in initially engaging, good engagement and rapport between Nicole and Mrs B. seem to be beginning, as demonstrated below.

BOX 6.7 Focus on Practice

Moving on with the Work Together

Mrs B. stated that she knew that she had given me the impression that she didn't want to speak to me but was angry that I did not persevere. Mrs B. and I spent a session discussing the difficulty Mrs B. was experiencing with a number of intense and sometimes conflicting emotions and how difficult it was for Mrs B. to access help. Mrs B. disclosed that she was concerned that she may have said something to me

Continued

that may have changed the way that I perceived her. Mrs B. decided that she wanted to continue seeing me for assistance and that it was helpful that I was able to "take the criticism without getting angry at me."

1. At what level of engagement would you see Mrs B. and Nicole engaging?
2. What would you have done in Nicole's situation?
3. What key points stand out for you in this example?
4. What practice skills are important in this example? (e.g., reviewing plan, roles, and expectations)
5. How do you receive disagreement or dissatisfaction from clients? Do you take feedback personally or do you see this as an opportunity to reflect on practice?

> Each theoretical perspective would understand these interactions differently. These understandings of Mrs B.'s situation will be revisited in Chapters 11 through 14.

These engagement difficulties illustrate that clarifying the initial reason and ongoing basis for contact is critical. In some settings, clients can be overwhelmed by the sudden arrival of a worker, for example. They may not know why a referral has occurred, what is known about them, and what the role of the worker is all about. In other situations, as in Mrs B.'s case, her own assumptions, needs, and expectations strongly influenced what occurred. These are all important introductory clarifications that may need revisiting throughout the length of work together.

The discussion of engagement so far has focused on working with clients who choose to engage in the process. Some clients, however, will not want to talk with you at all, and the process of engagement becomes more challenging. Trotter (2006) identifies some of these questions:

> How do you help someone who has no interest in being helped? . . . How do you counsel someone who does not even recognize they have a problem? How do you work with someone who has a totally different set of values from yourself? (p. 1)

> This section explores the initial contracting of the relationship. In Chapter 9, we will look at the processes involved in contracting around specific goals once an initial assessment has been done.

In these situations, role clarification and contracting are even more important factors in the establishment of a working relationship. Role clarification refers to the process of establishing clear understandings of purpose. That is, to answer as clearly as possible why it is you are meeting together. In some instances, this will involve explicitly addressing the lack of interest or free will in the contact; for example, you might say, "I doubt you want to be here, talking about what's happened. What if we agree on talking for 10 minutes about some things the court is going to need to know to make their decision?" It also involves talking very explicitly about the purpose of the contact and what the outcome or next step may be:

Worker: Hi, Brandi, my name is Joseph. I'm a social worker with the Ministry for Children and Family Development. I'm here because concerns were raised about your daughter being home alone and we need to understand what's going on. Given that a notification's been made, we will need to assess whether there are ongoing concerns about your daughter's safety.

Other issues that may need to be addressed in the initial contracting phase include the following:

- the length of time in this contact and ongoing contact
- the purpose of the conversation
- the purpose of the conversation from the client's perspective
- any concerns or questions the client has at the onset
- what will happen with the information discussed—that is, what are the limits of confidentiality?

This initial conversation is about establishing the when, where, why, and how of the work. A respectful and empowering strategy is to have an explicit discussion about the anticipated contact (Trotter, 2006). However, to make an assumption that our mandate as a worker—our theoretical orientation or the limitations of confidentiality, for example—are immediately understood by a client can be very wrong. These parameters may need to be outlined in detail so that the client is empowered to make decisions within that conversation.

One central tenet of the process of engagement is to begin where the client wants to begin. Starting "where the client is at" is illustrated in Karen's work with Myrtle and the setting of the priorities for their work together. An initial priority may seem to be the grief issues, but another priority emerges.

BOX 6.8 Focus on Practice

Engagement Is about Starting Where the Client Is

A single, 80-year-old woman, Myrtle was referred for a social work assessment following the death of her sister. The two women had lived together for their whole lives, and cared for their mother, who had died when the sisters were in their sixties. Myrtle was, not surprisingly, distressed at the death of her sister, but her worry on the first day of our meeting was what to do with the sister's body, as the two had both decided that their bodies should be donated for use by medical science. Ensuring that this occurred brought her significant relief.

Subsequently, over some years of contact, we explored her loss and revisited much of her life story. Myrtle wrote little notes to herself to remind herself of what she wished to discuss with me on my regular visits. On one such occasion the note revealed the question, "When I go (she had no fear of dying, now that her sister was gone) who is going to turn off the fridge?" I viewed this question as having multiple meanings, and in answering her practical question was able to begin also to deal with the larger question of what will happen to what remained of herself and her sister.

Starting with "where the client is at" sounds like a relatively straightforward positioning. Some challenges, however, include

- cultural differences—How does the worker know where the client really is at? Is the outset of relationship sometimes more a matter of where we *think or assume* the client is at?

- communication barriers—How do we ensure that the client's perspective is heard and understood when communication barriers are present, such as language differences or hearing impairments or audio-processing deficits?
- disagreements with where our client is at—How do we ensure this positioning of where they are at actually respects his or her humanity, when it may be so fundamentally opposed to our own world view, as in the case of a perpetrator of violence or sexual assault?
- What are the first steps to engage the client in the direction of a plan that includes the above points, is ethical, and facilitates the best interests of the client?

This is where some of the skills we will look at in Chapters 7 and 8 come into play as ways of exploring these dimensions and ensuring, as much as possible, that the client's views and preferences remain central.

People's unique communicative styles should be attended to, either directly or indirectly, in this time of relationship formation. Koprowska (2005) identifies experiences of deafness, visual impairment, learning difficulties, and dementia as influencing communication. The engagement process is about finding ways to work with these dimensions and establish a working relationship.

The degree of cultural awareness is an important consideration in initial contact. As Jane mentions in her experience with the bereavement group, sensitivity in relation to culturally safe practices is important. Decisions about initial interactions may consider whether to engage in a formal handshake, or who to address in the group. These issues can always be enquired about in the initial encounters. For example, "I would like to talk with you, but I'm wondering if we should have someone else here with us from your community?"

Cultural identities also influence engagement experiences—for example, when a female worker is engaging with a male client and the client's cultural background does not permit contact with women. Other differences will be more fundamental, but perhaps more subtle, in relation to different world views and beliefs. The Canadian Association of Social Work (CASW) *Guidelines for Ethical Practice* contain a section titled "Demonstrate Cultural Awareness and Sensitivity," which states that social workers must, "strive to understand culture and its function in human behaviour and society, recognizing the strengths that exist in all cultures." Further, the practice guidelines affirm that "social workers acknowledge the diversity within and among individuals, communities, and cultures" (2005, p. 4). The practice guidelines review the need for the social worker to take account of his or her personal beliefs and heritage and how they influence practice with clients. Perhaps most important is a commitment to obtain the training required to maintain competence pertaining to diversity issues in practice.

Confidentiality

Maintaining the confidentiality or privacy of a person's information is an important professional requirement, essential to creating a "safe" space for the client to talk about concerns. Agencies will have different practices, however, in relation to expectations of reporting and accountability around client information. Agencies involved in writing court reports, for example, have different recording and reporting arrangements compared with therapeutic and voluntary agency settings. Being aware of your agency's requirements and talking with your clients about mutual understandings of confidentiality from the outset are two practices of paramount importance.

Melissa provides an excerpt from a presentation based on her doctoral thesis, which examined people who had been engaged in suicidal behaviours and the impact of an intensive support program on their behaviour (Petrakis, 2004). She describes how the worker's decision might be influenced by the legal and agency context, as much as by the immediate client–worker situation.

BOX 6.9 Focus on Practice

Acting on Client Disclosures of Risk

Confidentiality is a cornerstone of professional social work practice. Note in the CASW Code of *Ethics* that "Social workers demonstrate respect for the trust and confidence placed in them by clients, communities and other professionals by protecting the privacy of client information and respecting the client's right to control when or whether this information will be shared with third parties" (CASW, 2005). With a client at risk, a therapist needs to use careful professional judgement about the balance between potential harm to the client by either disclosing information or maintaining confidentiality. A disclosure in the absence of a strong belief that the client presents an immediate risk to him/herself and/or others potentially creates a situation in which the therapist could be sued by the client for breach of confidence (Bond, 2000); however, failure to disclose when there is a strong belief that the client presents an immediate risk to him/herself and subsequently takes his/her own life may lead a therapist to having to defend him or herself in court against the accusation of failure in duty of care (Daines, Gask, & Usherwood, 1997; Jenkins, 2002).

Increasingly, therapists and clinicians are concerned with the risk of litigation (Reeves & Seber, 2004). The risk of clients harming themselves can debilitate the therapist from acting creatively and collaboratively, making their actions defensive and focused "solely on risk assessment rather than therapeutic change" (Sharry, Darmody, & Madden, 2002). Understandably, then, in an under-resourced system, focus shifts to at least keeping these clients safe. The focus shifts to risk assessment.

Using Self-Disclosure

Establishing a good relationship relies to a large extent on the client's willingness and capacity to engage in it. It is taken for granted that clients in most situations will disclose extensively about their life circumstances. The degree to which a worker should self-disclose, however, is more controversial. To self-disclose is to explicitly talk to the client about your own experiences. **Self-disclosure** occurs when the practitioner shares a personal experience that might be of value in helping the client feel they are being heard and understood (Coggins, 2016). For example, "I also lost a family member to a heart attack." We are always revealing things about ourselves through both our verbal and non-verbal interactions, but our use of self mediates these decisions and provides a boundary around some information. Bitter (2009) defines self-disclosure as simply "sharing part of oneself or life with a client" and notes that it is "highly valued in feminist family therapy" (p. 428). In addition, it involves "a judgment on the part of the therapist: that sharing some aspect of the therapist's life will directly benefit the client" (p. 428). Self-disclosure, then, refers to your explicit use of your own circumstances, either past or present, in ways that overstep the usual boundaries, as the following example illustrates:

Client: I'm just not coping anymore. I don't go out; I can't go out. I sit at home and cry and eat. That's all I do. I can't see how this will ever change.

Worker: When my dad died, I found it really hard to go out, too. It felt much safer at home. But I found if I forced myself to go out, I'd sometimes have an OK time. Gradually, it just got easier.

Client: So I'm not going crazy? This will change?

In this example, the worker is emphasizing the skills he found helpful in overcoming a similar situation. Such disclosure *may* help the client feel less alone and overwhelmed, as the response in this example implies. It may provide some modelling as to how someone else coped with a difficult and distressing time. On the other hand, the client may feel resentful that the worker is saying the pain will lessen, when that is not how he feels right now, and that the worker has been able to adapt to something the client feels he will never be able to adapt to. The use of self-disclosure is controversial because it highlights some of the major differences in expectations of the boundaries and purposes of helping relationships. It draws a much more complex set of assumptions about similarities and differences between interviewer and client into the interaction.

Some workers are adamant that self-disclosure should always be avoided, whereas others are just as adamant that it is one of the most powerful, equalizing skills of practice. This diversity of points of view raises questions as to why the field is so divided and whether an absolute position is possible to maintain over time and in all situations.

Consider the situation Suzie found herself in, in her work with clients with drug issues.

BOX 6.10 Focus on Practice

Disclosing Personal Details to the Client

It is inevitable in any counselling session that the client will ask a personal question, such as "So, do you have any kids—do you really know what it is like for me?" or "You don't look old enough to have teenagers" or "So, do you use drugs or what?"

I found that the first time this happened I had not given enough thought to what my response would be and it is the type of issue that requires thought, reflection, and ongoing discussion within a supervision session. For me, the question I had to ask myself was, how useful to the client would disclosing my personal experiences be, given that every person has such a unique set of circumstances that are individual to them? Sometimes by divulging and exploring your own experiences the focus of the session becomes diverted, and it is this diversion that is worth exploring with your client in more detail.

Suzie's examples of the questions she has been asked in practice about her own private life highlight the dilemma: To answer or not? Directly or indirectly? One way of understanding these kinds of questions is to ask whether they are questions about you, whether as a worker you will understand them or view them in a particular way. Will you understand what it is like to feel so overwhelmed as a parent, for example? How might the way you answer these questions impact your practice approach?

BOX 6.11 Practice Questions

How would you respond to the following questions?

- Do you have children?
- How old are they?
- You look too young to have a teenager.
- Do you have a boyfriend/girlfriend?
- Do you earn a lot of money doing this job?
- What time do you finish work today?
- Where are you off to for your holidays?
- Have you ever had an abortion?
- How old are you?
- Where do you live?
- Do you believe in a divine presence like God or Allah?

1. Would you respond to each and all of the questions? Why?
2. In what ways are the above questions relevant to your working relationship—or are they?
3. Who could ask these questions and get an answer from you? Why?
4. Do you feel prepared as a practitioner to address this type of a situation? If so, how? If not, what do you feel you need to practice?

The usual argument for the use of disclosure is that, in a professional context, self-disclosure helps to build trust and authenticity in a relationship. That is, the worker joins with the client through self-disclosure as another human being, facing similar challenges or successes. This sharing reduces inequalities in the relationship by reducing the sense that the worker is somehow outside of life's problems and challenges. The norms of reciprocity that operate in many relationships are considered to be enhanced by mutual disclosure and intimacy levels. The argument against the use of self-disclosure is that it detracts from the focus on the client's story. The purpose of the relationship is to hear and support the client's story, not to hear and support the worker's. Some argue that self-disclosure not only shifts

What are some reasons that a client might ask their human service worker to self-disclose? How can self-disclosure help establish a good working relationship with a client? How might it impede a good relationship?

the focus onto the worker, but also burdens the client with the worker's issues and with personal values that perhaps should not enter the agency arena. Another argument is that self-disclosure can place the worker at risk in certain situations. Clients may find out where you live or if you have children, and use this information to threaten you or to intrude into this private space. Once this information is known, it can neither be retracted nor controlled, and can lead to serious breaches of privacy and safety. Managing self-disclosure is about managing privacy and vulnerability—dimensions that differ from individual to individual, as well as cross-culturally. As with other relationships, over time, the capacity to tolerate or trust different levels of vulnerability or reciprocity within the context of a client–worker relationship can increase.

Melissa, a social worker in the mental health field and teacher of communication skills, recounts a discussion of self-disclosure in one of her classes, which shows how she resolves these issues in practice. These conversations are presented with the permission of the students. Melissa was working with a group of students who were about one month into their first field placements. She presents her experience below.

BOX 6.12 Focus on Practice

Issues in Self-Disclosure

We watched a video showing a counsellor opening an interview. The counsellor stated her name, asked the client in an open-ended manner what the client hoped to gain from the interview, and then explained the types of questions that would be asked in counselling and the rationale. The counsellor had described the process of counselling, but had not disclosed anything about herself, her qualifications, or her life. I reflected on this with the students. Exchanges with two students were particularly instructional regarding the issue of self-disclosure:

Student Situation 1—Wanting to Disclose

Student: I know I shouldn't self-disclose, but . . .

Melissa: It feels as though self-disclosure would help with rapport?

Student: Yes.

Melissa: What was the context?

Student: I am working in a mental health setting. We go out on home visits to families with a member with a mental illness. My brother has bipolar.

Melissa: It feels as though it could help to share this information.

Student: But I know I shouldn't.

Melissa: It sounds as though you know there is a rule but your gut is telling you something else.

Student: I guess so.

Melissa: I'm a big believer in following our gut in counselling, but when we start out, our gut isn't trained yet to how counselling is different from everyday conversations. In everyday conversations, we assume two equal parties who can contribute confidently and assertively. Counselling is not like that. One party is feeling very vulnerable and is being asked to reveal something he or she has tried to resolve, and often with the help of family and friends and even other professionals, yet the person is still very troubled. Such people will feel embarrassed about sharing and unsure what we will think of them if they tell us everything they are thinking. If we talk about ourselves, the client will gladly let us, relieved to be off the hook, at least for a while, and out of the spotlight. This is not good because we have missed this early opportunity to show our curiosity and concern and to indicate that we can focus exclusively on the client in this space because we consider her or him and their experiences important.

Student: Yeah, I don't want to make it about me.

Melissa: There's just one other thing, too. It might be that, if the family's experience is similar to yours, they do feel a quicker rapport established by your self-disclosure. However, it will become evident quickly that yours and their experiences are not exactly the same. The gender of the family member with bipolar may be different; that age of diagnosis probably was different; the level of chronicity also will be different; your family and theirs may differ in financial resources or social supports available. . . . Suddenly, as these differences come out in conversation, the family can feel betrayed that they thought you understood, when you don't understand at all.

Continued

Student Situation 2—Not Having the Experience to Disclose and Share

Student: My situation is different. My lack of experience makes me feel less skilled to help my clients.

Melissa: Tell me how self-disclosure would help with feeling less skilled.

Student: I am working in a women's health service where all the clients are pregnant. My supervisor has two children.

Melissa: So it feels like your supervisor has legitimacy or expertise because she has been pregnant before, like these clients, while you have not?

Student: Yes. I feel like I don't have that knowledge to offer.

Melissa: You feel that the knowledge isn't something book-learned or learned through your work in the service, that you need to have gone through it yourself?

Student: Yes.

Melissa: This situation is not so different from the first one we looked at.

Student: How do you mean?

Melissa: Your colleague is feeling that in her setting, rules prevent her from disclosing when it would be helpful. You are feeling that in your setting rules would support disclosure and it would be helpful, but you have no material to disclose.

Student: Yes.

Melissa: The dilemma is the same, though. Our self-disclosure shifts the focus away from the client and is personal and specific, therefore, limited. Even your effective supervisor, who uses her self-disclosure incidentally as part of her genuine use of self, will get into trouble sometimes because the client will note the differences in their experiences: that the gender of their babies is different; that their experiences of labour were different; that one did have and the other did not have postpartum depression; the involvement or lack of involvement by their partner/spouse and extended family was different; they were affected differently by cultural beliefs surrounding diet, child-rearing practices, the question of circumcision, and by difference in beliefs around religion and faith and rituals, such as baptism and naming rites. We need to be very careful not to fast-track rapport at the expense of real empathy.

The following questions may assist you in deciding whether or not to self-disclose:

- Is change in the client possible without self-disclosure?
- Is the disclosure client-centred and client-focused or does it shift the focus to you and your circumstances?
- Is it a necessary condition of practice? Or is it always contextual?
- How does your use of disclosure change as you practice and what determines those boundaries?
- What do you want to disclose and, more importantly, why?
- Is it possible or desirable to generalize from your experience or to distance yourself by offering a useful story without creating the burden for the client of its being your story? For example, "Some women have found . . ." or "Some people have found . . ."
- What are your beliefs about the comparative values of book-knowledge, work experience, and lived experiences? How do your beliefs impact your choices around self-disclosure?

Chapter Summary

In this chapter, we have explored some of the skills in establishing a client–worker relationship. This has included the skills of creating a safe and supportive environment in which to meet, the skills of an initial contact, and the skills of active listening. In looking at engagement, the use of minimal encouragers, empathy, and self-disclosure, it is apparent there is no one right way to be using these skills. Rather, they need to be thought about in context.

Questions for Analysis

1. What have you learned about
   - empathy?
   - engagement? In both urban and remote practice settings?
   - minimal encouragers?
   - self-disclosure?
2. Which skills of engagement do you find relatively easy to apply and which not?
   - Provide specific examples.
   - How will you practice in areas you identify as difficult?
3. What do you notice about people's reactions to emotion in
   - your family?
   - your work place?
   - your community?

Recommended Readings

Bishop, A. (2015). *Becoming an ally: Breaking the cycle of oppression*. Halifax, NS: Fernwood Publishing.

Bitter, J.R. (2009). *Theory and practice of family therapy and counseling*. Belmont, CA: Brooks/Cole.

Bougher, E. (2015). Pathways through grief to hospice volunteering. *Qualitative Sociology*, 30(3), 305–26.

Corey, G. (2015). *Theory and practice of group counseling*. Boston, MA: Cengage Publishing.

Dodge, R., Daly, A., Huyton, J., & Sanders, L. (2012). The challenge of defining wellbeing. *International Journal of Wellbeing*, 2(3), 222–35.

Duros, P., & Crowley, D. (2014). The body comes to therapy too. *Clinical Social Work Journal*, 42(3), 237–46.

Egan, G., & Reese, R. (2018). *The skilled helper: A problem-managementandopportunity-development approach to helping* (11th ed.). Toronto, ON: Brooks/Cole, Cengage Learning.

Gibney, P. (2003). *The pragmatics of therapeutic practice*. Melbourne: PsychOz.

Goleman, D. (2005). *Emotional intelligence*. New York, NY: Bantam Books.

Goleman, D. (2006). *Social intelligence: The new science of human relationships*. London: Hutchinson.

Hole , R., Evans, M., Berg, L., Bottorff, J., Dingwall, C., Alexis, C., . . . Smith, M. (2015). Visibility and voice: Aboriginal people experience culturally safe and unsafe health care. *Qualitative Health Research*, 25(12), 1–13.

Neumann, C.B., & Neumann, I.B. (2015). Uses of the self: Two ways of thinking about scholarly situatedness and method. *Millennium Journal of International Studies*, 43(3), 798–819.

Pugh, R., & Cheers, B. (2010). *Rural social work: An international perspective*. Bristol: Policy Press.

Scales, T., & Streeter, C. (Eds.). (2004). *Rural social work: Building and sustaining community assets*. Toronto ON: Nelson.

Scannell, L., & Gifford, R. (2017). The experienced phsychological benefits of place attachment. *Journal of Environmental Pshycology, 53*, 256–69. http://dx.doi.org/10.1016/j.jenvp.2017.04.001

Schmidt, G. (2017). *Social work practice in remote communities*. New York, NY: Linus Learning.

Internet Resources

Canadian Association of Social Workers, *Guidelines for Ethical Practice*
www.casw-acts.ca

Canadian Counselling and Psychotherapy Association (CCPA)
www.ccpa-accp.ca

Daniel Goleman's website (social and emotional intelligence)
www.danielgoleman.info

Social Care Institute for Excellence
www.scie.org.uk

PART THREE

Basic Skills: Focusing the Communication

In the previous chapters, we have explored the ways in which workers might approach practice and begin to think about the professional process and relationship into which we are entering. In this next part of the book, important verbal skills are identified in order to establish the client's particular situation and to identify a working agenda using specific forms of questioning. Typically, this phase of work involves, first, using probes such as useful and relevant questions (Chapter 7) and, then, seeking further clarification and understanding of the situation through inviting, reflecting, paraphrasing, and summarizing (Chapter 8). This process adds another dimension to the interview and assessment process of working with clients.

PART ONE Framing the Relationship

- the purpose of human service work
- your value base, professional ethics, and regulatory guidelines in Canada
- your theoretical and factual knowledge.

PART TWO Forming the Relationship

- your use of self
- your organizational context
- your ongoing support and professional development needs
- meeting the people involved
- opening the communication

- active listening and working with silence
- listening empathically
- using self-disclosure.

PART THREE Focusing the Communication

- establishing the story
- forming an assessment
- goal setting.

7 Establishing the Story

Learning Goals

- Understand the purpose of minimal encouragers.
- Describe and use a range of probing skills.
- Differentiate the types of questions and their purposes.
- Understand the skills involved in asking questions and making requests.
- Begin to understand and identify specific interview skills and there purpose.

The Task of Establishing the Client's Story

As Chapter 1 outlined, your focus will be on building a multi-dimensional understanding of the client and the client's story. This means understanding the client's story in relation to both inner and outer worlds. Specific verbal skills are used to support and encourage the client's telling of her or his own story. We look at minimal encouragers and probing skills in this chapter.

As discussed in Part One, establishing a professional worker–client relationship is the foundation of ethical practice. Prior to facilitating the following aspects of interviewing to gain further details of the clients story, this is a good time for the worker to pause and reflect on the aspects of the worker–client relationship currently being developed. For example, has an environment of trust, safety, and free from judgement, been created? Are appropriate professional boundaries clear to the client? How have you demonstrated care and empathy to encourage self-determination? The skills discussed in this chapter build on the worker–client relationship by creating structure and purpose to the interview process.

As discussed in Chapter 6, engagement is critical to establishing a good working relationship. Prior to applying skills aimed at establishing the client's story, the client must be engaged in the problem-solving process.

Using Minimal Encouragers

In Chapter 2, we looked at the verbal and non-verbal skills that enhance or inhibit a conversation. In order to keep talking in a conversation, we need some feedback from the other person that it is all right to continue speaking. The verbal and non-verbal cues we give to another person are often **minimal encouragers**. That is, they are minimal in the sense of not being major statements or questions or reactions, but they encourage the person to continue talking. Minimal encouragers can be verbal or non-verbal. Verbal minimal encouragers include

Yes!
Uh-hunh . . .
Mmm . . .
Right . . .
Sure.

Non-verbal minimal encouragers include all the facial and postural reactions we display—nodding, smiling, or the raising of eyebrows; leaning back, leaning forward, making a gesture—that inform the speaker you are listening attentively and that she should continue. Minimal encouragers are regarded as a way of keeping the conversation going. They are part of the conversation, too, however, and their impact can be significant, both in intended and unintended ways. The following example highlights the unintended impact, when a minimal encourager was interpreted by the client as an end to the conversation rather than as an affirmation to continue.

BOX 7.1 Focus on Practice

A Need for Minimal Encouragers

At a professional development seminar, a woman from a severely war-torn part of the world spoke of the impact for her of minimal encouragers when she encountered professionals. When she advised them of her nationality, she was often greeted with a response of "oh." She said she did not want that as a response to her communication because she did not know what it meant. She was left wondering what the person was thinking and meaning by "oh." Did it mean they assumed she'd been raped, that she'd been directly affected by the war, or that it was too hard to speak about? She wanted to know more of what the other person meant by "oh" rather than feeling as though she was on the end of someone else's assumption about her.

In this example, the meaning to the client of the minimal encourager was not clear, impeding the effectiveness of communication. Similarly, if the minimal encourager "right" or "sure" is used, a very specific meaning as well as a general meaning can be conveyed. People can be affirmed unintentionally in what they are saying, whereas the use of the minimal encourager is intended only to affirm the continuation of the conversation, not the meaning of it. Minimal encouragers should be well-timed, appropriate, and sensitive to the situation. Considering the above scenario: What are some other ways a minimal encourager might be misinterpreted? Think about a time this has happened in your own communication with someone. If a similar misinterpretation were to occur with a client, how might it impact the worker–client relationship?

BOX 7.2 Focus on Practice

A Need for Sensitivity

An Indigenous woman required a medical assessment that involved extensive arrangements to travel from her community to the urban centre where the assessment could be completed. Riya was very nervous, as she had not travelled outside her community often and was worried about talking with a new doctor, who was a stranger to her. In my role as community wellness worker, I reviewed the process with Riya and suggested that she share her concerns with the doctor when they met. Upon Riya's arrival she told the doctor she was scared about what was going to happen and the doctor responded with, "I'm sure you're scared . . ." What Riya heard was "You should be scared." Riya completed the assessment and returned to share her story; and I wondered how accurate the assessment could be, given how it began.

The above example highlights how misunderstandings can occur unintentionally. The doctor's statement was meant to support Riya, by acknowledging that he understood that it must be frightening for her having travelled so far and not to know him. Unfortunately, Riya interpreted his words differently, raising questions around the accuracy of her assessment outcomes.

Cross-cultural communication is an important skill for social work practitioners. It encourages workers to deepen their knowledge and respect for the many values and cultural norms of people from diverse groups. How would you ensure appropriate communication, considering the above example?

Kohli, Huber, and Faul (2010) expand on the term "cross-cultural communication" and express the importance of culturally competency, noting:

> Cultural competence engages the development of abilities and skills to respect differences and effectively interact with individuals from different backgrounds. This involves awareness of one's biases or prejudices and is rooted in respect, validation, and openness toward differences among people. Cultural competence begins with an awareness of one's own cultural beliefs and practices, and the recognition that others believe in different truths/realities than one's own. It also implies that there is more than one way of doing the same thing in a right manner. (p. 257)

Using Probes

Another set of skills is termed **probes**, because they are an active way of encouraging the client to relate the many dimensions of a problem situation. The verb "to probe" means to "examine or look into closely, especially in order to discover something; investigate; interrogate closely" (Brown, 1993, p. 2362). This definition brings to the forefront both the strengths and the risks of these skills—the strengths being about discovery and investigation; the risks being that a client can feel violated in the interrogation. Essentially, probing skills assist workers at the interview stage of working with a client, as a method of clarifying communication and gaining further required details. These important details ensure the worker understands the client's view of their situation.

Egan and Schroeder (2009) state that practitioners should "use probes to help clients engage as fully as possible in the therapeutic dialogue" (p. 161). They describe the key components of probing as the use of prompts, statements, requests, questions, and single word phrases (p. 150). Probes are one of the major groups of verbal skills that enable us to follow the client's story and get to the details. As Hepworth et al. (2017) state, focusing an interview is a complex skill, requiring three distinctive tasks. The first is selecting the topics for exploration; the second involves exploring the topics in depth; and the third involves maintaining a focus and keeping on topic. The use of probes is one way of moving through each of these phases. These skills enable us to stay with the client's story and where they want to head with it. At the same time, we use these skills to diverge from the seemingly dominant story to expand the focus of the interview. Therefore, probes are as critical for following the details of what the client is telling us as for exploring the unspoken dimensions of the experience; for asking about the history of an issue, or to explore the range of impacts of a situation in terms of feelings, actions, thoughts, and contexts.

Probes can be applied in a few different ways. For example, phrases such as

1. "Can you tell me a bit more about . . . ?"
2. "When you say hurt, can you help me understand what that means for you?"
3. "Say what you mean by . . ."
4. "When you say . . . what are you doing?"
5. "How do you do that?"
6. "If I were there with you, what would I see?"
7. "Why does that matter?"
8. "Why does that stand out in your memory?"

Well-formed probes gently guide and inform the client of the need for further clarity. Minimal encouragers can also be applied here through nonverbal nods and short encouragers, indicating to the client to continue with their story.

What Questions Will I Ask?

The skillful use of questions is a potent device for initiating, sustaining, and directing conversation (Dickson & Hargie, 2006, p. 121).

In Part Two, we looked at the importance of understanding the agency context and the worker's role. Your context and role will strongly influence where, when, how, and why you work with your client, and will inform the ways you go about asking particular questions. How we ask and what we ask is inextricably linked with the purpose of the contact. In Chapter 8, we will explore the skills of paraphrasing and summarizing as ways of minimizing such an outcome.

See Chapter 3 for discussions of paradigms and factual knowledge that form coherent practice. Reflect on how coherence influences your approach to interviewing.

Questions can be very intimidating—they can ask people to think about things that they have never thought of before or to recall traumatic issues and events. They can stigmatize and blame, inadvertently. If people are questioned continuously, they may feel interrogated rather than heard—that it is more important that the facts be established than it is for the individual to be heard. Depending on the focus of the agency, questioning can sometimes be purposefully designed. Discussed further in Chapter 9, standardized assessment tools are designed to gather information that help determine if a client has a particular diagnosis or requires further assessment. Some examples of standardized assessments might include a mini mental status exam, suicide risk assessment, or an ADHD assessment. Understanding how to facilitate assessment style questioning is important to best practice outcomes.

This following discussion brings together some of the current thinking about the nature of questions in general. Questions can be effective in opening up an interview and gathering the necessary information, or they can alienate, marginalize, or disempower people even further. Knowing how to ask effective, empowering questions is an essential skill.

Asking Open-Ended or Closed Questions

Questions can be open-ended or closed in their structure, influencing the kind of response that is elicited. An **open-ended question** invites the client to provide further elaboration of the details of the story. Questions beginning with the words "how," "what," "why," "when," "who," and "where" are open-ended because they invite some kind of descriptive, expansive response, not mere confirmation of information that has been provided by the person asking the question. When applied correctly, open-ended questions can assist clients in sharing the context and meaning of their situation as they understand it. Consider the following examples:

Worker: When did you first notice you were feeling this way?
Worker: How many children do you have?
Worker: What do you think is the most important issue to work on right now?
Worker: Where were you when you felt your hands starting to shake?
Worker: Who was there?

Closed questions, by contrast, seek confirmation or negation of information—with a simple "yes," "no," "maybe," or other singular word response such as "never." When applied correctly, closed questions can also assist with transitions in the interview process and closure. Closed questions do not call for further elaboration on detail:

Worker: Have you spoken with anyone about this?
Worker: Can you get another job?
Worker: Do you think it will happen again?
Worker: Are you feeling sad?
Worker: Is Tammy your sister?

Some authors suggest that any question eliciting a short answer is also a closed question—that a closed question is one where the topic is defined and the client's response is restricted to a few words or to a "yes" or "no" response (Hepworth, Rooney, Dewberry-Rooney, Strom-Gottfried, & Larsen, 2017). A question as to how far someone had travelled could similarly be seen as a closed question, although this is moving to a different interpretation of confirmation or negation of information, which is typically considered to be the defining feature of a closed question.

Some questions, while structured as closed questions in a grammatical sense, can function as open-ended purely through your vocal intonation: "Can you tell me about that?" can be understood as an encouraging **invitation** to talk more about a problem situation rather than as expecting a "yes" or "no" response.

Closed questions can lead to more detailed, descriptive responses, but they rely on the client taking up the intent of the question and initiating further response. To illustrate how a closed question can lead to further elaboration, notice the responses here:

Worker: Have you spoken with anyone about this?
Client: No.
Worker: Do you think you should speak with someone, perhaps at work?
Client: No.
Worker: Isn't there anyone else?
Client: Maybe . . .

In this instance, the conversation was not getting very far. Closed questions can present a number of risks—the risk of getting the question "wrong" or becoming too directive, and the risk of having to negate the other person's position, as well as the risk of lapsing into an interrogation, or of limiting the options.

The first risk, where the onus is on the interviewer to get the question "right," means that the interviewer can become too directive of the agenda—if the asking of closed question after closed question is not working to open up the discussion. In using closed questions, try to find the right lead. It can become a hunt for the right question—looking for a point of engagement. At these times, it may be more useful to reflect on what is not being heard in the situation or to pause to summarize what has been stated to that point in the conversation. It may be that the story has been difficult to establish because the client is not forthcoming—and why this is so should be reviewed. The client may not wish to talk to you or to trust you, he may not perceive you as competent, she may not be confident about her view of events, or they may not have the words to express what they think and feel.

Persistent questioning in the face of little response can result in the client becoming reluctant or resistant to the process. In some cases, reluctance and resistance are developed by the client as a personal safeguard measure based on fear, previous experiences, or the belief he or she has been wrongly accused. Egan and Schroeder (2009) explain that "defense mechanisms are unconscious processes that serve to maintain our self-esteem and keep our sense of self intact. They may be adaptive or maladaptive. Adaptive defenses lower anxiety. Maladaptive defenses prevent development of insight. Reluctance and resistance may stem from the unconscious use of defenses to protect the self" (p. 231).

Resistance can be particularly difficult when working with mandated clients. Consider the following example.

A young male client is forced to attend sessions with an alcohol and drug worker due to having breached his probation and sustaining a second charge of possession of drugs. The counsellor is faced with the client's resistance to attending his appointments.

Worker: Can you tell me what brings you here today?
Client: My probation officer says I have to come.
Worker: What would you like to discuss?
Client: Nothing . . . I don't want to be here, but I don't have a choice.

In this example, the client clearly states not having a choice in attending. It is important that the practitioner have the skills required to work with resistance. The practitioner needs to work from where the client is at, which in the above example is the fact of forced attendance. Here are some examples:

Worker: You said your probation worker is making you attend?
Client: Yes.
Worker: Can you tell me a bit about why you think he is making you come?
Client: I guess because this is my second time.
Worker: Second time with what?

As the conversation continues it increases the opportunity for engagement and leads to a decrease in resistance and reluctance. Additional engagement skills or statements may include the following:

Worker: I am not sure I would like someone making me attend, and I can't force you to stay. [*pause*] How about if we meet for two sessions and decide from there how to proceed?
Client: Okay.
Worker: Where should we start?

Is there a time when you felt resistant to a directive or order? How did you react? What was your first thought? It is important that practitioners recognize that some level of resistance and/or reluctance from clients is normal. Further, it is the practitioner's role to assist the client in working through these feelings and to find an incentive to follow through with the process. What are your skills in working with resistant or reluctant clients?

If the question is poorly chosen, the client is put in the situation of having to negate the person who has asked the question. For example:

Worker: Are you waiting to see me?
Client: Uh, no; I'm waiting to see Doug.

However, asking an open-ended question—"Who are you waiting to see?"—would have led to the person asking to speak to a particular person. This may seem like a trivial example, but when a closed question is asked with more serious implications, the issue of having to negate another person becomes significant. In disempowering situations, the client is less likely to have the confidence to negate someone else's statement.

Worker: So, your partner didn't give you the support money?
Client: [Who knows he did but she spent it on drugs.] Yes.

Closed questions can be coercive and manipulative, either intentionally or unintentionally. A closed question such as "Are you going to leave?" presents only one possible line of action to the client. There may be many other options to consider, so an open-ended question such as "What do you want to happen?" may not exclude these options because it implies choice.

Closed questions, however, have a very important role in assessment and intervention processes. They enable the clarification of the intensity of mood states or intentions of the client, for example, or details of a past history that may be critical to an understanding of the current circumstances. The use of open-ended questions tends to be encouraged in practice over closed questions as the more exploratory and less presuming style of the two forms of questioning.

BOX 7.3 Focus on Practice

Interrogation and Human Service Work

Watch any of the television programs showing courtroom scenes or police investigations and observe the way questions are framed to force particular answers. In these situations, the answer is anticipated—a "leading question" has been asked. One of the major differences between police interrogation and human service interview skills is that we want to ask questions that will not assume the answers but instead encourage the client to discuss their circumstances as openly and fully as possible.

Why is it important not to presume to know the answers? What are the key differences between these two interview approaches? Write down several of the questions you observe in the television show. Then, rewrite the leading questions into human service interview questions.

Asking open-ended questions, however, can also present challenges. Some workers, for example, propose that "why" questions should be avoided, on the basis that asking people for explanations of situations is too difficult and that these questions can be experienced as "accusatory and blaming" (Trevithick, 2005, p. 163). Others argue that "why" questions should be avoided because they tend to encourage the client to look for a preconceived response, which may even include "excuses or rationalizations" (Geldard & Geldard, 2005, p. 74). The other reason that "why" questions may be difficult to answer is that when we are caught up in personal difficulties it can be very difficult to answer issues of causation or reason—that is, to understand why we are facing difficulties in the first place. Other schools of thought see open-ended questions and issues of explanatory power as a fundamental part of a person's story, which we will explore later in Chapters 11 through 14. For example, psychodynamic theory looks at the connections and interpretations we make as to what is happening in the present. Similarly, narrative approaches emphasize the importance of what meaning we are making of particular situations.

Safer and more adaptable questions to ask are questions beginning with "what," because they are "consistent with a systemic perspective that stresses that no one person is responsible for a problem or a difficulty that exists" (Trevithick, 2005, p. 163). Here are some examples of these kinds of "what" questions:

Worker: What do you think led to the argument?
Worker: What was happening before the argument began?
Worker: What is your reaction to that situation?

These open-ended questions using "what" are particularly useful in the narrative approaches, which emphasize externalizing the problem.

Asking the Opening Question

An open-ended question is often used to start off a conversation—and it is the one question with which you can be relatively prepared. It is useful to think of the opening questions that appeal to you and why. Beginning with the very vague and open-ended question:

What are some questions that may be helpful in opening an interview with a child? What kinds of questions that are appropriate for an adult client may be less helpful with a child? What additional strategies might you need to question a child about their experiences?

Worker: How are you?
Client: Not good at all. I've had some tests recently and it looks like I have cancer.

The question has worked as a vague, open-ended question to engage the client around the issue to discuss. At other times, though, the question can be seen to be a social question we ask as a greeting rather than an authentic question about the client's well-being. As an open-ended question, it is too vague and too socially anticipated. So the reply can be:

Client: Fine. How are you?

And the conversation has not gone very far in relation to the specific issue. A further open-ended question is required to get to the specific issues. Some other opening questions could be:

Worker: What's been happening?
Worker: Can you help me to understand what brought you in today?

These questions imply that something has occurred to trigger the contact with you as a human service worker, but they do not imply that the person needs or wants help in the way that other opening questions do:

Worker: What can I help you with?
Worker: What would you like to focus on today?

The questions about what has been happening or going on also do not imply that the person is the one with the "problem."

The opening question you ask will not only influence the initial information the client shares but can impact the level of client engagement. The goal of an opening question is to invite the client to share some of the broader details associated with their story and what they would like support with. What would be your response to the above opening questions? Which question feels the most comfortable for you to work with and why?

Some scenarios were presented in earlier chapters for general discussion. Now that we have discussed open-ended and closed questions, opening questions, and probing for further details, consider the ways in which each of these conversations would require very different opening statements or questions, and probing skills. The goal here is to develop your skills in how open-ended and closed questioning, opening statements and probes work together in the interview process.

BOX 7.4 Practice Questions

1. How would you open discussions under the following circumstances?
   a. A child protection worker is going to meet with a parent, against whom allegations of child abuse have been made. The worker, on arrival at the family home, notices that the parent has blood-shot eyes, drooping eyelids, speaks slowly, and moves slowly with a stooped gait. The parent stares angrily indicating she is not happy at all about the notification to Child Protection Services.
   b. A worker in a seniors' centre is assisting a client 80 years of age who has recently lost his spouse. The man expresses that losing his spouse of 60 years has created feelings he is not sure what to do with. With tears rolling down his cheeks he continues by saying that he can't wait to be with his spouse again.
   c. A duty worker on a telephone crisis line receives a call from a young, distressed woman who has been assaulted by her partner. The caller doesn't know what to do—whether to leave her apartment or to stay.
   d. A worker has been involved with a separated family for many years, since the time when their child was diagnosed with cancer right through to her death six months ago. The worker wants to invite the siblings to a sibling support group, which will involve contact with the parents now divorced and the siblings who live apart (the oldest son lives with dad and the daughter lives with mom). There is little contact between the parents and siblings due to the parent's separation.

Individually, answer questions 2 to 4.

2. What are the key points to consider in the four scenarios?
3. What would be the first question you would ask in each scenario and why?
4. Following the opening question, what questions would you want to ask to assess the situation? Why?

Then in small groups of 3 or 4, complete questions 5 to 10.

5. Share your the questions that you wrote above with your group. How different are your questions from the ones your colleagues wrote?
6. Did the different questions result in different answers? If yes, how?
7. Was your interpretation of the situation similar to or different from the interpretation of the others? In what ways?

Reflecting on process:

8. What did you learn from this exercise about your interview skills?
9. What was revealed about potential conflicting interpretations or ideas?
10. Are there aspects of your interview style that you will change or be more aware of? Why?

Asking Succinct Questions

A succinct question is a brief and concise one. Lengthy, imprecise questions can confuse both the worker and client. The worker can lose track of what the "trigger" was for asking the question and the client can be left wondering what is being asked. For example, how would you answer this question if you were the client?

Worker: Why do you think, I mean, what caused him to be so angry, or if not angry so frustrated when you spoke last with him, um, or was it, um, when he called you?

Notice that in the question above, the worker has not hesitated in order to gather thoughts about what the question should be. The extraneous language used, such as "I mean" and "um," also breaks up the flow of the communication. Lengthy questions also can become multiple questions, where a client is asked:

Worker: Do you talk with anyone about this? I mean, have you spoken with your family? Or your friends? What do they think?

In this "question," there are now three different questions all wrapped up in the one delivery. It is as if the worker has found a flow and is rolling out all those thoughts in one go. The dilemma for the client becomes which of these questions to answer first. As a general rule, one question at a time should be asked.

Worker: Have you spoken with anyone else about this?
Client: Yes, my sister.

Worker: What does your sister think about what is happening?
Client: She is worried about me and . . .

Short, specific questions provide clearer focus to the interview, even if you have to pause to work out exactly how that question should be framed. A momentary pausing and gathering of thoughts is often better than rushing headlong into a series of questions.

Asking Relevant Questions

Your agency context and purpose will determine what questions are relevant to ask. Even in a specific setting, however, each one of us will ask different questions. What we think is relevant is, therefore, a question of our subjective and objective positioning.

BOX 7.5 Focus on Practice

Group Task

In a role-play, one "client" is interviewed by a number of "interviewers" (other students in the class) for about 10 minutes. The other students each take a turn at asking a question. After 10 minutes has passed discuss as a group how differently each interviewer was thinking about the situation. For example, were there any assumptions made, areas that lacked clarity leading to miscommunication, or was there confusion on where to focus? Ask the client which interview questions felt best to them, and which did not. It is a good opportunity to reflect on why you wanted to know about certain aspects of the client's story, what you saw as relevant in this interview, and if it matched the client's thoughts.

Take note of the following:

1. What questions were asked that resulted in gaining insight into the client's story?
2. What did you learn about your approach to interviewing? (Were you focused in a particular way? Why?)
3. What areas in your interviewing skills do you want to improve?
4. Where are your strengths?

In our time-limited client contact, we need to be quite selective about what we ask and why we ask it. Armstrong (2006) states,

> When we know another person . . . there are often large blank spaces in their history. . . . We may have only a sketchy—and probably one-sided—grasp of what occurred over substantial stretches of that person's life. And yet our encounter with them is not puzzling or missing something. (pp. 19–20)

Armstrong is highlighting a fundamental process of engagement with another human being—that engagement is not necessarily a matter of knowing the client's whole story, but about the narrative that is established together. Working with a client to establish her story is about building up an understanding of what has occurred in relation to specific events or experiences. It may be a sketchy picture, but the work together is about building as relevant a picture as possible, even though it is not complete.

The narrative picture that is created should be understood to be a result of co-authoring by the client and the worker. Payne (2006) explains that note-taking is a collaborative process in which the counsellor takes notes and scripts them for the client's review or invites the client to script the session. Corey (2008) suggests one technique for consolidating the gains a client makes is by writing letters. Narrative therapists have pioneered the development of therapeutic letter writing. These letters that the therapist writes provide a record of the session and may include an externalizing description of the problem and its influence on the client, as well as an account of the client's strengths and abilities that are identified in a session. Letters can be read again at different times, and the story that they are part of can be re-inspired.

To facilitate narrative counselling effectively and ethically, the counsellor must ensure that the client is part of the note-taking process so that it is the client's narrative being documented and not the counsellor's viewpoint of the client's narrative. It is a collaborative effort, and this means the client having access to session notes or participating in the documentation of session notes as part of the therapeutic process.

Reflecting on your practice is an important skill. See Chapter 5 for discussion of the importance of reflexivity and self-awareness, or "bending back on one's self."

Given that we gather selected information, the question of relevance is paramount. Important self-reflective questions to keep in mind throughout all your practice include the following:

- Why am I asking this question? (What is the purpose?)
- Who am I to this person and therefore is it valid that I ask these questions?
- For whom is the information important and/or relevant? (Is the question client-centred?)
- Am I listening to the client's story?
- Which elements of the story need to be clearly established, and which ones do not?
- What other sources of information are available—for example, through case file notes—rather than repeatedly asking the person the same questions?
- How would I feel about answering that question?

A major dimension of relevance is cultural relevance. What cultural dimensions of this person's experience may impact whether this question is relevant or not? For example, in many cultures, providing information about mental and physical health experiences is taboo. As Youssef and Deane (2006) draw to our attention, "Social reputation (soma) is a valuable asset in Arab culture and great efforts are made to avoid any shame that may threaten or compromise the family reputation" (p. 5). An awareness of all such issues is fundamental to sensitive and focused communication. Discussing these issues first may be more important than trying to move into a conversation that will be experienced as culturally insensitive. Working through cultural dimensions of a person's experience may also help the worker to identify areas where they need to learn the context from the client to assist with good communication outcomes.

Relevance can be considered not only in relation to the nature or breadth of issues that are discussed but also in relation to the depth of questioning that occurs. One comment made frequently by students in debriefing after role-play is, "I wanted to ask that question but I thought it might upset them." Clearly, this is an important consideration in all of our conversations—the intention is never to cause harm and distress. This highlights the importance of checking the client's comfort level with such questions and the direction of the conversation, as well as us checking your own comfort levels and knowledge bases. What this hesitation may mean, however, is that if a worker avoids some questions for fear of upsetting a client, a client may not have the opportunity to tell the story. We live daily with the issues and preoccupations of our own lives, so telling a sad, tragic, or otherwise painful story is not necessarily distressing to the client, who may welcome the opportunity to talk. It may seem overwhelming to the worker, but it may not be a new or "out of control" experience for the client. Similarly, if the question does upset a client, inviting her or him to explore a part of the story perhaps not verbalized previously may not *necessarily* be a bad outcome, but rather a step in the process of establishing the story and those experiences.

Relevance can also be a point of engagement. For example, inquiring about a client's cultural background creates the opportunity for the client to share personal and expert knowledge and at the same time assists the practitioner with understanding the client's background. When used correctly, this opportunity can engage the client in the process.

In considering the depth of questions and their relevance, it is also important to consider some of the assumptions we carry as workers about the ease of answering questions. Working in the human services, we can become very familiar with a language of emotions and of the inner world, and of valuing self-disclosure and self-reflection. These ways of being are not ways in which all people are comfortable, and yet we can expect answers to the questions we ask. The question of relevance remains crucial in determining whether or not we need to ask these types of questions.

Asking Specific Questions

As the worker in the situation, you have the responsibility for keeping a sense of direction and purpose—for avoiding a sense of "drift" (Trevithick, 2005, p. 170). Drift emerges when the direction and purpose of the conversation disappear and either the client and/or the worker is left wondering what the conversation is about.

The aim is to elicit specific information in relation to a client's story, not generalities. We need to know the detail of a client's experiences, which can then lead on to specific interventions. If we do not know how unhappy someone is, for example, we are not going to know enough about that person's current mental health to adequately undertake a **risk assessment** of him/her. If we do not know how difficult the person's financial circumstances are, we may not make the referrals or seek the assistance the situation requires.

In exploring stressful situations with clients it can be useful to think about the dimensions of events that make them stressful. Martin (1997) highlights the duration, timing, predictability, and controllability of events as the important dimensions to explore. For example, a client self-reports spending a great deal of time alone in his room, but until an assessment of duration, timing, predictability, and controllability of this behaviour is undertaken, it is very difficult to discern what kind of situation this is from the client's point of view or from the point of view of normal or understandable behaviour. It may be the extremely problematic behaviour of self-isolation accompanying drug abuse or bipolarity or schizophrenia, or it may be entirely functional behaviour in the client's context as it gives him time and space to work out issues or to avoid conflict in other areas of the family home.

The following scenario shows how important it is for you to think about all of what is implied when you are listening to a story. Taking the response at face value, as all the information you require, could be a serious mistake. With the person who is spending a lot of time in his room, further questions are required, such as

When did this start?
Is this new behaviour?
Has something recently changed?
How often does he go to his room?
How long does he stay in his room?
What is happening prior to his going to his room?
Why do you think it is a problem?
What concerns you about it?
What does he say or think about it?

Only after asking some of these more assessment-style interview questions can we begin to establish genuine understanding of how significant this behaviour is and whether or not it is a problem.

Asking specific questions can also mean raising taboo or difficult issues. Sometimes just asking a question gives a client permission to discuss a previously taboo issue or even, in some instances, the elements of language to discuss it. In a conference presentation, Dora Black (Black & Trickey, 2005) from the Tavistock Clinic in London spoke about her work with children recovering from experiences in family situations where one parent has murdered the other parent. Black's own therapeutic training had been within the psychoanalytic model, where specific questions were not asked. Interpretations of free associations or thoughts of the client were made, but questions rarely asked. In working with these children, and particularly in discussing the art work they created about what they had witnessed, she has discovered that because of their developmental stage at the time of the murders, these children did not actually have the language to name the experiences they needed to talk about. Asking specific questions as well as commenting on the drawings was one way of bridging this gap in the client's story.

For many people, some specific questions can be highly culturally and personally inappropriate. As individuals, we have different levels of tolerance for questions affecting privacy. Similarly, as families and communities we have spoken and unspoken rules in relation to information that is public and that is private. For some families, saving face and not airing private problems is a primary value, whereas for other families, the boundaries of family extend to the community, and nothing is private. In asking questions, we can be intruding across the boundaries of another person's private world. When questions are experienced as intrusive, it is important that opportunities to decline questions are provided. How will you ensure you understand the spoken and unspoken rules mentioned above? In rural and remote settings aspects of isolation, small populations, and community structure play an important role in how information is shared. The practitioner will need to be aware of the existing boundaries, social structure, and process for community decision making.

In addition, James and Gilliland (2017) outline multicultural perspectives revealing that a large majority of the world's population lives by a non-Western viewpoint. The authors continue by noting it is the practitioners' responsibility to evaluate their processes and emotional attitudes from a multicultural perspective to work towards addressing issues of institutionalized racism, ethnocentrism, ageism, sexism, and other forms of cultural and personal bias that clients may encounter in their workers. Kiselica (1998) outlines four qualities that mental health workers should consider when working with clients from a multicultural perspective: self-knowledge, awareness of one's own cultural bias; and understanding of different cultural groups; skill in culturally appropriate intervention; practice experience with counselling and working with culturally diverse clients (p. 6).

Building an understanding of the specifics of a person's situation is critical. What we do with the responses to questions, therefore, requires careful consideration so that we continue to develop detailed understandings of what the client has said. Sometimes we might ask only one question and regard that as having explored the issue. Consider this example:

Worker:	How does that leave you feeling?
Client:	Oh, I'm just so disappointed.
Worker:	What do you think you'll do now? Look for more work?

In this scenario, the worker has asked about the emotional state and has been told one specific dimension of this experience, but on hearing an answer, has not explored it any further. The worker has moved on to the next issue, having spent only a moment focusing on the emotional response the client has expressed. One person's disappointment is very different from another's—one person might be very depressed and make that statement but another might be quite recovered and be expressing a manageable feeling. Moving on after a singular response does not necessarily provide the depth of understanding that might be required.

So, revisiting that situation, a follow-up question begins to provide some further elaboration on the disappointment:

Worker:	How does that leave you feeling?
Client:	Oh, I'm just so disappointed.
Worker:	Tell me more about feeling disappointed?
Client:	Well, I thought the money stress was going to go away with these extra hours of work, but I'm still behind. It just isn't fair. Every time I try to get on top of things, they just keep on collapsing around me. I'm just useless!

Chapter 9 explores assessment further and presents more of these assessment frameworks.

Now the worker has a sense that the client is possibly feeling both angry about the situation and disappointed with herself. A lot more exploration of this situation is required to really understand what is going on.

In many settings where you work, specific psychosocial or risk assessments will be used by your organization to focus the information that is considered crucial.

Asking Neutral Questions

Questions can be very loaded; that is, questions can carry very strong assumptions within their wording or expectations about the answer. Particularly in the early stages of a working relationship, minimizing these assumptions is important, and asking questions that are more neutral in their language is a way of building the relationship and finding out the necessary information.

As discussed in earlier chapters, language can marginalize and stigmatize people. Questions need to be framed as inclusively as possible so that a client's story can be explored with as few barriers as possible. Assumptions about relationship status and sexuality, about financial capacities, about abilities and capacities, about beliefs and culture, about normative world views and a range of other dimensions of our lives can be made through the questions we ask or are asked. Rather than illustrate a whole range of possibilities, the reflection task below encourages you to think about the underlying assumptions that may be present in those questions.

BOX 7.6 Practice Questions

1. What underlying assumptions could be present in the following questions?
   - Have you talked to your friends about that?
   - What does your wife think?
   - Why didn't you write to them to lodge your complaint?
   - Are you going away for Christmas?
   - Can't your children help you?
   - Why didn't you move out?
   - Why don't you get home support services involved?
   - Can you tell me about why you've been so upset lately?
2. Once you have listed the underlying assumptions, share your list with another student and discuss how each of you developed your thoughts.
3. How would you reframe each of these questions so that some of the assumptions in each question are minimized?
4. How would you reframe the closed questions above as open-ended questions?

Some questions are very "leading" in their intent, such as, "Don't you think it really would be important to tell them what's going on?" In this type of leading question, the answer that the worker wants to hear is present in the question. Leading questions such as these have either the intention or the outcome of trying to "coerce the other person into agreement" (Koprowska, 2005, p. 84). For all these reasons, framing questions as neutrally but as specifically as possible is important.

Another way to address these issues is to clarify with the client whether the process of asking these questions is appropriate.

Worker: Is it OK to be asking these questions?
Client: Actually, I feel really uncomfortable.

Or alternatively, asking an open-ended question:

Worker: How do you feel about me asking these questions?
Client: It's fine. I just find it difficult to talk about these things.

Either of the answers could have been given to those questions—again, it is a matter of judgement as to whether you frame the question in terms of your role with the client or more as a question of how the client is feeling in the situation. Depending on the reasons for the human service contact, this situation could be re-contracted so that a mutual understanding of why such questions are being asked, and whether they are essential or not, can be reached.

Preparing for Difficult Conversations

Workers new to practice may find it challenging to facilitate a difficult conversation. For example, a conversation that involves informing a client of a death, loss, critical or terminal injury, or an incident involving extreme violence are demanding. Therefore, it is important for the worker to fully explore and prepare for difficult conversations, to maintain client-centred practice. While there is really no way to know how you may personally respond to any given situation, reflecting on the impending conversation prior to engagement can help you to prepare, or recognize if you should step back and seek supervision.

It is important to gather all the information required to address questions that may come up during the conversation, before meeting with the client. For example, if the conversation involves a client that is being informed that a loved one has died, the surviving family members may have specific questions about how, when, or what exactly caused the death, therefore, you should make sure you have all of the available facts prior to speaking with the clients. Having detailed facts is also important to assist clients who may respond highly emotionally or defensively. Accurate facts are important to aid clients with processing the event/situation. As a method of preparation, you may want to seek supervision prior to meeting with the client, to talk through the purpose and intended outcomes of the conversation, and to discuss what potential issues or challenges might arise.

Once you have gathered the required facts and have worked through the intended purpose of the conversation, it is important to consider the possible emotional responses the client may have. For example, the client's high level of stress (at work or financial) may intensify or shut down their verbal and non-verbal reactions and responses to the conversation.

The final point to consider is your potential reactions once you begin. Take some time to reflect on how your non-verbal cues and demeanour can help or hinder the conversation and make sure you feel prepared to maintain a calm and present position throughout the duration of the conversation. Then, once the conversation has occurred, make sure to conclude with clear next steps so the client has a sense of direction.

Asking "Difficult" Questions

In addition to managing difficult conversations, in some areas of practice, very difficult questions need to be asked. They are difficult questions because they relate to extreme human situations and, often, ethical dilemmas. Many of these questions emerge in medical and legal contexts, such as the question as to whether or not a patient is consenting to resuscitation, whether a family is consenting to an organ donation of a deceased family member, or whether a child is a victim of abuse within a family. In these situations, seeking supervision or case consultation can provide important feedback prior to engaging in an interview process with the client. The following are some general principles (see, e.g., Evans, Tulsky, Back, & Arnold, 2006):

- taking time to prepare in your own mind what the purpose of the conversation is about
- finding the optimal time to talk with the key people
- speaking clearly and slowly about the issues, even considering the possibility of using a warning or preface to what you are about to say

- being aware that on breaking bad news, very little is heard and remembered subsequently, so repeating and revisiting issues is essential
- checking in with people as to what they have heard, so that you can affirm that the message has been accurately conveyed.

In addition, the practitioner should feel prepared to state things clearly and not use words that are less clear but easier for the practitioner to say. For example, phrases like "she is no longer with us" and "he has gone to another place" are ambiguous, and can be confusing and create additional crisis if the statement is initially misunderstood. See the following example.

A mental health intake worker was recently assigned a file of a young woman presenting with high anxiety and depression. During the first meeting, the practitioner discovered the woman had been assaulted, leading to intense fear, which resulted in the client not being able to go to work, sleep, leave her room, or talk with family for over a month. During the discussion the practitioner wondered if the client was suicidal. When the practitioner approached the topic with the client, the client responded with, "I am so relieved you said the word. . . . I was afraid if I said the word 'suicide' my family would be angry at me for thinking that way, or think I was crazy, and I'm not crazy." This was the beginning of the client being able to address her situation openly from where she was at.

Asking Questions at an Appropriate Time

Sometimes a question may be an excellent question to ask, but the timing is wrong in the context of either the working relationship or the session itself. For example, we may not have established enough rapport with the client or we may be at a point in a conversation where it is inappropriate to ask such a question.

Carolyn identifies timing as a key issue in reflecting on her psychodynamically oriented practice, as outlined below, in the context of complexity, too.

BOX 7.7 Focus on Practice

Helping Clients Face Painful Truths about Themselves

One of the tasks of the psychodynamic therapist is to take in the verbal and non-verbal communications of their clients and to try to understand unconscious thoughts, imaginings, and feelings about themselves, their relationships, and their difficulties.

As some of our clients are struggling with experiences of lifelong losses, trauma, and rejection, or painful realities such as disability, terminal illness, or complicated mourning, our timing and way of making the "unthinkable" thinkable is crucial.

With the therapist's support, their capacity to explore and integrate this aspect of themselves (and the attitudes of others towards them, which is arguably more difficult) will strengthen them and free them up to engage more with life. However, this may be a highly painful and confronting experience.

Discussing her clinical work with adults presenting with an intellectual disability on a background of trauma, Sinason (1992), describes this well: "Some of their histories and life stories are extremely harrowing, and the process of recovering them has made me understand why their authors numbed their memories and minds for so long" (p. 319).

Within the counselling literature, in particular, a great deal of emphasis is placed on the experiences of reluctance and resistance (Shulman, 2009; Egan 2013). Reluctance, as in a hesitation, is seen to emerge when a client knows that "managing their lives better is going to exact a price" (Egan, 2009, p. 163) and is related to hesitating in the face of change. **Resistance** is often a strategy to avoid stressful events that a client may not feel prepared for or may want to change. Resistance can also refer "to the reaction of clients who in some way feel coerced" (Egan, 2009, p. 165). A strengths-based approach is to understand these processes more positively as processes of timing and readiness—to focus on why a person might be able to look at change at one point as distinct from another. The idea of change can be difficult for some clients as it often requires a shift in their current coping methods.

Resistance can also present itself when a client feels challenged by the practitioner. In some cases the client may believe their situation is fine and express frustration that the expectation is they should be doing something differently. In these situations any challenge from the practitioner becomes disregarded and stresses the worker–client relationship.

Responding to resistance requires careful reflection. Resistance can be a normal reaction to feeling vulnerable, fear of change even when it is a small change, or what may happen if the client shares their story (will I be judged?). Resistance can also be connected to uncertainty of what will, or is going to happen. A skilled practitioner will not react to resistance, focusing instead on what information is required for the client to engage actively in the problem-solving process.

Some important self-reflective questions to ask yourself in relation to reluctance and resistance, specifically regarding the timing of questions, include the following:

- What's going on here?
- Am I as the worker adequately addressing the issues with this client?
- Are there barriers to good communication within the relationship in relation to effective engagement?
- Am I asking appropriate questions?
- Are there other problematic dimensions of this communication process—that is, not so much the focus of the interview but the way I am talking about issues or the language I am using?
- What is it about the timing of these questions that may be contributing to this reaction?

Asking Questions that Lead to New Insights

We seek assistance primarily for new insights—to manage situations or emotions differently, to gain information or to understand situations more fully, or to learn new skills and behaviours. Talking with someone else or in a group is an opportunity to see things differently. Below, Karen describes her work with Max and a moment of new insight.

BOX 7.8 Focus on Practice

Challenging with Creativity

It is sometimes important to have clients see the other person's viewpoint in order to recognize their own.

Max presented at the community health centre at age 50, referred by his doctor for "support." With a recent acrimonious marriage breakdown and estrangement, avoiding his role as bank manager, and a serious health issue, Max was in need of much more than support. Max was suffering situational depression, sleeping problems, poor nutrition, and financial difficulties. Over a number of sessions, Max reassessed some of his previously insignificant relationships and was able to regain some feelings of happiness from a sporting interest, a daily walk, and a "cooking for one" class.

His relationship with his adult children remained strained by his former wife's bitterness, leaving him feeling embarrassed and belittled by the experience. This was compounded by a lack of status, and hence self-esteem, associated with the recent loss of his job. He felt unworthy of his son and daughter's offers of support and consistently refused them, although his ill health meant that he was unable to complete some tasks himself.

No amount of challenge regarding reciprocity in family relationships was effective in budging his view that "I am the father, I should be providing for my children and I don't deserve their help," until one day I asked him about his own role with his parents. He told me that for many years before they died he had maintained their house and garden.

Karen: So how was it that you did this for your mom and dad?

Max: They weren't well, I am their son, and I wanted to help them stay in their home.

Karen: What would it have been like for you if your parents had refused your help, because they felt they should have been able to cope?

Max [hesitates, then bursts into tears]: My pride has got in the way of letting my kids be my kids!

What kinds of questions might be useful to coordinate a group discussion? What kinds of self-reflective questions might be particularly useful to a human service worker coordinating a group activity?

While we will look at these issues in greater detail in Chapters 11 through 14, this section raises the importance of questions that open doors for clients. Questions that lead to new insights can be oriented around previous perceptions and experiences of coping so that a client begins to reflect on her/his strengths and capacities. People can become oriented around what they think the future could be for them and what would need to change in order to bring that about. It is an important emphasis to maintain throughout a communication process, as questions so frequently focus on risk, problems, and difficulties, rather than on exploring protective factors, successes, and strengths.

Suzie's example from her practice highlights the use of these sorts of questions.

BOX 7.9 Focus on Practice

The Change Process Requires Small, Manageable Steps

Chris:	Could I show you some of the poems I have written?
Suzie:	Yes, I would be happy to see them.
	[Chris shows his writing.]
Suzie:	They are creative. I can visualize the water you are describing in this poem.
Chris:	The gallery asked me if I would consider framing one for display, but I just can't. Every time I think about my work on the wall I feel like I am going to have a heart attack. . . . First I feel anxious and like I will have a panic attack. I just think I am terrified I will fail or what people will expect if I succeed.
Suzie:	What does success mean to you?
Chris:	That everyone will expect me to do better and better every time and I don't think I can do that . . .
Suzie:	Can you give me an example?
Chris:	Well, if someone likes my writing they may want me to do more and what if I can't or if they don't like my next piece?
Suzie:	Is it possible for you to just focus on this first poem with no commitment to provide any more—just that one piece of work?
Chris:	I don't know. I never thought about just one.
Suzie:	I am curious. . . . Could the request for one of your poems to be displayed be considered a success?
Chris:	Hmmm, yes, I guess that could be a success.

Suzie says of this interaction, "Concrete examples of problem solving can provide opportunities from which to draw parallels with other, more complex issues such as addressing substance use that a client is finding problematic." This process allows the client to identify success in smaller pieces and how to transfer success into other areas of his life. The client can then determine what success means in his life and how to build on each smaller success. This is particularly important in this example as the client identifies success as being "all or nothing," which creates feelings of being overwhelmed.

Advocates of a strengths perspective suggest asking the following types of questions (Saleebey, 2017):

1. Survival questions: for example, "Now that you have testified, can you tell me what you mean by feeling free?"
2. Support questions: for example, "Your friend seems to care a lot about you; can you tell me a bit about your relationship?"
3. Exception question: for example, "Can you tell me about a point in your life when you weren't stressed?"

BOX 7.10 Practice Questions

1. Conduct a 10-minute role-play with a "client," having an observer present. Debrief around the probing skills you have used throughout the interview.
2. Try to conduct the interview again using
   - only open-ended questions
   - only closed questions
   - no questions—only comments or statements
   - only problem-focused questions
   - only strengths- or problem-focused questions.

Following each round of practice styles, ask the person in the client role how the exercise felt from a client perspective.

- Did they feel heard, respected, and understood?
- What questions or style felt the most comfortable for you as the interviewer, and for the client?
- What did the observer notice about the interviewer's style and non-verbal skills?
- What did the observer notice in the client's reactions throughout the process?

This exercise helps you to identify your preferred questioning style—for some of us, asking questions is easy, whereas highlighting and reflecting back emotion is more challenging, and vice versa. This exercise highlights that we can use different questions to explore different dimensions of a situation. There is no one right way, but there are a lot of choices throughout an interview as to where we head with the conversation. It can be helpful to have a very active observer who will call a halt to an interview when certain skills are being demonstrated or are not present. This can be a useful way to increase confidence in the various aspects of interview skills and begin to identify your style and skill preference.

4. Possibility questions: for example, "You have established three different times that will work for you to take a walk. Which one do you want to try?"
5. Esteem questions: for example, "How did it feel to meet your goal?"

These questions will be looked at more closely in Chapter 13. The following exercise encourages you to think about how you use questions.

Additional Verbal Skills

Questions are clearly not the only verbal skills used in exploring a story. Questions or comments using single words or statements also keep the conversation flowing. Without being formally structured as questions, by using tone of voice and non-verbal encouragers, the following can be used to establish further the details of the client's situation:

Worker: You're angry?
Worker: It was due on Monday?
Worker: Confused?

Another type of probe is a request—an invitational or encouraging way of asking the client to explain more about the situation, in a genuinely interested way:

Worker: Tell me more about that.
Worker: Go on . . .
Worker: What do you mean by . . . ?
Worker: Say more about when she . . .

Carl Rogers, the founder of person-centred counselling, appears in a well-known video interview with a client called "Gloria" (Rogers, Ellis, & Perls, 1977). One of the striking features of this interview is that throughout the half-hour interview Rogers rarely asks a question. The rest of the interview is conducted using the skills of empathy, paraphrasing, and summarizing via which he clarifies Gloria's story and works with her towards a deeper understanding of her predicament. This interview highlights that questions are not always needed—that information can be shared through an engagement in a different form of dialogue. This is an important point. While many human service interactions are not going to be in the therapeutic context in which Rogers was working, many people tell their stories through means other than the more interrogative style of prompting. In the next chapter, we will explore the specifics of these skills of paraphrasing and summarizing, again looking at their strengths and limitations.

Do's and Don'ts in Questioning

Asking the right question shapes the therapeutic relationship with clients. Workers should always consider why they are asking the questions they are: Are your questions relevant, helpful to the client's situation, focused, and purposeful? Here are some examples of do's and don'ts in the questioning process.

TABLE 7.1 Do's and Don'ts of Questioning

Do's	Don'ts
1. Specific questions: What would you like to discuss? Who is your current support system? What thoughts do you have?	1. Ask multiple questions: Can you tell me, or what do you think might be the reason for your coming today, do you think?
2. Reflective questions: How did that make you feel?	2. Assign an emotion: That is awful. (This statement may not be an accurate reflection of how the client feels.)
3. Relevant questions: Can you tell me more about the accident?	3. Irrelevant questions: Aside from the accident, how is your day-to-day life going?
4. Strength-based questions: Tell me how it felt to walk for an hour yesterday.	4. Defensive questions: Did you do your walk yesterday?
5. Solution-focus questions: Given what you have shared, what would be your ideal solution?	5. Advice giving: So I think perhaps you should just try . . .

Chapter Summary

In this chapter, the key verbal probes for exploring a client's story have been described and analyzed. The ways in which asking open-ended (who, what, where, when, why, how) or closed (can, will, would, do), succinct, relevant, specific, neutral, well-timed questions that may lead to new insights have been explored, highlighting both the strengths and limitations of each of these styles of questioning. As much as possible, avoid leading questions, or questioning styles that are confusing and lack clarity. Purposeful or specific questioning in all areas is critical to help guide clients through the process of problem solving. When done correctly, purposeful questioning provides structure and often results in the client becoming aware of specific details of their situation they may not have considered previously.

Questions for Analysis

1. What are some of the risks involved in asking questions? Review your list of risks and reflect on areas you want to further develop your skill. What are some of the key considerations in asking effective questions? Review your list and reflect on the following exercise.
2. Read the following statements and create three questions for each statement that results in a more detailed or purposeful response:
   a. I feel overwhelmed.
   b. This just makes me feel sad.
3. Create a list of the various types of probes. From your list create another list of the probes you would likely use in practice. Then, construct a few reflective points explaining how your chosen probes align with your communication style, and what that tells you about your professional framework.

4. What are the differences between an open-ended and a closed question? Quiz yourself with the following questions:
   - Do you have a dog? (open or closed or potential interpretation for either)
   - Who were you with on Friday?
   - How did your walking go last week?
   - Can I call you?
   - What time is best for you to meet?
   - Did you find the office okay?
   - Can you tell me about your dad?
5. The "You" in practice: Now that you have practice open-ended and closed questions, what is your preferred style of questioning?
6. How do you think you will go about opening an interview or point of contact with someone? Over the next week, practice this process with people you interact with and note the various responses to your approach. After you have practiced opening a conversation a few times, think about what went well, what felt congruent to you, and what felt awkward.
7. What assumptions have been evident in some of your questions to date?
8. What are some of the key challenges for you in asking questions?
9. How will you challenge or improve your questioning skills?
10. How will you know you have met your skill development goals?

Group Activity

In small groups, read the following scenario and create a list of questions you would like to ask Robert to establish his story (open-ended and/or closed questions, succinct questions, difficult questions). Reflect on why you are asking the questions you create. (What is your purpose in asking each question, and who benefits?)

> Robert is a 77-year-old man living alone in an apartment building for older adults on Vancouver Island, British Columbia. You are an adult protection social worker responsible for responding to reports of abuse or risk. Together, Robert and his wife, Lindy (73), owned and operated a small, furniture company for 50 years, until they determined it was time to sell when Lindy became ill. Lindy was diagnosed with an aggressive form of cancer, and died a year later. Robert, now living alone, has few close friends because most of his time was spent managing the business and then caring for Lindy. Robert's children (one daughter and two sons) live in Ontario and are not able to visit often due to cost and their own family demands.
>
> You receive a call from Robert's daughter concerned that Robert might be unable to manage alone at home. You meet with Robert and he tells you that he was a daily rum drinker for 20 years, until he developed serious stomach problems and persistent high blood pressure. In addition to medication, Robert states he was only drinking on special occasions, until the loss of his wife Lindy. Robert admits that since Lindy's death he has been drinking daily to deal with feeling lonely, and to help with how much he misses Lindy. As a result, Robert is not sleeping or eating consistently and is having trouble remembering when he last ate or if he has taken his medication.

1. Reflecting on the forms of questioning described in this chapter, how would you start with Robert? What would be your opening question?
2. What questions would you ask to identify the potential problems, issues, and risks that could be part of this situation?
3. What information would you need to get from Robert and what questions might you ask to gain the needed information?

Recommended Readings

Al-Krenawi, A., Graham, J.R., & Habibov, H. (2016). *Diversity and social work in Canada*. Toronto, ON: Oxford University Press.

Bland, R., Renouf, N., & Tullgren, A. (2014). *Social work practice in mental health: An introduction*. Sydney: Allen-Unwin.

Davis, S. (2013). *Community mental health in Canada, revised and expanded edition: Theory, policy, and practice*. Vancouver, BC: University of British Columbia Press.

Egan, G. (2013). *The skilled helper: A problem-management and opportunity-development approach to helping* (10th ed.). Belmont, CA: Brooks/Cole Cengage Learning.

James, R.K., & Gilliland, B.E. (2017). *Crisis intervention strategies* (7th ed.). Pacific Grove, CA: Brooks/Cole Cengage Learning.

Hepworth, D.R., Rooney, R.H., Dewberry-Rooney, G., Strom-Gottfried, K., & Larsen, J.A. (2017). *Direct social work practice: Theory and skills* (10th ed.). Boston, MA: Cengage Learning.

Miller, L. (2012). *Counselling skills for social work* (2nd ed.). Thousand Oaks, CA: Sage.

Shulman, L. (2009). *The skills of helping individuals, families, groups and communities*. Belmont, CA: Brooks/Cole, Cengage Learning.

Trevithick, P. (2012). *Social work skills: A practice handbook* (3rd ed.). New York, NY: McGraw Hill Open University Press.

Wakefield, H. (2006). Guidelines on investigatory interviewing of children: What is the consensus in the scientific community? *American Journal of Forensic Psychology, 24*(3), 57–74. Retrieved from http://www.ipt-forensics.com/library/ajfp1.htm

Internet Resources

Breaking Bad News website (for strategies and guidelines)
www.breakingbadnews.org/publications

BC Guidelines, Cognitive Impairment: Recognition, Diagnosis and Management in Primary Care
www2.gov.bc.ca/assets/gov/health/practitioner-pro/bc-guidelines/cogimp-full-guideline.pdf

Oxford Bibliographies: Interviewing
www.oxfordbibliographies.com/view/document/obo-9780195389678/obo-9780195389678-0046.xml

8 Paraphrasing and Summarizing

Learning Goals

- Describe reflecting skills and their use.
- Understand the structure and function of summarizing skills.
- Understand the purpose of paraphrasing.
- Understand the difference between paraphrasing and summarizing.
- Learn how to manage emotions and the process of normalizing.

Building the Dimensions of People's Experiences

In the previous chapter, we explored the use of questioning skills. Questions help to probe further into a person's story and to more fully understand some of the specific dimensions of thoughts, feelings, events, and behaviours. However, you will need other skills to support people in the telling of their stories. If you only ask questions, the conversation can become an interrogation, as if running through a checklist. You need other skills to open up the story further; specifically, you can encourage someone to elaborate on the story through the use of paraphrasing, reflecting, and summarizing skills.

In facilitating reflecting skills such as paraphrasing and summarizing, it becomes important to reflect on how this occurs culturally. As a practitioner, it is your responsibility to be sensitive to, and familiar with, multiple cultures and world views. Bitter (2009) defines cultural sensitivity as "An awareness of cultural issues in families and a willingness to make these issues a central part of family practice, including an understanding of different values and beliefs, different levels of acculturation experiences, and the need to consider the marginalization, discrimination, and oppression of some cultures by the dominant culture" (p. 415). Bitter defines culture as "Shared experiences, language, and ways of being based on ethnicity, nationality, gender, age, ability, sexual/affectional orientation, and/or location" (p. 415). As a practitioner, if you are engaging in an attempt to assist the client in elaborating his or her story, you must consider the lived experience of the client in your working relationship. It is important to be mindful not to make assumptions about what you may think you understand about a client's lived experience, and be sure to seek the required understanding directly from the client. Paraphrasing and summarizing are the skills we use least in our everyday conversations. Paraphrasing and summarizing are explored throughout this chapter. It is important for workers to understand the differences between paraphrasing and summarizing when apply these skills. Paraphrasing focuses on capturing the essence of what a client is saying and restating it back to the client (not parroting what the client has said) to make sure you are understanding the client's story accurately. This technique can occur several times during your conversation. Here is one example of a worker's paraphrase:

Client: I have just separated from my wife, Susan. The way she was treating me was just too hard. Every time I tried to talk with her, she would just remain silent. I feel so much better now, and it makes me sad saying that to you.

Worker: You feel much better after separating from Susan and it's difficult for you to say out loud.

Summarizing is the process of taking the clients story over a prolonged period and condensing it into a few short summary sentences. Summarizing is often applied at the end of a counselling session to help the client bring closure to your session, and consider to next steps. For example:

Worker: You have tried several different ways to communicate with Susan about your concerns, and she has not responded, which lead to you deciding to separate from Susan, and while you feel good about your decision, you are feeling sad about the loss of your relationship.

We tend not to actively reflect back to someone what we think we are hearing. Instead, we pick up the threads of a casual conversation and ask questions. In a professional conversational context, paraphrasing and summarizing skills are a useful way of ensuring a number of things are occurring. In reflecting and summarizing, you can confirm the details of the story with the client. In doing this, you can confirm that you are hearing the story as she or he wants and needs you to hear it. This confirms that you are listening, and, in particular, listening to the key dimensions of the experience.

> Remember the process of communication presented in Chapter 2, where messages are encoded by the sender and decoded by the receiver. The skills of paraphrasing and summarizing enable these messages to be confirmed or represented.

Reflecting Skills

Reflecting skills are used in many ways—to affirm, challenge, clarify, or normalize a person's situation. Bitter (2009) notes that "the solution-oriented practitioner often will reframe problems as normal, everyday occurrences when the family or family members have been pathologized or have begun to self-pathologize their situation. Normalizing problems implies that because it is not so extreme, it can be addressed and solved" (p. 226).

Summarizing usually occurs at the end of a session or at a pivotal point in the conversation in an attempt to ensure clear understanding. Bitter (2009) states, "the summary lets the client know what the therapist(s) has heard and understands about the family's problem, and seeks to clarify anything that the interviewer might have missed" (p. 225). This summary includes recognition of the emotional burden the client or family is facing.

Generally speaking, "reflecting" is a process of "mirroring back to the interviewee what the interviewee has just said, as grasped by the interviewer" (Dickson, 2006, p. 167). The term "**paraphrasing**" is similarly used to describe this process of relating back, in your own words, what you think you have heard the other person say. The risk in using the term "mirroring" to define these processes is that it implies a static echo of what has been said, which is not the aim of the skill. Paraphrasing can also provide the practitioner with the opportunity to present information back to the client from a different perspective.

A distinction sometimes is made between the two types of responses—reflecting and paraphrasing: "while paraphrases are restricted to what is actually said, reflections concentrate upon less obvious information frequently revealed in more subtle ways" (Dickson, 2006, p. 171). Paraphrasing is seen by others to be reflecting of "cognitive aspects of messages rather than feelings" (Hepworth, Rooney, & Larsen, 2002, p. 141). However, these distinctions are not maintained by everyone, and the terms are often interchanged. Ultimately, paraphrasing provides the ability for the practitioner to gather information and further details in a non-direct conversational manner.

In contrast to paraphrasing, James and Gilliland (2017) state that most practitioners would agree that they would like to increase their accuracy in communication through two steps: restatement and reflection. Restatement of ideas involves making simple statements back to the client to ensure you are "on the same page." Clients may have difficulties expressing what is happening, particularly in situations of trauma. Purposeful restatement helps to clarify that the practitioner is accurately interpreting what the client is thinking and feeling. It allows for clarification surrounding the details of the client's experience, ensuring the client feels heard and understood. Restatement can also act as a natural pause in situations where clients are feeling overwhelmed retelling their story.

When done correctly, reflection skills can assist with the aspects of an assessment regarding the client's current state, potential resiliency, and ability to cope. Reflection of feelings involves sending the client a message that you understand what the client is feeling emotionally. During this process, if miscommunication has occurred or clarification is required, it provides the client with the opportunity to provide the practitioner with additional information.

Accurate reflection is also a critical component of assessment. For example, if a client is scoring between 9 and 10 on an anxiety scale (where 1 equals not anxious, and 10 is severe physical anxiety), their self-reported level of emotion is high and does not require immediate extensive reflection. In this case, the reflection could focus more on the client's current thoughts or affective state and how best to assist the client in lowering their current level of anxiety to a more stable level.

Egan (2013) (see also Egan & Schroeder, 2009) provides tactics for communicating your appreciation of important facts and feelings:

- Give yourself time to think.
- Use short responses.
- Gear your response to the client but remain yourself.

Restatement and reflection are critical skills that allow clients to feel understood and provide them with an opportunity to correct any miscommunications. How does restatement differ from paraphrasing? How can you practice these skills of restatement and reflection?

Being empathic and engaged in a story involves actively conveying that you are hearing how the person feels, as well as understanding the "facts" of the story. The "formula" is demonstrated in the following example:

Client: I'm exhausted. He's terrifying. He's so controlling of my every move, and any attempts I've made to break out of the situation, he's right there. When I moved out, he tracked me down and made me move back in. He threatened to beat the crap out of me if I didn't. And he would have if I hadn't returned. When I changed my phone number, he got it by tricking my best friend that there was an emergency.

Worker: You feel controlled and trapped by this guy because he's right there, wherever you turn in your life.

Client: Yeah, that's it. I'm trapped by him. It's useless trying to escape him.

In most situations, however, the essence of this formula is applied in a more abstract way. That is, we listen for the feelings and events that are at the heart of what is going on for the client, but we actively convey this using other responses. The following example uses a more abbreviated form:

Worker: So, he's trapping and controlling you, wherever you turn?

Alternatively, a more extended form would read,

Worker: And what I'm hearing is that while you're really trying to deal with this situation with this guy, whenever you do, he's able to get back in your life, and that's why you're feeling so tired and controlled.

"Owning" the reflection as the worker listens is achieved through the use of expressions such as "What I'm hearing . . . ," "It seems like . . . ," or "I wonder if . . ." and gives the client the opportunity to respond by refuting, correcting, or agreeing with the view. If a reflection is correct, it is often greeted with the response: "Exactly!" But the client needs also to be able to say, "No, that's not what I meant" or "Well, he didn't actually say that . . . ."

Egan and Schroeder (2009) discuss the importance of expanding this topic to include empathetic highlights as a way of bridging diversity gaps. Interacting with clients who differ significantly from you can create the opportunity for you to be the learner. Scott and Borodovsky (1990) refer to empathetic listening as "cultural role taking." In this instance, it is important for the practitioner to understand the client's cultural background to avoid assumptions based on the worker's personal beliefs.

In most instances, a reflection should move the conversation in some way. Notice the lack of movement in the following conversation:

Client: I'm absolutely fit to be tied about this whole situation.
Worker: You're feeling fit to be tied about this situation.

This worker is merely repeating or mirroring directly, not reflecting what has been said. In some instances, however, mirroring might be useful, depending on the tone of voice and the intent—it might help the client hear how angry he is in a particular situation. The risk is that the person may feel mimicked, and that the conversation has gone nowhere. In fact, the client could feel more frustrated and unheard:

Client: I'm absolutely fit to be tied about this whole situation.
Worker: You're feeling fit to be tied about this situation.
Client: That's what I just said.

It raises the question as to what conditions in the client–worker relationship enable us to feel best heard. It is rarely about repeating the story or echoing feelings, but more about what kind of purposeful response we give and receive.

In some instances, however, reflecting is helpful to just "sit" with the emotion or the experience that has been described and share it for a moment. Rather than finding out more detail through the use of questions, or challenging perceptions through reflections and summaries, sometimes reflecting back the emotion—be it heartache, exhaustion, or excitement—is a way of sharing in the reality of the client's experiences. Returning to the case of the harassed partner, this sort of response might go something like this:

Client: I'm exhausted. He's terrifying. He's so controlling of my every move, and any attempts I've made to break out of the situation, he's right there. When I moved out, he tracked me down and made me move back in. He threatened to beat the crap out of me if I didn't. And he would have if I hadn't returned. When I changed my phone number, he got it by tricking my best friend that there was an emergency.

Worker: It sounds really tough, and exhausting, and frightening.

Client: It is. It's lonely, it's frightening, and I can't see it ever ending.

Here, the worker does not draw out the events or the feelings of the client in any extensive way. An affirmation of how the client may be feeling is reflected in a short, empathic statement. This type of response is a normalizing response. In this case, it draws out the client's fear that she has no alternatives.

Normalizing

Normalizing is a skill of affirmation. Typically, it draws on a wider pool of knowledge or experience to place a person's experience in context. For example, in grief situations, many people report that they feel as if they are going crazy, based on their experiences of auditory or visual hallucinations, or disturbances to their sleep or capacity to function, as they had prior to the loss (Raphael, 1983). Normalizing is used in these instances to reassure people that these experiences are shared human experiences. Normalizing can focus on these grief experiences, or on coping strategies. For example, this conversation shows how the focus is on normalizing the experience following the death of a child:

Client: It's just stupid, stupid stuff. I hate feeling so disoriented. I feel as if I'm losing my mind. It's as if she's right there beside me and it drives me crazy. Am I crazy?

Worker: You're feeling like you're crazy because of these different experiences. Many people who have been through a major loss, like you have, experience similar things and find that they ask themselves these questions. It seems to be part of the "making sense" of it. They're not crazy, nor are you.

Normalizing provides a useful reflection and reminder that people are not alone in their distress and difficulty. For some people, however, this is not what they need or want to hear. Their experience feels unique to them and any attempt by other people to presume to understand it is deeply offensive. Workers have different competencies and inclinations in using normalizing skills. The potential for the *least* authentic interaction is high in paraphrasing, as is the potential to offend with normalizing. The potential to deepen understanding and empathy, however, is also high and that is why these skills are encouraged.

Multicultural perspectives require further consideration when utilizing normalizing skills. It is imperative that the practitioner understand the world view of the client's cultural background to work effectively. If the worker does not understand the values and beliefs of the client, miscommunication can occur and damage the working relationship. How will you know what is "normal" when working with diverse populations? How will you determine when this concept of normal is appropriate to the context of your work?

Managing Emotion

Managing emotion in practice begins with the worker. In order for a worker to be present for a client who is experiencing a highly emotional situation, they must first understand the concept of emotional intelligence (Ingram 2012). **Emotional intelligence** emphasizes the ability of an individual to recognize, comprehend, and work through the emotional aspects of their relationships and experiences. Likewise, emotional intelligence involves an individual's capacity to be cognizant of their own emotional responses in different circumstances.

Once workers learn the skill of self-regulation and awareness, they are more equipped to identify emotional responses in their client. Emotional intelligence enhances an individual's capacity for empathic understanding and by extension their communication skills (Ingram, 2012). This process is the framework to establishing positive relationships with clients.

Emotional intelligence aids workers with their paraphrasing and normalizing skills with clients. It encourages awareness of the workers role with clients and brings attention to the importance of professional boundaries. It is also a critical skill to aid workers in competently responding to a client's emotional state.

Why Use Reflecting Skills?

In using reflecting skills, thinking about why you are using these skills is important. A major argument for the use of these skills is that they actively convey that you have understood where the person is coming from. These responses do more than simply clarify (Hargie, 2006). These responses can lead to new insights because people

- can feel heard, respected, and affirmed in what they are experiencing;
- may not have thought about the situation in that way or may never have listened thoughtfully to what they themselves were saying. Clients who listen can hear a different account of events because of additional new experiences, because they listen to the worker or to themselves more insightfully, or because their emotional distance from their troubling situation has improved, which is so often why a counsellor is sought out as a listener;
- may not realize the full implications of what they were saying about their problems; or
- may not realize the levels of contradiction and complexity in their situation, which can be hard to hear or to articulate. Reflecting or paraphrasing often normalizes these complexities of emotions and experiences, through naming them and recognizing them as significant dimensions of the overall situation.

> Remember that minimal encouragers (discussed in Chapter 7) help to encourage the client to continue sharing the details of their story.

The worker's listening skills in these situations are primarily about acknowledgement, and they provide a way of actively demonstrating to the client the values discussed in Chapter 1.

Sometimes you will be aware of the other layers of experience through the client's conversation or interaction. For example, someone describing feelings of sadness, both verbally and non-verbally, seems to you also to be feeling helpless or angry or ambivalent. It is important for the worker to be able to "read" the total communication message in any conversation—the message involves both the verbal and the non-verbal in fundamental ways.

As with questioning, reflecting and paraphrasing are your means of influence—of your own opinion and world view—in the interview. Your choice of response will depend on what you are listening for, as the following exercise demonstrates.

BOX 8.1 Focus on Practice

A Group Role-Play

A group role-play or discussion can be a useful way to explore how you use paraphrasing or summarizing skills and what connections they may have with your initial effort to learn the client's story and assessment from the start of an interview.

One person can role-play the client. Alternatively, you could watch a short piece of a DVD conversation where a client is describing her or his situation. The whole group, with the exception of the student playing the client, becomes "the worker" and each person is invited to say what she/he would reflect back to the client.

1. The student role-playing the client: From your perspective, which reflection did you prefer and why?
2. How varied were the perspectives on describing the role-play within your group?
3. What was the reflection? Paraphrase, summary?
4. What are the consequences of each kind of technique in terms of the direction of the interview, the impact on the client, and the theoretical assumptions behind this focus?
5. What did you learn about your skills? Are there things you were not aware of?

Overusing paraphrasing can convey that you are listening, but may also mean that you have established few of the "facts" of the story, leaving you without the information you need to assess the client's situation. Again, it depends on your context and purpose as to whether you need to be probing for details or adopting a more reflective approach.

Summarizing Skills

Summarizing skills are used in a conversation to draw together the various issues that have been discussed. While reflecting and paraphrasing are used throughout an entire interview, the use of summarizing is connected to some important timing issues. A summary can be used after the initial overview of the issues with which someone is grappling:

Worker: So you're saying you've been into Child Services, you've spoken with the duty worker there, and she referred you to me to follow through on your complaint?
Client: That's right.

It can also be used when you feel the conversation has come to a standstill or if you want the client to know exactly how you have heard what has been discussed. In some cases, summarizing may address potential assumptions made by the practitioner through a process of clarification. It enables the client to clear up your summary and highlight areas of miscommunication.

Worker: So you're saying you've been to Child Protection Services, you've spoken with the duty worker there, and she referred you to me to follow through on your complaint?

Client: No, that's not what I said. I spoke with someone on the phone and she said I have to go to Child Protection Services, *after* talking with you, to put in my complaint.

Worker: Thank you for helping me understand correctly what you've said.

This summary establishes the details of a complex sequence of events, which the worker had misunderstood. Had he or she not summarized at this early point in the conversation, the misunderstanding could have caused major confusion. Clarifying statements like "Let me see if I have this right . . ." can also be added to actively seek the client's view on what you are summarizing (Trevithick, 2005, p. 166). It can also assist the client with connecting pieces of their story in ways they had not previously considered, opening up opportunity for change particularly when a client is describing multiple challenges.

A summary also can be used as a way of setting the direction of the next stage of conversation. It can close off some issues, too, and enable a focus to be agreed on for the rest of the discussion:

Worker: So, we've talked now about what's going on with your drinking and how it is impacting your family. You have said how urgent you think it is for you to attend treatment, but you are feeling unsure of the process and about leaving home. What do you think we should focus on now?

A summary can also be used at the end of a meeting to bring together the essence of the conversation:

Worker: We've talked about a lot of things today—your relationship and whether or not you will leave, and your current level of stress, which is affecting your ability to focus at work. We have decided that a good step for you is to focus on applying stress reduction skills so you can begin to feel clearer. You stated then that you would like to discuss your relationship further. We'll talk again in a few days to see how things are going and if coming back to discuss your relationship is something you'd like to do.

In general, a summary should be short. A long or mistimed summary can seem laborious. A long summary can sound as if it is just repeating what the client has said or is presenting a "shopping list" of issues. A summary should aim to pick up the complexity of issues to date and, typically, to open the next phase of the discussion. In addition, conveying accurately the language and emotional intensity of the client is important. A mismatch to the client's emotional intensity can leave the person feeling very misunderstood or misrepresented:

Client: [Having discussed in detail her sexual harassment case and the need to access legal representation] So I'm a bit concerned about what this is all going to cost.

Worker: So with the hassle of finding a lawyer, the ongoing complications at work where you are enduring this person each day, your ongoing stress at home, you're now also really overwhelmed by the enormous cost of the lawyers.

Client: [Having discussed in detail her sexual harassment case and the need to access legal representation] So I'm a bit concerned about what this is all going to cost.

Worker: You have shared very clearly the impact the harassment case has had on your work and home life and now you have the added concern of legal costs as your case moves forward.

Example of a potential next question:
What are you doing to take care of yourself throughout this process?

In the first instance, the worker has used unnecessarily intense emotional language—the client said she was a "bit concerned" and the worker has said "really overwhelmed"—and the client has been inundated by all the issues they have discussed, when in fact she only asked about the issue of legal costs.

Summaries are particularly important in situations where cultural or linguistic misunderstandings can occur. For example, when working with interpreters, it is sometimes difficult to know what the interpreter has communicated to the client, both from the standpoint of what the interpreter heard you say and from the standpoint of what the client has said to you through the interpreter. Regular summaries by both the client (through the interpreter) and the worker (likewise) can mediate some of this communication difficulty as to what has been heard and understood.

Chapter Summary

This chapter presents an overview of some of the skills you can use to consolidate the details of a person's story, with an emphasis on reflecting and summarizing skills. These skills help to establish a mutual understanding of a conversation, and of the overall work. They are skills that we tend not to use much in our everyday conversations, but they are one way of ensuring that the client's story is heard accurately and from his or her point of view.

Questions for Analysis

1. When would you use reflecting and summarizing skills, and when would you not?
2. When have you experienced the effective and/or ineffective use of these skills?
3. How is active listening important in summarizing and paraphrasing?
4. What potential miscommunication may occur in summarizing or paraphrasing?
5. What skills do you need to develop further in this area? Provide some examples.

Group Activity

In small groups of three or four, read the following paragraph and capture the essence of Mary's conversation by paraphrasing in one statement the main points of Mary's story. Share your group's paraphrased statement with another group and discuss each group's process.

> Mary came in for her session extremely upset and crying. "I have been awake for days walking the floors and can't even remember how I made it here. . . . I can't stop seeing the car accident every time I hear a loud noise. It causes me to see the details of the crash visually as if it just happened and then I have extreme night terrors. In my dream I see the car coming towards me, it was red, and I hear the brakes screaming as the two vehicles collide. The sound of the metal crunching as my car slides in circles to a sudden stop plays over and over in my mind. I have not eaten or showered in days and cannot seem to remember if I have taken my medication or seem to remember simple tasks that I need to do . . ."

Create your paraphrasing statement.

1. What key points did your group hear from Mary's story?
2. How did your group determine what the main points were?
3. Was your group's paraphrased statement similar or different from other groups?
4. What main points did you include in your paraphrasing statement?
5. Did another group include different points?
6. How might the skill of emotional intelligence be helpful in the case of Mary?
7. What specific aspects of emotional intelligence would you be aware of?

Individual Exercise

1. What are some feeling words stated by Mary? Create a list of Mary's feeling words and highlight the words you feel are critical to Mary's story.
2. Reflect on your interpretation of Mary's feeling words. What made you think the way you did?
3. Did you assume understanding of any of the words?
4. What skills helped you to determine your understanding?
5. How do feeling words assist us when working with clients?

Partner Practice

In pairs, take turns summarizing one another's statements. One student starts as the counsellor and one student the client (this could also be done with a friend or family member). Have the student in the client role share a short story of something that happened over the summer (planting a garden, learning how to . . .). Then, have the person in the counsellor role practice summarizing the client's story. Complete three rounds of summary practice with the goal of working to achieve a clear, crisp summary that your partner feels accurately reflects his or her story.

Recommended Readings

Bitter, J.R. (2009). *Theory and practice of family therapy and counseling*. Belmont, CA: Brooks/Cole.

Davies, K., & Jones, R. (2016). *Skills for social work practice*. New York, NY: Palgrave Macmillan.

Egan, G. (2013). *The skilled helper: a problem-management and opportunity-development approach to helping* (10th ed.). Belmont, CA: Brooks/Cole Cengage Learning.

Egan, G., & Schroeder, W. (2009). *The skilled helper: A problem-management and opportunity-development approach to helping* (1st Cdn ed.). Toronto, ON: Nelson Education.

James, R.K., & Gilliland, B.E. (2017). *Crisis intervention strategies* (7th ed.). Pacific Grove, CA: Brooks/Cole Cengage Learning.

Hargie, O. (2006). Training in communication skills. In O. Hargie (Ed.), *The handbook of communication skills* (3rd ed., pp. 553–65). New York, NY: Routledge.

Hirvela, A., & Du, Q. (2013). "Why am I paraphrasing?": Undergraduate ESL writers' engagement with source-based academic writing and reading. *Journal of English for Academic Purposes, 12*(2), 87–98. Retrieved from www.sciencedirect.com/science/journal/14751585

Ingram, R. (2012). Locating emotional intelligence at the heart of social work practice. *British Journal of Social Work, 43*(5), 987–1004.

Kadushin, A., & Kadushin, G. (2013). *The social work interview*. New York, NY: Columbia University Press.

Schmidt, G., & Jarrett, L. (2000). *Mental health and northern Aboriginal people: An annotated bibliography*. Prince George, BC: Northern Interior Regional Health Board and UNBC Social Work Program.

Internet Resources

Basic Counselling Skills, Paraphrasing
www.basic-counseling-skills.com/paraphrasingtone.html

For the helpers by the helpers (blog)
https://2105rocks.wordpress.com/the-beginning-stage/listening-response-2-paraphrasing

Social Work Skills Demonstrated: Beginning Direct Practice, Paraphrasing
http://wps.ablongman.com/ab_socialworkskills_1/149/38245/9790914.cw/-/9790916/index.html

9 Forming an Assessment—Setting the Agenda

Learning Goals

- Understand the purposes of assessment.
- Consider some of the inherent challenges in assessment.
- Understand the focus of assessments.
- Describe the process of setting goals for the work.

Revisit Chapter 7 and the process of establishing the story, what questions to ask, and how to gather important details of the client's story.

In the previous chapters, we have focused on some of the ways in which you can meet with people, engage in conversation, and begin to explore the circumstances that have led to your contact. Each time you ask a question or reflect back to someone what you have heard you are making decisions about what to respond to, what to hear, and what to remember from the conversation, and perhaps address at a later point. You are beginning to focus more on particular dimensions of this individual's situation. As you work through aspects of the conversation and begin to focus on specific areas, you are forming an assessment of someone's circumstances and how he or she is placed within those circumstances. The example below highlights that an interview or conversation will need to move to a particular focus after an initial period of exploration of the issues and concerns.

BOX 9.1 Focus on Practice

Moving from the Story to an Assessment

Your client, Mohammed, has described his difficult transition to life in Canada. He arrived several months ago on his own, after 14 months in a refugee camp adjoining his home country. He has some distant relatives living in Canada, but not locally, and contact has been difficult. His wife and two children are still in his home country and he is working towards bringing them to Canada, but it is not an easy process, especially given the language barriers and financial resources required.

Continued

Mohammed has found accommodation, but is experiencing great difficulties in adapting to Canadian life. He has come to your service for assistance with a number of urgent issues:

- his housing circumstances, which are temporary accommodations
- his health—given both his lack of financial resources and therefore inadequate nutrition—and his traumatic memories, which combine to keep him from sleeping
- his difficulty finding employment
- fear for his family and the need to bring them to Canada.

1. What else would you want to know about Mohammed and his situation?
2. What would you see as some of the major issues to address and how would you go about setting the priorities?
3. Are there other issues you would want to explore and possibly focus on in your conversation?
4. Think about the biopsychosocial-spiritual assessment (described in the next section) and how it might assist you here.

Understanding Different Types of Assessments

The term "**assessment**" is very broad, meaning different things in different professions. In Chapter 1, we looked at the general purpose of human services: working with people to alleviate adversity and oppression, and to promote well-being and health. Assessment, therefore, focuses on exploring how people are functioning and how optimal functioning and well-being can be enhanced through the provision of specific resources for their inner and outer worlds. An assessment process helps workers to understand a client's situation and evaluate outcomes of progress made. Assessments can also assist a worker to recognize when a chosen intervention is working or is ineffective in a particular client situation.

The type of assessment required from the worker varies according to your agency context. In work that is oriented towards a social care agenda, where change is a mutual goal, the assessment process focuses on setting goals for the work that will be engaged in together. Where you may be in a position of imposing a change agenda, assessment may be driven more unilaterally by you. You will be making judgements and decisions about coping capacities, risk, and resources. This work will still focus on change as the outcome, but it may not be so mutually determined.

Prior to conducting an assessment, a worker must consider factors that might influence whether or not the assessment can continue or how best to proceed. The following factors must be explored prior to commencing:

- The client's thoughts on participating in an assessment process.
- Are there any legal considerations that need to be addressed, such as capacity to provide consent, or a pending trial?
- Are there any safety or personal risks for the client?

Once all legal and safety factors are considered and addressed, the worker can begin to determine the best questions to ask (specific to the assessment being completed).

Revisit the values, knowledge bases, and theoretical perspectives explored in Chapters 1 through 3. These provide the basis for your assessment.

© rancorn/123RF

As a human service worker, what kind of information would you require from your agency prior to completing an assessment? What kind of information would you need from your client?

Social work assessments can vary agency to agency and are often designed to meet the needs of the population the agency is serving. For example, a biopsychosocial approach can be applied more broadly, whereas, a Mini-Mental Status Exam or the Beck's Depression Inventory have a more specific focus.

You might consider these questions when getting started:

1. What is the reason for the assessment and does the client agree? (Is the assessment voluntary, forced—e.g., suicide risk assessment and potential hospitalization, a suspected illness such as dementia—or required—e.g., to remain in school a behavioural assessment is required?)
2. What is the cause of the problem that led to the need for assessment? (Was it a sudden request, has the issue recently developed, or been a concern for a while?)
3. Who all is involved? (For example, if client is a minor, are the child's guardians involved?)
4. History details: How long has problem been present? What its duration, intensity, frequency, patterns, etc.? How does the problem present in the client's daily life?
5. What are the client's views of the situation (concerns, potential fears of consequences)?

6. What are the client's resources (level of resiliency, skills, strategies in place)?
7. What would the client like to see change following the assessment?

In most practice settings when you meet with a client for the first time, an assessment focused on broader details can help form a picture of the client's presenting problem and available resources.

For example, the biopsychosocial-spiritual (BPSS) assessment offers a historical context and assesses the client's strengths, and available resources. The BPSS assessment is meant to identify potential barriers for clients in addition to their current strengths , by considering four aspects of a client's life:

1. Biological: focuses on the individual's basic needs (housing, food, clothing, medical conditions, and environment).
2. Psychological: focuses on the client's history (including previous or current diagnosis and medications), personality traits, mental health, and self-identity.
3. Social: focuses on who is in the client's life, work, volunteering, education, cultural factors and connections (e.g., race, sexual orientation, gender, age, religion).
4. Spiritual: focuses on the client's religious and spiritual identity and associated practices.

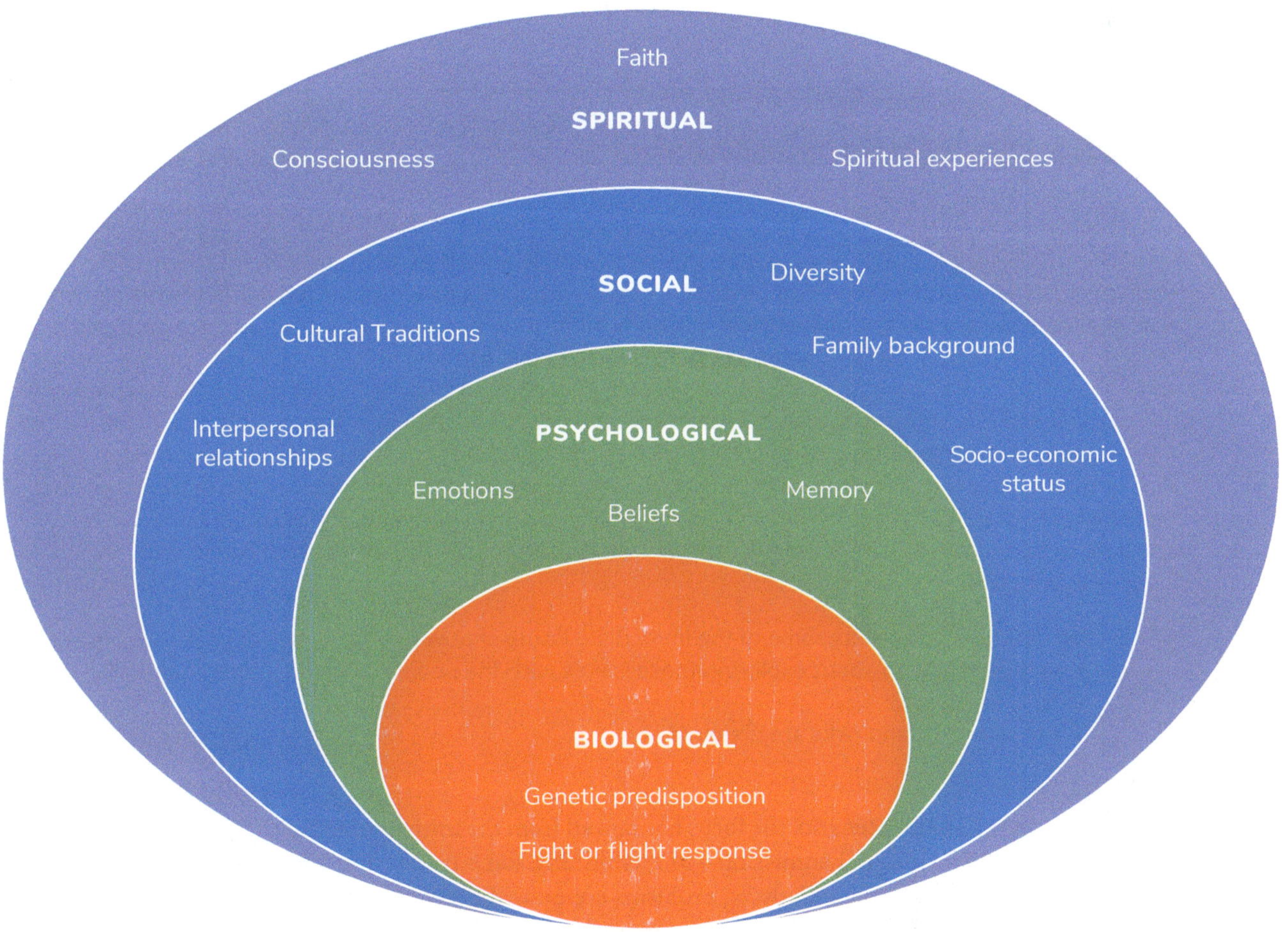

FIGURE 9.1 Biopsychosocial-Spiritual Assessment

Source: Adapted from Jonathan Singer, *The Social Work Podcast*, January 22, 2007. Retrieved from http://socialworkpodcast.blogspot.com/2007/02/bio-psychosocial-spiritual-bpss.html

Formal Assessments

Coggins (2016) describes a clinical assessment as comprehensive and critical to documenting a baseline from which workers can develop a client's treatment plan. Assessments are aimed at understanding clearly the client's presenting problem and how the client's current behaviours, level of emotional distress, and capacity to addresses the presenting problem will be considered in treatment planning and goals. Davis (2006) discusses the early phase of any intervention as including working with the client to define and set goals. Where necessary, this can include a formal assessment to assist with the recovery process. Davis describes a clinical assessment as "an ongoing process, one that involves interviews, gathering collateral information, using psychometric instruments, and in some cases laboratory tests as well as scanning and imaging techniques" (p. 191). Formal assessments are often developed to explore a specific group or population, for example, family assessments, multi-dimensional aging assessments, risk assessments, or substance misuses assessments.

The processes and purposes of facilitating an assessment are filtered by the influences we have discussed in earlier chapters: your values, knowledge bases, skills, and organizational context. You can see in the following scenario that you would be dealing with a number of different points of view throughout the assessment process and would need to juggle these.

BOX 9.2 Focus on Practice

Mr and Mrs Willis

Mr and Mrs Willis are in their late seventies and have been living in their own condo for 32 years. They have strong connections with a number of neighbours, and with their local Rotary Club. Mr Willis fell last week when he got up to answer the phone. He is currently in the local hospital with a fractured leg and wrist and diagnosed osteoporosis. Since his admission, the nurses have become very concerned about his memory and have organized an assessment for him, which has confirmed that he has dementia. The worker is to talk with Mr and Mrs Willis about a range of home-care options, including the possibility that he move into a supported living arrangement. Mrs Willis is distraught about the dementia diagnosis and the possibility that he might move out of their family home, where they have lived for so long. She has made it very clear that she wants her husband to come back home and live there. In her mind, this hospital admission is only about his physical recovery from the broken bones and she is terrified of any suggestion that he should no longer live with her.

1. What would you see as some of the immediate issues that would form part of your assessment?
2. How would you go about exploring these issues with the people involved in this situation?
3. Who is the client?
4. What strengths and risks are present?

In this scenario, the focus has moved from the initial presenting problem or concern—Mr Willis's hospital admission—to establishing some underlying concerns. In this instance, the presenting and underlying problems are quite different, depending on who you talk to about the situation.

Mental State Examination

One of the specific assessment frameworks that may be applied in the above scenario is a mental state examination (MSE) (Bloch & Singh, 2007). An MSE is designed to assess the cognitive status of a client in many different settings. It is included below as an example of a very specific set of questions that can be asked. Other agencies may have standardized psychosocial assessment questions that are used—they ask specific questions so that specific issues of risk and protective factors can be addressed.

BOX 9.3 Focus on Practice

Folstein Mini-Mental Status Examination

Orientation

What is the year?

- Season?
- Month?
- Date?
- Day?

Where are we?

- Province?
- City?
- Community?
- Hospital?
- Floor?

Registration

I am going to name three objects and I want you to repeat them after me. [Interviewer: give one point for each correct answer. Repeat the objects until the patient can name them all—Six attempts maximum. If more than one attempt, how many attempts completed?]

Attention and Calculation

I am going to ask you to do some subtraction. Think of the number 7.
I want you to subtract 7 from 100. Now subtract 7 from that and keep on going. 100, __, __, __, __, __. Stop.
Alternatively, spell "world" backwards.

Recall

Please name the three objects that I had you repeat after me just a short while ago. [Interviewer: give one point for each correct answer.]

Language

Please name these for me [interviewer: show client a watch and a pencil].
Now please repeat the following: "no ifs, ands, or buts."

Now I am going to ask you to do something for me. Take a paper in your right hand, fold it in half and put it on the floor. Now I want you to read this and do what it says. [Interviewer hands the client a card that says, "close your eyes."]
Now please write a sentence for me on this blank piece of paper. [Interviewer gives the client a blank piece of paper and asks him or her to write a sentence. Do not dictate a sentence. It must be written spontaneously. It must contain a subject and verb and be sensible. Correct grammar and punctuation are not necessary.]

Visual Motor Integrity

Please copy this design. [Interviewer: on a clean piece of paper, draw intersecting pentagons, each side about 1 inch, and ask him or her to copy it exactly as it is. All ten angles must be present and two must intersect to score 1 point.]
Total score (30)

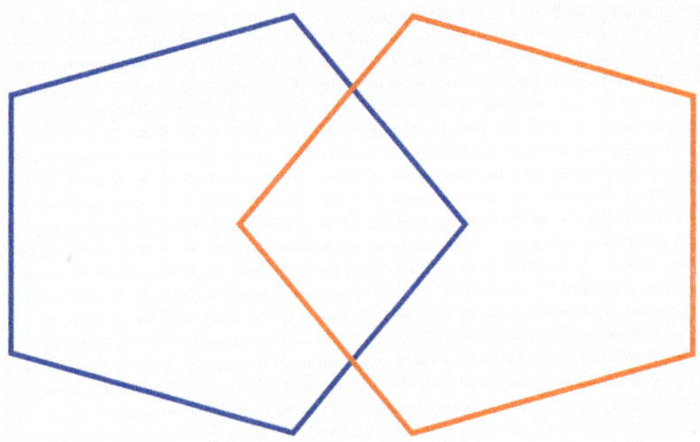

Interviewer: assess client's level of consciousness along continuum:

alert drowsy stupor coma

Source: Adapted from Coulehan and Block (2006, pp. 222–3).
Jfdwolff. https://commons.wikimedia.org/wiki/File:InterlockingPentagons.svg

Who Is the Assessment For?

Ideally, an assessment process enables the establishment of a mutual agenda for future action. In exploring the story with the client, the assessment process provides the step towards establishing the basis for further work and the ongoing purpose of the relationship. It is about moving from "starting where the client is at" to working towards where the client wants to be, or, in mandated circumstances, where others consider the client should be.

The different formats and requirements for assessments raise some major challenges in the assessment phase, depending on who the assessment really is for. For example, the following assessment formats are identified by Lloyd and Taylor (1995):

- third-party assessments
- investigative assessments
- eligibility/needs assessments

- suitability assessments
- multidisciplinary assessments.

In addition to these are assessments within the context of a more therapeutic client–worker relationship, where the assessment is conducted to ascertain what should be the focus of the work together. Some of these challenges raised in the assessment process are described now, before moving into an exploration of assessment frameworks.

Challenges in the Assessment Process

Forming an assessment is a challenging task. An assessment needs to capture the diversity of a client's life and the complexity of their unique and current situation. An assessment can have a profound impact on a person's life; for example, if it denies them eligibility for a service, or concludes that their child can no longer live with them. In the scenario outlined above, an assessment may lead to a strong recommendation that Mr Willis not return to his home. A comprehensive assessment, therefore, is critical. Some major challenges inherent in the process of assessment are briefly discussed, including the focus of the assessment, the adequacy and accuracy of the information gathered, the fluidity of assessment, who sets the agenda, and cultural diversity. Davis (2006) cautions practitioners to consider that the initial assessment may occur at a time of crisis for the client, and therefore may influence the accuracy of the information being gathered.

Assessing for Risks or for Strengths?

In the context of resource limitations and a focus in Western society on risk management (Giddens, 2002; Lupton, 1999; Webb, 2006), many assessments remain risk assessments, adopting a primarily pathogenic approach to understanding of people and their circumstances. Morley (2004) defines a risk assessment as a "process of categorizing and recording particular information about clients to make predictions about the likelihood of particular future events occurring" (p. 127). Examples of "risk" may include reckless actions, neglect involving personal health or safety, or suicidal thoughts.

Assessment is, therefore, about highly subjective predictions being made by someone who may not have gathered all the relevant information (Giddens, 2002; Lupton, 1999; Saleebey, 2017; Webb, 2006). A focus on capacity building, both within the person and within their wider families and communities, is an essential component of an assessment. A comprehensive assessment should incorporate not only a risk but a strengths perspective. Strengths-based assessment questions can include these:

1. What strengths do you think you have?
2. What is your most confident skill?
3. Can you tell me about a time when have you successfully faced a barrier, and what you did to overcome it?
4. What are the things you are good at?
5. Who/what is important to you in your life?
6. Tell me about a time when you felt like most things in your life were going well. What were you doing to achieve that success?

7. What inspires you?
8. What do you find you learn most easily?
9. What do you value about yourself?

Correct Information

In some situations, a systematic, detailed assessment may be possible. This enables an in-depth discussion of many dimensions of a person's life. Assessments, however, are often conducted quickly with people under less than optimal conditions. The available time and place can impact, therefore, quite profoundly on the outcome of an assessment. Similarly, what clients know of you—and what the information they give you will be used for—influences willingness to disclose, or even the perception that disclosure of certain information is relevant or required.

Gathering correct information with diverse populations requires that practitioners consider a client's cultural background and world view. The practitioner should consider any possible barriers the client is facing throughout the process and take steps to ensure the client understands purpose in gathering the information required.

Issues related to northern and remote locations also require consideration when gathering information. If the client is from a remote community, her or his experience in a larger urban centre may be limited and therefore, overwhelming. The client may require assistance in understanding what the purpose of the assessment is and how the process is designed. Bitter (2009) suggests the following diversity questions to consider in practice:

- What cultures are in the family background of each of the family members?
- In what culture or region is the family currently living?
- Is immigration or migration a recent family experience?
- How do economics, education, ethnicity, religion, race, regional affiliation, gender, and age affect family process?
- How is the fit between the therapist and the family with regard to economics, education, ethnicity, religion, age, race, majority/minority status, and regional background? (p. 368)

Fluidity of Information

People and circumstances change over time, sometimes very rapidly and sometimes more slowly. For example, someone with great enthusiasm for life who is developing dementia may become preoccupied with thoughts of suicide and appear to recent acquaintances as severely depressed. Poverty is another experience that, in Western contexts, often shifts for people across their lifespan, rather than remaining a constant (Room & Britton, 2006). People acquire different coping capacities or different stressors. Assessments can be written up and placed in client files, and become the source of information about the client over many years, without ever being revisited or verified. Details of a client's life can be handed on as "fact" when it may long since have changed yet again.

As a worker, too, you will change over time as you develop your knowledge base and practice wisdom. Perceptions of risk, for example, may change the more you are confronted with people in a particular setting. You may realize you were more cautious or liberal in an assessment of a client situation a few years ago than you would be now. The information gathered in any assessment process therefore necessarily changes over time.

The monitoring of changing needs and issues is important in situations where ongoing contact is maintained. This is why assessment is both a single process done in a first interview and an ongoing process throughout the length of any contact with workers.

Howatt (2000) suggests the following procedure for an initial interview:

- Introduce yourself: *"Hello, I'm (title) (name). And you are ———?"*
- Explain what an assessment is for, or ask what they are expecting.
- Explain what your role is, or ask the client to define what your job is, and then clarify.
- Explain the concept of choice, and that the counsellor cannot make or fix a person; the work is to help the client work through areas of concern.
- Explain any orientation information the client may need to know.
- Explain how long the interview will be, and that a break for any reason (for example, restroom) is okay.
- Explain that the assessment process is ongoing, and that all decisions are made in a collaborative manner. Also that the client's goals can change or be fine-tuned at any time.
- Explain that this is a helping process, and that at any time (unless court ordered) the client can terminate the process.
- Explain, if applicable, that you have already read any reports; however, the emphasis for today is on what the client has to say and wants to do.
- Explain your qualification.

Who Sets the Agenda?

Your aim is to set a mutually agreeable agenda for the work to be done together. At another level, you as the worker, and as part of a particular agency, influence that assessment and agenda, either implicitly or explicitly.

Depending on the context, you and your client may disagree in your assessments of a situation. For example, in acute psychiatric service settings different perceptions often arise as to whether someone requires an involuntary hospital admission; disagreement may arise as to whether or not a parent should be allowed to continue living in the family home following allegations of sexual abuse; or questions may occur as to whether a young person's non-attendance at school is indicative of more serious underlying problems at home or at school.

Making an assessment with clients in involuntary circumstances is a more fraught process. Important information is likely to be missing if a strong engagement and rapport has not been established. It is also critical to explain why the assessment process is important—that is, clarifying the role accurately. This can be done through ongoing, honest discussion. People's experiences of trust in both personal and professional relationships may have been poor, and so this is an opportunity to promote collaborative problem solving (Trotter, 2006).

An organizational context will also profoundly shape what assessment can be made and what subsequent interventions can occur. As a result, an assessment may be limited by what

> Remember the diagram reflecting the communication process in Chapter 2. In any assessment process, the worlds of the worker and the client are present.

> Reflect back on Mohammed's situation earlier in this chapter, and on the ways in which your assessment may be influenced by an agency's resources.

resources are available rather than what the person actually needs or has a right to access (Ife, 2001; Trevithick, 2005).

Diversity

Assessment processes have the potential to amplify all sorts of assumptions about world views. Assumptions about consent, agreement, and commonality of goals can be imposed without a worker realizing it. Similarly, assumptions about ways of living and perceptions of coping and adaptation (Rigney & Cooper, 2004; Smith, 2001) can be imposed. You can build optimal understanding by asking open-ended questions about the meaning of events or actions and by using paraphrasing. Workers have a professional responsibility to develop and sustain cultural awareness in relation to all diversity issues—including sexual, religious, and cultural diversities—and to their own prejudices and assumptions. As Miller, Donner, and Fraser (2004, citing Goodman, 2001) note, "Most people with agent status do not view themselves as having power and privilege" (p. 380).

Davis (2006) notes,

> in considering the mental health needs of Canada's culturally diverse population, one can identify a number of potential barriers to establishing and maintaining a constructive relationship between service providers and minority clients. These barriers include language, different world views as to what constitutes mental disorder and mental health, stigma, distrust, and how services are designed and allocated. (p. 299).

In addition, it is important to go beyond defining culture as solely linked to ethnicity. Some groups may define the term "culture" to include contextual variables such as, rural, urban or suburban settings; language, age, gender cohort, family configuration, race, ethnicity, religion, nationality, socio-economic status, employment, education, occupation, sexual orientation, political ideology; migration, and stage of acculturation (Falicov, 1995).

Consider the following questions to help you explore your understanding of culture.

1. How do you define the term "culture"?
2. What are some of the ways you have experienced culture being defined?
3. In a small group discuss how culture could be defined from the above list, for example, family configuration, or sexual orientation.

Corey (1996) suggests, "effective diversity practice demands an open stance on the part of the practitioner, a flexibility, and a willingness to modify strategies to fit the needs and the situation of the individual client" (p. 30). Corey continues, "it is important to realize that it takes time, study, and experience to become an effective diversity counsellor. Diversity competence cannot be reduced simply to cultural awareness and sensitivity, to a body of knowledge, or to a specific set of skills" (p. 31).

Mussel, Cardiff, and White (2004) define cultural competency as "a specific set of values, attitudes, knowledge and skills that sensitize and improve sharing of information and assistance between people of different cultural orientations" (p. 7).

What Assessment Frameworks Are Used?

As we listen to someone speak, we begin to form an assessment. In this sense, assessment begins as the work begins. Typically, though, after an initial exploration of the client's story, the communication needs to become focused in a purposeful way around specific issues of concern and action. Given the diversity of the specifics of each particular context, no single assessment framework exists. Many agencies have standardized intake and assessment forms and procedures, reflecting the assessment of the particular dimensions they focus on in service delivery.

Why we come to emphasize some dimensions and not others within these assessment processes is an important question to reflect upon. The theoretical dimensions we privilege as a worker and/or as an organization profoundly influence the listening we are capable of. As Fook (1993) states, assessment is "the phase of casework helping where a theory is formed about the particular causes of a particular person's particular situation" (p. 74). This knowledge returns our discussion to some of the earlier chapters, when we noted that theoretical perspectives influence what we hear and why.

Many assessment frameworks focus primarily on a client and the client's inner-world dimensions. The individual's personal stories and circumstances are understood as follows (Egan, 2002): "Stories tend to be mixtures of clients' experiences, behaviors, and emotions. Traditionally, human activity has been divided into three parts: thinking, feeling, and acting" (p. 77). From this theorizing of human experience, a framework for listening includes the following questions:

- What are the main points?
- What experiences are most important?
- What themes are coming through?
- What is the client's point of view?
- What is most important to him or her?
- What does he or she want me to understand?
- What decisions are implied?
- What is he or she proposing to do?

This framework will enable you, the worker, to listen to the things you consider priorities in the client's story as well as the client's evaluations of priorities. It provides an insight into clients' inner world by linking their thinking, feeling, behaving (both in the past and the future), and events. These dimensions begin to provide the basis of "what" to listen for.

Often underemphasized at this point is a sense of clients' circumstances in relation to their outer-world connections—their relationships, their social and cultural contexts, and the nature of their **structural contexts**. As Fook (1993) notes, "The structural element will always interplay with personal factors such as biography, current life events, emotional and psychological characteristics, genetic inheritance, physical health, and so on to create a unique personal situation" (p. 75). This appreciation for the client's context shifts an assessment from focusing only on thinking, feeling, behaving, and events to include the mediating dimensions of social context.

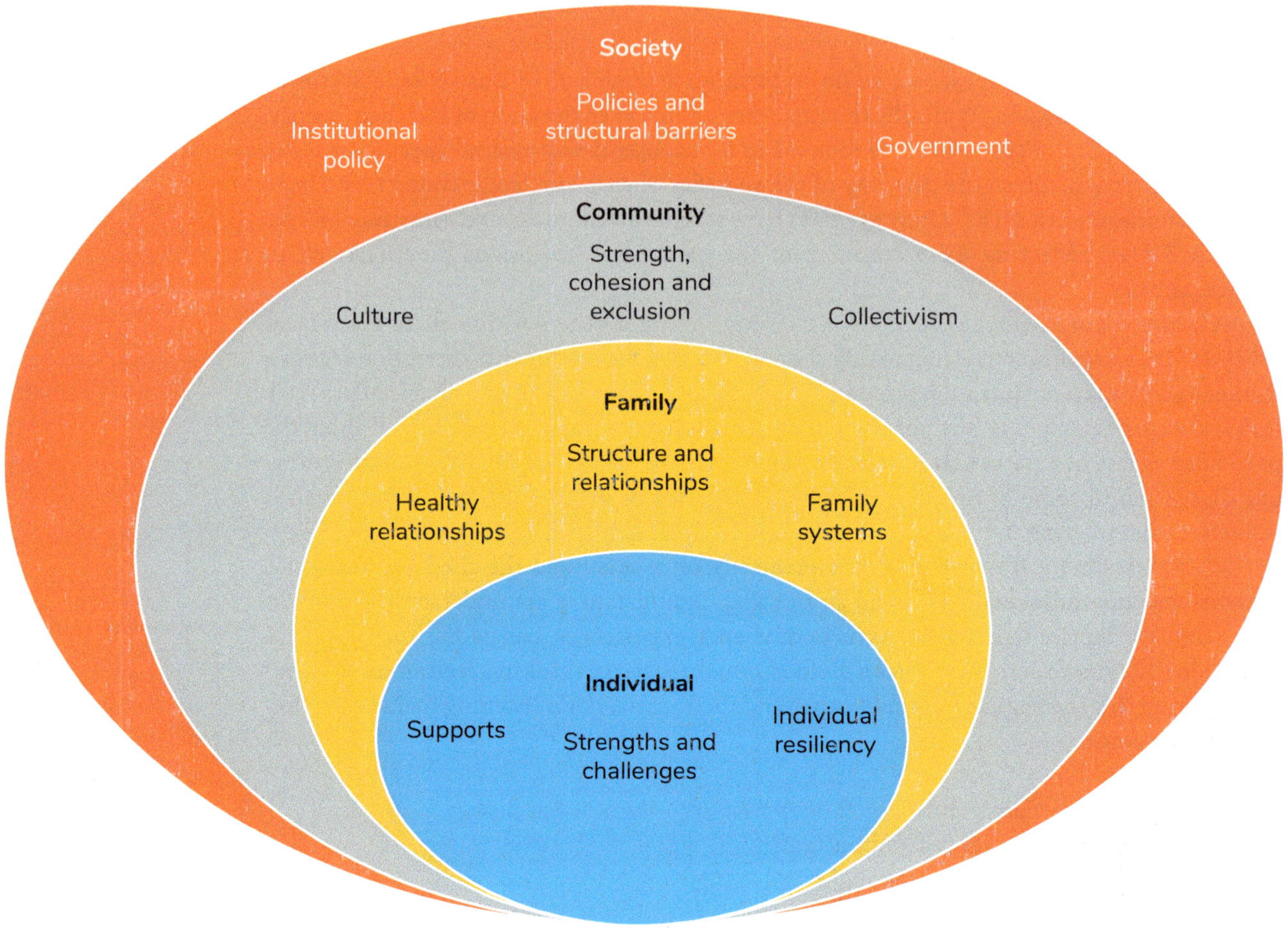

FIGURE 9.2 Dimensions of Social and Structural Contexts

This way of thinking about assessment focuses primarily on the individual and his/her inner world. Other assessments consider outer-world dimensions that impact these experiences, taking into account factors such as poverty and marginalization. Later chapters will elaborate on these themes in greater detail.

A Multi-Dimensional Assessment Framework

A multi-dimensional framework includes the other dimensions of individuals' lives: the social, structural, and cultural contexts. The ways in which the environment enhances or inhibits the person's coping become part of the assessment. Frameworks that assess behaviours, thoughts, and feelings place the individual at the centre of the construction of the problem, as opposed to frameworks that position the person as having been acted upon by external forces or circumstances. Assessment within human services involves inquiry about these external dimensions as much as about the client's internalizing of situations and events.

A multi-dimensional approach seeks to understand both the inner- and outer-world dimensions of a person's circumstances. The inner-world dimensions include the biological, psychological (thoughts and feelings), and spiritual dimensions. The outer-world dimensions include the relational, social, structural, and cultural dimensions. A broad, multi-dimensional assessment framework should include, then, each of these specific dimensions (Anglem & Maidment, 2004; Fook, 1993; Harms, 2005; Hepworth, Rooney, Dewberry-Rooney, Strom-Gottfried, & Larsen, 2017).

The difficulty with many of the more overarching practice approaches is that they position problem management entirely with the individual client. Human service workers focus on the client's problem and the environmental origins or contributors to these problems. Social work and the human services, therefore, take the additional step of listening to, assessing, and effecting change in outer-world issues, not just the inner-world dimensions of the client's problems. For this reason, human service work and social work have drawn on ecological (Bronfenbrenner, 1979; Germain, 1991) or multi-dimensional understandings of the person in his or her environment.

For example, the box below provides some key themes of a multi-dimensional approach described by Harms (2005).

BOX 9.4 Focus on Practice

A Multi-Dimensional Approach

Theme 1: An individual's inner world is multi-dimensional.

Each person can be thought of as having unique inner-world dimensions. Broadly speaking, these dimensions are biological, psychological, and spiritual.

Theme 2: The outer world or context in which individuals live is multi-dimensional.

Each of these inner-world dimensions of a person in turn influences, and is influenced by, the dimensions of the outer world—the physical, social, structural, and cultural contexts that shape daily experience.

Theme 3: Time is multi-dimensional.

Five dimensions of time—biological, biographical, historical/social, cyclical, and future—influence human behaviour and experience.

Theme 4: Human experience is multi-dimensional.

Human experience is a combination of an individual's unique developmental trajectory and unique life events. An understanding of both the more normative tasks of development and the non-normative tasks provides a more holistic understanding of a person's adaptive capacities and resources.

Theme 5: Adaptation is multi-dimensional.

Just as the causes of adversity are multi-dimensional, so, too, are the consequences—an understanding of the consequences of adversity for individuals, families, and communities needs to incorporate the possibilities of adaptation and maladaptation. This involves understanding notions of risk and protective factors, and notions of vulnerability and resilience. It also involves acknowledging who is making the assessment of adaptation.

Theme 6: Attempts to theorize human development and adaptation should be multi-dimensional.

Human experience, behaviour, and adaptation all can be understood from multiple theoretical viewpoints—theories of the inner world, theories of the outer world, and theories that attempt to bridge the two. Rather than suggesting that human service professionals do not have a firm theoretical base from which to work, a multi-dimensional approach acknowledges that there are many ways of understanding human experience.

Continued

The task is to discern how we reach understandings and to work towards as good a fit as possible between the identified issues and the possible human service responses.

Theme 7: Human service responses must be multi-dimensional.

Responses by human service professionals must be multi-dimensional, including practices, programs, and policies that incorporate prevention, intervention, and post-intervention strategies.

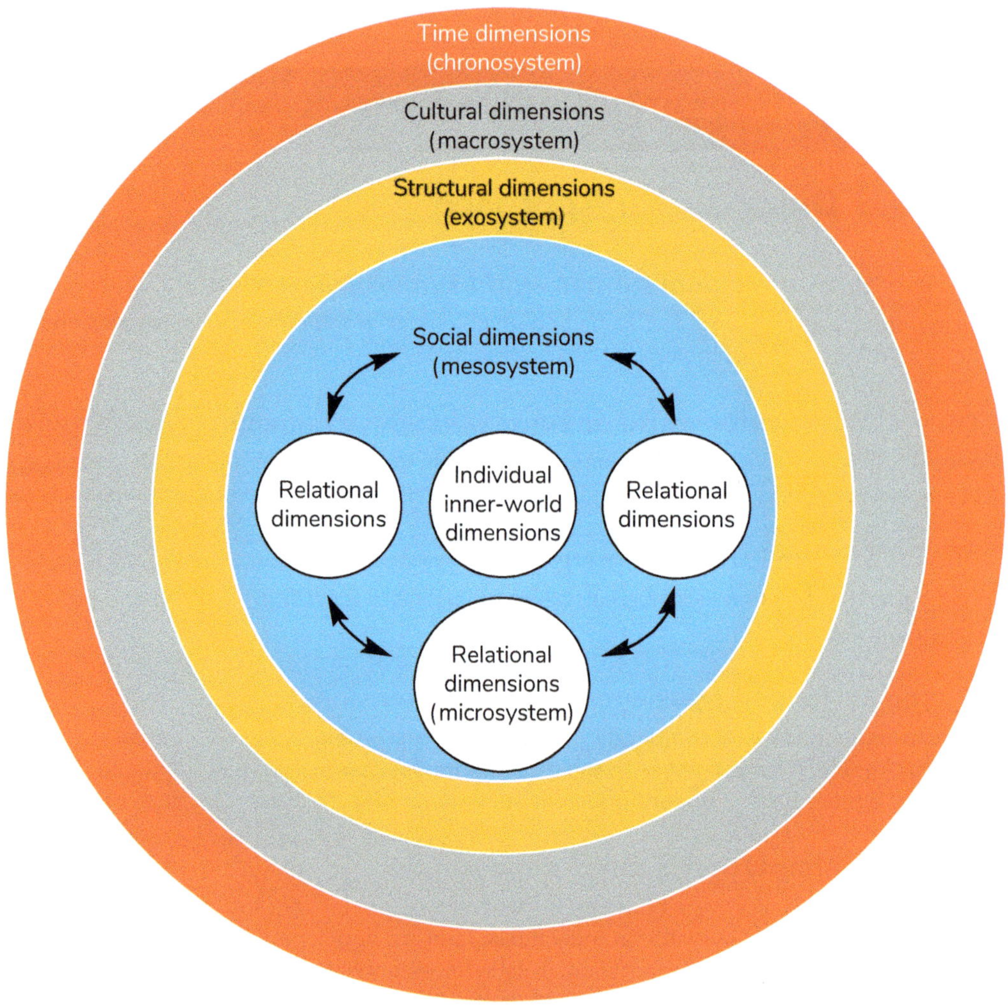

FIGURE 9.3 A Multi-Dimensional Approach

Source: Harms, L. 2005. Understanding Human Development: A Multidimensional Approach. South Melbourne: Oxford University Press.

Links to specific websites with assessment tools are provided at the end of this chapter. Examples will also appear in Appendix 2.

Assessing Sources of Stress and Vulnerability

Exploration of each of the dimensions in the box below includes an assessment of whether they are significant sources of stress and vulnerability or are significant sources of protection and resilience. In some instances, you may need to ask very direct, closed questions to establish an understanding. In others, you may develop your understanding from a more descriptive conversation, so that specific questions do not need to be asked. Each of these dimensions can become the focus of further exploration and intervention.

BOX 9.5 Focus on Practice

Exploration of the Client's Physical Dimensions

In what ways do the following dimensions impact a person's current circumstances and coping capacity?

- age
- sex
- family configuration
- general presentation and appearance
- general health or medical status—drug and alcohol use
- housing environment
- physical changes and their impact on well-being
- sources of physical stress
- physical coping strategies and resources

Depending on the circumstances, a range of other questions about specific dimensions may be relevant. Within the physical dimension, for example, specific assessment tools are available to assess drug and alcohol use and abuse or general health (Goldberg, 1978).

Assessing Psychological Function

Thousands of scales have been developed to assess a person's psychological functioning. For example, scales are available to measure intelligence; emotional intelligence; the impact of trauma, stress, and grief; and personality traits. *The Diagnostic and Statistical Manual of Mental Disorders* (APA, 2013) is a major resource, a collation of psychological assessment guidelines, used in many mental health settings (although some theorists and practitioners take a strong stance against this tool because of its misuse in practice and its shifting, ever-expanding view of what constitutes mental illness; see, e.g., Cech, 2015; Coggins, 2016; James & Gilliland, 2017). For any psychological phenomenon, a scale seems to be available.

BOX 9.6 Focus on Practice

Exploration of the Client's Psychological Dimensions

In what ways do the following dimensions impact a person's current circumstances and coping capacity?

- intellectual capacity
- language capacity

Continued

- self-image, self-esteem
- sense of agency and motivation
- mental health status
- subjective perceptions of the problem situation
- psychological changes and their impact on well-being
- sources of psychological stress
- psychological coping strategies and resources

Assessing Spiritual Dimensions

Similarly, spiritual dimensions of a person's life can be measured using a range of assessment tools, such as Fowler's faith development framework (Parker, 2006), as described below.

BOX 9.7 Focus on Practice

Exploration of the Client's Spiritual Dimensions

In what ways do the following dimensions impact a person's current circumstances and coping capacity?

- importance of spirituality
- spiritual practices
- importance of religion
- religious practices
- spiritual changes and their impact on well-being
- sources of spiritual stress
- spiritual coping strategies and resources

Assessing Social Networks

Many dimensions of a person's social network also can be analyzed, using a range of available tools.

BOX 9.8 Focus on Practice

Exploration of the Client's Social Dimensions

In what ways do the following dimensions impact a person's current circumstances and coping capacity?

- qualities of relational networks with partners and family
- qualities of social networks with neighbours, friends, colleagues, clubs, church groups, etc.

- perceived and received social support
- significant power relationships
- qualities of social roles the person engages in: occupation, education, schooling, university, or paid/unpaid work
- major family and life events and history
- sources of social stress
- relationships with social institutions (past or present)
- social changes and their impact on well-being
- sources of social stress
- social coping strategies and resources

A comprehensive assessment of a client's social dimensions or environment networks can be undertaken by talking through and drawing an eco-map, for example. In an eco-map, you document each relationship a person has with those in his/her immediate networks, according to its particular qualities or resources. You can also show the interconnections between people in a person's network. Each relationship can be illustrated by using different connecting lines, according to the legend in Figure 9.4.

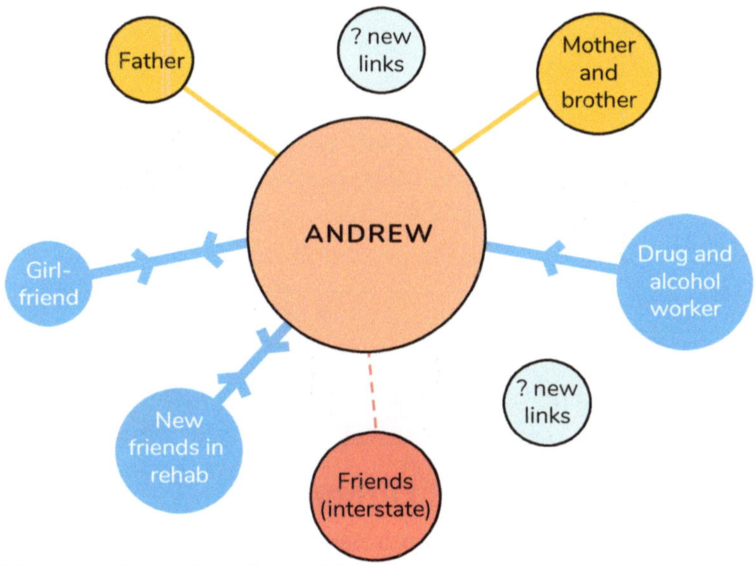

Fill in connections where they exist.

Indicate nature of connections with a descriptive word or by drawing different kinds of lines:

strong — tenuous - - - stressful

Draw arrows along lines to signify the flow of energy, resources, etc.
Identify significant people and fill in empty circles as needed.

FIGURE 9.4 Mapping a Client's Social Network Using an Eco-Map

Source: Harms, L. 2005. Understanding Human Development: A Multidimensional Approach. South Melbourne: Oxford University Press.

Assessing Structural and Cultural Dimensions

An eco-map can also identify workers in various organizations who may be contributing to a particular situation. In this sense, they are the front line of the structural dimension; that is, the broader systems that profoundly restrict a person's coping capacity, and, indeed, often create the difficulties in the first place. It is equally important to assess the structural and cultural dimensions of people's lives.

The assessment tools for the structural dimensions are used less in many organizations, and are often more the focus of discussion than of formal assessment.

Cultural assessment tools are also available and address a range of issues within this critical dimension. For example, the checklist of social dimensions (Fook, 1993) provides a way of reflecting on the dimensions not only of your social identity but also those that may be influencing your client's experience.

BOX 9.9 Focus on Practice

Exploration of the Client's Structural Dimensions

In what ways do the following dimensions impact a person's current circumstances and coping capacity?

- financial circumstances
- legal circumstances
- socio-economic status and roles
- political circumstances
- gender roles
- occupation and education level
- structural changes and their impact on well-being
- structural sources of stress
- structural resources

BOX 9.10 Focus on Practice

Exploration of the Client's Cultural Dimensions

In what ways do the following dimensions impact upon a person's current circumstances and coping capacity?

- culture and ethnicity
- culture and sexuality
- subculture or cultural minority status
- socially held beliefs and myths
- cultural changes and their impact on well-being

- cultural sources of stress
- cultural coping strategies and resources

Assessing Ability to Cope

A sound assessment should focus on the risks and on the strengths in a client's circumstances. Listening for strengths is paramount in any assessment process. While such a focus by no means diminishes the difficulties a person has been encountering and may be facing (Saleebey, 2017), your understanding of how someone is addressing or coping with other demands or similar demands is an extremely important evaluation to include in an overall view of how the person can change and adapt in regard to the main problem.

BOX 9.11 Focus on Practice

Unexpected Strengths

Many practitioners within prenatal care services have been concerned about women's non-attendance at clinics when substance abuse issues have been identified. However, a study (Tobin, 2005) of 23 women attending a major women's hospital, combined with a data analysis of 1,250 hospital records, found that

- contrary to popular opinion, less than half (47 per cent) of the women identified that a lifestyle preoccupation with drug and alcohol issues posed a barrier to attendance for pregnancy care; and
- the overall attendance rates for women with substance abuse issues . . . do not differ greatly from those without substance use issues. (p. 7)

These findings have enabled workers to rethink their understandings of women's efforts to attend prenatal care while they also are dealing with drug and alcohol issues.

BOX 9.12 Focus on Practice

Addiction Assessment Tools

The CAGE tool is widely used in emergency rooms because it is quick and simple to administer. CAGE is an acronym using keywords from each question as follows:

(a) Have you ever felt you should **C**ut down on your drinking?

(b) Have people **A**nnoyed you by criticizing your drinking?

(c) Have you ever felt **G**uilty about your drinking?

(d) **E**ye opener: Have you ever had a drink first thing in the morning to steady your nerves or get rid of a hangover?

A score of 2 or 3 on the CAGE is recommended as a cutoff for identifying individuals with alcohol-related problems.

Source: Adapted from http://counsellingresource.com

Davis (2006) provides an example of a self-assessment focused on relapse prevention/crisis plan adapted from a model created by Eric Macnaughton of the Canadian Mental Health Association:

> Signs that suggest I am doing well:
> Events or situations that triggered relapse in the past:
> Early warning signs that I experienced in the past:
> Effective ways that I can cope if I experience early warning signs:
> What early warning signs indicate that I need help from others:
> Who I would like to assist me (names):
> What I would like them to do:
>
> If in crisis:
>
> Ways I can manage stress, regain balance, or claim myself:
> People I can call and their phone numbers:
> Resources that I can use (agencies, support groups):
> Things that I or other people can do that I find helpful:
> Medications that have helped in the past:
> Medications that have not helped or that have caused an adverse reaction:
> Medications that I am currently on:
> (p. 228)

Specific questions, however, can be used to manipulate responses or they can also mean we miss out on critical information. In asking about "x" and not "y," we may then not realize that "y" is the problem. Being too specific can mean that, because we do not ask the "right" particular question, we do not establish what is going on or a particular detail of the circumstances. Again, using open-ended questions and clarifying responses further can help in avoiding some of these difficulties.

Additional assessment tools commonly used in addiction assessments are the Michigan Alcohol Screening Test (MAST) and Drug Abuse Screening Test (DAST). The MAST is a self-test consisting of 22 questions that may assist clients in becoming aware of their alcohol misuse. Similarly, the DAST is a self-test consisting of 20 questions that may assist clients is becoming aware of their drug misuse.

Types of Assessments

An assessment process can vary from a very brief discussion and assessment of needs or rights, through to a planned assessment period over a specified time period or number of sessions. For example, the Metta Youth Psychotherapy program (Harms & McDermott, 2003), which provides intensive psychotherapeutic support for at-risk young people for up to three years, has a four-session assessment period, at the end of which both the client and the worker discuss the continuation or cessation of therapy.

Assessments are often a part of client intake or referral for specialized services. Tools for assessment can include depression scales, anxiety scales, attention deficit hyperactivity disorder (ADHD), and other specific mental health disorders. This may involve a practitioner

© istock/Marizza

Try completing one of the self-assessment forms listed in this chapter or Appendix 2. What kinds of information and reflection are these exercises attempting to elicit from a client?

facilitating the initial assessment as part of determining the best plan of care for a client and the most appropriate referral.

Assessing Suicide Risk

See **Appendix 2** for examples of various assessment forms.

Davis (2006) points to an example of problematical suicide assessment; he states, "a study of a large Canadian community mental health program found that the forty-three documented completed suicides over a three-year period by clients of the program represented a rate twenty-five times higher than that seen in the general public" (p. 194). Davis notes that it is imperative that practitioners regularly consider clients' "thoughts and intentions concerning suicide, a process that involves assessment, documentation, and consultation with colleagues and supervisors" (p. 194). Risk factors for suicide completion can be categorized as follows:

1. *Vulnerable populations:* includes males, persons with a mental illness, youth, First Nations, the elderly, widowers, and those suffering from a painful, chronic, or terminal physical illness or condition.
2. *Historical factors:* previous attempts; history of suicide in the family or among friends; history of abuse or trauma; history of impulsivity; the proximity of anniversaries of significant events, such as the birthday of a child who was taken away.

You will learn more about suicide ideation and prevention in Chapter 10.

3. *Current risk factors:* current symptoms of mental illness, such as "command" hallucinations or delusions that support suicide; loss of job, social standing, or relationship (or anticipation of same); living alone or in isolation, recent death by suicide of another significant person; rigid "black-and-white" thinking; perfectionism, recent discharge following hospitalization for psychiatric reasons; use of substances that are depressive or disinhibiting (such as alcohol).
4. *Current thinking:* a sense of hopelessness; thoughts of suicide that are frequent, persistent, and specific; having a plan and a means to carry it out. (p. 195)

In Figure 9.5 James and Gilliand (2017) provide an assessment model to apply in crisis/risk situations. The seven steps are easy to remember, and offer workers a structured series of step to work through challenging situations.

What Interventions Are Used?

At the end of an assessment process, possible interventions typically are discussed. A "contract" is sometimes formally undertaken, in that there is agreement around the problem areas or difficulties, and the ways of addressing some or all of these issues. Typically, you will discuss

- the perceived areas of work for change;
- how that may be achieved;
- your mutual responsibilities and commitments as the worker and the client; and
- the time limits on your work together.

From this, a plan for intervention emerges. Interventions can address resources in the inner and/or outer worlds of the person. For example, inner-world interventions can help clients develop new ways of coping with behavioural or belief restrictions that they impose on themselves, or others impose on them. Intervention strategies include counselling, **psycho-education**, social support strategies, and group work. Outer-world interventions can help clients manage and change the structural restrictions in their worlds, and may involve very active worker action to bring this about with the client. Intervention strategies include resource provision, referral, liaison, advocacy, capacity building, group work, and community development.

How Do We Set the Goals for the Work?

Remember Mrs B.'s work with Nicole in Chapter 6 and their ability to reset the goals of their relationship.

Whereas the assessment process establishes the overall problem and strengths areas in a client's circumstances, and resource requirements, contracting and **goal setting** are important processes in establishing the priorities for intervention, both from the client and worker perspectives. That is, when you have explored with your client the key themes of their difficulties, priorities need to be set as areas for work. It is not possible to address everything at once, and a process of goal setting enables a plan to be developed around the tasks and timelines.

The goals for the kind of intervention need to be articulated and, ultimately, even if only in a small way, mutually satisfactory. In the following box, Burstow (1987, p. 21) recounts her own experience of encountering a therapist who worked in such a different way from what she wanted and needed in terms of intervention at a particular point in her life.

Assessment

Overarching and continuous throughout the crisis.
Evaluating the client's present situational crisis in terms of the client's coping ability, mobility, support systems needed, physical resources required, and degree of threat to self and others.
Making judgments as to type and kind of actions needed, based on the crisis worker's action continuum.

Tasks

Overarching Default Task: Ensuring Safety
Continuous assessment of how safe the client, others in the environment, and the worker are throughout the crisis, Putting in place and implementing procedures that will ensure the safety of all those involved in the crisis, including the crisis worker.

1. **Predispositioning/engaging/initiating contact.**
   Making initial positive contact with the client. Setting the stage for what the worker is going to do, what the client can expect from the worker, and how the worker will operate throughout the crisis.
2. **Exploring the problem.**
   Defining the problem as it currently manifests itself across the affective, behavioral. and cognitive domains of the individual. Exploring the intrapersonal, interpersonal, and systemic effects of the crisis as it operates in the current environment within which the person operates.
3. **Providing support.**
   Determining what kinds of support systems have worked in the past, what support systems are currently available, and what support systems will be needed. More specifically. determining how much the worker will need to function as the main support system during the crisis and indicating to clients how that will happen.
4. **Examining alternatives.**
   Considering immediate short-term options to de-escalate the crisis and defuse the situation. Examining the choices the client currently has available in a realistic and time-efficient manner; includes finding situational supports, installing coping mechanisms, and reframing thinking to be more positive and solution focused to generate achievable Short-term goals.
5. **Making plans.**
   Generating a short-term plan from the alternatives that are positive and doable, and translating into immediate action steps the client can comprehend, own, and implement.
6. **Obtaining commitment.**
   Obtaining a verbal or written commitment to a plan that can be comprehended, owned, and put in operation by the client.
7. **Follow-up.**
   Immediate, short-term follow-up by the worker to ensure that the plan is working and that the client and others are safe.

Crisis Worker's Action Continuum

Crisis worker is nondirective | Crisis worker is collaborative | Crisis worker is directive

(Threshold varies from client to client) | (Threshold varies from client to client)

Client is mobile | Client is partially mobile | Client is immobile

The crisis worker's level of action/involvement may be anywhere on the continuum according to a valid and realistic assessment of the client's level of mobility/immobility.

FIGURE 9.5 Model of Triage Assessment Form for Crisis Intervention

Source: James, R. K., and B. E. Gilliland. 2016. Crisis Intervention Strategies, 8th edn. Toronto: Nelson.

BOX 9.13 Focus on Practice

Mutual Goals

From a client's perspective, Brian said, "I was in the process of making a major move and found myself panic-stricken. The therapist I sought help from was client-centred. He was very empathic, very kind, very respectful, but he gave me nothing on which to hold. He offered no clue about what I might do in a situation that demanded that I act almost immediately and in which I was paralyzed. I emerged from the session more terrified than ever and by now markedly suicidal. Eventually, I did what I should have done in the first place. I sought help from someone who would offer me what was missing in myself, who half-gave-me, half-helped-me-find some preliminary sense of direction. I sought help, that is, from a helper who did not ask me to be an equal at a point where I clearly could not be."

Reflecting on this experience, Brian suggests that the therapist "failed" because

1. He did not acknowledge or understand how vulnerable Brian was.
2. He assumed that everyone at all times was equally able to get their needs fulfilled, as long as the counsellor is empathic.
3. He did not take an active leadership role when such a role was required.

One possible explanation for why Brian's situation occurred was that the client and the worker did not explicitly discuss the goals of the work. An opportunity to discuss goals together is vital.

Goal setting occurs in a number of ways, depending on the context and the theoretical orientation of the worker. Goal setting is also influenced profoundly by the client's engagement in the change process. Some general views on the nature of the goal(s) that are set are expressed by Marsh and Doel (2005):

> In common with the selected problems, the chosen goal should be one which is feasible and desirable for the person to achieve within the agreed time limit, relatively specific, something he or she feels motivated about, and a clearly understood link between the problem and how the goal will alleviate it. (p. 117)

Breaking this process of goal setting down further, an emphasis is often placed on developing SMART goals (Marsh & Doel, 2005, p. 36), where the well-known acronym SMART stands for specific, manageable, achievable, realistic, and timely.

1. *Specific*—Goals should be focused on particular issues, not generalized states of being, for example. This may involve transforming the following statements, where the worker is talking with his client about his goals in moving in with his new partner and her two children from another relationship:

Worker:	What would your goal be with these kids?
Client:	I really want to be a good dad to these kids [goal statement 1].
Worker:	How will you know when you're being a good dad?
Client:	I'd be doing things that would be natural, like taking them to the park that's just around the corner, and those things that I know

> we already share. But I'd also be able to be clear with them when they start fooling around and not having to worry that they're "not mine" [goal statement 2].

The first goal statement is global and it may be hard to know when it has been achieved. Notice that the second goal statement is much more specific to certain situations, so the client will know when he has, by his criteria, met his goals.

2. *Manageable*—Notice that the goals set in the above scenario are manageable goals, in that they involve some small steps about the kinds of changes he wants to see. Many people set unmanageable goals, in a number of different ways. They may take too long, or require resources that are unattainable, for example. Goals need to be manageable in the sense that adequate resources are available—be they time, energy, condition, or personal resources (Hobfoll, Ennis, & Kay, 2000).
3. *Achievable*—The client in this scenario can probably easily achieve the goals; he has specified two ways in which he can make immediate, tangible changes in his interactions. Many people set unachievable goals that are incompatible with where they are at. The goal may be too ambitious or may require too much of a major change in too many dimensions of the person's life. For women leaving situations of violence, a major barrier is often the prospect of leaving so many dimensions of their lives—including, sometimes, children—to ensure their own safety.
4. *Realistic*—This client is talking about realistic goals; visiting a park is probably possible in a local community during the course of a week. Realistically, he recognizes that differences in parenting style may be a source of difficulty in the new family arrangement. He is not setting ambitious goals, for example, by promising a trip to Disneyland or that he is always going to be able to maintain his commitment without fail.
5. *Timely*—His goals seem to be appropriate in terms of timing in that he is anticipating moving into a new situation. If he was presenting in the midst of a high-conflict situation around parenting issues, these goals may not be so timely. They may be too late! The timeliness of goals is an important determinant of their success.

BOX 9.14 Practice Questions

1. Think of a time when you have wanted to change a specific dimension of your life. What was your goal?
2. In retrospect, would you describe it as a SMART goal, using the definition above?
3. What were the challenges or barriers to making the change in the first place?
4. How did you go about trying to make the change?
5. Did it work? Why or why not?
6. What would you do differently if you wanted to make that change again?
7. Try to apply the SMART model to a current situation you would like to change.

The Egan model is a very structured way of working and, in some settings, can be applied fully. Processes like these enable us to talk through goals with clients or to even write them down on paper or on a whiteboard or flip chart so that they are clear and can be easily remembered.

BOX 9.15 Focus on Practice

THE EGAN MODEL

Egan's problem-management and opportunity-development model has been used internationally as a framework for an interview or series of counselling sessions with clients. It is based on a process of goal setting, and includes the following questions within each stage of the model.

Stage 1—Problem clarification and ownership

What's going on? What are the problems, issues, concerns, or undeveloped opportunities I should be working on?

- Help clients to tell their story.
- Help clients break through blind spots.
- Help clients choose the right problems/opportunities to work on.

Stage 2—Goal setting and commitment to goals

What solutions make sense for me? What do I need or want?

- Help clients use imagination to spell out possibilities for the future.
- Help clients choose realistic and challenging goals that will equal real solutions (agenda for change).
- Help clients find incentives—what am I willing to pay for what I want?

Stage 3—Strategies for accomplishing goals

What do I have to do to get to what I want?

- Help client see possible actions—many ways to achieve goals.
- Help client choose best fit.
- Help client to craft a plan.

Source: Egan, G. (2007). *The skilled helper: A problem-management and opportunity-development approach to helping* (8th edn). Pacific Grove: Brooks/Cole.

One way of further opening up the goal-setting process is through brainstorming. Brainstorming involves either verbally or in writing proposing every possible solution or course of action even vaguely relevant to the current situation. The important feature of a brainstorm is that it is done without any censoring of ideas. Brainstorming enables the opening up of new possibilities. In some situations, the lack of new coping strategies is part of the problem. As a discussion between the client and worker, brainstorming enables a pooling of resources, without any pressure towards a particular option at that point in time.

Worker: Let's think about what the possibilities are here, without putting any limits on our imaginations at this point. What have you thought about doing?

Client: I'm stuck. I can't think of anything.

Worker: OK, that's one option. To stay stuck, to keep things as they are!

Client: [laughs] I hadn't thought about that! No way, I couldn't bear that. You know, when I felt more on top of things, I did half wonder about going back to school and finishing that.

Worker: And what would you then do?
Client: Well, I'd be able to work, you know. Get a job. Get out of the house, get some money. Have some time out from my kid, who drives me nuts sometimes.

Already in this scenario, six different goals have been identified as possibilities, all of which would need some further exploration:

1. not doing anything.
2. going back to school.
3. seeking a job.
4. seeking a job after a further educational experience.
5. getting out of the house—either through employment or through other options like community involvement.
6. time out from the children.

"Not changing" is a goal to explore equally with a client, when so much of the emphasis is on changing. It provides a safe place to explore why change really is so often necessary, and emphasizes that any change beyond staying the same brings new challenges and possibly new territory.

Some goal setting will require negotiation and possibly compromise, where the goals with clients are not mutually agreeable. Some actions will be imposed on clients, as a result of court orders, and in these situations the goals that need to be met are not always mutually agreeable. Working through the SMART dimensions of goals, however, can go a long way towards finding mutually agreeable grounds for continuing the work together.

Chapter Summary

In this chapter, the assessment process has been explored, highlighting its usefulness in focusing the client's story on intervention and action. Importance was placed on understanding the purpose of an assessment and in what situations an assessment is appropriate. A multi-dimensional assessment framework was presented as a very broad way of understanding a client's situation and resources. The risks inherent in assessment have also been examined, particularly in relation to perpetuating fixed and assumptive assessments of people and their circumstances. The chapter briefly outlined some of the interventions human service workers use in relation to both outer- and inner-world change for clients. The chapter concluded with an exploration of the process of goal setting, often used in practice to set the agenda for action and intervention.

Questions for Analysis

1. What have you learned from this chapter about
    - assessment processes?
    - interventions?
    - goal setting?

2. What are the dimensions you find relatively straightforward to ask about in an assessment process and what do you find more difficult? Why?
3. What are the risks in an assessment process?
4. How often do you consciously use goal-setting processes to work through issues? What impact do you think this has on your practice?

Group Activity

In groups of three or four, read the following assessment and discuss what you think the next steps are for Mr Jordan.

After several falls, Mr Jordan's family doctor has referred him for in-home services from Home Support Services. As part of the doctor's initial assessment, you as the hospital social worker were called to meet with Mr Jordan. The purpose of your involvement is to complete an assessment of Mr Jordan's physical, social, and psychological strengths, and arrange for access to relevant services within the community.

Initial assessment

Mr Jordan is an elderly white male who resides in a two-storey house 30 minutes from town. He is currently 81 years old and has lived in the same community for all of his adult life. He has a high school education, and has worked mainly in skilled labour jobs, including construction, pulp mills, and forestry. Mr Jordan speaks very happily of his career. He sporadically drives to the grocery store, approximately 30 minutes from his home, but avoids driving in the rain or dark. Mr Jordan was married for over 50 years; his wife suddenly died approximately 5 years ago. He repeatedly speaks about how he misses her and feels quite lonely without her in his life. The client struggles with a number of chronic medical conditions including Type 2 diabetes, hypertension, arthritis, and gout. He states that he smoked cigarettes for 40 years, but quit the year before his wife died. In addition, he was hospitalized in the 1990s for a hernia and required a four-week stay in hospital. Over the past several months, Mr Jordan has been experiencing recurrent falls, which he blames on his "clumsiness." His interests include fishing, carving, and sitting outside when his arthritis is not flared. Overall, Mr Jordan seems comfortable and relatively outgoing. Although he was not intoxicated, several beer cans were noticed on the kitchen counter.

With regard to social supports, Mr Jordan lives alone, but his neighbour, Betty, a 73-year-old woman, visits him two to three times per week. Betty stops by to visit Mr Jordan to check on him and sometimes they have lunch together. Occasionally, Betty will drive Mr Jordan to town to buy groceries and pick up medications if he is unable to drive. He has a son, James, who works in construction and lives in Port Alberni, about four hours away from Mr Jordan. James is not married and has no children. Mr Jordan states that his son stops by once per month and phones him every Sunday evening.

Mr Jordan manages to take care of himself in regard to most daily living needs, although he does have Meals on Wheels deliver him lunch three times per week. He still cooks his breakfast each morning. After talking about the client's diet, it was identified that Mr Jordan seems to eat a lot of meat and dairy products and fewer fruits and vegetables. He did not seem concerned about falling. The client also described his desire to not ever be admitted to an extended care facility regardless of how sick he became.

1. What do you think are critical points in this initial assessment and why?
2. What strengths are present?
3. What concerns might you have?
4. What would you like to have more detail about?
5. Is there information missing?
6. What steps would you take to begin creating a plan for Mr Jordan, and why?
7. What are the priorities in your plan?
8. What are the barriers to your plan?
9. How will you proceed?

Recommended Readings

Anglem, J., & Maidment, J. (2004). Introduction to assessment. In J. Maidment & R. Egan (Eds.), *Practice skills in social work and welfare: More than just common sense* (pp. 112–26). Crows Nest: Allen & Unwin.

Bitter, J.R. (2009). *Theory and practice of family therapy and counseling*. Belmont, CA: Brooks/Cole.

Brownlee, K., Graham, J., & Dimond, P. (1997). Strategies for community assessment. In K. Brownlee, R. Delaney, & J. Graham (Eds.), *Strategies for northern social work practice* (pp. 113–28). Thunder Bay, ON: Lakehead University Centre for Northern Studies.

Corey, G. (2008). *Theory and practice of counselling and psychotherapy* (8th ed.). Pacific Grove, CA: Brooks/Cole.

Davis, S. (2013). *Community mental health in Canada, revised and expanded edition: Theory, policy, and practice*. Vancouver, BC: University of British Columbia Press.

Egan, G. (2013). *The skilled helper: A problem-management and opportunity-development approach to helping* (10th ed.). Belmont, CA: Brooks/Cole Cengage Learning.

Fischer, B., Russell, C., Murphy, Y., & Kurdyak, P. (2015). Prescription opioids, abuse and public health in Canada: Is fentanyl the new centre of the opioid crisis? *Parmacoepidemiology & Drug Safety, 24*, 1334–6.

Harris, J., & White, V. (2018). *A dictionary of social work and social care* (2nd ed.). Oxford, Oxon: Oxford University Press.

Hepworth, D.R., Rooney, R.H., & Larsen J.A. (2017). *Direct social work practice: Theory and skills* (10th ed.). Boston, MA: Cengage Learning.

Miller, L. (2012). *Counselling skills for social work* (2nd ed.). Thousand Oaks, CA: Sage.

Mussel, B., Cardiff, K., & White, J. (2004). *The mental health and wellbeing of Aboriginal children and youth: Guidance for new approaches and services.* Report prepared for the British Columbia Ministry for Children and Family Development, Victoria, BC.

Regehr, C., & Glancy, G. (2014). *Mental health social work practice in Canada* (2nd ed.). Toronto, ON: Oxford University Press.

Trotter, C. 2006. *Working with involuntary clients: A guide to practice*. Thousand Oaks, CA: Sage.

Internet Resources

American Psychiatric Association and the DSM-5
www.psych.org
www.appi.org/products/dsm-manual-of-mental-disorders

Canadian Centre on Substance Use and Addiction
www.ccdus.ca/Eng/Pages/default.aspx

Canadian Resource Centre for Victims of Crime
www.crcvc.ca

Health Canada, Mental Health–Depression
www.hc-sc.gc.ca/hl-vs/iyh-vsv/diseases-maladies/depression-eng.php

National Native Alcohol and Drug Abuse Program
www.canada.ca/en/indigenous-services-canada/services/addictions-treatment-first-nations-inuit.html

PTSD Association of Canada
www.ptsdassociation.com

Trauma-Informed Practice Guide
http://bccewh.bc.ca/wp-content/uploads/2012/05/2013_TIP-Guide.pdf

World Health Organization, International Classification of Diseases-11
www.who.int/classifications/icd/en

10 Assessing Risk Situations

Learning Goals

- Understand the dimensions of situations of conflict.
- Review your safety and appropriate responses when you are threatened by others.
- Learn to use smoothing skills for difficult situations.
- Learn the practical considerations for outreach work.
- Understanding risk and confidentiality.

Working with Conflict

In Chapter 4, we looked at the concept of your "use of self." The focus in that discussion was primarily on how you engage as a worker in empathic and supportive work. For many workers, however, the work is characterized by frequent or occasional incidents of physical and/or verbal abuse. You need to respond to these situations with some additional priorities, using some different communication skills.

It is important for practitioners to become familiar with the safety procedures of their workplace and/or agencies with which they work that require an on-site presence on a regular basis, such as prisons. The Canadian Centre for Occupational Health and Safety (CCOHS) has a detailed list of what falls under violence in the workplace. The CCOHS (2019) includes actions from other employees and/or clients that include incidents of verbal bullying or threats, physical or psychological abuse, and whether the act occurs on or off the worksite. Working with the public is at the top of the list factors that may increase exposure to incidents of work-related violence. Specifically, social work practitioners and health care service providers (for example, this would include hospital social workers) are listed in the top three at increased risk for violence. The CCOHS also highlights that the time of day you are working (night), time of year, and geographic location should be considered as added levels of potential risk requiring assessment.

Here are some questions to consider:

1. What is your agency's policy for working with potentially aggressive or violent clients?
2. Does the agency have a safety committee?
3. What specific steps are in place to address a potential incident?
4. Is there an alarm system, or how do you gain assistance?
5. Are the numbers for police/security posted?
6. Do you have experience working with potentially aggressive or violent clients?
7. If not, how do you know you are prepared should an incident arise?

To this point, the examples we have looked at have been interventions where a relatively positive engagement is possible, even if not in the initial stages of working together. Below, Joanna describes one such practice experience where initial engagement seems to be progressing relatively smoothly.

BOX 10.1 Focus on Practice

Joanna Works with Conflict

I was a counsellor working in an addictions recovery centre. I was assigned a client with a history of violence who spoke English as a second language. The client was charged with assault and was agitated about his pending court appearance. He asked to meet with me and I was concerned with his visible level of anger. I decided to see him in my office but informed him the door needed to remain open. We talked through his concerns for some time, and as he spoke, his anger would increase, his face became red, and sweat ran down the side of his face. Gradually, as I continued to remain calm, he became less distressed.

1. How do you think Joanna approached this conversation to help reduce her client's agitation?
2. What concerns would you have?
3. How would you feel about seeing this client?
4. What do you think you would do in this type of situation?

Recall that in Chapter 7 we discussed forms of questioning. Which interview style would Joanna's scenario require?

At this stage, Joanna and her client have managed to engage together in conversation. The client seemed to be experiencing a highly agitated physical and emotional state, influenced not only by his stressful circumstances but likely through the communication difficulties and cognitive difficulties created by his difficulty understanding English. Some of the skills Joanna may have used at this time include the following:

- Speaking slowly and calmly, avoiding getting caught up in the emotion of her client's agitation.
- Speaking clearly and in plain English so as not to compound her client's disempowerment through use of his second language.
- Emphasizing an alliance or joint problem-solving relationship, alleviating the isolation that the client may have been experiencing—for example, focusing on statements like, "Let's see what we can sort out together."

- Containing the emotion, through not mirroring the distress and agitation of the client but mirroring a calmer state that may reduce the client's agitation; and, in some instances, maintaining a distance so that the client does not feel enclosed or trapped, and maintaining steady eye contact to help engage him in a different mood state.
- Establishing an appropriate and structured agenda for the conversation. If someone is feeling overwhelmed by circumstances, remember the goal-setting tasks outlined in the previous chapter, where goals are SMART. In this instance, a very small goal may need to be set in discussion to establish a focus among the chaos.
- Using repetition: the "broken record" technique encourages the use of one message until it finally is "heard" by the other person. In Joanna's situation, she may say something like, "Let's just sit over here and talk." And she would repeat that one statement calmly until that can happen. In some situations, this technique could cause the situation to escalate, but in others it helps restore focus and agreement on the next step in the conversation.

Joanna's approach addressed worker safety (keeping the door open, and remaining calm) and facilitated client safety, by reassuring the client that his concerns were being heard and assisting the client in returning to a more grounded state through purposeful communication strategies.

Refer to Chapter 9, and review the steps to SMART, and apply them to Joanna's situation.

All of these skills are examples of **smoothing skills**. They aim to reduce agitation and the escalation of emotions that can make communication difficult to sustain. Joanna also took steps to ensure her physical safety and, potentially, that of her client. It is not always appropriate to move into private spaces if you have concerns for yourself and/or your client, and so Joanna's responses were active and assertive. Despite all of Joanna's efforts, further communication escalated into a more violent interaction. We will return to this situation in the next section for further discussion.

The situation to this point, however, highlights the differences between passive, aggressive, and assertive responses. Workers need well-developed assertion skills, particularly in response to aggressive encounters. The advantage is that assertion,

> unlike aggression, respects the other person's rights and dignity through the use of non-hostile verbal content and verbal attributes. Assertion is expected to produce strong relationships and relatively few negative emotions, whereas aggression is predicted to result in a strained, emotionally charged relationship. (Rakos, 2006, p. 348)

The non-verbal communication skills discussed in Chapter 2 could be helpful in challenging situations, and if applied incorrectly have the potential to add to a challenging situation.

Rakos identifies four behavioural components of what he terms "conflict assertion" (pp. 350–1) Related to the above situation, these components include the following:

- the content of the conversation—that is, what Joanna says in response to her client's distress and agitation
- paralinguistic elements or how the communication sounds to the other person—that is, does Joanna speak loudly, warmly, or gently?
- non-verbal behaviours or how people appear to be physically reacting—does Joanna disregard her client's personal space or step back and allow him some space?
- social interaction skills—Rakos identifies "the timing, initiation, persistence and stimulus control/skills that enhance the impact of the verbal behaviour" (p. 351); what does Joanna choose to do by way of focus in the conversation, for example?

TABLE 10.1 Dealing with Criticism

If it is accurate	Accept it.
If it is clearly wrong	Disagree and affirm yourself.
If it is unclear	Clarify it.
If it is about you rather than your behaviour	Accept the behavioural part if it is true, but reject the personal label.
If it is nagging, too frequent, or destructive; if you are stunned, overwhelmed, or confused by the criticism	Seek security through law and order.

Source: Adapted from Kotzman, A. 1995. Listen to Me, Listen to You. Camberwell: ACER.

Assertive feedback is characterized, therefore, by these elements:

- "I" statements—as the worker, you clearly own your feelings, beliefs, or thoughts. The other person can disagree with your view.
- behaviour-focused statements—you provide feedback or criticism of the behaviour, not the person. Behaviour can be changed.
- seeking a response back from the person—through asking, for example, "What do you think?"

Other strategies can be used to deal with criticism and feedback that is directed towards you, as indicated in Table 10.1.

In managing conflict, it is important to consider what the best strategy may be. If the situation is too confronting or unexpected, it may need to be dropped and dealt with at a later time. Opportunities for direct conversation about a conflict normally should be offered; however, one way of de-escalating tension is to deprive people of opportunities for open, albeit difficult, communication. Clients have often experienced major disadvantage and oppression in prior circumstances, and the opportunity for them to be heard and for a solution to be worked towards is critical. Intense emotions can be compounded through a lack of resolution mechanisms. Mediation, in some instances, can facilitate a resolution.

Threatening Behaviour

As mentioned above, Joanna's situation with her client escalated further. The scenario continues here.

BOX 10.2 Focus on Practice

Joanna's Next Step in Work with a Client

Joanna reflects on the next steps in her work with her client:

> I spoke with the client at length to make sure I fully understood his concerns. We discussed his frustration regarding his language barrier, which made him feel misunderstood. During our conversation, he stated the word "assault," and as I tried to clarify what he was saying, he started to

become agitated and threatening before storming off. The situation was becoming unsafe, so I decided to remove myself to avoid it from escalating any further.

This example reinforces how factors such as limited language skills can inhibit clear communication, and the importance of assessing potential risk from both verbal and non-verbal cues prior to and during work with distressed and agitated clients.

1. What is your immediate reaction to the situation Joanna and her client were in?
2. What do you think you would do in a similar situation?
3. What cross-cultural issues could be influencing this situation?

Joanna's example is one where finding common ground was not possible. Joanna's safety, the client's safety, and the safety of others in the environment became the most immediate issues of concern. In reviewing the situation, the following conclusions might be made:

- It was an unsafe situation to stay in and physical evacuation was needed. In some instances, police or guards may need to be called.
- The client's agitation was indicating something very important about what was going on for him—the disempowerment, frustration, and anger he was experiencing.
- He had a low frustration tolerance—in this case, as a result of feeling unable to successfully communicate his story, and he felt unsafe and vulnerable.

In this instance, the client returned later and smashed furniture in the reception area, and the police were called to manage the situation.

People considering social work as a profession should realize that human service workers often may face circumstances of **violence**, stalking, or threatening behaviours (Ogloff, 2006; Warren, 2006). Some key principles or skills for potentially threatening situations include the following:

- Maintain a high alertness for your own safety, both physical and emotional, and trusting any of your own intuitions about a lack of safety, even if not immediately manifest in a situation; the situation may rapidly become physically unsafe and you may need help or you may need to leave.
- Follow your agency's report and accountability requirements, including *always* alerting someone in your organization as to your whereabouts.
- Use high levels of proactive planning, e.g., use supervision as a preventive strategy for your safety and well-being.

Community Outreach

Practitioners who work in community settings may find themselves isolated and detached from a formal agency environment. In outreach practice it is important for the worker to take time to ensure their environment meets personal safety needs. Prior to departing from your agency, a worker should review the agencies safety protocols for working at a distance.

Have you previously lived or worked in a remote community? What additional steps would human service workers need to take to ensure safe travel to and from their work?

Safety begins with ensuring the worker arrives safely at their destination. Consider the following elements:

- car maintenance (access to road side assistance; road side safety provisions)
- time of year (winter road conditions, construction delays, traffic)
- access to services (how remote, cellphone service, or emergency service if required).

Once a worker has arrived, consider these:

- parking (on the street to avoid potentially being blocked in and ensuring an easy exit)
- environment (who else may be in the home, what potential hazards are in the house)
- exit strategies (what is the process for leaving should you feel unsafe).

The following example highlights the importance of safety.

BOX 10.3 Focus on Practice

Working Outside the Supervised Office

A worker travelled away from her agency for community outreach two days per week. Her outreach office was located in the basement of a designated professional building in a remote community. One day, a client came in very angry at someone else and became violent, threatening to hit someone in the reception area while pounding his fist on the counter. In that moment, the worker realized she was in the basement and the only way out was blocked by the angry client. In addition, she was alone.

What are the important questions to ask yourself when you are working outside a supervised agency setting?

Risk and Confidentiality

The Canadian Association of Social Workers' *Guidelines for Ethical Practice* (2005) remind social workers,

> Social workers who have reason to believe that the client intends to harm him/herself are expected to exercise professional judgement regarding their need to take action consistent with their provincial/territorial legislation, standards of practice, and workplace policies. Social workers may in this instance take action to prevent client self-harm without the informed consent of the client. In deciding whether to break confidentiality, social workers are guided by the imminence of self-harm, the presence of a mental health condition, and prevailing professional standards and practices (Standard 1.6.3)

In thinking about the worker's situations of risk, it is important to revisit the issue of confidentiality. Remembering Mark's situation and his expressed thoughts of suicide (Chapter 4) and considering Joanna's client who was threatening violence and became violent, some additional considerations come into play in confidentiality. It may be necessary to breach the confidentiality standards we usual adhere to with low- or no-risk clients when the risk level escalates. Within the ethical guidelines of various human service professions, this "duty to warn" is identified as follows:

> Take a few minutes to review the CASW Code of Ethics and Guidelines for Ethical Practice regarding risk: https://www.casw-acts.ca/en/Code-of-Ethics

- Social workers uphold the right of society to impose limitations on the self-determination of individuals, when such limitations protect individuals from self-harm and from harming others, and
- Social workers uphold the right of every person to be free from violence and threat of violence. (CASW, 2005, p. 5)

In becoming aware of a public safety risk, social workers, in this instance, "when disclosure is necessary to prevent serious, foreseeable and imminent harm to a client or others" (p. 7).

At times when you have concerns about a client's safety, or the safety of others because of what the client is saying, a careful consideration of whether to breach confidentiality is required. If possible, this breach should always occur with the support of a supervisor or manager, and, if it seems safe to do so, the client can be advised of your intended actions. For example, you might have a conversation with Mark about his suicidal thoughts and feelings and then discuss with him your concerns for his safety before contracting together on a safety plan. The safety plan may involve discussions with other significant people in his environment, or it may involve a hospital crisis assessment and treatment team if the danger of self-harm or suicide is high.

Some of the myths surrounding suicide include the following:

Myth 1: Suicide occurs without warning.
Myth 2: People who talk about suicide are not serious about killing themselves.
Myth 3: Bringing up the topic gives people the idea.
Myth 4: People who try suicide are just trying to get attention.
Myth 5: The best response to a threat is to say, "Go ahead." (Shebib, 2000; James & Gilliland, 2017)

Suicidal ideation can emerge as a result of extended exposure to trauma, loss, or feelings of ongoing failure. Suicidal ideation can also occur as the result of a sudden event that overwhelms an individual to the extent they feel unable to understand and cope with what has occurred. The *Diagnostic and Statistical Manual of Mental Disorders* (DSM-5) contains categories for discussion regarding both suicidal behaviour disorder and self-injury.

Facilitating a suicide assessment involves first evaluating if the individual is at acute suicide risk, chronic suicide risk, or the potential for risk-taking that results in self-harming behaviours (Regehr & Glancy, 2014).

A client categorized as at acute suicide risk is experiencing a profound wish to die. Clients in this state often describe the precipitating event as life shattering and unchangeable or mobilizing in a manner they are unable to recover from. In acute situations, symptoms can escalate quickly but are often transitory, leaving opportunity for the situation and the client's emotional state to shift with appropriate intervention (Regehr & Glancy, 2014).

Chronic suicide risk is most commonly present in clients presenting with persistent mental health disorders or individuals facing a lifelong illness that impacts their quality of life in ways they describe as unending. When assessing risk in this type of situation, it is important to recognize that the client's state is less impulsive (as you might see in acute suicide risk situations). Often, due to the length of time they have endured their situation, the decision made tends to be more in response to not having control over a permanent diagnosis and a lack of ability to change their circumstance (Regehr & Glancy, 2014).

If suicidal thinking is suspected, bringing up the topic of suicide has proven to relieve the client of the stress of hiding his or her intent. Practitioners should take specialized training to competently assess if a client is suicidal. A suicide assessment includes the following questions/considerations:

1. Talk about suicide: Are you thinking of hurting yourself? Or, Are you having thoughts of suicide? This eases into the conversation and opens communication regarding

potential suicidal thoughts or self-harm. Clients tend seek clarification indicating the direction the conversation will proceed.

2. Past attempts: Have you ever hurt yourself before? When? What did you do? What happened? Ask questions that clarify any services provided and what was helpful or not helpful.
3. Physical and mental status: Does the client have a current mental health diagnosis or are they currently taking any medication? If yes, what medication are they taking?
4. Presence of a viable plan: If the client confirms they are having thoughts of suicide, or self-harm, it is important to ask if they have thought about how they intend to harm themselves.
5. A means to kill one's self: Explore means by asking about access to weapons, or medication. Ask specific questions. How many pills do you have?
6. Efforts to put affairs in order: Has the client described details in their plan that indicate notifying someone, planning for children, or ways of sending a goodbye (letters to family).
7. Substance misuse: Does the client have a history of addition or are they currently engaged in self-medicating behaviours?
8. Personal losses: Has the client lost anyone to suicide? Have there been any recent losses for the client?

The third category, self-harm or self-injury, is an action taken by a client resulting in some form of harm that is not life threatening. Self-harming behaviour such as cutting is often described by clients as a means to achieve relief from the psychological distress.

As a final step in assessing risk, it is important to remember for workers to conclude their assessment by inquiring what the client thinks they will do once they leave your office. Asking about future plans can indicate the potential immediacy of risk and assist workers with decision making and safety planning (who to involve). Regehr and Glancy (2014) offer guidelines in Table 10.2.

If a worker determines a client is actively suicidal, you should consider the *Code of Ethics* and follow the appropriate guidelines. Social workers are obligated to report suspected harm to self or others. Some general points to consider in decision making are as follows:

- Have you explained the limits to confidentiality clearly to your client at the onset of your work together?
- What level of risk is the client displaying resulting from your risk assessment? (moderate risk, high risk?)
- What process does the *Code of Ethics* state to follow in these cases?
- Consult with your immediate supervisor to review the situation and your thoughts on the appropriate next steps.
- Involve additional support if required (for example, police or ambulance).

Chapter Summary

In this chapter, we have looked at some of the main strategies for dealing with high-risk situations. These strategies are not prescriptions for success. Rather, they provide some points of departure for thinking about what to do in certain situations; all have been found to be

TABLE 10.2 Assessment of Suicide Risk

Static Risk Factors	Demographic considerations	• Gender (males are at higher risk) • Age (highest risk for youth between 15 and 24, followed by men over 65) • Upper or lower socio-economic group • Unemployed or retired • Single, widowed, or divorced • Social isolation	Increasing Risk ↓
	Past psychiatric history	• The person and his or her family – Affective disorders have 15 per cent mortality by suicide – Among suicides, 45 to 70 per cent have affective disorders	
Modifiable Risk Factors	Alcohol use	• Alcoholics have 15 per cent eventual mortality rate by suicide • Suicide attempts are preceded by alcohol intake in 50 per cent of men and 50 per cent of women	
	Present mental status	• See Folstein mini-mental status exam in Chapter 9 • Severe depression • Hallucinations that command the person to act in a harmful manner	
	Precipitating events	• Recent loss or separation • Is there a clear precipitant? • Can there be some resolution to the problem?	
	Resources	• Limited personal resources • Limited resources within the person's network • No community resources	
Intent	Method or plan	• Abstractly considered suicide • Has given thought to method • Has prepared for suicide – saving pills, purchased gun • Level of intent to die • Lethality of method – drug overdose common in Canada (1/3 suicides, 2/3 attempts)	
	Future plans	• No plans to do something other than suicide today • No longer-term plans	

Source: Regehr, C., and Clancy, G. Mental Health Social Work Practice in Canada, 2nd edn. Toronto: Oxford University Press.

effective in situations in the past. The potential for risk is present in human service work and it is important for workers to understand the various levels of risk that may occur in their particular work setting and how you respond to potential violence, anger, or incidents of threat.

The risk situations of suicidal behaviour, threatening behaviour, and conflict have been explored here only very briefly, and you are encouraged to expand your reading on appropriate supervision and awareness in practice in relation to these experiences. Risk cannot be eliminated in the work that we do—people in stressful situations often respond unpredictably, and that applies to ourselves as much as our clients. Good ongoing support and supervision are two ways of working preventively, but they are also critical buffers in the aftermath of high-risk encounters. Risk also highlights the importance of reviewing agency policies regarding safety and what the processes are should a risk situation arise.

Questions for Analysis

1. What have you learned about assessing risk situations—specifically, the topics of violence, threatening behaviour, suicide, and self-harm? Work through your ideas with another student and discuss areas you want to learn more about.
2. What are some of the personal and professional dilemmas that such risk situations raise for you? For example, do you have any personal values or cultural beliefs that may impact your practice regarding the topics in question one?
3. What are some of the essential skills required in dealing with risk situations?
4. Reflect on situations of conflict or risk that you have been in and on the ways you responded. Do you respond well in crisis situations? If not, what will you do if you find yourself in a crisis with a client?
5. What further training do you require to work with clients who present risk? How will you obtain this added knowledge to ensure you are prepared in practice?

Group Activity

In a small group of three or four, brainstorm some of the structural aspects of violence, threatening behaviour, suicide, and self-harm, and how they may present in casework with clients (e.g., oppression, poverty, or systemic barriers). Then answer the following questions:

- What did your group conclude?
- What is your role in attempting to address some of the aspects your group identified?
- How does this link to anti-oppressive practice?

Recommended Readings

Brownlee, K., & Graham, J.R. (Eds.). (2005). *Violence in the family: Social work readings and research from northern and rural Canada*. Toronto, ON: Canadian Scholars' Press.

Canadian Women's Foundation. (2016). The facts about violence against women. Retrieved from www.canadianwomen.org/facts-about-violence

Cutcliffe, J. (2005). Toward an understanding of suicide in First Nation Canadians. *Journal of Crisis Intervention and Suicide Prevention, 26*(3), 141–5.

Gigerenzer, G. (2014). *Risk savvy: How to make good decisions*. New York, NY: Penguin.

Laming, C. (2006). *A constructivist approach to challenging men's violence against women*. Melbourne: University of Melbourne Press.

Morley, C. (2004). Conducting risk assessments. In J. Maidment & R. Egan (Eds.), *Practice skills in social work and welfare: More than just common sense* (pp. 127–45). Crows Nest: Allen & Unwin.

Ogloff, J. (2006). Advances in violence risk assessment. *InPsych*, 28(5), 12–16.

Shebib, B. (2017). *Choices: Interviewing and counselling skills for Canadians* (6th ed.). Toronto, ON: Pearson.

Sicora, A. (2017). *Reflective practice and learning from mistakes in social work*. Bristol: Policy Press.

Sinha, A., & Kozlowski, A. (2013). The structure of Aboriginal child welfare in Canada. *The International Indigenous Policy Journal*, 4(2). Retrieved from https://ir.lib.uwo.ca/iipj/vol4/iss2/2

Taylor, B.J. (2017). *Decision making, assessment and risk in social work* (3rd ed.). London: Sage.

Trotter, C. (2006). *Working with involuntary clients: A guide to practice*. Thousand Oaks, CA: Sage.

Internet Resources

Canadian Association for Suicide Prevention
www.suicideprevention.ca

Canadian Mental Health Association
https://cmha.ca

Canadian Child Welfare Research Portal
http://cwrp.ca

CAMH Mental Illness and Addiction Index
www.camh.ca/en/health-info/mental-illness-and-addiction-index

Ending Violence Association of Canada
http://endingviolencecanada.org

Department of Justice, Get Help with Family Violence
www.justice.gc.ca/eng/cj-jp/fv-vf/help-aide.html

PART FOUR

Applying the Skills: Focusing the Intervention

In this next part of the book, we explore briefly some of the specific tasks and skills of human service practice.

As you may recall, Chapter 9 identified human service interventions that target change within the inner and/or outer worlds of people. Change strategies that focus on people's inner worlds—strategies of counselling, psycho-education, social support, and group work—can help clients develop new ways of coping with behavioural or belief restrictions that they impose on themselves or that others impose on them. Change strategies that focus on people's outer worlds—strategies of resource provision, referral, liaison, advocacy, capacity-building, group work, and community development—can help clients manage and change the structural restrictions in their worlds, and may involve very active worker intervention to bring about changes with the client.

Each theoretical approach has a long tradition that informs its current understandings and uses of skills. It is beyond the scope of this book to explore the developmental processes that inform that tradition, but resources are provided at the end of each chapter for you to follow up with your own reading on these topics. The aim here is to provide you with an introduction to some of the skills used in practice.

The emphasis throughout these next four chapters is on how these skills can be applied in different settings. Some workers adopt a "purist" theoretical approach; that is, the worker self-identifies as a psychodynamic worker or as a feminist worker. Most workers, however, incorporate a range of skills into their practice—drawn from a range of theoretical perspectives—using a theoretical base. Skills are presented in relation to their particular theoretical paradigms rather than under the design of a single, overall approach. The aim of these four chapters is to illustrate how to choose which skills will positively impact the work you do.

PART ONE Framing the Relationship

- the purpose of human service work
- your value base, professional ethics, and regulatory guidelines in Canada
- your theoretical and factual knowledge.

PART TWO Forming the Relationship

- your use of self
- your organizational context
- your ongoing support and professional development needs
- meeting the people involved
- opening the communication
- active listening and working with silence
- listening empathically
- using self-disclosure.

PART THREE Focusing the Communication

- establishing the story
- forming an assessment
- goal setting.

PART FOUR Focusing the Intervention

- drawing on theoretical perspectives
- doing the work.

11 Task-Centred and Crisis-Intervention Skills

Learning Goals

- Identify the core skills of task-centred and crisis-intervention approaches, particularly in relation to the establishment of the relationship between a worker and client and specific interventions.
- Understand the strengths and limitations of these approaches.
- Understand crisis intervention.
- Apply a model of crisis intervention.

Task-Centred and Crisis-Intervention Approaches

Task-centred and crisis-intervention approaches do not fit so easily into one dominant paradigm and cannot be described as "pure" theories. They are, however, important approaches in practice, and these are included here as a demonstration of more practitioner-led and practitioner-developed theoretical frameworks currently in use.

Crisis-intervention theories arose from work with people during the immediate crisis time of particular critical incidents. Lindemann's (1944) study of grief, for example, identifies that typically, a four- to six-week period following major losses or stressors occurs during which people's usual functioning is significantly reduced, requiring particular supports throughout this change in functioning, both emotional and practical. One of the major emphases of crisis intervention is on assisting people to manage their initial extreme emotional responses, and to return to a more balanced cognitive and emotional state (Caplan, 1990; Granot, 1996). Crisis-intervention approaches are often about initially quite directive and/or assertive outreach, supporting people to make decisions and to vent emotion, while over time these reactions resolve (James and Gilliland, 2017).

A study of family members of a patient in the intensive care unit at the Alfred Hospital, for example, showed that family members were experiencing very high levels of post-traumatic stress symptoms (Harms, Rowe, & Suss, 2006). The implications of this finding are profound for the family's capacity to process the information they receive from medical staff and to make decisions on behalf of the patient. One of the major approaches of social work in this setting is to help people to become grounded again through tasks shifting them back into cognitive and practical activities that will help to mediate or settle some of their emotional responses. Emotional containment and support are also key considerations. As Trevithick (2005) notes, the only social work theory developed by practitioners is the task-centred approach (Marsh & Doel, 2005), where the methodology is more about the doing than about theorizing behaviour in particular ways. More recently, Doel and Marsh (2017) encourage social workers to apply a task-centered model, stating, "Task-centered social work provides both a broad framework and detailed practice guide which bridges the care and control divide" (p. v). It assists the worker and client towards highlighting "what works" and addresses straightforwardly the power inherent in professional authority, promoting anti-oppressive practice (Doel & Marsh, 2017).

The power inherent in professional authority is an aspect workers should reflect on carefully. Refer to Chapter 3 and the discussion on anti-oppressive practice.

Task-centred and crisis intervention approaches rely on the rapid establishment of empathy and trust with clients during what is typically a short period of intervention (Healy, 2005; Doel & Marsh, 2017). They apply to interventions in both the inner and outer worlds, but view the restoration or the introduction of resources in the outer world as major facilitators of change and adaptation. They also are based on strengths perspectives.

Task-centred approaches are sometimes criticized for seeming to prioritize task- and goal-setting over the client–worker relationship. As a human service worker, what steps could you take to build and maintain a positive client relationship within a task-centred practice?

Core Skills of Task-Centred Practice

The Ahmed family arrived at your agency seeking assistance with their multiple stressors. Depending on what agency the Ahmed family chooses, the focus of the work will differ. Some agencies are focused on outer-world or practical tasks associated with living in a new country, whereas others are focused on inner-world tasks of adapting to life in a new culture.

BOX 11.1 Focus on Practice

Immediate Needs

Two years ago the Ahmed family came to Canada from Somalia. They have five children—three attending school, a three-year-old, and a one-year-old infant. They are living in shared housing with another family, all of whom have been granted refugee status. They have been able to connect with the local school. They miss many aspects of life back home, specifically their rural village, traditional foods, and less extreme changes in seasons. They have been able to build connections with some other members of the Somali community. They feel emotionally torn about their migration. They have left behind family and many friends. They are learning English but find it very difficult to fit into Canadian culture. Being unemployed, they are also finding it difficult to afford the expenses of daily life.

Mrs Ahmed has found their situation much easier than her husband. She enjoys living in a shared house and sharing the cooking and domestic duties with the other family. Mr Ahmed is frustrated by his difficulties finding work. He sees himself as solely responsible for earning the family's income, and feels deep shame that he has not been able to do this so far. He has become very withdrawn and depressed.

Source: Adapted from Harms (2005, pp. 68–9).

Establishing and Sustaining the Relationship

From a task-centred perspective, your engagement with your client is established through the focus on task- and goal-setting. Given the multiple concerns for this family, this may need to occur in a culturally empathetic space for exploring the needs and goals, with adequate time and space for a full exploration of their circumstances (Marsh & Doel, 2005; Doel & Marsh, 2017). In order to engage in problem solving, which is the main goal of task-centred practice, a worker typically engages using emotional warmth, optimism about finding solutions, and, in some situations, considerable **assertiveness**. Engagement is with the details of the person's circumstances and the possibilities for solutions.

A major criticism of task-centred approaches is that they fail to acknowledge the importance of rapport in the client–worker relationship. This imbalance is considered a misrepresentation of the centrality of relationship to positive change, as Marsh and Doel argue (2005; Doel & Marsh, 2017), with the relationship emerging

> from the doing, rather than the doing arising from the relationship. We believe this mirrors what happens in our everyday lives, just as a complete stranger can feel like a lifelong friend if you happen to find yourselves mutually dependent in a short, intense crisis. (2005, p. 115)

Nevertheless, the task-centred relationship is seen primarily as an active and "doing" relationship, in contrast to some of the other approaches described in the next few chapters. In this way, the knowledge of potential resources you bring to this interaction is just as important as your interpersonal engagement skills.

Specific Interventions

Task-centred practice has evolved from a more pragmatic approach to human service delivery. It is a time-limited, contracted, and highly structured approach, and therein rests both its strengths and limitations. Interventions focus on "doing"—on activities, either within the context of the contact itself or outside, as "homework" (2005, p. 38).

The skills of task-centred practice relate to the Task Planning and Implementation Sequence (TPIS), first outlined by Reid and Epstein (2005, p. 78; Tolson, Reid, & Garvin, 2003). As seen below, once the client's circumstances have been explored, seven steps are followed, drawing on the exploration and goal-setting skills we have looked at in previous chapters. Using the example of the Ahmed family, task-centred practice proceeds as follows.

BOX 11.2 Focus on Practice

The Seven Steps of Task-Centred Practice

1. Task Selection

Drawing on the probing, paraphrasing, and summarizing skills discussed in Chapters 7 and 8, you work with the Ahmeds to identify a key task to work on—you ask the question "What do you think you might be able to do about this issue?" This question then begins a brainstorming exercise to find possible solutions. In this instance, the solution could be to connect Mrs Ahmed with a local food bank and to address Mr Ahmed's isolation and lack of income possibilities, linking him with more prosperous members of the community who are willing to help other newcomers to get started.

2. Task Agreement

Talking with the Ahmeds about a number of possible goals, you then discuss each goal to arrive at one task that you all think will be the most achievable.

3. Planning Specifics of Implementation

An implementation plan is then discussed—"how, who, where, when, and why" are often important questions to explore during this phase.

4. Establishing Incentives and Rationale

In this phase of exploration, you look together at why the change should occur—what are the motivations, and why is it necessary?

5. Anticipating Obstacles

In this exploration, you turn the focus from those listed above to look at all the potential barriers to the successful achievement of the goal. Both inner-world and outer-world barriers are important to explore. This is about exploring the "what if" questions (Marsh & Doel, 2005, p. 78).

6. Simulated and Guided Practice

Exploring a process thoroughly is important—the technique of role-playing prepares us to put into practice new skills and helps us to experience some of the potential new emotions we may experience in a situation. We can learn how we might react to a number of different dimensions in an experience.

7. Task Review

A further seventh step might happen in another session: task review. Review and evaluation are critical in a task-centred approach. What worked and what did not work? Why? It enables a review of goals and whether or not they were SMART goals.

Healy (2005, pp. 113–15) outlines eight practice principles related to this structured approach, which translate further into the skills you could use. Each of these is applied to understanding the Ahmeds' situation.

> It is important for the worker to be aware of their role. See Chapter 4 for more on self in practice.

1. *Seek mutual clarity with service users.* Explore the story extensively, and come to understand the story fully from the Ahmeds' perspective and your own using the skills we have looked at in Chapters 7 and 8. Shared concerns would be raised and a particular emphasis on cultural empathy would be required. A cultural consultant may be a very useful ally for the Ahmeds and also for you in this situation, so that solutions are culturally sensitive and appropriate.
2. *Aim for small achievements rather than large changes.* With the Ahmeds, so many needs are being expressed by them that it could feel overwhelming both to them and to you as a worker. Achieving small steps helps to build a sense of efficacy and accomplishment (Bandura et al., 2003), thereby building the confidence and capacity to continue to make changes.
3. *Focus on the "here and now."* A major difference from other approaches is that the problem is identified as in the present, not in the past, or even the future, as other approaches might locate issues. Change is brought about in the present to enhance current coping and functioning, and to build coping capacity for the future. In this sense, a way of coping is being taught or developed further with the client.
4. *Promote collaboration between the worker and service users.* You can establish a sense of collaboration with your client through sharing the solution-focused process, which uses collaborative language such as "'we" or "when we have done that." The solution becomes shared so that a sense of isolation can be somewhat reduced for people in overwhelming situations. The collaboration, however, must be authentic and viable, rather than becoming a series of false promises.
5. *Build client capacities for action.* As Healy (2005) notes, "While acknowledging that the problems may have their origins in other 'causes' such as 'deeper' psychological problems or unjust structural conditions" (p. 114), these are not the focus of task-centred interventions. The focus is on dealing with an identified problem and targeting immediate practical or psychological resources to solve them. Capacities for action emerge from the provision and receipt of resources (Hobfoll, Ennis, & Kay, 2000).
6. *Plan on brevity.* Task-centred approaches are short-term and time-limited approaches, not extending beyond 15 sessions. You may even focus on task-centred work within the

context of a single session with a client. The Ahmed family would be advised of this in your initial contact and a close scrutiny of these time limits would be maintained once the goals for the work have been set. This approach is consistent with a strengths perspective, which sees people as capable of influencing their own lives and functioning adequately when adequate resources are in place.

7. & 8. *Promote systematic and structured approaches to intervention, and adopt a scientific approach to practice evaluation.* These last two principles highlight that the model outlined above gives you and your clients a very clear map of how you will work together and what you will aim to achieve. The Ahmeds are empowered in the process as they are informed of the process. Healy (2005) identifies the **mutual clarity** and the "external accountability" of applying a standardized practice model as two of the approach's major strengths. In contrast to the less structured and arguably less measurable interventions outlined in the following chapters, this approach uses and provides ongoing evidence for practice.

In summary, the skills relied on extensively in task-centred practice are

We explore the process of making a referral in Chapter 15.

- exploring, probing, and clarifying skills;
- contracting and problem-solving skills;
- goal-setting skills for teaching, advising, and directing clients to resources in ways that are task-focused, strengths-focused, and solution-focused; and
- resourcing and referral skills.

Core Skills of Crisis-Intervention Practice

Recall the Willis family, presented in Chapter 9, who are experiencing difficulties after Mr Willis suffered a fall and had to be hospitalized, where the staff recognized and diagnosed his dementia and suggested a radical change in living arrangements. As Mrs Willis is facing an immediate **crisis**, task-centred skills could be successfully used, but crisis-intervention skills may be more appropriate.

Crisis-intervention skills are based more on an understanding of the mood and cognitive state of the person at the time of the intervention, which means the immediate context or state of the person determines the way of thinking and intervening at that time. As a result of this focus, your intervention is about enhancing the immediate functioning of people affected by the crisis, both practically and emotionally.

A crisis is typically defined as "Crisis in a clinical context refers to an acute emotional upset arising from situational, developmental, or sociocultural sources, and results in a temporary inability to cope by means of one's usual problem solving devices" (Hoff, Hallisey, & Hoff, 2009, p. 4). This understanding is vital, as Caplan (1990) and others have argued that crisis presents an opportunity for the development of new coping skills, as well as the threat of loss.

Davis (2006) notes, "a more common method of psychiatric crisis response in Canada is the mobile crisis team, which generally is a seven-day-a-week service with some after hours capacity that provides brief crisis intervention through telephone contact or home visits" (p. 141). Davis describes the team as including trained nurses and clinicians who have access to an on-call doctor.

> Examples of mobile crisis teams include: Vancouver's Mental Health Emergency Services, which offers a crisis line that clients and other citizens may access and which

> can provide home visits with a nurse, sometimes with a plainclothes police officer as back-up; the police officer provides more security for evening calls in higher-crime areas and can also invoke a provision of the Mental Health Act whereby persons can be taken to hospital for an assessment. (p. 141)

James and Gilliland (2017) offer a basic crisis intervention model, as outlined in Figure 9.5 (Model of Triage Assessment Form for Crisis Intervention), that focuses on "ongoing [assessment] throughout the crisis" (p. 59) in terms of such factors as the client's coping ability and threat factors, so that the crisis worker can judge the "type of action needed" throughout the course of the crisis.

The James and Gilliland (2017) model of crisis intervention is meant to offer crisis workers an integrated problem-solving model that is simple to follow and adaptable for any crisis situation. It can be particularly helpful to workers new to crisis work with seven steps that assist workers with working through the main areas of a crisis response.

Establishing and Sustaining the Relationship

Like task-centred approaches, crisis-intervention approaches do not typically focus on understanding the nature of the relationship between the worker and the client to the extent that other approaches do. It is fundamental to the success of the work, however, and therefore is still regarded as being the "glue" in the relationship and important to the process of stabilization.

Intense and strong bonds often form during crisis from a sense of the shared experience and from (as others argue) the psychological regression and dependence that can occur in the midst of a crisis. The regression and dependence, however, are viewed as temporary, resolving typically within weeks of a particular crisis.

Early in the crisis period, particularly in disaster situations, the worker fosters a highly directive and assertive role, expressing warmth and a highly empathic engagement. Over time, as individuals resume their pre-crisis levels of functioning, the worker is no longer as directive or assertive.

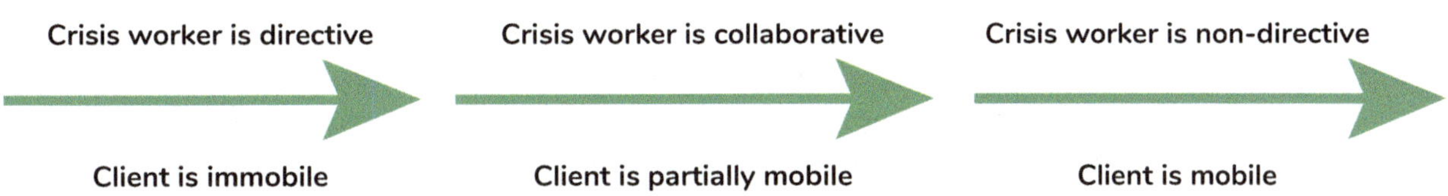

FIGURE 11.1 Crisis Worker Model

Source: Adapted from James, R. K., and B. E. Gilliland. 2016. Crisis Intervention Strategies, 8th edn. Toronto: Nelson.

BOX 11.3 Focus on Practice

Confronting a Crisis

You have been assigned to work with the Stewart family. Mr and Mrs Stewart, who both hold professional positions, have one child, Melissa (age 16). Melissa, who had been struggling with addiction issues, recently disclosed to her parents that she is questioning her sexual orientation and has been seeking counselling

Continued

supports. This resulted in Mr and Mrs Stewart throwing Melissa out of the house. That evening, distressed by her parents' reaction, Melissa went drinking with a friend and ended up being critically injured in a car accident. Both Mr and Mrs Stewart feel responsible but refuse to see Melissa.

1. How might you address the immediate crisis state of Mr and Mrs Stewart?
2. How would you address the immediate crisis state of Melissa?
3. How would you establish a working relationship?
4. Following a crisis-model approach, what might you identify as immediate concerns in assessing this situation?
5. In order, how would you approach this crisis situation?

Specific Interventions

Crisis-intervention skills support people, helping them to cope in the immediate aftermath of traumatic or stressful situations. James and Gilliland (2017) describe an individual's response to crisis as "a perception or experiencing of an event or situation as an intolerable difficulty that exceeds the person's current resources and coping mechanisms" (p. 8). Based on understandings of how people cope in crises, they focus on an immediate restoration of cognitive and emotional control, as well as on resuming normal functioning as quickly as possible, through the re-engagement with daily tasks and defusing of mood and emotion. Some of the key skills required by the worker include the following.

1. *A rapid assessment of functioning.* As a worker, you need to assess very quickly how well someone is functioning. This is important because often in the midst of a crisis serious decisions need to be made. If someone is unable to make decisions clearly, then different strategies may be required. Many formal tools are available for this assessment. For example, the Triage Assessment Form: Crisis Intervention (Myer et al., as described in Myer & Conte, 2006, pp. 968–70), which establishes a person's functioning in relation to three domains: the affective or emotional domain, the behavioural domain, and the cognitive domain, assessing each of domain on a rating scale from 1 to 10. This test helps to determine levels of functioning, and changes over time. James and Gilliland (2017) offer an ABCs of assessing a crisis situation. The worker begins with assessing the client's affective state (A), looking for impairment that causes symptoms of withdrawal or detachment. The behavioural state (B) consists of acting out, what steps are being taken to address a crisis, or any of the psychomotor activities as a result of the crisis. Psychomotor activities can be complex and may include jumpiness or involuntary twitches such as leg or arm movement, as well as more long-term activities such as irritability, poor sleep patterns, insomnia, levels of depression/anxiety, and, in acute cases, psychosis. The third area focuses on the client's cognitive state (C), assessing thinking patterns, ability to organize, or level of response (p. 60).
2. *Reassurance of safety.* While Mrs Willis is in a safe situation, in another circumstance—such as that of Melissa—you may be working with people who have been confronted with life-threatening situations, such as sexual assaults, road accidents, or violent incidents. In trauma situations, reassurance of basic physical safety is most critical and the highest priority (Herman, 1992). In addition to ensuring client safety, it is important

for the crisis worker to ensure their own personal safety in all crisis work. Some aspects to consider include: Where is the crisis? Are you alone in the response? Who knows your plan? If the response is outreach-based, what assistance might you require once you are on scene? Who else is involved in the crisis? Are there known potential dangers, mental health concerns, or other aspects that increase risk?

3. *Maintaining a needs and rights focus.* Despite the above comments about coping capacity, decisions are often made *for* people during a time of crisis when they knew nothing of what was decided for them. Other people affected by crisis can remain empowered to make decisions for themselves and others. Overlooking when people have not been allowed to act in ways they wanted to or might have been able to during a crisis has been a major criticism in many debriefing efforts (Crumpton-Cook, 1996). Crisis intervention skills focus on empowering the affected person to make necessary decisions in a supported environment. This involves exploration of what may have worked in the past for the client, and how they wish to move forward from the crisis.
4. *Validation of feelings.* As distinct from the task-centred approach, crisis intervention focuses on the intense emotional state someone may be experiencing. Mrs Willis may be experiencing a wide range of emotions. Similarly, Mr and Mrs Stewart are experiencing a mixture of intense emotions stemming not only from their daughter's disclosures but from their multi-level feelings of responsibility for the accident. Melissa's emotions, if she is conscious and not too heavily sedated, may range from confusion to anger to pain in her feelings of abandonment over her parents' reaction. A crisis intervention encourages the **ventilation** or expression of all these emotions, if that is consonant with her physical condition. In this sense, it is connected with psychodynamic approaches, with the cathartic release of all emotions in all their complexity—the first step in being able to consciously control them. Listening and supporting—through probing, reflecting, and paraphrasing—is important. The listening is characterized by validating all emotions. While a cognitive behavioural approach may then move on to challenge some of these feelings, assessing them as irrational or rational thoughts or emotions, crisis-intervention approaches see this non-judgmental listening as the first step in dealing with the disequilibrium in emotions and thinking that crises create.

   The term "**containment**" is used frequently in relation to the ventilation of feelings and the skill of the worker who is supporting the client so that the emotions are experienced without overwhelming the person. The term originates from psychodynamic understandings, so the skills of containment will be discussed in Chapter 12.
5. *Information and resource provision.* Mrs Willis has been confronted with a lot of new information. Not only will she need to support her husband in his recovery from his fractures, but she also admits she knows nothing about dementia or of the processes involved in moving her husband to new accommodation. She has been confronted with a range of new emotions and is finding it hard to cope with their disorientating impact. Overwhelming feelings can be observed in the Stewart family, although not to the extent that they are willing to see their daughter. Here, the crisis worker begins to formulate a plan that includes education the client requires to regain their pre-crisis state.

   Crisis-intervention strategies are "immediate, active and directive interventions such as education, clarification, and reassurance about the normative, expectable reactions to trauma" (Gelman & Mirabito, 2005, p. 481) or crisis. Your knowledge of crisis and trauma, and the expectable immediate and longer-term reactions, is drawn on at this time. It may involve you making a normalizing statement like the following (apply this statement to both the Willis and Stewart family examples):

> You said you're feeling really strange, as if it's all happening around you, but you're not part of this. You may find that over the next few days, these feelings come and go, and then pass. This is a normal reaction to the distressing information you've been given.

With these skills, you are providing a psycho-educational base for your clients to understand themselves in their world. This approach is different from a more supportive or reactive approach that might be used in other situations. Here, you are actively drawing on your knowledge base to provide resources for your client to draw on.

6. *Direct influence*. In addition to the more active stance outlined in the previous section, in some instances you may use directive or influencing skills (Walsh, 2006). The person may not be able to make decisions because of the overwhelming nature of the circumstances. For example, after the conversation with the doctors about Mr Willis's newly diagnosed dementia, Mrs Willis may not be able think clearly about whether she should go home, contact their children, or stay with him. In this instance, a worker might be quite directive about suggesting a plan if no priority seems to be emerging:

> How about we go and make the phone call to your children and see what they would like to do? If they decide to come in, you can wait here with your husband and meet them. If they can't come in now, we can think about how you will get home and what you might do tomorrow.

This set of suggestions sets some limits around what Mrs Willis needs to think about in the midst of her crisis. They do not take away any of her rights or disempower her because the response to these suggestions will be driven by what she wants to do. However, the suggestions contain (limit) her options to make it easier for her to come to a decision in a heighten emotional state that is clouding her ability to think clearly.

Maslow's hierarchy of needs was presented in **Chapter 4**.

In other situations, you might make some suggestions about what she could do if she is unable to make a decision. Remembering Maslow's hierarchy of needs is important in this kind of work—people in crisis often need the basics attended to, such as shelter, food, clothing, and communication. For example, Mrs Willis may forget that she hasn't eaten since dinner last night, and she may need support in ensuring these basic needs can be met.

As you can learn from the above example, the skills you employ sometimes are assertive and directive skills because people's usual coping capacities are disrupted in life crises. A crisis-intervention approach acknowledges that crises are both threats and opportunities because new coping strategies can be introduced when usual coping strategies do not work, so growth and development may occur even in severely stressed circumstances (Caplan, 1990; Maslow, 2013; Poindexter, 1997).

In the previous chapter, we examined strategies for dealing with risks the worker encounters. Another type of risk—or crisis—is that of physical harm to the client. The Department of Justice has several tools for assessing risk specific to violent relationships and, while geared towards correctional workers, the questions are applicable to social work practice when assessing risk. One of these tools is the Aid to Safety Assessment Planning (ASAP), which is currently being used in New Brunswick and British Columbia collaboratively between Victim Services and criminal justice personnel. The ASAP focuses on identifying risk from the victim's perspective and assists the worker in the following five-step protocol:

1. Gather the information.
2. Identify the presence and relevance of abuser and safety support factors.
3. Develop risk scenarios.
4. Work with the person (usually a woman) on her safety plan.
5. Note priority actions.

Strengths and Limitations of Task-Centred and Crisis-Intervention Skills

The skills outlined in this chapter have emerged relatively recently in human services work practice in recognition of people's immediate reactions to circumstances of trauma and crisis. In using these skills, you are aiming to provide resources to people to help them cope with immediate problems and to find active solutions for them. These skills are less pathologizing of people's coping capacities. They encourage people to develop or regain a sense of control and empowerment as quickly as possible. The client's engagement with a supportive and encouraging worker can be a vital step, providing an ally and a resource through times of particular difficulty.

The skills within a task-centred approach are primarily task-focused, whereas crisis-intervention skills are both task- and emotion-focused strategies. Many critics fault task-centred approaches in relation to what is regarded as their conformity with a neo-liberal political agenda. As Webb (2006) states,

> The danger with adhering to this kind of perspective is that it can result in crude unreflective instrumentalism, in the bid to water things down to tasks, to dilute difficulty, to make things so simple that they no longer carry any depth of meaning or value for service users. (p. 123)

Furthermore, task-centred and crisis-intervention approaches both come under criticism for the potentially disempowered location of the client in relation to the worker. Another concern is that of the pragmatic, evidence-based nature of both approaches and their tendency towards a linear approach to problem solving (Healy, 2005), which may be inconsistent with the world views of people who carry more cyclical notions of time and change such as Indigenous cultures. Brown and Rainer (2006) suggest that when an individual faces a crisis their experience occurs in relation to their psychosocial cultural context. If aspects connected to social identities are overlooked by the crisis worker the response from the individual will be largely ineffective.

Baskin (2005) suggests, "Aboriginal Peoples cannot look outside their cultures for their self-image. Aboriginal traditional values, especially in the area of relationships, carry the instructions for healing" (p. 172). Baskin outlines the following steps from the Vancouver Native Education Centre for creating healthy relationships and communities:

- focusing on self-esteem and self-worth as Aboriginal peoples
- offering support
- using symbols that engage the senses and the gifts of the earth to heal, rather than only words
- teaching respect for the self, family, community, and the earth
- taking the focus away from an individualistic approach to the situation
- balancing the four aspects (psychological, physical, emotional, and spiritual) of the person, so she/he can use all of her/his resources
- promoting ways of achieving harmony and integration within.

Another consideration noted by Baskin (2005) is the circle. "The circle implemented both culture-based and some Western healing practices (as long as these were compatible with the values of Aboriginal cultures)" (p. 174). Baskin describes the purpose of the circle as a safe, supportive, and confidential group forum for discussion and learning.

CP PHOTO/Winnipeg Free Press – Ken Gigliotti

Men participate in a drum circle at the Aboriginal Healing Range home at the Stony Mountain Institution in Stony Mountain, Manitoba. Healing Lodges, like the one at Stony Mountain, seek to address the needs of Indigenous inmates through ceremonies, visits with Elders, and time spent in nature.

In some instances, task-centred and crisis-intervention skills clearly are inappropriate. More insight-oriented problems require more insight-oriented skills and understandings. These are considered in later chapters.

Chapter Summary

In this chapter, some of the key skills that are used in task-centred and crisis-intervention approaches have been introduced. The goal-setting and problem-solving skills of a task-centred approach were applied to the complex circumstances of the Ahmed family to demonstrate how finding solutions is the focus of the work together. The emotion-and task-focused skills used with Mrs Willis and the Stewart family illustrated the short-term, multi-dimensional emphasis of a crisis-intervention approach. These skills are primarily used in situations where communication is under time constraints. They focus on optimizing people's strengths and capacities in the face of the more extreme difficult circumstances of life.

Individual Exercise

Would you be effective in crisis work? Ask yourself the following questions:

1. What makes a good crisis worker?
2. How is self-care critical to crisis practice?
3. Which of the task-centred and crisis-intervention skills appeal to you? Why?
4. When would you find these skills helpful?
5. What are some of the strengths and limitations of these skills?
6. What skills would you like to develop further?
7. What cultural issues would you need to consider?

Group Activity

Your personal safety is important. Have you considered the risk to your personal safety in practice and how you might mitigate potential personal risk? What are the work safety aspects of crisis work? As a class, or in small groups, create a list of personal safety considerations for crisis workers in the following situations:

- hospital emergency room crisis worker
- outreach community crisis worker (going into clients homes)
- critical incident response crisis worker (attending accidents, or disaster scenes).

Once the safety aspects in each area have been considered, discuss other possible areas of practice that may require further consideration when developing worker safety procedures (for example, cultural considerations, gender issues, or potential added barriers when working with vulnerable children or seniors).

Partner Practice

With a partner, work through the scenario below listing the steps your group would take in responding to Jacob's crisis situation.

> Jacob is a 40-year-old man who has been out of work for more than one year. He is a trained mechanic but has been unable to gain stable employment. Jacob has one child, Michael (eight years old), who has some challenging behaviours. Most frustrating for Jacob is Michael's refusal to go to sleep. Last night Michael refused to go to bed, screaming loudly, throwing things, and repeatedly running out of his room. Jacob becomes increasingly angry with Michael and spanks him. Jacob's reaction only increases Michael's behaviour so Jacob decides to take Michael for a drive hoping he will fall asleep in the car. As they make their way down the street, Michael throws his toy at Jacob who turns to grab Michael and does not see an oncoming truck, which crashes into the car head-on. Jacob walks away with minor injuries but Michael is critically injured. Jacob has not spoken since the accident occurred and is in the hospital waiting on news regarding Michael's condition.

You are the crisis worker for this incident. You approach Jacob to discuss the incident. How would you handle this crisis situation? What factors need to be considered? In order, what task-centered or crisis-intervention steps would you take? In addition, outline the safety procedures you would take to address potential risk for you as the worker in this scenario.

Recommended Readings

Brown, F., & Rainer, J. (2006). Too much to bear: An introduction to crisis intervention and therapy. *Journal of Clinical Psychology, 62*(8), 953–7.

Brownlee, K., & Graham, J.R. (2005). *Violence in the family: Social work readings and research from northern and rural Canada*. Toronto, ON: Canadian Scholars' Press.

Davis, S. (2013). *Community mental health in Canada, revised and expanded edition: Theory, policy, and practice*. Vancouver, BC: University of British Columbia Press.

DeAngelis, T. (2011). Helping kids cope in an uncertain world. *Monitor on Psychology, 42*(8), 67–70.

Doel, M., & Marsh, P. (2017). *Task-centered social work*. New York, NY: Routledge.

Flannery, R., & Everly, G. (2000). Crisis intervention: A review. *International Journal of Emergency Mental Health, 2*(2), 119–25.

Galynker, I. (2017). *The suicide crisis: Clinical guide to the assessment of imminent suicide risk*. New York, NY: Oxford University Press.

James, R.K., & Gilliland, B.E. (2017). *Crisis intervention strategies*. Pacific Grove, CA: Brooks/Cole.

Marsh, P., & Doel, M. (2005). *The task-centred book*. London: Routledge.

Maslow, A.H. (2013). *Toward a psychology of being* [E-reader version]. Start Publishing LLC.

Miller, L. (2010). On-scene crisis intervention: Psychological guidelines and communication strategies for first responders. *International Journal for Emergency Mental Health, 12*(1), 11–19.

Myer, R., & Conte, C. (2006). Assessment for crisis intervention. *Journal of Clinical Psychology, 62*(8), 959–70.

Rzepnicki, T.A., McCracken, S.G., & Briggs, H.E. (2012). *From task-centered social work to evidenced-based and integrative practice*. New York, NY: Oxford University Press.

Tolson, E., Reid, W., & Garvin, C. (2003). *Generalist practice: A task-centered approach*. New York: Columbia University Press.

Zeiders, K.H., Roosa, M.W., Knight, G.P., & Gonzales, N.A. (2013). Mexican American adolescents' profiles of risk and mental health: A person-centered longitudinal approach. *Journal of Adolescence, 36*, 603–12. doi:10.1016/j.adolescence.2013.03.014

Internet Resources

Canadian Association for Suicide Prevention
www.casp-acps.ca/home.asp

Canadian Critical Incident Stress Foundation
www.ccisf.info

Center for Response-Based Practice
www.responsebasedpractice.com

Critical Incident Stress Management
www.criticalincidentstress.com/what_is_cism_

Department of Justice (Canada), Aid to Safety Assessment Planning (ASAP)
www.justice.gc.ca/eng/rp-pr/cj-jp/fv-vf/rr09_7/p3.html

National Center for Crisis Management (US)
www.nc-cm.org

12 Psychodynamic and Cognitive Behavioural Skills

Learning Goals

- Identify the core skills of psychodynamic and cognitive behavioural approaches, particularly in regard to establishing the relationship between a worker and client and specific interventions.
- Understand transference and countertransference, the unconscious and conscious, and defence mechanisms in psychodynamic practice.
- Understand how "thoughts-feelings/emotions-behaviour" are applied in cognitive behaviour therapy approaches.
- Explore the process of negative automatic thoughts and beliefs, as part of a cognitive behavioural approach.
- Understand the strengths and limitations of these skills.

Psychodynamic Theories

Of all the theoretical dimensions, **psychodynamic theories** place most emphasis on the client–worker relationship and on the communication processes within that relationship. Psychodynamic theories are primarily concerned with the inner worlds of individuals and how difficulties arise in functioning because of their past and present inner-world preoccupations. As a result, psychodynamic theories are concerned with human drives or motivations in relation to pleasure, power, conflict, and anxiety. The effects of these experiences are thought to develop across the lifespan through various psychosocial or psychosexual phases. One of the major arguments within psychodynamic theories is that "psychopathology arises from early childhood experiences" (Sommers-Flanagan & Sommers-Flanagan, 2004, p. 41). Relating Jahzara's situation in Chapter 3 to psychodynamic theory, a worker with this understanding would want to know about conscious and unconscious memories of experiences to see how Jahzara's own past patterns of being parented are being replayed in her adult context, as well as the fantasies and drives that motivate Jahzara's behaviour or relationship difficulties.

Psychodynamic theories are intensely focused on verbal and non-verbal communications, which are messages directed consciously and unconsciously to the worker. These processes behind the client's telling of the story are to be interpreted as much as the story's content. The client's relationship with the worker is seen as an opportunity to work through and experience a "corrective emotional" relationship or the "training ground" (Shulman, 2016) with the worker that may repair or address some of the difficulties experienced in previous relationships, primarily those with parents. Underlying this is an argument that the relationship enables the opportunity for the establishment or re-establishment of a secure attachment. That is, the secure base of the relationship with the worker provides a sense of meaning and coherence that can be carried into other contexts. Transference and counter-transference (Gibney, 2003) are an essential purpose of the work undertaken together. Thus, the experience of connection with the worker, or the therapeutic alliance, is considered one of the major change agents (Trevithick, 2005).

More recently, psychodynamic theorists have focused on the concept of therapeutic action, suggesting that Freud's theory of talking freely was successful in bringing the unconscious to the conscious, but that the need for therapeutic action is more complex (Cabaniss, 2017). The core idea of therapeutic action suggested by Cabaniss (2017) has two main points:

- thoughts and feelings that are outside of awareness can affect and motivate people, often leading to habitual but maladaptive ways of thinking and behaving; and
- becoming aware of these thoughts and feelings can be therapeutic (p. 8).

Core Skills of Psychodynamic Practice

Payne (2005) describes psychodynamic theory as "based on the work of Freud and his followers, and developments of their work. They are called 'psychodynamic' because the theory underlying them assumes that behaviour comes from movements and interactions in people's minds" (p. 73). Payne outlines the main points of psychodynamic theory as follows.

1. Psychodynamic perspectives are an important historical source for basic social work skills.
2. Their long history means that application to different forms of practice is fully developed.
3. Recent developments in attachment theory are relevant to child care and protection and loss and bereavement.
4. Recent developments in ego psychology have influenced therapeutic work with adults, particularly in the United States.
5. Psychodynamic ideas are a rich source of complex ideas for interpreting behaviour.
6. Wide understanding and study of psychodynamic theory make for good connections with other professionals and across national boundaries.
7. Lack of a strong evidence base and the use of models of integral thinking have led to criticism.
8. The historical, Eurocentric, and Jewish cultural origins of psychodynamic theory lead to victim-blaming and stereotypical assumptions about women and LGBTQ behaviour.

A central belief of psychodynamic theory is that if appropriate nurturing is not provided in an individual's primary years, emotional states can remain infantile, unconscious, and unresolved across the lifespan. In psychodynamic theory the process of exploring unresolved issues is done through externalizing. Externalizing is an unconscious defence mechanism resulting in individuals projecting their own internal characteristics onto the outside world, specifically at other individuals or society. An example of externalizing is an exceedingly argumentative client who complains about other people's difficult personalities while seeing herself or himself as faultless.

Miller (2012) describes the process of externalizing in the following three ways:

- the process of identifying an ideal object (such as another person or society) that is just right, which leads to feelings of satisfaction
- the process of rejecting an object that frustrates needs, which leads to anger
- the process of discovering an object that excites needs, which leads to longing (p. 58).

Some of the main concepts in practice are anxiety and ambivalence, coping, defences and resistance, transference and counter-transference, and relationships, which will be discussed in more detail in this chapter. To illustrate some of the key skills within a psychodynamic approach, Karen describes her work with Julia, a 40-year-old woman.

BOX 12.1 Focus on Practice

Letting the Client Take Control

Julia requested counselling because her friends had told her she was depressed. During the first and many subsequent interviews Julia revealed a complex and detailed examination of her life events through the perspective of all her family members, friends, and work colleagues. It was impossible to gain from Julia any view that she expressed alone. She apparently was incapable of identifying—or perhaps even of developing—an opinion on a subject apart from the input from others.

It became clear that her unconscious expectation of counselling was to gain further insights into her situation from yet another person. The challenge for the worker was to not be drawn into this pattern but reflect it back to Julia to assist her in examining how she habitually places herself in relation to others. The concepts of transference and counter-transference were helpful in this instance.

A further pattern that appeared during counselling was the client regularly appearing in a chaotic state, with a range of apparent crises to report from the previous week. Counselling sessions involved deconstructing and reframing these experiences to help Julia view them in a more positive light and to restore a sense of efficacy in her own capacity to act and interpret her own experiences. Due to her longstanding habit of having others (particularly her mother) define the events in her life negatively, she found it quite challenging to break this habit and have hope for change.

This experience of **repetition** was challenging for me as the counsellor, but Julia began to learn how she could take control of her understanding of events.

1. What is your initial reaction to hearing about Julia and Karen's work?
2. What would you focus on in work with Julia? Why?

Notice that the emphasis in this scenario is on

- lifelong patterns of behaving and relating;
- family and significant others and their impact on the client's sense of self;
- conscious and unconscious motivations and drives;
- parallel processes occurring in the client–worker relationship;
- transference and counter-transference experiences;
- working over time to address patterns of behaving, thinking, and feeling that keep repeating themselves; and
- developing insight and, ultimately, changes to an experience of the self as chaotic.

Each of these conceptual areas will be addressed throughout this discussion of psychodynamic skills.

Establishing and Sustaining the Relationship

The client–worker relationship is central to any work with a strong psychodynamic orientation. The focus is on the relationship dynamics (Walsh, 2006, p. 30). A client can resolve problematic issues from the past by experiencing a positive relationship in the therapeutic relationship or "working alliance" in the "here and now." The relationship provides a "corrective emotional experience" (McCluskey, 2002) and internal working models of relationships that a client may have developed through poor earlier relationships can be influenced for the better.

The relationship becomes the vehicle for change, as issues of unconscious motivations and desires, conflicts, and anxieties repeat themselves in the client–worker relationship. The intention is that the client projects these conscious and unconscious experiences and expectations onto the therapist, forming a **transference**—a transfer of earlier and current significant relationships—onto the current therapeutic one. As a result "the client perceives the helping professional in a distorted way and brings his or her past relationships into the present relationship with the counselor" (Corey & Corey, 2007, p. 67).

By developing insight about transference over time, change can occur as these needs and desires come under more conscious control. Transference is theorized as a part of every relationship in which people engage. In the therapeutic context, however, it is analyzed for what it tells us about ourselves and our ways of relating to ourselves, significant others, and the world around us.

Counter-transference is the parallel process that occurs for the worker. As Corey and Corey (2007) note, "Broadly speaking, helpers may have unconscious emotional responses to a client that result in a distorted perception of a client's behaviour" (p. 67). Corey and Corey explain that counter-transference can block the neutrality of the worker. The therapeutic relationship is based on the assumption that the worker is in an objective, neutral position as a sounding board for the client. However, this assumption in psychodynamic practice is being increasingly challenged. In Julia and Karen's situation, focusing on the counter-transference would involve Karen continually reflecting on how she feels and to what in the client's story she reacts. Supervision for Karen is an essential condition for such issues to be discussed and addressed.

The therapeutic relationship dynamic was symbolized by Jung as a series of links, an image that today we might replace with the metaphor of a complex web of relationships, as shown in Figure 12.1.

The aim of engagement throughout your work with your client is to foster a positive transference relationship so that trust and insight can be achieved. Unlike other client–worker relationships, the contracting of the work is not expected to occur from the outset within a psychodynamic approach (Howard, 2006). Instead, the emphasis is on experiencing the relationship first and on analyzing what emerges in that interaction. The relationship itself is as much a focus of the work as other issues raised in the conversation.

When reflecting on the processes of transference and counter-transference, it is important for practitioners to distinguish between their own emergent emotions and the emotions that originate with the client. In addition to engaging in this ongoing reflective process, seeking supervision is central to the process of exploring feelings that surface in work with clients to prevent them from impacting the practitioner's work (Miller, 2012).

The early psychodynamic view of the worker was as a "blank screen"—an objective and neutral listener whom the client would "project" her or his earlier relationships that had influenced the individual's **psychosexual development**. Eventually, the impossibility of maintaining such an unnatural relationship became evident. The term "intersubjectivity" is now used to denote the complex, reciprocal relationship between the worker and client (Gibney, 2003). Nevertheless, close boundaries are prescribed for work and the relationship, unlike some of the Indigenous practice approaches.

Psychodynamic processes are thought about in many different and sometimes contradictory ways. This complexity has a major impact on the types of skills that you might use. Two major schools of thought are the object-relations and ego-psychology approaches. The object-relations approach proposes that we relate to people in the present on the basis of

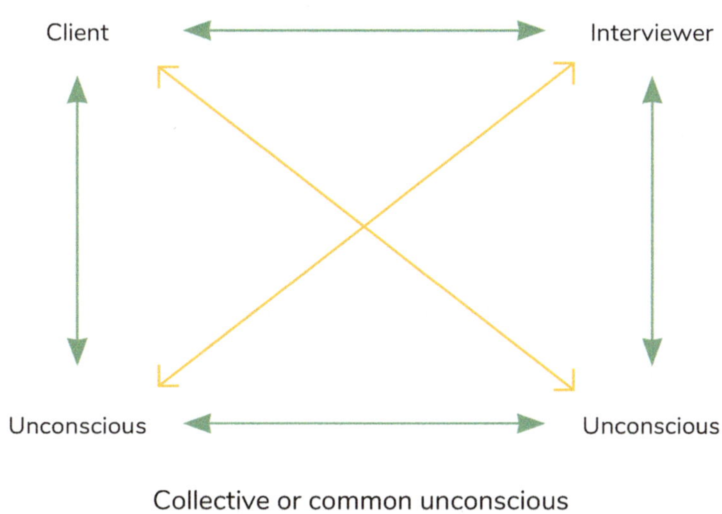

FIGURE 12.1 Conscious and Unconscious Levels of Communication within Relationships

Source: Jacoby, M. 1984. The Analytic Encounter—Transference and Human Relationship. Toronto: Inner City Books.

expectations formed by early experiences within significant relationships. During infancy, we develop internal working models of relationships based on our relationships with those around us, and it becomes necessary in adult life to explore and repair faulty unconscious object relationships internalized since infancy. How the external world is taken in and how the resultant internalizations influence psychic structure and later personality functioning are the focus of this approach (Goldstein, 1995).

Many psychodynamic theories also maintain theories of attachment at their core. For example, the infant's primary need for attachment to a caring person (Bowlby, 1984), realizes itself in the good object (Klein, 1962) or the holding environment (Winnicott, 1987), respectively. A mature ego develops into one that can accommodate ambivalence and complexity in life rather than to the dichotomized concepts of "good" and "bad."

Ego psychology argues that we learn a coping repertoire across the lifespan that has various strengths and deficits, and that later difficulties are associated with this lifelong coping repertoire. The focus of intervention is on building **ego strengths**, where the ego is seen as "a mental structure of the personality that is responsible for negotiating between the internal needs of the individual and the outside world" (Goldstein, 1995, p. xi; Walsh, 2006, p. 32).

Specific Interventions

In light of the above, assessment typically involves taking a detailed history and examining the following dimensions of a person's life:

- drives as related to pleasure, aggression, and mastery/competence (Walsh, 2006, p. 31)
- management of anxiety
- personality
- experiences across the lifespan
- defence mechanisms.

Some of the specific psychodynamic skills or techniques (Gibney, 2003; Nelson-Jones, 2006; Walsh, 2006, pp. 40–3) you might use include the following.

1. *Promoting a corrective emotional experience.* As outlined in the previous section, the development and maintenance of the relationship over time is considered one of the most critical skills within psychodynamic approaches. This relationship enables the experience of a positive transference to emerge and for insight-oriented work to be done in a supportive environment despite the challenges the client faces on a daily basis.
2. *Offering containment.* In the previous chapter, containment was mentioned as an important skill within crisis-intervention approaches. Containment refers to "an exquisite empathy and thoughtfulness with which the [worker] responds to the client throughout the session" (Gibney, 2003, p. 46). Containment enables a sense of psychological safety and is therefore crucial in situations of crisis. It is also crucial in Julia's situation, where she normally does not experience herself as psychologically centred and strong. Containment can be offered within the conversation, in relation to external threats, and in context.

- *Within the conversation.* At the core, Gibney (2003, p. 51) describes this as relating to the fact that the client feels absolutely understood—accurately and genuinely. This, he and others argue, leads to the client being able to get in touch with her or his feelings, irrespective of the nature of those feelings. As a result, there is containment and affirmation of the client's inner-world experiences.
- *In relation to external threats.* By giving advice and direction in decision making, the worker in many ways models adult decision-making processes and does not hesitate to advise on particular situations, particularly those of risk. In these ways, the role of "good" parent may be enacted.
- *In context.* Unlike other approaches, a psychodynamic approach typically is employed in a structured setting, with clear boundaries around your meeting times and space. This routine is viewed as providing "containment" for the anxiety of uncertainty. The certainties of this contract provide some safety and boundaries and therefore provide an opportunity for the client to experience safety and boundaries in their inner world as well. In crisis situations, it is important to contain the emotional chaos through clear structuring and planning of actions. This notion of containment is similar to Winnicott's (1987) notion of a therapeutic "holding environment"—a safe, consistent, surrounding environment that is predictable in terms of time and event.

3. *Providing interpretations, particularly through exploring internalized relationships across the lifespan.* In Julia's case, where she is seemingly quite articulate about her circumstances, using imagery or analogy (Macnab, 1989, p. 101) to explore her inner objects might include suggesting that it is as if she has a backseat driver directing her. The worker might reflect what part of Julia's "self" this process applies to: "Every time you want to make a turn it's as if someone else is directing you." To regain a sense of ego strength, she can begin to listen to herself as the driver and trust her own feelings and sense of knowing.

   In conducting what Walsh (2006, p. 43) calls a "developmental reflection," specific skills outlined in the earlier chapters are emphasized. The tendency within psychodynamic approaches is to emphasize non-directive "uncovering" techniques to listen to her or his circumstances. The relationship, typically, is high in empathy, although a participant-observer role is strongly encouraged. Some approaches are amplified, such as skills of interpretation, using summaries, making observations or invitations, and using "why" questions. For example: "Earlier, you were telling me about your difficulties in finishing a project and just now you're telling me about how you're finding it difficult to leave this relationship." Or: "Notice that each time you talk about Brent you become quite choked up and you stop talking about him as freely as you do others."

   The timing of interpretations, however, is critical. Interpretations are usually made only in the context of well-established, trusting relationships, where they can be discussed fully in insight-oriented work.
4. *Encouraging the management of anxiety and insight into defence mechanisms.* Anxiety experiences are understood to lead to a distorting of reality, a loss of control, and inner conflict. Major anxiety in the form of trauma can lead to "dissociation" as a defence against such severe stress. Dissociation is the separation of thinking and feeling, leading to alterations in memory, identity, and consciousness, where there can be a separating out of various aspects of the self. According to the theory, in the face of anxiety we unconsciously use these sorts of defence mechanisms, which enable us to channel impulses "into acceptable behaviors" (Walsh, 2006, p. 31).

Returning to Karen's discussion of her work with Julia, a number of areas of ego "damage" might be assessed, including Julia's high levels of disorganization in practical terms and in emotional terms, self-sabotage, and vulnerability to the needs of others. On the other hand, in talking with Karen it seemed she identified ego strengths that she had underestimated or not developed and was able to begin to focus on these to influence her future functioning.

A key term used in understanding change is "resistance." This term is originally from the **defence mechanism** of resistance, or the "opposition to making what is unconscious conscious" (Reber, 1985, p. 642). Healthy defence mechanisms are a natural tool that alerts the mind to a potential threat. Unhealthy defence mechanisms typically result from a previous trauma that has been left unresolved and is unconsciously altering the individual's current behaviour. For example, someone who experienced a robbery at a store they frequented as a child now experiences social anxiety as an adult. Defence mechanisms help to explain the unconscious process of pushing back against change in the face of potentially overwhelming anxiety.

Overall then, some of the goals of intervention in psychodynamic approaches are to

- free individuals and family members from unconscious restrictions and therefore establish less "neurotic" patterns of relationship and communication;
- work towards eliminating unhelpful patterns of relating;
- delineate roles clearly, by comparing the fantasy with the reality of expectations;
- find a balance of autonomy and mutuality;
- develop affect tolerance and impulse control; and
- restore or develop an integrated self-identity.

These goals are about expanding the person's inner capacities and his or her capacities to function in daily life. While psychodynamic practice requires extensive training to facilitate, the principles of this approach can assist workers with paying close attention to a client's emotional state, the influence of unconscious awareness and potential defence mechanisms, and the process of engaging in building relationship with clients (Miller & Rollnick, 2014).

Cognitive Behavioural Theories

Cognitive and cognitive behavioural theories usually are located within a positivist paradigm. The early theorists (Ellis, 1995; Beck, Freeman, & Davis, 2004) proposed that a person's difficulties emerged in relation to three domains: the way the person thinks, the way the person feels or reacts emotionally, and the way the person acts. Cognitive behavioural therapy is based on an understanding that creating change in any of these domains and change in the other domains will follow necessarily.

The reciprocal links between thoughts, feelings, and behaviours in the cognitive behavioural model are clearly evident in other current interviewing models, such as Egan's (2007) problem-management and opportunity-development model (p. 81). He presents these three dimensions as pivotal to what the clients talk about:

- their experiences—that is, what happens to them
- their behaviour—that is, what they do or refrain from doing
- their affect—that is, the feelings, emotions, and moods that arise from or are associated with their experiences and both internal and external behaviour.

Others refer to these dimensions of conversation as the "Think-Feel-Do" framework (Thompson, 2002, p. xvii). A major criticism of this approach is that many people's difficulties occur within the outer world—for example, Jahzara's poverty or some men's violence towards women—but the therapeutic approach does not address change at these social levels that affect individuals in society broadly or collectively. Change in the cognitive behavioural model is theorized at the level of each individual's thinking, feeling, and behaviour (Egan, 2007, pp. 7–8).

Cognitive behavioural therapy has tended not to emphasize the client–worker relationship to the same extent as psychotherapeutic approaches, apart from acknowledging the collaboration in which the worker helps the individual to reflect critically on her or his thinking, feeling, and doing.

Core Skills of Cognitive Behavioural Practice

Cognitive behavioural approaches are incorporated in many models of counselling, both implicitly and explicitly. **Cognitive behavioural therapy** (CBT) focuses on an individual's thought process and how their thoughts can trigger certain emotional and behavioural responses. At its foundation, CBT combines cognitive therapy and behavioural therapy techniques to generate change. CBT assists individuals in becoming aware of inaccurate or negative thinking, challenging the client's view of their situation and encouraging more effective response. CBT can be helpful in treating mental health disorders, such as anxiety, stress, depression, social phobias, post-traumatic stress disorder (PTSD), and eating disorders. CBT also contains skills that clients can learn and practice independently of a practitioner.

Payne (2005) breaks down CBT into two parts, which are viewed frequently in practice as one: first, behavioural models of therapy, deriving from psychological learning theories; and second, cognitive models of therapy, deriving from psychological theories of perception and information-processing (p. 119). Payne outlines the main points of cognitive behavioural theory as follows.

1. Cognitive behavioural work focuses on defining and addressing people's behaviours, particularly social phobias, anxiety, and depression.
2. Careful assessment and monitoring of progress often uses behavioural measurements.
3. Research evidence of effectiveness is strong and important to theory and practice.
4. The main techniques are well defined and technical, including respondent and operant conditioning, social learning and skills training, and cognitive restructuring of the person's belief system.
5. Social learning techniques, such as assertiveness and skills training, are widely used, particularly as part of group work, and are taken up in feminist practice.
6. More specific techniques are used in clinical settings where supervision and training in their use are available to practitioners.
7. The use of cognitive behavioural models of practice has been controversial because of their association with politically controversial "whatever works" standards of interpersonal control. Also controversial in the profession are "evidence-based practice" perspectives. The proponents of cognitive behavioural models are known for their sometimes intemperate critiques—supposedly from a scientific and evidence-based perspective—of pre-existing and broader perspectives on social work practice.
8. Cautious concern about the potential for ethical problems has been raised in regard to cognitive behavioural models. These theories have been widely applied according to rigid

> political doctrines in Eastern countries, where scientific methods are less influential, and in countries where broad goals for the revision of society are conceived of as relevant to social work and coercive methods are permitted (adapted from Payne, 2005, pp. 119–20).

In its traditional form, cognitive behavioural practice works on a model of change that sees inextricable links between feeling, thinking, and behaving. This model was represented by an "equation" or theory of change by Ellis (1995):

$$A + B = C \rightarrow D \rightarrow E$$

A represents an "activating event" or circumstance; B represents beliefs, which Ellis describes as being initially either irrational or rational; and C represents the consequences of the event and beliefs about it in terms of thoughts, feelings, and behaviours. In this equation, Ellis locates B as the mediating process on any event or circumstance and the main area of focus in any intervention. D then represents the conflict between beliefs and emotions and the attempts to establish more rational beliefs in lieu of irrational ones. Finally, E represents the evaluation or reexamination of both the event and beliefs and, therefore, the perceived level of consequence should shift because change in the original thinking pattern has occurred.

The basis of cognitive behavioural therapy is that in changing one dimension of a problem situation—for example, what the client believes about a particular situation—change is inevitably influenced in the other dimensions, as Holly's description of her work with Craig later in this chapter demonstrates.

Simmons and Griffiths (2014) summarize the value of cognitive behavioural practice:

> The CBT model hypothesizes that situations in themselves do not cause psychological distress, but rather what is important is the way that people interpret, make sense of and react to situations. People will experience distress if they construe a situation negatively, or react to it in a negative way. (p. 21)

The CBT model focuses on negative automatic thought (thoughts) and how the thought process influences emotions (anger, guilt, sadness, etc.), physical sensations such as anxiety, stress, or other bodily reactions, and the resulting behaviours (what the person then does as a result of their emotional or physical state).

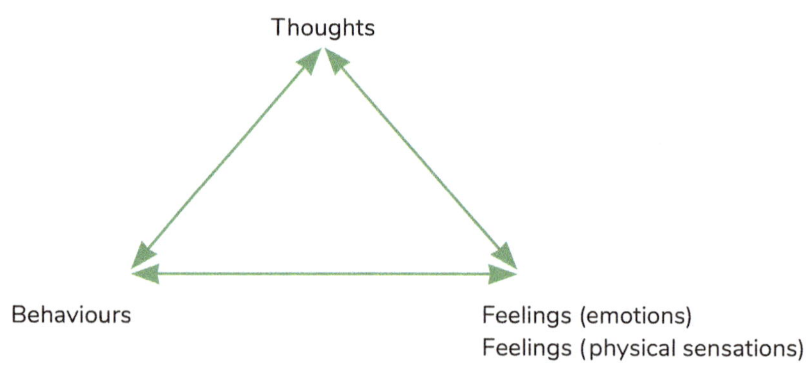

FIGURE 12.2 The CBT Model

Establishing and Sustaining the Relationship

Engagement in CBT work is usually within a short-term, time-limited client–worker relationship. The relationship is understood primarily as a means to critically reflect on habits, patterns, and self-defeating behaviours. The relationship is not reflected on as a particularly significant component of the change agenda in the way that psychodynamic approaches are, as described in the previous chapter. The key focus in engaging with someone is to develop an empathic relationship in which emotions, behaviours and thoughts can be reviewed and challenged while necessary and realistic goals can be set.

A second important element to engagement is education. Ensuring the client understands the process of CBT is critical to successful outcomes. Not only does understanding the rationale and process of CBT enable a collaborative working relationship, it supports the client's ability to understand and reflect on their current situation. Simmons and Griffiths (2014) suggest that visual examples of the CBT cycle are a helpful way for clients to begin to understand how they are active participants in their situation and to recognize how they want to create change, see Figure 12.3.

BOX 12.2 Practice Exercise

In pairs of two, think of a fear that you have had in your life and work through that fear following the visual example in Figure 12.3.

Here is an example: Imagine that you are petrified of spiders. Every time you see one, you run in the other direction because you believe that all spiders are poisonous and will bite you. Now, if you want to understand why you are so scared of spiders you might eventually discover that you were bitten by a spider when you were a young child, which is the cause of your current and persistent fear of spiders.

The issue here is that even though you know the cause it does not change the fact that you are terrified of spiders, sprint away from them, and think of them as scary creepy crawlers that bite.

How would this thought process fit in the above model?

Now work through your own example.

Specific Interventions

Assessment focuses on a number of themes in relation to patterns of thinking, feeling, and behaving. Traditionally, the emphasis was on identifying **rational and irrational thoughts** or beliefs. Ellis (1995) and others argue that our counterproductive behaviours are sustained by the beliefs we hold onto in our everyday lives. As a result, unhelpful or unhealthy behaviours and feelings are the target of interventions.

Some of the specific skills originating from a cognitive behavioural approach include challenging the client's self-defeating or unhelpful beliefs so that the client learns to control and monitor his or her thoughts.

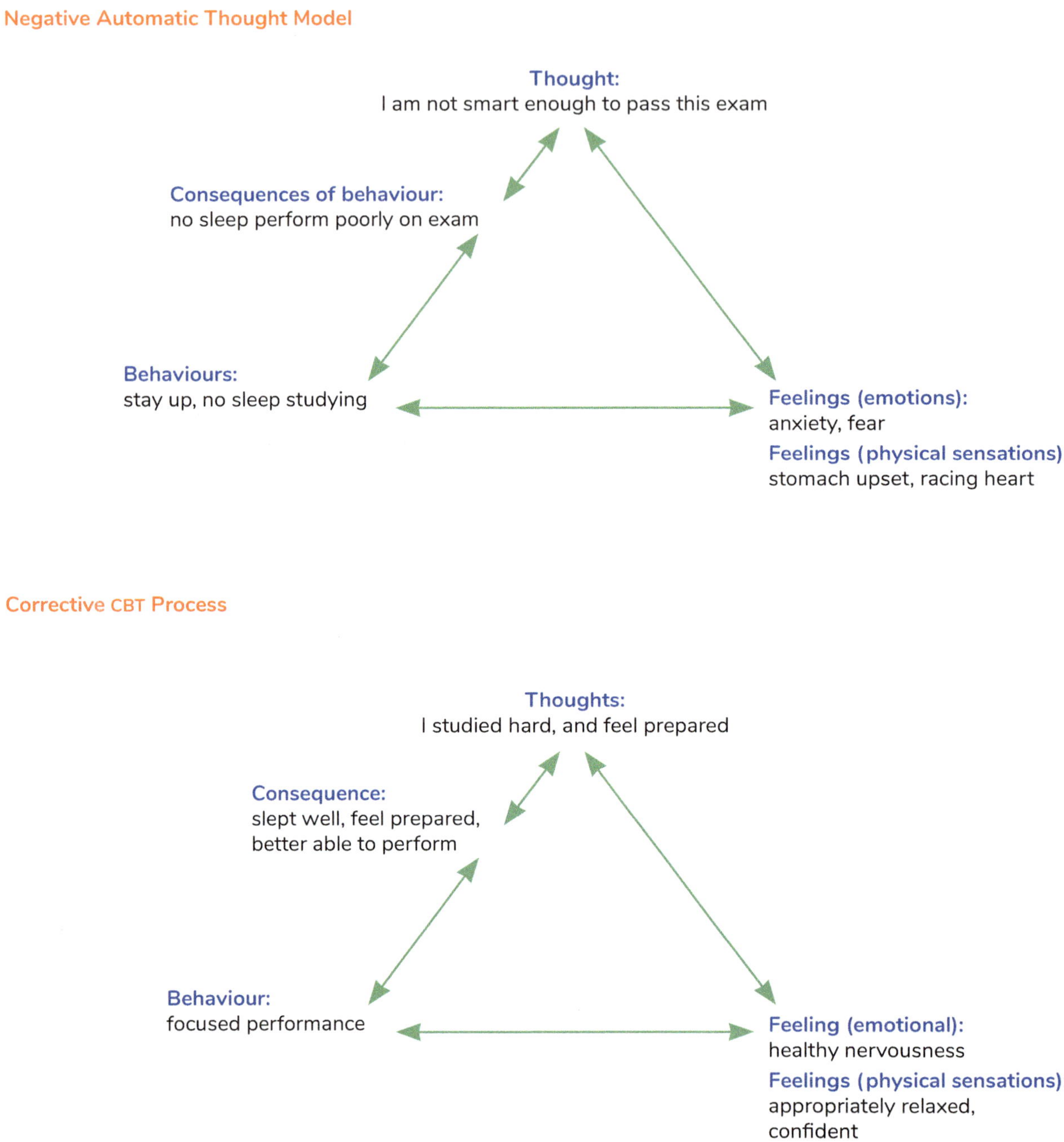

FIGURE 12.3 Visual Example of CBT Cycle

Source: Adapted from Simmons, J. and R. Griffiths. 2014. CBT for Beginners, second edition. London: SAGE.

Challenging Self-Defeating or Unhelpful Beliefs

In earlier chapters where we have looked at the processes of assessment and goal setting, an assumption of rational **decision making** on the part of the client has been implied. CBT approaches have been instrumental in demonstrating the need to challenge beliefs, behaviours, and feelings in order to bring about change. Ellis (1995) and others encourage identification of the following self-defeating messages:

I should . . .
I must . . .
I always . . .

These messages reflect our beliefs in behaviours that are compulsory or are absolute and, therefore, leave us without room to move. For example, we may distort beliefs about ourselves and others through catastrophizing and awfulizing (amplifying the negative consequences) or by generalizing. The reason for **challenging** these unhelpful beliefs is that more of a "middle ground" can be reached through a "reality check." We may not even be aware of the place in our thinking of many of these taken-for-granted ways of thinking about the world and our behaviour. An outsider (in this case, you as the worker) may be able to hear the ways in which patterns of thinking are unhelpful cognitive patterns for the client.

Ellis (1995) identifies a number of core beliefs that he considered to be the irrational beliefs and illogical deductions responsible for creating human experiences of panic, self-blame, and self-doubt, as listed below. These beliefs have been used extensively as a starting point to explore the extent to which irrational beliefs create unrealistic expectations of ourselves and those around us.

Ellis (1995) argues that beliefs that are considered irrational or unhelpful can be challenged or neutralized by more rational or helpful beliefs. Fook (1993, p. 86) identifies resolving or tolerating conflicting beliefs and challenging false beliefs as critical strategies. These techniques are skills of reframing—of learning to think about something differently as a consequence of:

- challenging its helpful or unhelpful characteristics;
- including more information into the picture of understanding; and
- hearing another point of view.

The above three points are explored in Figure 12.3.

BOX 12.3 Focus on Practice

Irrational Beliefs

Ellis's "irrational beliefs" include the following:

- It is a dire necessity for an adult to be loved or approved by virtually every significant person in [his or her] community.
- One should be thoroughly competent, adequate, and achieving in all possible respects if one is to consider oneself worthwhile.
- Human unhappiness is externally caused and people have little or no ability to control their sorrows and disturbances.

Continued

- One's past history is an all-important determinant of one's present behaviour, and because something once strongly affected one's life, it should indefinitely have a similar effect.
- There is invariably a right, precise, and perfect solution to human problems, and it is catastrophic if this perfect solution is not found.
- If something is or may be dangerous or fearsome, one should be terribly concerned about it and should keep dwelling on the possibility of its occurring.

Source: Adapted from Ellis (1974, pp. 152–3).

Controlling Thoughts: Thought-Stopping

Another central tenet of CBT approaches is that thoughts are controllable. The argument is that due to habit or a lack of conscious attention we are unaware of the thoughts, feelings, and beliefs that govern our behaviour. Strategies that combine both behavioural and cognitive strategies, such as "thought-stopping," are used as interventions into these thought processes. In thought-stopping the worker can interrupt the client's unhelpful thoughts during a conversation by literally saying "stop." Then the client is encouraged to similarly stop his or her own thoughts when he or she becomes aware of that thought pattern and replace the negative thought with a corrective thought. For example, "I should be working harder, I am a failure" (STOP). "I work hard and it is healthy to have time off." It is recommended that the client keep track of their thoughts on a client-thought record sheet so that they can gradually bring these automatic, unhelpful thoughts under more conscious control.

Date	Situation	Emotions	Thought/ Images
	(Where were you when the situation happened? Who was around you? When did the situation occur, and how? Describe it.)	(What were your feelings at the time, on a scale of 1 to 10?)	(What did you think? On a scale of 1 to 10, how much do you believe your thought?)
12/2/17	*I had a panic attack at my friend's house with several people watching.*	*Everyone is staring at me. I am freaking out inside and they are judging me.* *I am at a 10 of 10.*	*I thought they could see me shaking, felt I was weird, and they would not want me around ever again.* *10 of 10.*

FIGURE 12.4 Sample Client-Thought Record Sheet

Monitoring Thoughts

Other strategies focus more on tracking unhelpful behaviours, for example, through the use of a journal (either around specific behaviours or thoughts). Below, Holly elaborates on how she worked with Craig to address this interconnection.

Have you tried keeping your own thought record, as shown in Figure 12.4? How would your own experience keeping thought records inform how you presented this tool to clients?

BOX 12.4 Focus on Practice

Using CBT Techniques

Craig is a 27-year-old man who came to see me for psychotherapy and follow-up, due to suicidal behaviour and an underlying anxiety disorder. He is on long-term disability. Craig's mother died of leukemia when Craig was 19 years old. Craig's sister Joanne was murdered 13 years ago. He has one older brother with an intellectual disability and another brother who Craig alleges tried to molest him when the brother was eight or nine years of age and Craig was three. Craig lives alone and has a number of entrenched OCD [obsessive compulsive disorder] behaviours that he believes help to manage his anxiety, such as checking that taps are off, never having the gas turned on in the house, and washing and rewashing his hands.

Craig does not use alcohol or other substances. He does smoke cigarettes, however. He says, "I don't drink tea or coffee or Coke because it makes my heart go too quickly." Craig does not use public

Continued

transport because he generally feels uncomfortable around people. He says that "I can't get on public transport: people stare at me. I ride my bike everywhere. I haven't got on public transport for at least 10 years."

Craig is also self-conscious of his appearance. He is typically dressed in somewhat worn tradesman's clothing and he wears woollen gloves on his hands, even on very warm days, noting this is "because I've got tattoos." These tattoos are from the time Craig spent in prison.

Craig notes that it takes him 60 to 90 minutes to leave the house. He has a lot of rituals to complete prior to departing. He is meticulous in tidying and cleaning behaviours with regard to the back garden, the house, and his own body. He checks and rechecks the taps.

> I turn 'em off with a wrench because I think they're dripping. But they're not. I wreck the washers, I turn it so tight.

Specific to his self-harming behaviour Craig says

> The voices tell me what to do. The other day I remember the voices telling me what to do: to take five and another five.

And

> I keep looking at the knife on the stove. I think about ending things.

After four weeks of talking to me, at his third outpatient appointment Craig describes his anxiety and suicidal thoughts as "like a toothache in my heart."

What would you see as some of the possibilities for intervention with Craig?

Two interventions significantly impacted Craig's perceived level of coping, the regularity and severity of his presentations to the hospital emergency room, and his optimism. The first was his increased role in his church community. He approached the minister about helping out. He began to visit an elderly church member and another with a physical disability on a weekly basis. He would help with odd jobs, often in the garden, and in return join them for a cup of tea in their homes. Craig felt useful and the structured activity seemed to help by keeping him occupied and his thoughts, for the most part, off anxious preoccupations.

This intervention is about changing the outer world, through focusing on behaviours and structures that promote well-being.

The second intervention, which used more traditional CBT approaches, was the introduction of a mood journal. Craig and I converted an exercise book into a journal. Each day Craig would write down any good thing that happened that day and any upsetting thing that happened that day, and he would give himself a score out of 10. He would then bring the diary with him to sessions and we would discuss his week. As we were able to reduce sessions, the journal enabled him to self-monitor between appointments.

Interestingly to me, I did not recommend the daily scorekeeping at all. I once asked him—when trying to gauge the extent of his depressed mood—what he would give himself out of 10, where zero was terrible and 10 was fantastic. He seemed to select this himself as a useful tool to include as part of the journal. Of course, since we were more than three months into treatment by then, he had undergone three formal assessments with me as part of the research element of the suicide prevention strategy. The depression measure Beck's Depression Inventory II uses 0 to 3 ratings as does the quality-of-life tool. The Manual Manchester Short Assessment of Quality of Life uses a seven-point Likert scale of 25 questions. It could be that Craig found the numbering helpful for self-monitoring or it could be that Craig interpreted assigning numbers to things as giving them extra legitimacy.

Interesting, too, was that Craig's use of the numbers was highly subjective, so it was important to gain an understanding of his coding over time. While I would hope for a seven- or eight-out-of-ten day as a baseline for myself, when discussing what would be the score for a "good" day Craig informed me that he was happy when he had a "five" day. On those days he did not suffer high anxiety or feel a desire to self-harm. On a "three" or "four" day he would try to carry out some task in the garden or around the house, phone or visit a friend, or engage in positive self-talk. We worked out a safety plan from there whereby if he was having a "one" or "two" day he would call me during business hours or Crisis Assessment and Treatment Team triage after hours to talk instead of engaging in self-harm. He liked this and felt in charge of the process and that he was knowledgeable about his thought processes after all. Always, though, he required validation through my making time in the next outpatient session to read over his entries since we had last met and ask him about them.

All of these strategies actively address the ways in which thoughts, feelings, and behaviours interconnect and potentially create restrictions on the ways in which we live. In a small group or with a partner, identify the CBT thoughts, feelings, and behaviours model in the case of Craig. What did each person in your group identify? What were the similarities and differences in your group?

Cognitive Behavioural Assessment

A CBT assessment involves gaining knowledge of when the situations first occurred. Typically, the problem is experienced in one of two ways: slowly with a gradual onset over time, or suddenly following a traumatic event (Miller, 2012). Exploring these two aspects tells us whether the issue is persistent, sudden, or fluctuates. This understanding assists with planning for the present and recognizing how the issue is impacting current day-to-day levels of functioning.

To understand the details of the origin, triggers, and impact of the issue, Miller (2012) describes six areas of assessment:

> Situational: which environmental factors were present.
> Behavioural: what the person did.
> Cognitive: which thoughts were present at the time.
> Affective: which emotional reaction occurred, i.e. overall mood.
> Interpersonal: who was present.
> Physiological: which bodily reaction was present. (p. 117)

The six areas of assessment are then explored through the process of using Socratic questioning. Socratic questions are purposefully systematic and guide the client through the CBT process actively linking thoughts, feelings, and behavioural aspects of the client's situation. There are six general areas of focus in Socratic questioning:

1. Questions focused on clarifying the client's story: *What makes you say that? How does this relate to our conversation?*
2. Questions that probe the client's assumptions: *Is this thought realistic? What could we assume instead? How can you confirm or reject that assumption?*

3. Questions that probe for why and ask for evidence: *What is the evidence for and against this idea? What would be an example of that? What is ___ similar to? What do you think causes ___ to happen? Can you tell me why?*
4. Questions about perspectives: *What would be an alternative to ___ be? What is another way to look at ___? Would you explain why you think it is necessary or beneficial, and who benefits from it? How are ___ and ___ similar? What is another way to view ___?*
5. Questions that probe possible implications and consequences: *What possible assumptions can you make? What are potential consequences of that assumption? What are you inferring? How does ___ affect ___?*
6. Questions that reflect on a question asked: *What does ___ mean? How does ______ relate to daily life? Why do you think ______ is important?*

Miller (2012) promotes Rutter and Friedberg's (1999) five-point model towards developing a Socratic questioning design:

- Elicit and identify the automatic thought.
- Tie the automatic thought to the feeling and the behaviour.
- Link the thought-feeling-behaviour sequence together with an empathic response.
- Obtain collaboration on steps 1 to 3 and agreement to go forward. [Here, the goal is to work collaboratively with the client to gain an understanding of how their thought process is influencing their emotions and behaviour. Once this understanding has been gained, the worker and the client can establish the next steps.]
- Socratically test the belief. [Testing the Socratic belief is the process of highlighting the changes in the client's thinking after the collaborative effort of working through the automatic thoughts that were present when they began sharing their story.] (p. 199)

BOX 12.5 Practice Exercise

In small groups of three or four, read Jeff's scenario below and apply the steps of Socratic questioning, facilitating a CBT assessment process to create a plan for Jeff.

> Jeff (48) is living alone and is described as having sustained high anxiety. He frequently behaves in disruptive ways to avoid having to go out and attend public meetings or interact with others. This behaviour is preventing Jeff from gaining employment and attending medical appointments. Jeff has been referred to you by his doctor who has concerns regarding the amount of time Jeff spends alone and his level of social isolation. Jeff says he will work with you, but refuses on several occasions to leave his apartment to attend appointments, saying he is okay and does not need to come. When you speak with Jeff over the phone he frequently admits he wants to be able to go out and would like to have a job, but he just can't. You arranged for a home support worker to meet Jeff and assist him with coming to meet you and Jeff agreed to try one appointment.

While there are other cognitive behavioural techniques, the client-thought record sheet (see Figure 12.4) and assessment model provided above are a good starting point for workers to begin to work with and understand the CBT process when working with people.

Strengths and Limitations of Psychodynamic and CBT Skills

CBT is often cited as the most successful form of psychological intervention. It has been found to be useful in addressing problems in a short-term, contracted way. Davis (2006, pp. 234–5) describes behavioural techniques as traditionally being applied to persons with anxiety disorders, behavioural problems, and sexual disorders such as pedophilia, and cognitive treatments as applied to distorted thinking—irrational, unrealistic, or self-defeating beliefs and interpretations. However, the reported success of CBT is due in part to the relative ease of measuring its inputs and outputs compared with some of the more process- or insight-oriented approaches.

A major criticism of CBT approaches is that the problem is seen to be located in people's inner worlds. The major interventions focus on changing individual behaviours, thoughts, or feelings, whereas many human service workers are aware that the issues many clients are grappling with are located, or have their sources, in the outer worlds in which they live. For example, poverty can be thought about differently and behaviours can be changed in relation to it, but the essential agenda should be to alleviate poverty, not blame the individual for feeling stressed because of its effects, such as lack of adequate food, shelter, and clothing. The lack of attention to structural concerns, so often at the heart of individual experiences of stress and depression, is the major criticism of these approaches.

Psychodynamic approaches have attracted controversy in social work and psychology. Three major criticisms are made of CBT. The first is that psychodynamic approaches are inherently intrapsychic and therefore fail to address the social, structural, and cultural causes of human distress and oppression. CBT'S inherently apolitical stance means that it is not a useful approach for social change; rather, it locates both the causation and responsibility for change at the level of the individual. Human service workers work constantly at the interface of the individual and the society, so psychodynamic approaches have major limitations in this regard. This critique is noted by Walsh (2006): "There is nothing that prohibits a social worker who practices ego psychology from helping clients engage in larger system change activities, but nothing within the theory itself encourages these interventions" (p. 45).

A second criticism of CBT is that many of the key theories of psychodynamic approaches lack an available evidence base from which to draw conclusions about efficacy. Related to this is further criticism that the theories are unfalsifiable. The condition of the client's inner world is defined by the therapist according to an unprovable theoretical model. Therapy is defined within a closed linguistic system (a tautological framework) and the client's progress within the model is not verifiable.

A third criticism of CBT is that psychodynamic approaches can disempower clients through a lack of explanation to the client about the theories being used to understand that individual's inner worlds, and that these theories assume the superiority of the beliefs and the authority of the therapist. Healy (2005, p. 57) also raises a question about the relevance of what she terms the "psy" (as in "psychologically oriented") theories where the relationship is mandated. The basis of the relationship with involuntary clients may not be trust (Healy 2005, citing Smith, 2001, p. 289), but a formal agreement. Yet, the assumptions about engagement in a therapeutic relationship are said to be based on trust and a positive attachment. Indeed, behavioural modification techniques can be seen as coercive, and when used with patients in mental hospitals or with prisoners in penal institutions, it can be argued that CBT violates a person's inherent civil rights. Healy also notes that psychologized approaches generally may "limit workers' capacities to undertake responsibilities associated with decision-making in high-risk situations" (p. 57).

However, psychodynamic approaches are, as Healy notes, so embedded within many ways of working in the twenty-first century that their use continues despite these limitations and drawbacks. Their strength has been in providing theories of human behaviour as well as a way of understanding the client–worker relationship dynamics. They link individual agency, motivation, and coping with persons' functioning in the outer world. Psychodynamic approaches not only provide a way of understanding individual behaviour in the context of a client–worker relationship but also behaviour and processes within organizations, groups, and families.

Chapter Summary

In this chapter, some key skills associated with psychodynamic and cognitive behavioural approaches have been explored. Psychodynamic skills focus on bringing to conscious awareness patterns of relating both to the self and to others, and beliefs from the past to understand their impact on present functioning and future expectations. Cognitive behavioural skills similarly focus on building insight into the present and establishing more conscious control over thinking, feeling, and behaving. A major focus of CBT is the education provided to clients so they are able to adapt negative automatic thoughts independently from the collaborative work they have completed with their practitioner. A limitation of these skills is that they seek to bring about primarily inner-world change for the client. They have been criticized for failing to address the social, structural, and cultural contexts of people's lives and for relying on practitioners to address these issues in conjunction with the therapeutic process they have facilitated.

Questions for Analysis

1. What dimensions of these skills appeal to you? Why?
2. When would you use CBT skills and when would you not?
3. What are some of the cultural assumptions embedded in each of the approaches?
4. What is the difference between transference and counter-transference in psychodynamic work? What would you watch for in your practice?

Partner Practice

With a partner, practice an initial interview using CBT techniques. Have your partner identify a problem such as "I feel like a failure in school," or "I should work harder." Once the problem has been shared, assist your partner in identifying the automatic thoughts associated with the problem (when they occur, where, what happened), then what associated emotions emerge in response to the automatic thoughts, and finally the action or behaviour that occurs.

Once you and you partner have both had the opportunity to practice, discuss how the process worked, the structure, what you found helpful, and why this approach worked or did not work for you as the counsellor.

Recommended Readings

Beck, J.S., & Beck, A.T. (2011). *Cognitive behavioural therapy: Basics and beyond* (2nd ed.) New York, NY: Guilford Press.

Beck, A., Freeman, A., & Davis, D. (2004). *Cognitive therapy of personality disorders*. New York, NY: Guilford Press.

Brandell, J. (2004). *Psychodynamic social work*. New York, NY: Columbia University Press.

Cabaniss, D.L. (2017). *Psychodynamic psychotherapy: A clinical manual*. Malden, MA: John Wiley & Sons Inc.

Davis, S. (2006). *Community mental health in Canada*. Vancouver, BC: University of British Columbia Press.

Dean, R. (2002). Teaching contemporary psychodynamic theory for contemporary social work practice. *Smith College Studies in Social Work, 7*(1), 11–27.

Dobson, D., & Dobson K.S. (2016). *Evidence-based practice of cognitive-behavioral therapy* (2nd ed.). New York, NY: Guilford Press.

Gibney, P. (2003). The pragmatics of therapeutic practice. Melbourne: PsychOz.

Greenberger, D., & Padesky, C. (2016). *Mind over mood: Change how you feel by changing the way you think* (2nd ed.). New York, NY: Guilford Press.

Howard, S. (2006). *Psychodynamic counselling in a nutshell*. London: Sage.

Lindblad-Goldberg, M., & Northey, W F. (2013). Ecosystemic structural family therapy: Theoretical and clinical foundations. *Contemporary Family Therapy, 35*(1), 147–60.

McAdams, C.R., Avadhanam, R., Foster, V.A., Harris, P.N., Javaheri, A., Kim, S., & Williams, A.E. (2016). The viability of structural family therapy in the twenty-first century: An analysis of key indicators. *Contemporary Family Therapy, 38*(3), 255–61.

Miller, W.R., & Rollnick, S. (2014). *Motivational interviewing: Helping people change* (3rd ed.). New York, NY: Guilford Press.

Payne, M. (2014). *Modern social work theory* (4th ed.). New York, NY: Oxford University Press.

Piet, J., & Houguard, E. (2011). The effect of mindfulness-based cognitive therapy for prevention of relapse in recurrent major depressive disorder: a systematic review and meta-analysis. *Psychology Review, 31*(6), 1032–40.

Robichaud, M., & Dugas, M.J. (2015). *The generalized anxiety disorder workbook: A comprehensive CBT guide for coping with uncertainty, worry, and fear.* Oakland, CA: New Harbinger Publications, Inc.

Shulman, L. (2016). *The skills of helping individuals, families, groups and communities* (8th ed.). Boston, MA: Cengage Learning.

Simmons, J., & Griffiths, R. (2014). *CBT for beginners* (2nd ed.). Thousand Oaks, CA: Sage Publishing Co.

Internet Resources

Beck Institute for Cognitive Behavior Therapy
www.beckinstitute.org

Canadian Association of Cognitive and Behavioural Therapies
https://cacbt.ca/en/conferences/vancouver-2018

Canadian Counselling and Psychotherapy Association
www.ccacc.ca

Canadian Mental Health Association
www.cmha.ca

Canadian Mental Health Association, Ontario
www.ontario.cmha.ca

Canadian Mental Health Association, Vancouver, Burnaby Branch
http://vancouver-burnaby.cmha.bc.ca

Canadian Network for Mood and Anxiety Treatment
www.canmat.org

Centre for Addiction and Mental Health
www.camh.ca

International Association for Cognitive Psychotherapy
www.the-iacp.com

13 Narrative and Solution-Focused Skills

Learning Goals

- Identify the core skills of narrative and solution-focused approaches, particularly in relation to the establishment of the relationship between a worker and client and specific interventions.
- Identify core skills in narrative practice.
- Understand dominant narratives.
- Understand externalizing and the process of re-authoring narratives.
- Understand the strengths and limitations of these skills.

Narrative and Solution-Focused Theories

An example of the **constructivist** paradigm, **narrative theory** places a major emphasis on the ways in which an individual constructs and relates the stories of their life, particularly their problem stories. This approach is grounded in the belief that meaning-making, through the formulation of narrative, is integral to well-being because it leads to an integrated inner state: "the establishment of some stability for meaning is an essential foundation to any claim for a meaningful sense of felt subjectivity" (Sharp, 2006, p. 66).

Solution-focused or strengths-based narratives are often emphasized, so that the client develops a sense of insight and control over the narrative. When people experience major adversity, reconstructing a sense of self that is able to influence their environment again is an important process. Unlike in psychodynamic and cognitive behavioural perspectives, the self (or subjective experience) is understood as a more fluid state of being rather than constructed across the lifespan through various developmental phases.

Narrative approaches have had wide appeal across a variety of settings and populations. Indigenous communities have used narrative extensively to retell stories of colonization and culture (Smith, 2001; Tamasese, 2000; Wingard, 2001), while Holocaust survivors have used narrative to recount and validate experiences of horrific trauma and torture (Laub & Auerharn, 1993; Reiter, 2000). Bearing witness to a person's experiences of adversity and suffering has been recognized throughout the literature of trauma and grief as a critical process in recovery. It also means that the telling of stories has the power to bring about change at other social levels, such as at program or policy levels. Applying narrative skills requires the practitioner to identify the power held by dominant narratives in society. By understanding the impact of a dominant narrative on multiple levels (micro, macro) the worker is able to address the client's needs at the agency level while challenging the larger societal structures that play a role in the dominant narrative.

Referring back to Jahzara's situation in Chapter 3, narrative work would focus on the ways in which she initially tells her story, and the ways in which it can be co-created to focus more on her strengths and so that she externalizes rather than internalizes her problems. The worker is influential in developing alternative narratives that empower Jahzara and her coping capacities.

CP Photo/John Woods

Justice Murray Sinclair, Chairperson of the Truth and Reconciliation Commission of Canada, speaks at a sharing circle, one of many events held across the country that were intended to provide a platform for those affected by the residential school system an opportunity to share their experiences. This truth telling was seen as a necessary prelude to the ongoing process of reconciliation. How does this approach to truth and reconciliation reflect the principles of narrative approaches to trauma?

Core Skills of Narrative Practice

Narratives or stories are expressions of our values, beliefs, and experiences. The manner in which a story is told is unique to the storyteller (pictures, song, verbally, etc.). Narrative practice approaches therapeutic conversation by focusing on how individuals tell stories to make meaning about their lives. It is human nature to relate a lived experience in story form. Miller (2012) observes, "we fantasize about our future, anticipate our dreams, and relay the horrors of life" through story (p. 131). Narrative therapy, similar to family therapy, looks at the external world and the problem as external to the person. It is important to recognize the power of a constructed dominant narrative at both the micro (immediate, extended family) and macro levels (larger society, structural). Bitter (2009) describes the narrative approach by citing Foucault:

> Foucault asserts that those perspectives that become dominant-culture narratives have to be challenged at every level and every opportunity, because their function is, in part, to minimize or eliminate alternate knowledge-positions and alternate narratives. Because of the power of dominant-culture narratives, individuals and families tend to integrate these positions as if they are the only possible ones to take—even if those positions are not useful to the individual or the family. (p. 249)

Narrative practice aims to understand and transform the stories people live by—individual stories as well as stories held by communities and even nations. Dowrick (2006), writing about the power of story and storytelling, reminds us that "storytelling is one of humankind's most basic arts and the drive to listen to and tell stories is deep in almost everyone. It's the telling of stories that allows us to explore a situation or interaction that matters to us, to make sense of it or to relive it" (p. 57). Narrative approaches seek to understand the client–worker relationship and how to listen to clients' stories in particular ways. The stories are important reflections of us as individuals and/or communities but also as interior narratives that profoundly influence and maintain our lives.

For the worker, narrative techniques include skills such as listening with curiosity, posing questions that make a difference, deconstruction and externalization of client's thought patterns, the presentation of alternate stories, and assisting the client with re-authoring. As Bitter (2009) explains,

> Diversity, multiple frameworks, and an integration/collaboration of the knower are all part of this new social movement to enlarge perspectives and options. For some social constructionists, the process of "knowing" includes distrust of the dominant-culture positions that permeate families and society today. For these people, change starts with deconstructing the power of cultural narratives and then proceeds to the co-construction of a new life meaning. (p. 259)

Some questions to assist in exploring the real effects of culture on the person while also developing avenues for re-authoring lives may include the following:

1. What influence has your culture had in your life?
2. What challenges have you faced growing up in your culture and how have you handled them?

3. What is significant in your life and the lives of your family and community that you feel I must know if I really want to understand you?
4. What resources within your cultural community support you and you draw strength from in times of need? (Bitter, 2009, p. 261)

The Dulwich Centre website provides a narrative example titled "The Story of My Driving," demonstrating how the process of developing a story can help clients to become aware of how they have linked certain events in their life through the meaning they have given each experience.

Establishing and Sustaining the Relationship

As a result of emerging from postmodern understandings of subjectivity and truths, narrative approaches adopt a strong focus on the ways in which problem stories are co-created (de Shazer, 1994, p. xvi). The client–worker relationship provides a safe, supportive engagement in which a person's stories can be heard, witnessed, and validated. In bearing witness to a person's stories and helping to co-create new stories of strength and healing, change can occur. This approach has proven particularly important in coping in the aftermath of trauma experiences (M. White, 2004; Knight, 2013).

Specific Interventions

The agenda for change in narrative approaches focuses on understanding and re-authoring the stories we live by. Changing people's stories about their lives "can help to change their actual lives. Furthermore, changing these stories often involves challenging larger social stories within people's problem-saturated stories about themselves and their lives. All individual stories are social stories" (Brown & Augusta-Scott, 2007, p. xvii). As a result, specific skills have emerged in relation to what is attended to in stories and how they are explored. As in other approaches, skills in validation and exploration are used—probes, reflections, and summaries all assist to establish the dominant narratives of a person's life, both their own narratives and those that others impose on them. Narrative therapy then aims to transform the unhelpful stories—the inhibiting and self-defeating stories—restoring (or re-storying) them with stories that are strengths-based.

Exploring the Dominant Narratives

For many people, their circumstances are not only difficult but not heard by anyone. Experiences of oppression, poverty, trauma, and grief are often "disenfranchised" from the dominant social stories—no one wants to pay attention to them or accord them legitimacy. Listening to someone's stories can be a transforming experience and listening to one's own story allows new perspectives to form. Moore (2004) notes, "The repeated telling of a story gradually allows the pieces of life experiences to find their relation to each other" (p. 58). The repetitions of a story of trauma allow the person to name and to find explanations for her or his feelings, diffusing the negative impacts of the trauma.

Some of the major skills involved in narrative work are good listening skills such as listening actively and empathically to what is being told, asking questions and summarizing along the way, and enabling the person to tell all she or he needs to tell, no matter how complex, ambiguous, or painful the story. Narrative approaches emphasize that we each carry multiple identities and roles that change and are reconstructed frequently. Listening for what is told and how it is told is the first skill in narrative practice.

To assist clients with authoring their story M. White (2007) suggests a mapping process that includes deconstruction questions, relative influence questions, and contextual influence questions:

- Deconstruction questions help the client to explore how the problem has been constructed, different perspectives, the limits to the current construction, and other possible narratives that might be present.
- Relative influence questions explore how the problem influences the client, those around the client, and the client's feelings about maintaining the current narrative.
- Contextual influence questions focus on structures in the dominant culture (gender, diversity, religion . . .) asking *"Where did you learn A?"* and *"What structures show you A?"*

What kinds of non-verbal communication skills could you use to demonstrate active listening while practicing narrative therapy?

After the narrative has been developed, preference questions are asked to help the client prepare for re-authoring their current problem narrative. Questions such as

What would you prefer to have happen?
Is this the way you would prefer for ____ to happen?
Do you see ____ as good or bad?
Is this to your advantage?

Deconstructing and Re-authoring: Externalizing the Problem

Unlike the approaches explored in Chapter 12, narrative approaches consider the problem external to the person. While the person has a narrative about the problem, its causation, and its consequences, the person is not the problem. This skill of **externalizing** the problem entails inviting the person to speak around and about the problem, but not about herself or himself as the problem. In other words, "the person is not the problem, the problem is the problem" (Russell & Carey, 2003). Specific questions are asked about the problem, understanding that it is an issue external to the person. Once the client is able to externalize the problem (taking the problem away from the person), there is opportunity for the client to re-author their story or to explore hidden meanings. Externalizing can also assist clients with redefining self-defeating emotions such as shame or guilt and support the client in exploring the root of these emotions in a more specific manner.

To apply the skill of externalizing successfully the worker must assist the client in identifying the problem separate from the self, where the problem is rooted in the client's history, and how the problem has shaped the client's narrative over time.

BOX 13.1 Focus on Practice

Questions That Aim to Externalize the Problem

- Tell me about a time that you stood up to, said "no" to, or resisted the problem. How was that situation handled differently?
- Have there been times recently when the problem has not played a role in your life?
- Can you think of any time in the past when the problem could have played a role in your life but it did not?
- Do you remember other times in the past when you have stood up to the problem?
- How did it feel when you stood up to the problem?
- How have you been able to keep the problem from getting worse?

Source: Brown & Augusta-Scott (2007, p. xxxv).

Listening for Strengths and Coping Capacities

In Heather's work with a client in a drug and alcohol service, she sets out to explore what has happened in the early days of someone's recovery, when that person has experienced difficulties, as illustrated below.

BOX 13.2 Focus on Practice

A Conversation with a Client Who Has Relapsed

Heather is talking with a client who attended one session, then missed two appointments, and has attended for a second time and has reported a relapse.

Heather:	Hi Tony, why don't you tell me how the last few weeks have been going for you?
Client:	Not so great.
Heather:	What hasn't been so great for you?
Client:	I relapsed . . .
Heather:	I can see that you aren't very happy about this relapse. Was it a shock for you?
Client:	Nah, I always relapse.
Heather:	It sounds like this is something that happens often for you?
Client:	Yeah, like thousands of times. I give up . . .
Heather:	What has happened in the past when you have relapsed?

Notice that rather than pathologizing the recurrence of a relapse, Heather moves on to explore this client's narrative of relapse. She invites him to explore this more fully rather than explore what he has "failed" to do, and by becoming aware of some particular patterns of risky behaviour it opens up the way to new coping strategies. This process normalizes and validates the person rather than challenging and pathologizing the person's story.

Re-authoring Stories through Listening for Unique Outcomes

As shown by Heather's questions above, another major skill of narrative approaches is to emphasize a time or times when the problem has not been a problem, or when ways of managing it differently have been available. This way of "thinking again" emphasizes the strengths in a person's coping and that, in some situations, the problem or the client's way of coping with it varies. This reframing of the negative experience is related to the technique of challenging some of the ways the client thinks about an experience, described in Chapter 12.

The challenge to think about **unique outcomes** encourages the client to think again about how a problem dominates his or her life. Unique outcomes, also applied in solution focus therapy as exceptions, are a strength-based approach that helps clients effect change in their lives by creating an opportunity to construct and then live their desired alternate narrative. Unique outcomes are not untruths but rather unseen pieces of the client's life experience that were not believed as credible because they did not fit with the dominant story. Highlighting these unique outcomes involves deconstructing the dominant stories of a person's life and re-authoring new, positive, and life-affirming stories.

White and Epston (2005) suggest four areas that invite clients to re-author their story: what was happening in their lives; what happened; how did it happen; and then, what could it possibly mean? Reflecting on these four areas assists clients in describing where their story originated, the ongoing or current impact, what it means to them, and potentially how they want their story to proceed. Once the foundation of the clients' current narrative has been explored, they are then encouraged to generate new proposals for action in their story, describe situations likely to be favourable to the newly formed action, and predict the outcome of the action steps taken in the process of re-authoring their preferred story.

Unique Outcomes Questions:
Was it easier than you expected, facing ____?
Could coming here today be a unique outcome and a step towards you overcoming ____?

Re-authoring Social Stories

Unlike the skills discussed in earlier chapters, which tend to affirm existing cultural and social realities, narrative approaches seek to challenge some of those dominant social stories. Through deconstructing and re-authoring individual or group stories, the representations of these broader social, structural, and cultural narratives can be changed too.

Individuals' life stories are socially constructed and influenced by socio-political structures. These repeat experiences result in dominant narratives in our lives and society. Swart (2013) reminds practitioners that a narrative approach takes the power of language seriously and therefore pays close attention to both written and spoken language, stating, "if a word creates a world, it calls on our ethical responsibility to be both wary of our speaking and always aware of what our speaking and use of language are creating" (p. 1).

Core Skills of Solution-Focused Practice

Narrative and solution-focused approaches share many skills including the use of extensive open-ended questioning around a problem and the strategy of externalizing the problem as separate from the person in order to establish a new perspective on that person's circumstances. Both approaches step away from the assumptions of other perspectives that assume "there is a necessary connection between a problem and its solution" (O'Connell, 1998, p. 14). A number of differences, however, are evident in the two approaches. Narrative approaches are based on a very fluid understanding of the story a person lives by. Solution-focused approaches work more within a systems perspective and notions of a continuous self. "Brief therapies are by definition solution-focused. Solution-focused therapists help clients craft fairly well-defined goals that can be accomplished in a reasonable time frame" (Egan and Schroeder, 2009, p. 295).

Solution-focused therapy is situated in the postmodern theory of social constructivism. Social constructivism is a sociological theory that suggests objective reality does not exist, but rather, knowledge is created through an individual's social interactions and cultural context. This idea fits well within solution-focused practice as it supports the idea that we can never truly know the reality of another person (Hoffman, 2002).

Establishing and Sustaining the Relationship

As with narrative approaches, solution-focused approaches emphasize that your relationship with your clients is a short-term, co-creating relationship. The emphasis during the listening phase of the process is to hear both exceptions and solutions to problems in daily life. The goal is "to identify and amplify client strengths and resources" (Walsh, 2006, p. 208), with much of the "work" being done by clients outside of any counselling or conversational time spent with you as the worker. Your role as worker is to stimulate a new way of thinking about problem situations with your client.

Dolan (2005) summarizes the major tenets of solution-focused brief therapy as follows:

1. If it ain't broke, don't fix it. If it works, do more of it.
2. If it is not working, do something different.
3. Small steps can lead to large changes.
4. The solution is not directly related to the problem.
5. No problem happens all the time. There are always exceptions which can be utilized.
6. The future is both created and negotiable. (cited in Bitter, 2009, p. 232)

A positive and rapid engagement is encouraged so that work can occur quickly—not within the context of a lengthy therapeutic relationship. A high emphasis is placed on clients' expertise and empowerment in finding the solutions they need. The emphasis in the client–worker contact is on translating that expertise and empowerment into everyday life (O'Connell, 1998, p. 85).

Specific Interventions

Many of the interventions are similar to those described in the previous discussion of narrative approaches. Questions are asked to explore fully the ways in which the client views her or his situation, with an emphasis on exceptions and solutions, as well as on the future.

Focusing on Exceptions and Solutions

Questions that reflect a solution-focused approach relate to the *exceptions* to problems and to their solutions, rather than to a lengthy exploration of the nature of the problems themselves. This difference in focus is the major reason for the differences in the use of skills and the emphases of the approaches described in the previous chapter. The narrative approach presumes that people have strengths and resources that have enabled them to overcome difficulties and problems, and that these strengths and resources are what should be amplified, rather than the potentially overwhelming nature of the problem situations themselves. The emphasis is less on insight into current behaviours, thoughts, feelings, and events, and more on foresight about the future and building on a capacity to influence that future.

Focusing on the Future

Solution-focused skills are designed to orient the client towards the future instead of the past or even the present in great detail. Asking questions about the maintenance of problem situations emphasizes the consequences of not changing and encourages the motivation to change—the realization that unless something happens, problems could remain as they are or become exacerbated, rather than diminishing.

At the heart of solution-focused therapy is the skill of the "miracle question" (de Shazer, 1985), an open-ended question that is designed to "enable people to pretend, to transcend the present and imagine a better state of affairs" (Manthei, 1997, p. 100). The miracle question was proposed by de Shazer (1994): "Suppose that tonight after you go to sleep a miracle happens and the problems that brought you to therapy are solved immediately. But since you were sleeping at the time you cannot know that this miracle has happened" (p. 95). The first part of the miracle question invites the client to think that her or his difficulties could be different.

The next step is to think about how they could be different. For example, asking questions such as, "Once you wake up tomorrow morning, how will you discover that a miracle has happened? Without your telling them, how will other people know that a miracle has happened?" These questions can be adapted in many ways to invite people to think how differently their circumstances could or should look and as a result help set the goals for what needs to shift, even if only in the story someone lives by. The language of the questions you ask is driven by this focus on the future and by an emphasis on possibility and change. It is an essentially positive, strengths-oriented approach to practice.

After the client–worker relationship has been established and the client has shared their broader concerns, the process of goal setting can begin. In solution-focused therapies goal setting should be specific and achievable. It is important that the goals are identified by the client, while the worker facilitates focus, ensuring the identified goal matches the client's current abilities. A defined and well-planned goal opens the opportunity for change.

Questioning in solution-focused therapies is formed using "change language." Change language is applied through the use of questioning that focuses on times when the client was able to achieve their desired goal. In this process, clients are reminded of their existing skill set. Some examples include the following:

> What is the first thing you would notice when things are going well?
> How will you know the work you are doing here has been helpful?
> What have you done previously that has helped?
> Where do you think is a good starting place?

Another form of goal setting in solution-focused therapies is the use of scaling questions. Scaling provides the client with the ability to be specific and, in some manner, measure their progress towards reaching their goal. For example,

Worker:	On a scale of 1 to 10 with 0 being the most stress you have felt and 10 being normal life stress, where are you today?
Client:	Today I am at a 1.
Worker:	What would be different if you were at a 3?
Client:	I would feel less shaky all the time.
Worker:	Tell me about being shaky?

From this initial scaling point the worker is able to assist the client with exploring specific aspects of the problem. Scaling can continue with questions such as

What would be the first thing you would notice if you were not feeling stress?
How would you know the difference between good stress (like being on time) and harmful stress (like avoiding going to work)?

This process can also help with identifying setbacks. For example,

Worker: Last week you stated you were at a 5 and today you are at a 3. What shifted?
Client: My boss rejected my report and I feel like a total failure. Now I can't seem to leave my house or even think about work without shaking uncontrollably . . .

Continued use of the scaling technique highlights client successes and empowers clients to recognize their progress independent from the counselling relationship. Clients are better able to understand what they want to achieve, potential barriers to their success, and how to work towards their goal independently.

Strengths and Limitations of Narrative Skills

Narrative skills enable the client to develop a coherent but constantly evolving story about who he or she is in the changing context of the problems. Solution-focused skills enable the client to think and talk about the person she or he would like to be and how that person would like to live. They are applied in a strengths perspective so that the client focuses on positive change rather than on inescapable negativity and oppression. These skills have the potential to transform circumstances far beyond individual lives, to cause change, and to re-author dominant social and cultural narratives.

Some of the limitations are that narrative and brief-solution approaches may not provide clients the opportunity, both in relation to time and to emphasis, to explore their past and present circumstances in depth. Some critics are concerned about the lack of depth and the lack of understanding of or insight into the nature of personal difficulties. Particularly with solution-focused approaches, critics suggest that there is an emphasis on the positive at the expense of understanding the despair and distress.

Others question the underlying assumptions that clients are telling socially desirable stories in shared strengths-oriented discourse. Many stories involve not-so-desirable actions and perpetrations against others, and the theory leaves unclear where these fit within an overtly positive view of human behaviour in the absence of a political, ethical, moral, or social position. Nevertheless, narrative approaches have been profoundly influential in community organizing and social action strategies.

Other critics suggest caution in relation to the extent that workers impose their personal views and dominant stories on the client (Walsh, 2006, p. 268)—a concern that is pertinent to all approaches in human services work. Further concerns apply to the absence of theories of human development and change in the narrative and brief-solutions methods. To what extent can stories be so subjectively located that a worker needs no basis in biopsychosocial assessments and understandings of a person's life? Bitter's (2009) response to these concerns is that "cognitive-behavioural therapists approach culture as a context and a reinforcing context at that—in which thinking and behaving are enacted. For those cultures that place less emphasis on talking, expression of feeling, and intrapsychic expression, cognitive-behavioural methods seem like a welcome relief" (p. 320).

In **Chapter 14**, we will explore how feminist and critical approaches adopt a strong structural and political critique, which address criticisms of the more subjectively located approaches.

Chapter Summary

In this chapter, the skills associated with narrative approaches have been discussed, including exploring dominant stories, deconstructing and challenging these stories, and re-authoring them using a strengths-based approach. The skills explored in Chapters 6 through 8 are foundational to successful practice. Knowing how to listen, be comfortable with silence, and paraphrase with clients is important to the storytelling process. The future- and strengths-focused skills of solution-focused strategies have also been examined, particularly through the use of the miracle question and scaling technique. In both narrative and solution-focus therapies, the focus is on change and assisting clients in realizing their strengths and skills towards achieving their goals.

Questions for Analysis

1. What have you learned from this chapter about
   - exploring the narratives?
   - externalizing problems?
   - unique outcomes?
   - asking a "miracle question"?
   - focusing on personal or community strengths and resources?
2. What do you see as the key strengths of these skills?
3. When do you think you would use these skills? Why?
4. What do you want to learn more about?
5. What skills will you seek further training in and why?

Group Activity

In a small group of three, read the following narrative and discuss what you see as Paige's dominant narrative. How would you work with Paige to externalize her situation and what questions would you ask to assist her with the process of externalizing and re-authoring her story?

Paige had her first panic attack when she was 15. She was in the hall at her high school. Suddenly, all the noise from the other students dulled and the bell seemed to ring forever. Everything started to spin and Paige felt sick. She doesn't remember what happened next because she fainted. She describes her experience in her own words:

> I opened my eyes to see a teacher and students staring at me. I felt unclear and embarrassed.
>
> After that day, I had more and more attacks, and worried all the time about when the next one would happen. I didn't know they were panic attacks until my mom took me to the doctor and he diagnosed me with panic disorder. I didn't really know how to

make the attacks stop. To avoid the anxiety of anyone seeing them happen, I stayed home and missed school.

This turned into not being able to leave the house at all. My anxiety got worse and I stopped eating. The doctor gave me antidepressants and suggested I see a counsellor to work on a plan to address my panic attacks. This meant going out on a daily basis to try and work through the attacks.

I ended up failing grade 10 because it took me the rest of the school year to work through my anxiety enough to be able to go back to school.

Now, I finally feel less scared that an attack will happen. I haven't experienced an acute panic attack for months, but I still take medication for generalized anxiety.

I found it very helpful when my counsellor helped me to understand what's physically happening during a panic attack, and I know now that each attack will eventually pass.

Partner Practice

1. Pair up with another student and discuss a time when you felt extremely overwhelmed. Explore how you were feeling during this time, specific aspects of your feelings, who was around you, and what influenced your feelings. Then, explore what helped you move past this time, what changed, and how it changed. What did you learn from this experience?

After both you and your partner have had the opportunity to work through your examples, reflect on the important aspects you need to be aware of when working with clients.

2. With a new partner, practice using the scaling technique. For example, choose one aspect of wanting to eat healthier or to improve your time management skills. Take turns applying scaling and then reflect on the process. What was helpful? What did you learn that will be helpful to your future practice?
3. In a small group of three or four, have one person tell a story about an event in their life. After the story has been told, have each listener share what they heard from the story and, as a group, explore the similarities and differences. Have the storyteller share what felt closest to their experience and why.

Recommended Readings

Bitter, J.R. (2009). *Theory and practice of family therapy and counseling*. Belmont, CA: Brooks/Cole.

Brown, C., & Augusta-Scott, T. (2007). *Narrative therapy: Making meaning, making lives*. Thousand Oaks, CA: Sage.

Coady, N., & Lehmann, P. (2016). *Theoretical perspectives for direct social work practice: A generalist-eclectic approach* (3rd ed.). New York, NY: Springer Publishing Company.

Denborough. D. (2014). *Retelling the stories of our lives*. New York, NY: Norton & Company Inc.

de Shazer, S. (1994). *Words were originally magic*. New York, NY: Norton.

Franklin, C. (2015). An update on strengths-based, solution-focused brief therapy. *Health & Social Work*, 40(2), 73–6.

Guterman, J.T. (2014). *Mastering the art of solution-focused counseling* (2nd ed.). Alexandria, VA: American Counseling Association.

Knight, C. (2013). Indirect trauma: Implications for self-care, supervision, the organization, and the academic institution. *Clinical Supervisor*, 32(2), 224–43.

Madsen, W., & Gillespie, K. (2014). *Collaborative helping: A strengths framework for home-based services.* Hoboken, NJ: John Wiley & Sons Inc.

O'Connell, B. (1998). *Solution-focused therapy.* London: Sage.

Payne, M. (2014). *Modern social work theory* (4th ed.). New York, NY: Oxford University Press.

Russell, S., & Carey, M. (2003). Feminism, therapy and narrative ideas: Exploring some not so commonly asked questions. *International Journal of Narrative Therapy and Community Work*, 3(1), 67–91.

Swart, C. (2013). *Re-authoring the world: The narrative lens and practices for organisation, communities and individuals.* Bryanston, South Africa: Knowres Publishing.

White, C. (2016). A memory book for the field of narrative practice. Adelaide: Dulwich Centre Publications.

White, M. (2004). Working with people who are suffering the consequences of multiple trauma: A narrative perspective. *International Journal of Narrative Therapy and Community Work*, 1, 45–76.

White, M. (2007). *Maps of narrative practice.* New York, NY: W.W. Norton & Co.

Zimmerman, J. (2018). *Neuro-narrative therapy: New possibilities for emotion-filled conversations.* New York, NY: W.W. Norton.

Internet Resources

Canadian Solution Focus Brief Therapy Center
www.canadiansfbtc.com/upcoming-events

Dulwich Centre, Canada
https://dulwichcentre.com.au/canada

Dulwich Centre, What Is Narrative Practice? A Free Course
https://dulwichcentre.com.au/courses/what-is-narrative-practice-a-free-course

Narrative Therapy Center of Toronto
www.narrativetherapycentre.com

19 Narrative Therapy Techniques, Exercises, & Interventions
https://positivepsychologyprogram.com/narrative-therapy

Solution Focused Brief Therapy Association
www.sfbta.org

14 Feminist and Critical Theory Skills

Learning Goals

- Identify the core skills of feminist and critical approaches.
- Identify skills specific to the critical/feminist paradigm for establishing and sustaining a working relationship.
- Understand the principles of feminist therapy.
- Understand the strengths and limitations of feminist skills.

Feminist Theories

Feminism is a theory located within a critical paradigm. That is, the agenda of feminism is to bring about structural change as a result of women countering the oppression they experience within male-dominated power structures. Feminism focuses its attention beyond the inner world of an individual, arguing that inner worlds are influenced profoundly by the wider social and political context (Dominelli, 2002; Trevithick, 1998).

Like psychodynamic theory, there is no single **feminist theory**—feminists profess a variety of views along a continuum from radical to liberal feminism (Tong, 1998). Within feminism, one of the major variations relates to the extent to which perspectives argue for separatist positionings of women and men.

Feminist approaches empower individuals facing adversity to change their circumstances externally, rather than to internalize them as private problems. Feminist theory grew from critical theory in that it locates oppression and disempowerment within the wider social environment as the major causes of individual difficulty (Ife, 1997; Maidment & Egan, 2004; Pease & Fook, 1999). Critical theory identifies and seeks to challenge multiple sources of oppression—for example, gender, economics, culture, and sex. The primary focus of change is on the wider social, structural, and cultural contexts, rather than on the individual. Practice methods range from therapeutic counselling to social action and advocacy strategies.

This Ottawa monument of the Famous Five celebrates the five Albertan women, led by Emily Murphy, who pushed the courts to acknowledge women as "persons" under the law—a goal that they accomplished in 1929. Together with women's suffrage, this push for legal and political recognition for women is today seen as part of the first wave of feminism, occuring mainly in the late nineteenth and early twentieth centuries.

In feminist analysis, Jahzara's depression (see Chapter 3) might be understood in the context of her structural and social disempowerment (Shin, 2015), and its resolution would be anticipated through appropriate social supports and recognition. Similarly, the stressors in parenting might be understood as arising from the privatization of mothering and the unrealistic expectations placed on women to provide care for children and other family members with little social support and acknowledgement.

Core Skills of Feminist and Critical Practice

Unlike the approaches discussed in the previous chapters, feminist and critical theory approaches have an explicit lens on outer-world dimensions as the focus of their work. Many texts relating to communication and counselling skills exclude a discussion of these approaches because change is not understood as occurring at the microskill or client–worker level of individual communication and interviewing. Rather, the focus of intervention is on social, structural, and cultural change. However, a number of key skills emerging from feminist and critical theory perspectives are readily transferable to communication at the client–worker interface. For the purposes of this discussion, skills unique to feminist and critical theory approaches are focused on within the same discussion, rather than under separate headings.

See the multi-dimensional approach in Chapter 9.

Payne (2005) provides a rationale for critical approaches:

> Critical theories question the idea of a set, continuous self and identity. Part of this has to do with language. For example, we tend to think of things as dichotomies: what we are and what we are not. However, critical ideas suggest that things can change, be contradictory and multiple: many things at once. We should see ourselves as a whole people who can develop more complexity and diversity. (p. 244)

In practice, this notion is centred around deconstruction, resistance, challenge, and reconstruction. In regard specifically to feminist theory, Payne (2005) explains,

> As our society has become more conscious of the complex and frequently unfair and unjust ways that we respond to women, and the effects it has on self-image and functioning, a growing body of relevant therapeutic theory is emerging. This theory is useful in situations when women are seeking to get a better understanding of themselves and their potential, and to find strategies to help set and achieve appropriate life, personal, and career goals. (p. 244)

BOX 14.1 Focus on Practice

Five Principles of Feminist Therapy

Corey (2008, 2001) describes feminist therapy as based on five interrelated principles:

- The personal is political, which implements social change.
- The counselling relationship is egalitarian, which encourages equality between the therapist and the client. The client should be aware that she has the power to change and define herself and the therapist is only a tool with new insight and information.
- Women's experiences are honoured and they should get in touch with their personal experiences and intuition.
- Definitions of distress and mental illness are reformulated involving the internal as well as external factors of distress. Pain and resistance are viewed as a positive confirmation of the desire to live and overcome distress rather than being viewed as weak.
- Feminist therapists use an integrated analysis of oppression, which means that they understand that both men and women are subjected to oppression and stereotypes and that these oppressive experiences have a profound effect on beliefs and perceptions. (p. 341)

Payne (2005) provides the following practice issues and concepts:

- *Consciousness-raising* (connected to the critical practice conscientization) as a strategy for stimulating awareness and change.
- *Reflexivity* as a research tool and its subsequent adaptation as an element of practice.

- *Dialogic, egalitarian relationships* as the vehicle of practice that values and empowers women.
- *Social and personal identity* as the social processes by which it is formed and by which it changes is an important aspect of creating and intervening in diverse relationships. (p. 252)

Establishing and Sustaining the Relationship

Within feminist and other critical approaches, the emphasis within the worker's relationship with people is on establishing equality and working in partnership to recognize the inherent human rights each has as a citizen (Healy, 2005, p. 186). Another way of thinking about working with your clients is about "becoming an ally" (Bishop, 2015).

Revisit Figure 9.3 in Chapter 9 as a framework for important aspects of establishing a relationship.

In becoming an ally or working in more egalitarian ways, your task is to emphasize the reciprocity of skills within the relationship. As Ife (1997) suggests, "the critical paradigm requires that skills be shared between the worker and the 'client,' that the 'client' be seen as possessing skills that are just as valid and important as those of the worker, and that each should share their skills with the other in a process of mutual empowerment and mutual education" (p. 150). Within this relationship context, you remain aware that the wider social context—and its issues of sexual, racialized, and class oppression and **discrimination**—is likely to be reflected. Individual client–worker relationships become the microcosm in which these power relations can be replicated. The client–worker relationship itself provides an opportunity to address power imbalances and to name and ultimately challenge these sources of oppression. In relation to the assessment of the "presenting problem" the personal is understood as inherently connected to the political. As a result, critical and careful attention to these dynamics is required and openly discussed throughout the client–worker contact. This approach is based on the belief that change occurs through the "integration of personal and socio-cultural transformational processes" (Bricker-Jenkins, Hooyman, & Gottlieb, 1991, pp. 291–2).

Remember, in Chapter 2 we looked at communication as a process. As a worker, practicing a feminist approach in communication is viewed through a gender–power filter or analysis.

Most feminist and critical approaches see the relationship as a short-term resourcing role or a longer-term collaboration, rather than as a "therapeutic" relationship. This strategy is based in the belief that individuals are dealing with the private pains of public problems and that the solutions should be structural and political. Many models of feminist therapy, however, embrace the opportunity for both personal insight and political change.

Specific Interventions

Underlying all of the skills of any critical approach is an analysis of individual problems through a wider structural and power analysis, whether in relation to gender, class, ability, culture, or ethnicity. Within feminist approaches, this analysis is of gender and power, and women's oppression by men specifically. As a result, you are not using different communication skills, but are using them in a particular way to focus on a specific way of understanding people and their circumstances.

Feminism exposes the glaring omission inherent in all four paradigms—that of gender analysis of women's inequality in society and of how the state contributes to women's oppression (Mullaly & Dupre, 2019). Consider the example in Focus on Practice 14.2.

BOX 14.2 Focus on Practice

Gender and Inequality

Susan, a recently widowed woman of colour, is facing several challenges. She is unable to find employment and feels strongly it is due to her visible disability, which requires her to walk with a cane. Susan feels she often is treated differently from other women and from the way she sees men being treated—for example, the difference in how much time is extended for discussion during job interviews and the wait time for an interview.

Susan is uncertain how to address these issues. She fears that broaching her concerns with a worker may cause further refusal of assistance for her and for her son, who requires daily assistance for autism. If Susan is unable to gain employment, her family may risk losing their home and the required services for her child.

Practice within critical approaches draws on many of the skills we have already explored in previous chapters, such as the skills of questioning, of developing a story or multiple stories of the self, of understanding thoughts, feelings, and behaviours, and challenging these where necessary. Feminist and critical approaches also incorporate goal-setting processes into the work. We now explore three additional skills that are unique to feminist and critical approaches: the three core practice skills (Bricker-Jenkins, Hooyman, & Gottlieb, 1991, pp. 292–5) of **validation**, **consciousness-raising**, and **transformative action**. These skills lead to interventions that mobilize resources to meet basic human needs through relationships that nurture and sustain uniqueness and create validating environments.

Using Validation

To validate someone or something is to "lend force or validity to; confirm; ratify; substantiate" (Brown, 1993, p. 3541). Validation, in an interpersonal relationship, affirms the "truth" of a person's subjective experience. In this way, reflecting skills are used to affirm someone's telling of her story and her perceptions about what has occurred. Validation has emerged as an important part of the recognition that so many people's stories, and particularly women's, have been invalidated, disbelieved, or rendered invisible. Naming what has occurred is a first step in the process of work together, particularly in relation to experiences of violence, assault, and disempowerment.

BOX 14.3 Focus on Practice

The Importance of Validation

Luanne is a 34-year-old mother of three children. She had difficulty succeeding as well in school as her several brothers and sisters, all of whom are university graduates. She did graduate from a post-secondary secretarial course. On one of her holidays in Mexico she met Rudy, a Colombian expatriate who wanted to immigrate to Canada. They formed an intimate relationship that resulted in Luanne's first pregnancy. She

Continued

helped Rudy immigrate to Canada and they married and had two more children. Rudy did not adapt easily to Canadian culture, but he has an artistic flair and has formed a rapidly growing interior décor business supplying ceramic tile and other home decorations in ceramic and stone to builders in Toronto. They enjoy a comfortable upper-middle-class lifestyle.

Luanne has suspected for some time that "things don't quite add up" with Rudy, who is physically aggressive and verbally abusive to her. Recently, he had been physically abusing their children when she was out. The morning she witnessed Rudy striking the children, she quickly packed up her important papers and clothing and toys for the children and took refuge with them in a women's shelter. She is very angry, very frightened, and does not know what action to take to protect her children and herself.

Validating statements you could make in your conversation with Luanne might include the following topics: her courage in standing up to the abuse; her values in wanting to protect her children from such harmful practices; her courage in leaving with her children despite threats of harm if she ever left; her spirit of adventure in travelling to get to know other parts of the world; her successful transition from a social setting of very modest income to a social setting that makes more complex demands on its members; and her willingness to learn what she needs to know about the legal system in order to protect herself and her children.

See Chapter 13 for more on narrative- and solution-focused approaches.

Your questioning, reflecting, and statement skills would focus on the wider structural and cultural dimensions of her experience, not only the personal dimensions of Luanne's self-esteem issues, which perhaps made her unwilling to acknowledge Rudy's overbearing, demanding, threatening, and abusive behaviours because their marriage let her match her economically successful family. The focus, like narrative and solution-focused approaches, is on externalizing the problem.

Encouraging a Process of Consciousness-Raising

Through validation and dialogue, your skills help your client to engage in a process of consciousness-raising that is not only focused on your client's personal attributes but also in your client's wider social context. This consciousness-raising process leads to a process of liberation, which is sometimes described as spiral in nature (Bishop, 2015). The process of liberation involves "breaking the silence, ending the shame, and sharing our concerns and feelings" (p. 81). The skills we use are storytelling, analysis, strategy, and action: "Story-telling leads to analysis, where we figure out together what is happening to us and why, and who benefits. Analysis leads to strategy, when we decide what to do about it. Strategy leads to action, together, to change the injustices we suffer" (Bishop, 2015, p. 81). Action leads to another round of reflection, analysis, strategy, and action. This is the process of liberation. Like narrative approaches, storytelling becomes an important process and so, listening and reflecting are critical skills. Feminist and critical theories, however, in politicizing problems, also consider the importance of how to name these issues in their wider social context as important steps in working together.

Talking with someone about her difficult relationship circumstances may lead to a wider discussion of power and gender, or power and age, so that the person comes to understand relational circumstances as emerging from wider social, structural, and cultural influences, not from the particular circumstances of her own situation. This may mean that the intervention focuses more on forming connections with others in similar circumstances to move beyond an individual client–worker relationship and to participate in transformative action, as described below.

Engaging in Transformative Action

Through the individual experience of validation and consciousness-raising, liberation from oppression comes about through transformative action. While individual counselling work might be an important step in building insight and strengths for a person, connecting with others in group or community work is seen as the ultimate step to recovery or adaptation (Herman, 1992; Mullaly & West, 2018), as the problem no longer resides "with" the person but is addressed in its wider social context.

Wakefield (2017) outlines the steps of transformative action (Table 14.1).

TABLE 14.1 Strategies for Building Transformative and Feminist Leadership

Modelling feminist purpose and principles	• Engaging in ongoing processes of self and interpersonal reflection • Signaling the feminist purpose and principles of a group through small initiatives • Creating specific opportunities for younger leaders to emerge
Inspiring shared vision based on personal and collective reflexivity	• Proving reflection space to help people to connect on a personal level to collective political vision • Enabling people to unlearn harmful habits • Using body work to enhance personal awareness and interpersonal connection • Providing space for groups to engage in collective practices to cultivate different qualities • Sharing knowledge about the development of just organizational cultures
Empowering and enabling others to act	• Recognizing and valuing the different contributions people make • Incorporating collective leadership where an individual's safety is at risk • Fostering interpersonal openness and trust in groups • Clarifying expectations for responsibilities and conflict resolution • Prioritizing development of skills in collaboration • Facilitating connections between women in positional power and constituents • Developing trust with stakeholders by linking personal struggles to political action
Challenging patriarchal norms and oppressive power	• Using tools and processes to surface harmful expressions of power embedded in institutions • Collectively identifying positive forms of power • Investing in structures, processes, and collective practices that disable patriarchal norms • Replicating values-based organizing principles when moving from organizational change to collaboration and movement-building work • Enabling multiple team members to benefits from training programs so they may better establish and hold each other accountable for new norms

Continued

Encouraging integration of heart, mind, and body	• Encouraging interpersonal-relationship building of teams reduces artificial separations between work and life that contribute to stress and burnout • Coaching and mentorship to help individuals work through ongoing challenges • Recognizing the direct and vicarious trauma women activists may experience • Valuing and providing opportunities to develop self- and collective-care strategies

Source: From Wakefield, S. (2017, p. 9), "Transformative and Feminist Leadership for Women's Rights." Oxfam America Research Backgrounder series. https://www. oxfamamerica.org/explore/research-publications/transformative-feministleadership-womens-rights

Within this perspective, your focus as a worker is not only on the work you undertake with your clients but also in your desire to bring about change with others in the immediate and wider contexts. An example of transformative action includes "bringing people together in order to present a petition or submission about a policy issue, or to advocate for change" (Ife, 1997, p. 168). Other actions include the development of groups and community activities. For example, the Canadian Resource Centre for Victims of Crime was established in 1993 to provide awareness and support for women harmed by an act of violence. The resource centre offers several programs to support women, such as emotional and legal services. Similarly, groups whose primary goal is to assist women in crisis—through counselling, legal support, and provision or direction to specific services such as shelter or abortion—are active also in organizing and participating in self-empowering public demonstrations. These groups support activities related to events such as annual Take Back the Night marches and vigils to commemorate specific tragic events like the Montreal Massacre of 6 December 1989, or more recently, the Women's March, which promote messages of inclusion, equality, and empowerment.

The communication skills required for feminist and structural interventions include all of those outlined earlier—both verbal and non-verbal—enabling you to explore the story of the individual or the community that is dealing with a particular issue, to challenge, when necessary, particular ways of thinking and acting, to externalize the problems, and to validate and affirm people and their strengths. The skills may also include working towards linkage with, and referral to, other transformative-action opportunities.

Examples used in work with clients includes assertiveness education, which focuses on women becoming aware of their interpersonal rights. This idea focuses on transcending traditional gender roles and challenging negative beliefs that impact or influence our daily lives. Assertiveness learning/education is often completed through the process of reframing. Reframing is a counselling technique where the worker supports a client in considering an idea from a different point of view. While the worker does not dispute the facts presented, they encourage discussion that helps the client to arrive at a different conclusion. Reframing teaches clients to create shifts in their thinking from an *intrapersonal* position to an *interpersonal* position, creating room for change.

Ultimately, your focus is on collective action, however, rather than individual responsibility as the way to bring about change. For example, women's groups have actively lobbied governments for the provision of refuges for women escaping domestic violence. This action requires clear communication and argument with key stakeholders. Your engagement and rapport-building skills are fundamental to these processes, as well as to your direct practice with clients.

Protesters at the second annual Women's March on Toronto in January 2018. Prompted by the 2016 US presidential election of Donald Trump, the march is used to protest the ongoing social and economic inequality of women in Canada and internationally.

BOX 14.4 Practice Exercise

Using Feminist Skills

Duty workers on telephone crisis lines frequently receive calls from distressed young women who have been assaulted by a partner. These women have been hurt, are frightened, and don't know what to do—whether to leave or stay. You are the duty worker taking calls when a woman calls the crisis line. The woman speaks English but has a heavy foreign accent, making her difficult to understand. In between her phrases punctuated by sobs, she informs you she has been pushed into a dresser so that her head caught the edge of its large mirror. She also states her arms have bruises and she does not know what she should do.

1. How would you go about assessing such a situation with this woman?
2. What else would you want to know about her situation?
3. What validation skills might you use?
4. What consciousness-raising strategies would you consider?
5. Would you encourage her engagement in transformative action at all and how?

Strengths and Limitations of Feminist and Critical Skills

The strengths of feminist skills are that they shift the focus of women's personal problems to the outer world, where so often the cause lies. They emphasize that people are both victims and survivors of these wider influences, and that through political and communal strategies, change can be achieved. Like narrative and solution-focused approaches, the emphasis is on changing the social and cultural discourses rather than regarding individuals as personally responsible and pathologizing their coping capacities. As a result of feminist discourse, radical change has been made in social attitudes, in legislation, and in social supports that affect the lived experience of women. The understanding and validation that a feminist critique has offered for relationships, workplaces, and family life have affected women in Europe and North America and are having an influence on the lives of women around the world.

The first and obvious drawback of the feminist approach is that it may be less than helpful or empathetic to the needs and problems of males. Even where the worker has general skills, the worker's enthusiasm for her own emphasis may provide less support and understanding than the male client needs.

The related second major criticism of feminist and other critical theory approaches is that the worker is imposing a particular world view on clients who may have a different world view. That is, the worker expects her or his lens to become the lens of the client. The dominance of Western, middle-class views in the development of many of these theoretical understandings has led to the criticism that they are themselves colonizing, polarizing, and disempowering theories, rather than theories that achieve what they fundamentally set out to achieve—equality and empowerment. As Healy (2005) notes, "A contradiction exists between anti-oppressive theorists' claim to promote dialogue in practice and their assumptions that they hold a true and correct analysis of the world" (p. 190). Within the diverse context of Canadian services, for example, significant challenges emerge for feminist workers in maintaining a particular critique of gender, power, and culture, while respecting cultural difference and diversity.

Chapter Summary

In this chapter, the skills privileged within feminist and critical theory approaches have been explored, including validation, consciousness-raising, and transformative action. Understanding your clients' experiences from a feminist, and therefore critical theory perspective, enables the focus to be shifted from an emphasis on individual responsibility for coping to structural solutions and strategies. Instead, the personal is deemed to be political, leading to different solutions and expectations of the client–worker relationship. Some of the challenges inherent in these skills, however, were explored in relation to the potential to replicate the very situation the perspective seeks to eradicate—disempowerment within a particular cultural community and the imposition of a particular world view and way of being.

Questions for Analysis

1. What have you learned from this chapter about
   - how listening is influenced by feminist or critical theory approaches?
   - the nature of questions and the focus of intervention within these approaches?
   - the six specific skills primarily used within feminist and critical theory approaches?
2. What do you see as the key strengths of these skills?
3. When do you think you would use these skills? Why?
4. What skills do you want to learn more about?

Group Activity

In a small group of three or four, choose a magazine or website of your choice that you would normally review. Then, identify examples in text, images, or pages that support or contest traditional gender roles and social or societal norms/stereotypes. How is the media constrained by these social/cultural norms and responsible for maintaining these ideals?

- How does this influence communication?
- How might your approach to work with clients be influenced?
- What would you want to be aware of in your practice?

Recommended Readings

Bishop, A. 2015. *Becoming an ally: Breaking the cycle of oppression*. Halifax, NS: Fernwood Publishing.

Bricker-Jenkins, M., Hooyman, N., & Gottlieb, N. (Eds.). (1991). *Feminist social work practice in clinical settings*. London: Sage.

Case, K.A. (Ed.). (2016). *Intersectional pedagogy: Complicating identity and social justice*. New York, NY: Routledge.

Chaplin, J. (1999). *Feminist counselling in action* (2nd ed.). London: Sage.

Collins, P.H. (2014, April). *Toward social justice: Sharpening intersectionality's critical edge*. Keynote address given at the Intersectionality Research, Policy & Practice: Influences, Interrogations and Innovations international conference at Simon Fraser University, Vancouver, BC.

Collins, P.H. (2015). Intersectionality's definitional dilemmas. *Annual Review of Sociology, 41*, 1–20. doi:10.1146/annurev-soc-073014-112142

Enns, C.Z. (2017). Feminist therapy and empowerment. In C.B. Travis & J.W. White (Eds.), *Handbook of the psychology of women* (pp. 273–97). Washington, DC: American Psychological Association.

Flasch, P., Murray, C.E., & Crowe, A. (2017). Overcoming abuse: A phenomenological investigation of the journey to recovery from past intimate partner violence. *Journal of Interpersonal Violence, 32*(22), 3373–401.

Fook, J. 2000. Critical perspectives on social work practice. In I. O'Connor, P. Smyth, & J. Warburton (Eds.), *Contemporary perspectives on social work and the human services: Challenges and change*. Frenchs Forest: Addison Wesley Longman Australia.

Fook, J., Collington, V., Ross, F., Ruch, G., & West, L. (2015). *Researching critical reflection: Multidisciplinary perspectives*. New York, NY: Routledge.

Grzanka, P.R. (2016a). Queer survey research and the ontological dimensions of heterosexism. *Women's Studies Quarterly, 12*(2), 130–48.

Grzanka, P.R. (2016b). Undoing the psychology of gender: Intersectionality and social science pedagogy. In K.A. Case (Ed.), *Intersectional pedagogy: A model for complicating identity and social justice* (pp. 63–81). New York, NY: Routledge.

Hesse-Biber, S.N., & Piatelli, D. (2012). The feminist practice of holistic reflexivity. In S.N. Hesse-Biber (Ed.), *The handbook of feminist research: Theory and praxis* (2nd ed., pp. 557–82). Thousand Oaks, CA: Sage.

Kondrat, E. (1999). Who is the "self" in self-aware?: Professional self-awareness from a critical theory perspective. *Social Service Review, 73*(4), 451–77.

Mullaly, B., & West, J. (2018). *Challenging oppression: A critical approach to anti-oppressive and anti-privilege theory and practice*. Toronto, ON: Oxford University Press.

Park, C. (2016). Intimate partner violence: An application of attachment theory. *Journal of Human Behavior in the Social Environment, 26*(5), 488–97.

Pillow, W.S., & Mayo, C. (2012). Feminist ethnography: Histories, challenges, and possibilities. In S.N. Hesse-Biber (Ed.), *The handbook of feminist research: Theory and praxis* (2nd ed., pp. 187–205). Thousand Oaks, CA: Sage.

Remer, P. (2014). Feminist therapy. In J. Frew & M.D. Spiegler (Eds.), *Contemporary psychotherapies for a diverse world* (pp. 397–441). New York, NY: Routledge.

Rempel, S. (2017). *Advocacy in practice: creating a culture of social change in the human services*. Toronto, ON: Oxford University Press.

Shin, R.Q. (2015). The application of critical consciousness and intersectionality as tools for decolonizing racial/ethnic identity development models in the fields of counseling and psychology. In R.D. Goodman & P.C. Gorski (Eds.), *Decolonizing "multicultural" counseling through social justice* (pp. 11–22). New York, NY: Springer.

Stoppard, J. (2000). *Understanding depression: Feminist social constructionist approaches*. London: Routledge.

Internet Resources

Canadian Journal of Developmental Studies
www.cjds.ca/cjds.html

Canadian Resource Centre for Victims of Crime
https://crcvc.ca/links

Canadian Women's Foundation
www.canadianwomen.org

Centers for Disease Control and Prevention, Intimate Partner Violence
www.cdc.gov/violenceprevention/intimatepartnerviolence/index.html

Domestic Violence and Incest Resource Centre Library, Hub of Helpful Information
www.dvirc.org.au/HelpHub/HelpIndex.htm

Feminist Majority Foundation
www.feminist.org

Women's and Gender Studies et Recherches Féministes
www.wgsrf.com

PART FIVE

Finishing the Work

In this final part of the book, we explore the tasks involved in finishing the work with clients and the tasks of evaluation. This last chapter brings together ways of thinking about practice that are multi-dimensional and that balance a number of different tasks within the client–worker relationship. Finishing the work is the final dimension in the framework of human service work.

PART ONE Framing the Relationship

- the purpose of human service work
- your value base, professional ethics, and regulatory guidelines in Canada
- your theoretical and factual knowledge.

PART TWO Forming the Relationship

- your use of self
- your organizational context
- your ongoing support and professional development needs
- meeting the people involved
- opening the communication
- active listening and working with silence
- listening empathically
- using self-disclosure.

PART THREE Focusing the Communication

- establishing the story
- forming an assessment
- goal setting.

PART FOUR Focusing the Intervention

- drawing on theoretical perspectives
- doing the work.

PART FIVE Finishing the Work

- ending well
- evaluating the work.

15 Finishing Work with Clients

Learning Goals

- Understand how finishing the work is conceptualized.
- Describe the tasks of finishing the work with your clients.
- Analyze the challenges in finishing the work.
- Consider the ways of evaluating your work.
- Understand how an effective evaluation is conducted.

Thinking about Finishing the Work

In contrast to all the attention paid to *establishing* a good client–worker relationship, many texts spend surprisingly little time on the process of ending it well. Your relationships with your clients will end for many reasons and in many ways, as they do in your other personal relationships. Ideally, a client–worker relationship ends when the work is done—that is, when the goals agreed upon have been met and change has been able to occur or begin to occur. In some settings, the work ends because the contracted time period ends or the mandate to attend an agency is fulfilled. These endings can be anticipated and planned for as part of the overall contact.

Other endings occur in unplanned ways. The circumstances of the client or worker may change, such as when the client relocates or the worker changes jobs. The relationship may end because of a poor engagement or rapport within a client–worker relationship. Clients may drift away because they are dissatisfied. In some more extreme situations, the worker or client may not be able to continue the process due to death or serious illness (Shulman, 2009).

In other circumstances, your relationships with clients may not end as expected. Some relationships continue over long periods of time and across different organizational contexts, particularly if you continue to work through a number of organizations within a particular field of practice. Some continue by virtue of you and the client living in the same small, rural, or remote community (Green, 2003; Taylor, 2004). In some instances, perhaps more controversially, client–worker relationships have become lifelong ones and are characterized more by friendship than by any professional stance (Crossley & McDonald, 1984; Stansfield, 2006). Organizational contact may not be the only context for contact, which breaks down the often artificial boundary between the world of a client and his or her worker.

BOX 15.1 Focus on Practice

Different Endings?

Different endings are typified in the stories we have explored throughout this book. Recall Karen and Mark from Chapter 4.

> Mark was in his thirties, presenting with suicidal thoughts when he met with Karen for a first interview. His story related to the recent traumatic event of having watched as his small daughter ran across the road, was hit by a car, and dragged a long distance. His daughter had suffered multiple injuries including some brain damage, and he was wracked with guilt as well as by the trauma of witnessing the terrible event. He had left his family and the province feeling empty and hopeless.

Recall Nicole and Mrs B. from Chapter 6.

> Mrs B. is the mother of an eight-year-old son diagnosed with a treatable but life-threatening condition. She talked with Nicole about the impact of the diagnosis on her, her son, and their family. Issues arose about subsequent contact over the following two-month period, until Nicole and Mrs B. were able to talk through their issues and expectations of each other. Mrs B. decided to continue seeing Nicole for assistance.

And recall Joanna and the client who became aggressive towards her, from Chapter 10.

> Joanna was working as a counsellor in an addictions recovery centre. She was assigned a client with a history of violent behaviour who spoke English as a second language. The client was charged with assault and was distressed about a pending court appearance. Throughout their discussions, the client became highly agitated and threatening before storming off.

Each of these circumstances could lead to very different endings of the worker–client relationships. In Karen's situation, through regular, supportive counselling, it was anticipated that a strong engagement and working alliance would be established over time. Karen's organization may have limits on the number of sessions she can work with Mark or she may be able to engage indefinitely with him. Each of these possibilities presents specific challenges about how clearly an ending is contracted in their work together, both at the beginning and along the way. The finishing process is likely to be a discussed, planned process in their work together.

In Nicole's working relationship, she will continue to see Mrs B. throughout her child's treatment and, if the treatment is not successful, possibly through her child's dying and death. The relationship could be long-term or relatively short-term, depending on the unpredictable trajectory of the illness. Any sense of when this client–worker relationship may end could be difficult to establish.

In Joanna's situation, the relationship did not end in this one scenario. The client returned and continued to be aggressive and threatening. Joanna continued in her assignment as the case manager for this client until the client left the agency, but she was also able to have little direct involvement with him. The relationship was crisis-driven and engagement remained tenuous. Given that a working relationship had been so difficult to establish, it was hard to think about how, why, and when it would finish. In fact, the relationship ended when the client left the agency. Joanna's client's needs were not met.

The Tasks of Finishing the Work

One of the challenges in understanding how to effectively finish the work is that there is little evaluation of what happens after it because there is no further contact.

Endings, like beginnings, are important influences on the work that is achieved subsequently. We often consolidate our skills and learning a considerable time after we first acquire them. As Loader (1995) states, "Certainly, we 'finish' counselling, we 'end' a supervisory or a collegial relationship, but the development is within us, within the other, not confined to time" (p. 38). Shulman (2009) discusses the importance of counsellors sharing their own feelings about the termination of sessions, as a way of teaching appropriate ways to manage endings and encourage the client to engage in expressing how they are feeling.

The Canadian Association of Social Workers' *Code of Ethics* (2005) notes the following points regarding the termination or interruption of services:

> **1.8 Practices for Termination or Interruption of Services**
>
> 1.8.1 Social workers renegotiate or terminate professional services when these services are no longer required or no longer meet the needs of clients.
> 1.8.2 Social workers respect the right of voluntary clients to discontinue service, engage another practitioner or seek a second opinion.
> 1.8.3 Whether the decision to renegotiate or terminate is that of the client or the social worker, social workers (where appropriate) initiate a discussion with the client to appreciate, and if possible, address any difficulties or misunderstandings that may have occurred. If the client desires other professional services, the social worker may assist in referral.
> 1.8.4 Social workers discuss client's needs, options and preferences before continuing or discontinuing services, or offering to seek transfer or referral.
> 1.8.5 Social workers at the earliest opportunity inform clients of any factor, condition or pressure that affects their ability to practice adequately and competently (p. 10).

What are the important tasks in ending a client–worker relationship? The following is a fictional conversation at the finishing stage of a group, as presented by Yalom (2005), dramatizing many of the important tasks. Jakob, a group member, asks how the group facilitator is feeling and he replies that he is tired but ready for the last group meeting that will take place the following week.

Jakob: Okay to bring a ceremonial cake for our last meeting?
Julius: Absolutely, bring any kind of carrot cake you wish. (pp. 335–6)

But there was to be no formal farewell meeting. The following day, Julius was stricken by severe headaches. Within a few hours he passed into a coma and died three days later.

This story accentuates four tasks that the worker should have in mind during a worker–client relationship about terminating that professional relationship:

- work towards a planned ending of an intervention
- manage an unplanned interruption to that ending
- participate in a ritual to mark the end of work together
- manage the evolving familiarity in the client–worker relationship.

Evident in this example is the shift from a worker-directed concern for the client to the point where the client can express concern for the worker, questioning him directly about his well-being.

Turner (2002) suggests there are four major tasks associated with termination: "(1) deciding when to terminate, (2) dealing with feelings associated with ending, (3) generalizing and maintaining gains made, (4) evaluating accomplishment as service provided" (p. 225). Three more essential tasks associated with termination include asking for a **referral**, providing follow-up, and critically reflecting on the client's status and on the worker's intervention. Termination tasks differ depending on the nature and the context of the relationship such as whether it has been a short-term or long-term relationship, a mandated or voluntary human service involvement, or a strong or a weak **attachment** bond.

Bitter (2009) cites two criteria for termination: "Termination is based on effectively reaching a state in which problems have improved or have been eliminated. That is, there is no need to keep clients in therapy once they have reached the desired goals" (p. 479). Sheafor and Horejsi (2008) state that termination should be expected and not come as a surprise to clients because ending should be part of the work from the beginning. Termination should be "discussed during the planning and contracting phase of the helping process and the client should be reminded from the beginning that intervention is goal oriented and time limited" (p. 479).

Working towards a Planned Ending

At the early stage of establishing a client–worker relationship, it is important to be thinking about how the work may be ending. Will it end as a result of agency-imposed time limits, workload issues, the end of a mandate, or through the attainment of agreed-on goals? Planned endings can occur when the work is clearly contracted around any of these dimensions. It raises the question of the timing of this discussion.

In some situations you can talk with your client from the beginning of your contact as to how and when the work will end. The process of disengagement is a purpose of your work, just as the process of engagement is. From the standpoint of the client's rights and empowerment, the client should always be informed about when and how an ending will occur. Not knowing about how and when a relationship may end creates unnecessary vulnerability, insecurity, and disempowerment, particularly when difficult or poor relationships are a prominent feature of a person's personal histories. In other situations an ending may be planned only after the goals are more clearly established through mutual agreement. Initially, some sessions remain relatively unstructured about the overall time frame but once the extent of work both parties wish to engage in becomes more evident the length of the client–worker relationship can be estimated. In other situations mentioning the inevitable ending too early in the relationship may jeopardize engagement. The early phases of most work and contact may need to focus more on building a strong engagement and rapport. Once a strong engagement is in place, the process of setting goals and completing them structures a natural termination point. In some cases goals change or, in the case of setbacks, require additional steps in the work, but practitioners should emphasize that ending is an important part of the work you do together.

Understanding endings involves reflecting on what were the intended outcomes of the work together. For example,

- What kind of change was being worked towards and how would you know if it had been achieved?
- What are the assumptions about recovery, adaptation, or efficacy that both you and your clients have being working with?

Christine Simpson, whose daughter had been murdered and who described her relationship with her grief worker, John, to a newspaper reporter saw the end of the work as relating to the following outcome: "I still have my pain, and my anger, but I am also very happy with my life as it is" (Stansfield, 2006, p. 16). Endings mean different things for different people, depending on their age and stage, their past experiences of ending relationships, and what the significance of the work has been for them. Since bad endings in human relationships are such a major contributor to human distress and suffering, ending a good working relationship well is one way of positively modelling the good relationship experience, even if the relationship has been a mandated one.

With planned endings, you can talk over what will be involved and what it might mean for the client and for you. Future contact and referral options can also be discussed, as described later in this chapter.

"Theorizing" Endings

How we think about endings influences what can and should happen at this point in the worker–client relationship. Each of the theoretical perspectives considered earlier has a different emphasis on the process of ending the work and whether the tasks discussed above are important. Bitter (2009) notes that "improvement in the form of movement forward is more than an acceptable end" (p. 199).

Psychodynamic approaches have dominated understandings of the termination process because of the centrality of the relationship to the goals of the work. In many discussions of the ending of a client–worker relationship or a therapeutic group, grief and sadness are identified as the dominant emotions in the finishing process. Perhaps in the intensity of therapeutic work, this can be reasonably anticipated. The goal of psychodynamic work is often the establishment or reparation of secure attachments or good inner objects, and so the focus is on ending well after having worked through both past and present feelings of loss and abandonment. Termination is a carefully planned and discussed stage of work (Walsh, 2006, pp. 43–4).

Consistent with the psychodynamic approach, authors such as Shulman argue that **denial** is the first stage of the ending process. He proposes that there is an inevitable change in the engagement in the relationship prior to its ending, and that there may be both direct and indirect anger. Using grief theory, ending is seen as a process of mourning, "acknowledging the client's ending feelings and sharing the worker's ending feelings" (Shulman, 1999, p. 209).

Sorrow and grief are not always the condition of the client, however, as it can be a time of realizing that change has been achieved and that a new phase is beginning. For many other people the end of a client–worker relationship can be an incentive to achieve goals. The attainment of goals may mean that the relationship can end because conditions of a court order, for example, have been met. Ending can be about a client's regaining a sense of control over his or her own life, free from the scrutiny of a worker (Trotter, 2006).

Task-centred approaches are based on the premise that ending work together is positive because it signals empowerment and achievement. As Marsh and Doel (2005) state, "there is the effect which we all experience as we move towards a deadline . . . in which our mind concentrates on the coming event with increasing strength. A time limit is, therefore, motivating" (p. 118).

Endings signify the achievement of clearly contracted work and the empowerment of the client to resume independent functioning. Short-term work is then seen to be all that is required so that people can resume connections or establish new connections with informal social networks and their own interior resources.

Providing Feedback and Reviewing Goals

Planned endings provide an opportunity for "systematically adding up the experience" (Shulman, 1999, p. 213) and identifying areas for future work if needed (p. 215). While engaging in the client–worker relationship opens up the story, ending closes off and sums up the story, identifying what has been addressed and achieved.

Clearly, direct conversations with people about what has been helpful and unhelpful will provide very useful feedback about how circumstances have changed and what has been effective in creating these changes. Marsh and Doel (2005) suggest a series of questions to ask in a final session as part of this review focusing on: the beginning; the problem, whether it was the correct one and whether it has changed; the agreement or the goals; how things have changed in general; and the expectations for the future.

Your review could include the following types of questions:

- Do you think we have worked on the right issue?
- How has the situation changed for you?
- How has the situation changed others?
- Do you think we achieved what we set out to achieve?
- What strengths can you now rely upon? How will you continue to apply these strengths?
- Do you think we could have done things differently?
- What questions haven't I asked?
- Have we explored everything?
- How near to your goals are you now?
- What do you think will happen in the future in relation to these issues? (Adapted from Marsh & Doel, 2005)

The termination review provides an important opportunity to look at the ways in which the client will sustain the gains beyond the contact period. Reviewing what she or he will now do differently emphasizes the strengths and capacities that have been acquired. In being aware of the stages of change model, you can also talk through the possibilities of encountering future difficulties and how they may be managed. Identifying your availability for future contact is also critical if this is a possibility. This is discussed later in this chapter.

In any feedback and review process, social desirability tendencies influence a lot of the feedback we give. That is, we often give positive feedback to maintain relationships rather than provide more accurate and potentially hurtful feedback. Below, Yalom (2005) suggests one form of feedback from a client who was asked to comment as to whether his worker had been effective.

Recall the stages of change model (Chapter 1), which describes the phases of change management: pre-contemplation, contemplation, action, maintenance, and relapse.

BOX 15.2 Practice Exercise

Consumer Feedback

Client: Eventually I realized you didn't know how to help me and I lost faith in our work together. I recall that you spent inordinate amounts of time exploring my relationships—with others and especially with you. That never made sense to me. It didn't then. It still doesn't.

1. How would you feel and what would you do if your client provided this feedback to you?
2. What would you do in your interactions with your clients to try to ensure that they could talk these issues through earlier?
3. What practice skills do you need to improve? (Yalom, 2005, p. 28)

In asking for feedback, we need to be prepared to hear both positive and negative remarks. If we are serious about a consumer perspective we need to take all feedback on board and talk it through with the people concerned. We need to talk about these issues in supervision and critically reflect on what has occurred in specific situations. Other ways of receiving feedback include client satisfaction surveys, used in many organizations, or feedback interviews with other staff members such as managers or supervisors. An anonymous survey gives clients the option of providing critical feedback without fear of any reprisals in terms of access to the agency in the future or other personal outcomes. An opportunity to talk with a supervisor can enable clients to talk about concerns they may have about their experiences with you as a worker.

Recall the process of giving and receiving feedback, outlined in Chapter 10.

Managing an Unplanned Ending

Yalom's example of a worker's sudden death is an interruption to a planned group ending. This can occur in practice, with circumstances such that either the client or the worker interferes with a planned ending. In many other instances, however, the work does not finish in a planned way at all. It ends because the client departs, because of a change in the client's circumstances and/or transient circumstances, or because there is no other way to address worker ineffectiveness.

Worker-Driven Endings

Workers can be in situations of unplanned endings for several reasons. In some cases workers transfer locations, receive a promotion, or choose to leave their employment, and each of these scenarios can result in unplanned endings.

In some instances, worker-driven unplanned endings can occur when a worker is faced with symptoms of burnout or vicarious trauma, which interrupt their ability to practice. Symptoms of burnout can include rigidity in work role, disengagement, irritability, and feelings of resignation about the potential benefit of the worker's role.

Vicarious trauma occurs when a worker is continuously exposed to the traumatic experiences of their clients. It results in emotional exhaustion, stress, anxiety, and in many cases longer term mental health issues. Workers facing burnout and vicarious trauma, should seek the support they require. It is also important for workers to be sure preventative measures are in place when they return to work. Consistent supervision and debriefing specific to the work environment, wellness planning, and healthy professional boundaries are foundational to sustaining practice.

Client-Driven Endings

Turner (2017) notes that some unplanned endings may be due to clients intentionally avoiding the ending process, due to reactions from significant others, because of conflicts, because the client is happy with the improvements but does not tell the worker, or due to factors that the client cannot control, such as a change in work schedule. Unplanned endings can be disconcerting—you can be left wondering what happened. Some strategies you can use at these times include the following:

- critically reflecting on your work with the client and what issues may have been influencing the decision to not return
- trying to follow up through telephone contact with your client to discuss what has happened
- sending a letter that leaves the door open for future contact, if this is possible
- fulfilling your reporting requirements in terms of the organization and duty of care to the client.

Agency-Driven Endings

In some organizations, clients are not informed when a worker departs. Even if contact is intermittent—for example, a client comes to the hospital only twice a year for an appointment—you may want to consider whether informing clients of your departure is desirable and possible. Unplanned endings can leave people feeling unsettled, angry, distressed, or unclear about what has occurred. In some situations, this outcome is preventable and worth working towards preventing.

Participating in Ending Rituals

Yalom's fictional group ends with a discussion about making a ceremonial cake. This sharing of food is not an uncommon gesture in the finishing of work together. Rituals in one-to-one work are similarly important. Rituals provide an opportunity to acknowledge beyond words what is taking place and what has taken place.

An ending ritual may be as simple as the review discussion outlined above, in which the ritual of closing is undertaken. Other rituals that can emerge in the ending of work together include the following:

- Creative reminders of the work can be developed, such as photos, scrapbooks, memory cards, journals, or a summary document of what has been achieved. This ensures the recognition of **continuing bonds**; that is, that a relationship can continue beyond the direct contact of your work in other forms such as good memories.
- Sharing food—particularly cross-culturally—is an important way of symbolically shifting the power imbalance to a shared power balance.
- Gratitude can be expressed through letters or cards.
- The worker/client can become involved in sharing significant milestones of the other's experience, such as attending a graduation or the funeral of a family member.
- Token gifts can be exchanged.

Each one of these gestures is a way to express sharing and gratitude, and symbols can remain lifelong reminders of important work that has been done together. Workers and organizations approach these gestures differently and important choices should be made about whether they are appropriate and empowering gestures.

Managing the Evolving Familiarity

In Yalom's group, concern is expressed by a group member towards the worker and the worker responds. This depicts a different direction of concern and attention within the client–worker relationship. Surprisingly little is written about the shifts that occur in client–worker relationships over time. Rural workers acknowledge the ongoing basis of relationship and connection (Green, 2003; Green, Gregory, & Mason, 2006), but within the urban context it is rarely noted. It is important to emphasize the inevitable familiarity that emerges in the context of a client–worker relationship. In many instances this continuity can lead to a curiosity and concern with someone's well-being to the point where ending the work does not occur when it perhaps should. That workers become attached to clients (and vice versa) for a variety of different reasons is inevitable, but it remains one of the less-discussed issues in practice.

The literature relating to self-disclosure we explored earlier, in some ways, addresses the issues of trust and vulnerability within relationships. The psychodynamic literature talks about relationship in terms of transference and counter-transference. Fiction and movies, such as *Reign Over Me* (2007) and *50/50* (2011), often depict relationships that would be regarded as gross enmeshment and a violation of professional boundaries, as is true, too, in older films—*The Prince of Tides* (1991), *Good Will Hunting* (1997)—where a psychiatrist or psychologist is a central figure. They demonstrate, however, that relationships are complex and cannot be neatly compartmentalized as professional or personal.

Ending rituals, such as writing cards, exchanging token gifts, or sharing food, can be helpful for workers and clients as they close their work together and transition to a different kind of relationship. How might these rituals vary depending on the kind of practice that you follow as a human service worker? What different kinds of ending rituals might you use for a group as opposed to individual practice?

Indigenous and cross-cultural models have increasingly challenged Western models of practice for their emphasis on the artificial boundaries between the personal and the professional. Western models have been based on a concern about the power differential and the potential disempowerment and exploitation that can emerge within the client–worker relationship, and as a result, authenticity and the growing trust and familiarity between clients and workers over time have tended to be minimized as key agents of change. Using supervision to address these issues of boundaries and appropriateness is vital so that work ends when and how it should.

Making a Referral

In many situations, a referral for ongoing or different services may be required. For example, the work may not be complete but circumstances for the worker or client may have changed. Alternatively, the worker and/or the client may realize that goals cannot be achieved within this setting and that working with someone else may be more appropriate. Ending one client–worker relationship may be about making transitions to "new experiences and support systems" (Shulman, 1999, p. 218). In all of these situations, a process of referral is needed.

Referral processes have been found to be most successful when the following dimensions are attended to:

- discussion of the reason for the referral
- discussion of the process of referral
- a joint meeting with the current and new worker, if appropriate, to enable the goals to be established for continuing work
- consent of the client to speak with another worker
- the writing of reports as required.

Providing Follow-Up and Keeping the Door Open

As many of the examples in this chapter have highlighted, not all human service work occurs in the context of neat, structured sessions, nor as unique occasions. Talking about the possibility of future contact is an important step, if this contact is possible within the resource context. This involves being clear about whether the work has definitely ended, whether no more contact is possible for whatever reason, or whether work can be re-contracted at a later date should other issues arise.

Some of the key reflections within this process include:

- Is the client empowered to access services when and how they are needed? For example, can he or she see someone else if that is the preference? Can the client continue talking with you within the context of a new "episode of care," as many organizations term it?
- How does the client reinitiate contact?
- Are there other ways in which the client can stay connected with the organization if that is her or his wish? Many organizations have extensive volunteer networks that enable clients of the service to contribute to the organization and to others experiencing similar issues. This turn-around can be an important marker of recovery and adaptation. (Herman, 1992)

In some situations a formal follow-up after a specified time interval is part of the organization's practice. For example, when a death has occurred some hospital workers will follow up at the time of the anniversary of the death, or invite people back to a memorial service. In some other instances the possibility of follow-up is more complex. For example, many clients will not inform other family members that they have been in contact with services, so any attempt at reconnecting may breach confidentiality for that person.

Follow-up can provide a beneficial opportunity for the client to reflect on the intervention experiences and possible changes and give feedback about the process. Clients can evaluate the longer-term effects of the work as they reappraise what they have experienced since the intervention and the efficacy of the intervention. For the worker, follow-up gives some insight into the ongoing changes people have made and satisfies professional curiosity about how things have progressed for someone. Below, a worker describes the experience of meeting a client a decade after their initial contact.

BOX 15.3 Practice Exercise

Connecting Again

I did not expect to bump into my client again. It was in another setting, where neither of us was in a work role. I was really surprised that after 10 years I still remembered so much of her situation and of the work we did together. For me, it was overwhelming to see how well she was doing and all that she had dealt with. I saw that she had survived so much. I am not sure what it was like for her to talk with me again. I think I gave her a fright, but I think she was also pleased to reconnect and to tell me about what she was now doing. We so rarely connect with people down the track and find out how they are doing.

1. What would you do in this situation?
2. What would you be curious about?
3. What do you need to keep in mind when engaging in the conversation?

The important question to ask is: Who is the follow-up for? Follow-up must first and foremost be for the benefit of the client.

Critical Reflection and Evaluation

Evaluating your work occurs in this final phase of contact in two important ways. The first is evaluating the work with the client to review his or her perceptions of what has occurred and the efficacy of that work, as we discussed above. The second is your own **evaluation** of your work in the context of all of your practice. This occurs through your own critical self-reflection and your supervision.

See Chapter 5 for extensive exploration of critical self-reflection and supervision.

Client perspectives, as discussed above, are important key to your evaluation, but so are the perspectives of other workers and key stakeholders. Supervision, peer discussions, and annual performance appraisals provide opportunities for you to receive feedback about your practice.

Reviewing the evidence base of your practice (Lewis, 2002) is also critical. Supervision and your own professional development opportunities provide instances to review the various sources of information you rely on. As Morris (2006) states in relation to social workers, they

> need to know what interventions and services improve a client's functioning, a community worker needs to know how her or his community can work together to solve its problems and prevent other community problems, and the administrator/policy maker often just needs to know who her or his client community is. (p. xxxiii)

A commitment to learning and self-reflection is essential for effective human service work.

Strengths, Optimism, and Communication

While we continue to know more about experiences of change and adaptation, and the role of intervention in these experiences, much remains unknown and open to question and research. Throughout this text we have explored many of those issues and hope you are left with many more questions as you begin your practice. Working with people is a life-changing experience—whether this work occurs in the classroom, in the counselling room, in the corridors of a hospital, in people's homes, or in our communities.

People's lives and opportunities can change for the better as a result of interventions and resources. Oppression and adversity can be alleviated by the concerted efforts of individuals, groups, and communities. Human strength, resilience, and optimism are not only traits we encourage in the people with whom we work, they are traits we need to foster and keep alive within ourselves as workers (Mancini & Bonanno, 2006). Throughout this book we have explored some of the ways in which these efforts can be enhanced by effective communication skills. You have been encouraged to try these skills and critically reflect on how they may be useful tools for your applied practice.

Chapter Summary

In this final chapter, we have explored how your work with people can end in planned and unplanned ways. Some of the meanings of endings have been considered, as have the skills required in managing the transition through to the end of the work together. Evaluating your work, both with the client directly and indirectly in your own supervision and reflection, has been emphasized as a critical dimension of your practice.

Questions for Analysis

1. What have you learned from this chapter about
   - planned endings to client–worker relationships?
   - unplanned endings to these relationships?
   - the tasks of termination?
   - evaluating your practice?
2. What has been your experience of ending relationships, both professional and personal?
3. How have you felt about these various endings?
4. How will you receive feedback if the client is not happy with the work and ends it early? How may you apply the feedback?
5. What do you think are the most important dimensions of finishing the work?
6. How will you improve or add to your practice skills, based on your evaluation of your practice, to ensure continued professional development?

Group Activity

In a small group of three or four, discuss a time when you experienced an ending. For example, it could be an ending such as leaving a middle school or graduating high school and moving away to attend university.

- What thoughts did you have about your ending? (too soon, not ready, cannot wait!)
- What emotions did you experience? (sadness, fear, excitement)
- Was there something that helped you work through your process of ending? What was it and how was it helpful?

As a group, discuss the key aspects of termination you feel are important to the client–worker relationship and why. Then discuss possible issues that could arise if the termination process is completed incorrectly.

Partner Practice

In pairs of two, reflect on the concepts of ethical practice, personal and professional boundaries, and potential power dynamics in the client–worker relationship discussed in Chapters 1 through 4. Create a list of the critical aspects of these concepts that are part of facilitating a successful termination process. Think through and identify links between how understanding the importance of ethical practice, personal and professional boundaries, and potential power dynamics in the client–worker relationship are important in the termination phase of your work.

Recommended Readings

Betteridge, L. (2014, Fall). *Early endings—Addressing the challenges of termination. Perspective.* Ontario College of Social Workers and Social Service Workers. Retrieved from https://www.ocswssw.org/wp-content/uploads/2014/11/PN-Early-Endings.pdf

Felton, E., & Polowy, C. (2015). *Termination: Ending the therapeutic relationship—Avoiding abandonment.* National Association of Social Workers, Utah Chapter. Retrieved from www.utnasw.org/?page=Terminationguide

Gil, E., & Crenshaw, D.A. (2016). *Termination challenges in child psychotherapy.* New York, NY: Guilford Press.

Hepworth, D.H., & Rooney, R.H. (2017). *Empowerment series: Direct social work practice.* Boston, MA: Cengage Learning.

Klass, D.P., Silverman, P.R., & Nickman, S. (1996). *Continuing bonds: New understandings of grief.* Washington, DC: Taylor & Francis.

O'Hara, A., & Weber, Z. (Eds.). (2006). *Skills for human service practice: Working with individuals, groups, and communities.* South Melbourne: Oxford University Press.

Patterson, J., & Williams, L. (2018). *Essential skills in family therapy* (3rd ed.). New York, NY: Guilford Press.

Payne, M. (2005). *Modern social work theory.* Chicago, IL: Lyceum Books.

Payne, M. (2014). *Modern social work theory* (4th ed.). New York, NY: Oxford University Press.

Reamer, F. (2006). Termination services. *Social Work Today – Eye on Ethics.* Retrieved www.socialworktoday.com/news/eoe_0506.shtml

Turner, F.J. (2017). *Social work treatment: Interlocking theoretical approaches.* New York, NY: Oxford University Press.

Internet Resources

Canadian Association of Social Workers, *Ending the Client Relationship*
www.casw-acts.ca/en/ending-client-relationships-webinar

Canadian Counselling and Psychotherapy Association
www.ccpa-accp.ca

InfoXchange: Technology for Social Justice
www.infoxchange.net.au

Statistics Canada—Investigating Social Justice Issues
www.justice.gc.ca/eng/rp-pr/jr/index.html

Appendix 1: Further Resources

Canadian Association of Social Workers (CASW) Contact Information

As a federation of nine provincial and one territorial social work organizations, the Canadian Association of Social Workers provides a national leadership role in strengthening and advancing the social work profession in Canada.

Canadian Association of Social Workers
383 Parkdale Avenue, Suite 402
Ottawa, Ontario K1Y 4R4
Tel: (613) 729–6668, 1–855–729–2279
Website: www.casw-acts.ca

Alberta College of Social Workers
#550, 10707 100 Avenue NW
Edmonton, AB T5J 3M1
Tel: (780) 421–1167, 1–800–661–3089 (Alberta residents only)
Fax: (780) 421–1168
E-mail: acsw@acsw.ab.ca
Website: www.acsw.ab.ca

The Association of Social Workers of Northern Canada (ASWNC)
Box 2963
Yellowknife, NT X1A 2R2
Tel: (867) 920–4479
Fax: (867) 669–7964
E-mail: ed@socialworknorth.com
Website: www.socialworknorth.com

British Columbia Association of Social Workers
Suite 402, 1755 West Broadway
Vancouver, BC V6J 4S5
Tel: (604) 730–9111, 1–800–665–4747 (BC residents only)
Fax: (604) 730–9112
E-mail: bcasw@bcasw.org
Website: www.bcasw.org

Manitoba Association of Social Workers/
Manitoba Institute of Registered Social Workers
Unit 101-2033 Portage Ave.
Winnipeg, MB R3J 0K8
Tel: (204) 888–9477
Fax: (204) 831–6359
E-mail: masw@mts.net
Website: www.maswmirsw.ca

New Brunswick Association of Social Workers
Mailing address:
P.O. Box 1533, Station A
Fredericton, NB E3B 5G2
Street address:
403 Regent Street, Suite 100
Fredericton, NB E3B 3X6
Tel: (506) 459–5595, 1–877–495–5595
Fax: (506) 457–1421
E-mail: nbasw@nbasw-atsnb.ca
Website: www.nbasw-atsnb.ca

Newfoundland and Labrador Association of Social Workers
P.O. Box 39039
St John's, NL A1E 5Y7
Tel: (709) 753–0200
Fax: (709) 753–0120
E-mail: info@nlasw.ca
Website: www.nlasw.ca

Nova Scotia Association of Social Workers
1891 Brunswick St., Suite 106
Halifax, NS B3J 2G8
Tel: (902) 429–7799
Fax: (902) 429–7650
E-mail: nsasw@nsasw.org
Website: www.nsasw.org

Ontario Association of Social Workers
410 Jarvis St.
Toronto, ON M4Y 2G6
Tel: (416) 923–4848
Fax: (416) 923–5279
E-mail: info@oasw.org
Website: www.oasw.org

Prince Edward Island Association of Social Workers
81 Prince Street
Charlottetown, PE C1A 4R3

Tel: (902) 368–7337
Fax: (902) 368–7080

Saskatchewan Association of Social Workers
2110 Lorne St.
Regina, SK S4P 2M5
Tel: (306) 545–1922
Fax: (306) 545–1895

Source: Canadian Association of Social Workers (CASW) *Code of Ethics*, 2005, www.casw-acts.ca

Additional Resources

Addictions Resources

Canadian Center on Substance Use and Addiction
www.ccdus.ca/Eng/Pages/Addictions-Treatment-Helplines-Canada.aspx

Centre for Addiction and Mental Health
www.camh.ca

Drug Rehab and Addictions Services in Canada
www.drugrehab.ca

Government of Canada, National Addiction Resource List
www.canada.ca/en/health-canada/services/substance-abuse/get-help/get-help-with-drug-abuse.html

National Anti-Drug Strategy, 2017–18
www.canada.ca/en/health-canada/campaigns/national-anti-drug-strategy/about-strategy/messages.html

Northwest Territories Health and Social Services
www.yhssa.hss.gov.nt.ca

Seniors and Aging

Alzheimer Society of Canada
http://alzheimer.ca

BC Psychogeriatric Association
www.bcpga.bc.ca

Canadian Association on Gerontology
http://cagacg.ca

Canadian Seniors Directory
www.canadianseniorsdirectory.ca

Mosaic Seniors
www.mosaicbc.org/services/settlement/seniors/

Programs and Services of Interest to Seniors
www.saskatchewan.ca/residents/family-and-social-support/seniors-services/programs-and-services-of-interest-to-seniors

Seniors Policy Lens
www.mentalhealthcommission.ca/English/document/269/seniors-mental-health-policy-lens-toolkit

Seniors for Seniors
https://seniorsforseniors.ca/resources

Mental Health

Access Mental Health
https://access-mentalhealth.ca

Accessing mental health care in Canada
www150.statcan.gc.ca/n1/pub/11-627-m/11-627-m2017019-eng.htm

Anxiety Canada
www.anxietycanada.com/what-cbt-1

Canadian Mental Health Association
https://cmha.ca

Centre for Addiction and Mental Health
www.camh.ca

Canadian Association for Suicide Prevention
www.suicideprevention.ca

Canadian Network for Mood and Anxiety Treatments
http://canmat.org

Crisis and Trauma Resource Institute
https://ca.ctrinstitute.com/workshops/cognitive-behavioural-therapy-toronto3-20-2

Mental Health Services
www.canada.ca/en/public-health/services/mental-health-services.html

Mood Disorders Society of Canada
https://mdsc.ca

Counselling

Canadian Art Therapy Association
www.catainfo.ca

Canadian Association for Play Therapy
www.cacpt.com

Canadian Association of Cognitive and Behavioural Therapies
www.cacbt.ca

Canadian Association for Marriage and Family Counselling
https://camft.ca

Canadian Association for Psychodynamic Therapy
https://psychodynamiccanada.org

Canadian Counselling and Psychotherapy Association
https://www.ccpa-accp.ca

Canadian Group Psychotherapy Association
http://cgpa.ca

Canadian Society for Spirituality and Social Work
www.spiritualityandsocialwork.ca

Solution-Focused Brief Therapy Association
www.sfbta.org

Culture and Diversity

Aboriginal Professional Association of Canada
www.aboriginalprofessionals.org

Association for New Canadians
http://www.ancnl.ca

Immigration and Refugee Organizations across Canada (CCR)
http://www.povnet.org/node/2915

Indigenous Peoples in Canada
www.thecanadianencyclopedia.ca/en/article aboriginal-people

Indigenous Works
https://indigenousworks.ca/en/resources/indigenous-organizations

Native Women's Association of Canada (NWAC)
https://www.nwac.ca

Thunderbird Partnership Foundation
https://thunderbirdpf.org/about-tpf/first-peoples-wellness-circle

Additional Resources

Access Alliance Multicultural Health and Community Service LGBTQ Resources
http://accessalliance.ca/programs-services/lgbtq-programs/lgbtq-resources

American Psychological Association
www.apa.org

Canadian Cancer Society
www.cancer.ca

Canadian Center for Gender + Sexual Diversity
http://ccgsd-ccdgs.org

Canadian Civil Liberties Association
https://ccla.org/focus-areas/equality/lgbtq-rights

Canadian Diabetes Association
www.diabetes.ca

Canadian Health Network
www.phac-aspc.gc.ca/chn-rcs/index-eng.php

Canadian National Institute for the Blind
www.cnib.ca

Canadian National Society of the Deaf-Blind, Inc.
www.deafblindcanada.ca

Canadian Virtual Hospice
www.virtualhospice.ca

Epidemic and Pandemic Alert response
www.who.int/csr/don/en

Family Care Office: Parenting Resources, University of Toronto
www.familycare.utoronto.ca/caring_children/pr.html

Pride at Work Canada
https://prideatwork.ca

Schizophrenia Society of Canada
www.schizophrenia.ca

Women North Network
www.womennorthnetwork.ca

Appendix 2: Practice Exercises

Practice Forms

Practicing human service skills with fellow students or human service workers can result in a reflective process that assists you in developing your professional framework. The following is a short feedback form that you can provide to a peer who has agreed to act as a client for your ongoing practice development.

I ____________________ understand that I am volunteering to participate in a practice skill session. I understand that I may end my participation at any time without consequence.

I consent to the practice session being video recorded for review after the practice session is complete and that the video recording will be destroyed within ____________________ (time period) following review.

I understand that the interviewer is not a counsellor and the purpose of this exercise is to assist the interviewer with feedback towards further development of human service interview skills.

I will answer the following questions to the best of my ability in my role as a participant.

______________________________ ______________________________

Signature Date

	Disagree		Neutral		Agree
	1	2	3	4	5

1. I felt comfortable during the session. ____________________
2. The questions were clear. ____________________
3. The interviewer helped me identify my issue more clearly ____________________
4. I was able to identify resources to assist me. ____________________
5. The interviewer helped me identify tools to increase my ability to cope. ____________________
6. I felt confident in setting a goal to work towards. ____________________

Any specific questions or moments you wish to highlight:

____

____

____

Feedback Form for Non-verbal Communication

Non-verbal communication is communication without words. It includes facial expressions, eye contact, touching, tone of voice, and dress, posture, and spatial distance between people.

________________________ ________________________

Name of Interviewer Date

____

Name of person completing this form

Answer the following questions highlighting observable non-verbal communication.

1. What body positioning did you observe? Was it open or closed? How did the client appear to respond to the interviewer's positioning?

   ____

   ____

   ____

   ____

2. Describe the interviewer's hand gestures, facial expressions, busy hands, head tilting, and overall appearance of being present.

   ____

   ____

   ____

3. Describe the interviewer's tone of voice. Was it calm, confident, and client centred?

   ____

   ____

   ____

Continued

4. Did the interviewer appear present or distracted and what tells you this?

____

____

____

5. Where there any non-verbal aspects that taught you something about the interview/engagement process? If so, what was it?

____

____

____

Feedback Form for Verbal Communication

Verbal communication is the use of sounds and words to express yourself.

______________________________ ______________________________

Name of Interviewer Date

____

Name of person completing this form

In a group of three (one interviewer, one client, and one observer) facilitate a practice session rotating through each role. Have the observer answer the following questions highlighting observable verbal communication. Once you have each taken a turn as the observer, discuss the answers to the below questions and what you have learned from this process.

1. How did the introduction feel? Was there a specific word or phrase that stood out to you?

____

____

2. Were the questions asked clear? What questions helped the process the most?

____

____

____

3. Were the questions strength based? Provide a few examples.

____

____

4. Were there any questions that appeared confusing or unclear requiring clarity?

____

____

____

Continued

5. What specific word choices appeared to have the most impact on the conversation?

6. Did the level of vocabulary appear to match the client? Provide an example.

7. Was the interview structured? What statements demonstrate this?

8. Were any goals discussed? Did they appear to be client centred?

9. Did the goal appear attainable? What specific statements tell you this? If the goal did not appear attainable why?

Ethics

Ethical dilemmas in practice are not difficult to navigate—especially when two guiding principles come into conflict. Ethical dilemmas occur when a situation calls for the worker to prioritize one ethical principle over another or if one's personal values come into conflict with one's professional values guided by the Canadian Association of Social Workers' *Code of Ethics* (www.casw-acts.ca/en/Code-of-Ethics).

The following pages present a few examples of ethical decision-making models. Choose a model and apply the ethical decision-making steps provided in your chosen model to the following scenario.

Scenario

You are a clinical social worker who works with couples. A few months ago you saw a mother and her 14-year-old daughter who has a mild intellectual disability. The mother was having some difficulty managing her teenage daughter. You referred the child to another clinical counsellor who specializes in these types of issues. The mother called you back because she was trying to get some information from the counsellor and the counsellor told her that the information was confidential. The mother is concerned that the counsellor and her daughter may be discussing her daughter's interest in exploring her emerging sexuality. What do you do?

Ethical Models for Practice

"The model uses six 'fundamental principles' for evaluating consequences of options for action and combines actions of the absolutist use of principles and the relativist emphasis on context and deliberation about consequences of actions" (Miller, 2007, p. 35).

Step 1: Identifying the problem or dilemma during information gathering and consultation about the nature of the problem.

Step 2: Identifying potential issues involved in the problem in terms of rights, responsibilities, and welfare of all involved.

Step 3: Reviewing relevant codes of ethics to see if and how they apply.

Step 4: Reviewing applicable laws and regulations.

Step 5: Consulting to get other perspectives about the problem.

Step 6: Considering courses of action.

Step 7: Evaluating consequences of various courses of action using the principle framework.

Step 8: Deciding on the best course of action.

Source: Pamela Miller. (2007). *Ethical decision-making in social work and counselling: A problem/inquiry-based approach*. Toronto, ON: Thompson/Nelson.

Tracking Harms's Model of Decision Making

"The focus of this model is primarily on the goals and motivations of the participants. For each option potential obstacles for achieving are calculated within this context of goals and strategies with the ultimate objective of choosing options that minimize harm" (Miller, 2007, p. 34).

Step 1: Construct arguments that justify the acts or omissions of participants to try to understand their motivation for their actions.

Step 2: Determine the actual goals of the participants and the means by which they thought they would achieve those goals. Determine what their goals ought to be and what means would be best for achieving those goals.

Step 3: Identify the harm of alternative courses of action and identify to whom the harm would occur, as well as the kind and degree of harm.

Step 4: Make a judgement about what is the best outcome and what will minimize harm.

Step 5: Determine how the outcome should be achieved in a way that will produce more good than harm.

Source: Pamela Miller. (2007). *Ethical decision-making in social work and counselling: A problem/inquiry-based approach.* Toronto: Thompson/Nelson.

First Nations Code of Ethics

The following is a *Traditional Code of Ethics* formulated by the Assembly of Manitoba Chiefs Youth Secretariat, which summarizes the most important values and teachings that are considered universal to all nations.

1. Each morning upon rising, and each evening before sleeping, give thanks for the life within you and for all life, for good things the Creator has given you and others and for the opportunity to grow a little more each day. Consider your thoughts and actions of the past day and seek for the courage to be a better person. Seek for the things that will benefit everyone.
2. Respect means to feel or show honour or esteem for someone or something; consider the well-being of, or treat someone or something with deference or courtesy. Showing respect is the basic law of life.
   - Treat every person, from the tiniest child to the oldest Elder, with respect at all times.
   - Special respect should be given to Elders, parents, teachers, and community leaders.
   - No person should be made to feel "put down" by you—avoid hurting others' hearts as you would a deadly poison.
   - Touch nothing that belongs to someone else (especially sacred objects) without permission, or with an understanding between you.
   - Respect the privacy of every person. Never intrude in a person's quiet moments or personal space.

- Never walk between or interrupt people who are conversing.
- Speak in a soft voice, especially when you are in the presence of Elders, strangers, or others to whom special respect is due.
- Do not speak unless invited to do so at gatherings where Elders are present except to ask what is expected of you, should you be in doubt.
- Never speak about others in a negative way, whether they are present or not.
- Treat the earth and all her aspects as your mother. Show deep respect to the mineral, plant, and animal worlds. Do nothing to pollute the air or the soil. If others would destroy our mother, rise up with wisdom to defend her.
- Show deep respect for the beliefs and religions of others.
- Listen with courtesy to what others say, even if you feel what they are saying is worthless. Listen with your heart.

3. Respect the wisdom of people in council. Once you give an idea to the council or a meeting, it no longer belongs to you—it belongs to the people. Respect demands that you listen intently to the ideas of others in council and that you should not insist that your ideas prevail. Indeed, you should freely support the ideas of others if they are true and good, even if those ideas are quite different from the ones you contributed. The clash of ideas brings forth the spark of truth.
4. Be truthful at all times and under all conditions.
5. Always treat your guests with honour and consideration. Give your best food, your best blankets, the best part of your house and your best service to your guests.
6. The hurt of one is the hurt of all; the honour of one is the honour of all.
7. Receive strangers and outsiders with a loving heart and as members of the human family.
8. All the races and nations in the world are like the different coloured flowers of one meadow. All are beautiful as children of the Creator and they all must be respected.
9. To serve others, to be of some use to family, community, nation or the world is one of the purposes for which human beings have been created. Do not fill yourself with your own affairs and forget your most important task. True happiness comes only to those who dedicate their lives to the service of others.
10. Observe moderation and balance in all things.
11. Know those things that lead to your well-being and those things that lead to your destruction.
12. Listen to and follow the guidance given to your heart. Expect guidance to come in many forms; in prayer, in dreams, in times of quiet solitude and the words and deeds of wise Elders and friends.

Sources: www.fnhssm.com/index.php/home/traditional-code-of-ethics
Aboriginal Information Series Office of University Accessibility, August 2006, Number 2

Core Social Work Values and Principles

The Canadian Association of Social Workers' *Code of Ethics* sets forth values and principles to guide social workers' professional conduct. A code of ethics cannot guarantee ethical behaviour. Ethical behaviour comes from a social worker's individual commitment to engage in ethical practice. Both the spirit and the letter of this *Code of Ethics* will guide social workers as they act in good faith and with a genuine desire to make sound judgements.

Social workers uphold the following core social work values:

Value 1: Respect for Inherent Dignity and Worth of Persons

- Social workers respect the unique worth and inherent dignity of all people and uphold human rights.
- Social workers uphold each person's right to self-determination, consistent with that person's capacity and with the rights of others.
- Social workers respect the diversity among individuals in Canadian society and the right of individuals to their unique beliefs consistent with the rights of others.
- Social workers respect the client's right to make choices based on voluntary, informed consent.

Value 2: Pursuit of Social Justice

- Social workers uphold the right of people to have access to resources to meet basic human needs.
- Social workers advocate for fair and equitable access to public services and benefits.
- Social workers advocate for equal treatment and protection under the law and challenge injustices, especially injustices that affect the vulnerable and disadvantaged.
- Social workers promote social development and environmental management in the interests of all people.

Value 3: Service to Humanity

- Social workers place the needs of others above self-interest when acting in a professional capacity.
- Social workers strive to use the power and authority vested in them as professionals in responsible ways that serve the needs of clients and the promotion of social justice.
- Social workers promote individual development and pursuit of individual goals, as well as the development of a just society.
- Social workers use their knowledge and skills in bringing about fair resolutions to conflict and in assisting those affected by conflict.

Value 4: Integrity of Professional Practice

- Social workers demonstrate and promote the qualities of honesty, reliability, impartiality, and diligence in their professional practice.
- Social workers demonstrate adherence to the values and ethical principles of the profession and promote respect for the profession's values and principles in organizations where they work or with which they have a professional affiliation.
- Social workers establish appropriate boundaries in relationships with clients and ensure that the relationship serves the needs of clients.
- Social workers value openness and transparency in professional practice and avoid relationships where their integrity or impartiality may be compromised, ensuring that, should a conflict of interest be unavoidable, the nature of the conflict is fully disclosed.

Value 5: Confidentiality in Professional Practice

- Social workers respect the importance of the trust and confidence placed in the professional relationship by clients and members of the public.
- Social workers respect the client's right to confidentiality of information shared in a professional context.

- Social workers only disclose confidential information with the informed consent of the client or permission of client's legal representative.
- Social workers may break confidentiality and communicate client information without permission when required or permitted by relevant laws, court order, or this *Code*.
- Social workers demonstrate transparency with respect to limits to confidentiality that apply to their professional practice by clearly communicating these limitations to clients early in their relationship.

Value 6: Competence in Professional Practice

- Social workers uphold the right of clients to be offered the highest quality service possible.
- Social workers strive to maintain and increase their professional knowledge and skill.
- Social workers demonstrate due care for client's interests and safety by limiting professional practice to areas of demonstrated competence.
- Social workers contribute to the ongoing development of the profession and its ability to serve humanity, where possible, by participating in the development of current and future social workers and the development of new professional knowledge.
- Social workers who engage in research minimize risks to participants, ensure informed consent, maintain confidentiality and accurately report the results of their studies.

The RESPECTFUL Model: Diversity in Practice

The RESPECTFUL model was developed by Michael D'Andrea and Judy Daniels around 1997. The goal of the model is to recognize the multidimensionality of all clients in an all-inclusive and integrative way. The ten factors are meant to influence an individual's sense of personal well-being. Using the 10 steps in the RESPECTFUL model, shown below ask yourself the following questions:

- How do I define myself in each of the ten points in the RESPECTFUL model?
- How will my multidimensional position influence my practice? And why?
- Are there potential ethical dilemmas or conflicts that may occur should you work with a client who differs from your position?
- If conflict occurs, how might you work through it?

The 10 factors of the RESPECTFUL model are as follows:

1. **Religious**
2. **Economic** Class Background
3. **Sexual** Identity
4. **Psychological** Maturity
5. **Ethnic**-Cultural-Racial Identity
6. **Chronological** Developmental Challenges
7. **Trauma** and Other Threats to One's Well-Being
8. **Family** History and Dynamics
9. **Unique** Physical Characteristics
10. **Location** of Residence and Language Differences

Self-Reflection for Professional Development

Working with a partner, video record a practice session. After, review the tape and take note of your interview skills answering the following questions.

1. Identify open-ended questions. ______________________________

2. Closed questions. ______________________________

3. An example of paraphrasing. ______________________________

4. An example of a summary. ______________________________

5. An example of an encourager. ____

____

____

____

____

6. An example of probing for further details. ______________________________________

____

____

____

____

7. What struck you about watching your video? What did you learn from this process? How could this contribute to skill development and aspects of supervision? _______________

____

____

____

____

Sample Forms and Assessments for Partner Practice Sessions

CLIENT INTAKE FORM

Name: ______________________ Date: ______________________

Parent/Legal Guardian (if under 18): ______________________

Full Address: ______________________

Home Phone: ______________________ May we leave a message? Yes ☐ No ☐

Cell/Work/Other Phone: ______________________ May we leave a message? Yes ☐ No ☐

Email: ______________________ May we leave a message? Yes ☐ No ☐

Have you ever attended counselling services in the past? ( ) no ( ) yes

If yes, what worked? ______________________

____

____

____

Are you currently taking prescribed medication? ( ) Yes ( ) No

If yes, please list: ______________________

What is the medication for? ______________________

MEDICAL INFORMATION

Do you currently have a primary physician? ( ) Yes ( ) No

Name of physician ______________________

Do you have any medical concerns you feel are important for me to know? ______________________

____

____

____

How is your sleep? ____

How many hours per night do you sleep? ___________________________________

Do you exercise? ____________ How many times per week do you exercise? __________

Do you have alternate ways of being active? (rec sports, hiking, fishing, etc.) ____________

____

EMPLOYMENT INFORMATION

Are you currently employed? ( ) no ( ) yes. If yes, who is your employer/position? __________

______________. How long have you been in your current position? __________

____.

SPIRITUAL BELIEFS

Do you have any specific spiritual beliefs or practices you wish me to know about? __________

____

____

____

ADDITIONAL IMPORTANT INFORMATION

What do you consider to be your personal strengths? ______________________________

____

____

What are effective coping strategies do you feel confident about? ______________________

____

____

____

What are your goals for counselling? ______________________

____

____

____

Do you have questions you would like to share? ______________________

____

____

____

Biopsychosocial Cultural Spiritual Model Example

A biopsychosocial cultural spiritual model explores the biology, the psychology, the socio-cultural, and the spiritual dimensions of an individual's life context. The biopsychosocial spiritual model is often referred to as the BPSS assessment.

The BPSS provides a brief historical background about the possible causes of the challenges the client is presenting, and assists with identifying the client's strengths and supports.

Review the following sections and create some questions that you think are important to each area. Then facilitate a practice interview with a partner using the model as a guide. After you are done, discuss the information that you gathered. Did you gather information that you may not have otherwise? Was it relevant? Was this helpful? How did this process assist you in developing your interview skills?

Briefly, the categories are as follows:

- **Biological:** Assesses the client's basic needs: food, shelter, clothing, medical, health, physical capabilities in a physical environment; explore illnesses (past and present), disabilities, sleeping habits, eating habits, substance misuse, recent medical attention, accidents, dental needs, or any relevant concerns associated with basic needs; consider medical history, including family history.

- **Psychological:** Explores suicidal/homicidal ideations and any history of suicidal attempts or hospitalizations; thinking and reasoning abilities; the client's judgement, mood, insight, personality characteristics; and strengths and weaknesses.
- **Social:** Assessment reflects the client's story; consider, for example, employment history, educational background, family and friends, legal issues, and supports such as peers or social groups. The client's stage in life, or age, is also important to assess to determine if the challenges are a stage in life events.
- **Cultural:** Explores any cultural beliefs and practices that are present in the client's life.
- **Spiritual:** Gathers a history and understanding of the client's religious/spiritual beliefs—e.g., the client's belief system, any church affiliations, or if there have been any recent changes in their spirituality. This dimension also explores how the client's spiritual beliefs, as evident by prayer or meditation, identify where the client finds meaning in their life.

Cognitive Behavioural Model

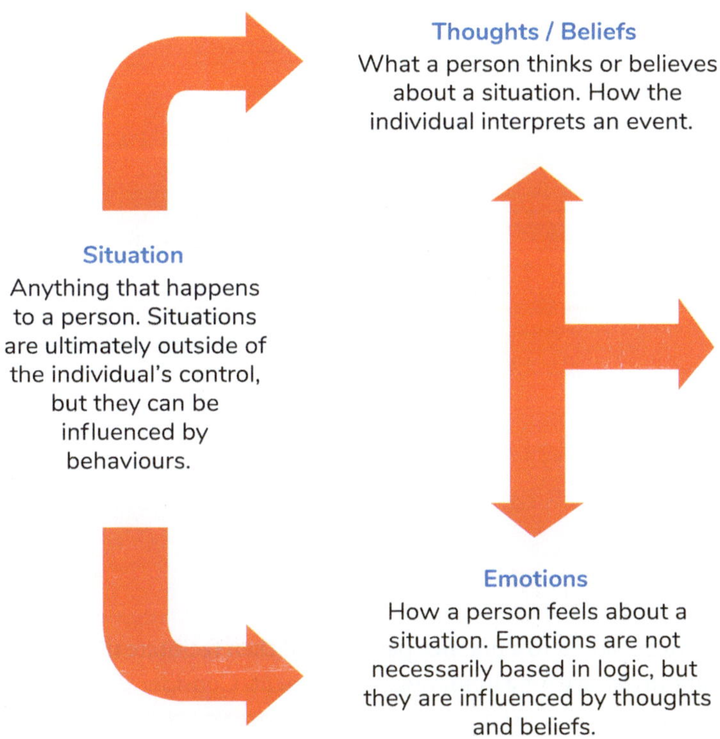

FIGURE A2.1 Cognitive Behavioural Model

Source: © 2013 Therapist Aid LLC. www.therapistaid.com

After reviewing the model, try to explain it to a practice partner and then facilitate the process of completing the Thought Log for a homework assignment. Consider this exercise from the perspective of a client and a worker. As a worker, what skills are you trying to develop with a client through this exercise?

Event	Thought	Consequence (emotion & behaviour)	Alternate Response

FIGURE A2.2 Thought Log

Beck Anxiety Inventory (BAI)

After reviewing the model, try to explain it to a practice partner and then facilitate the process of completing the Beck Anxiety Inventory for a homework assignment. Consider this exercise from the perspective of a client and a worker. As a worker, what skills are you trying to develop with a client through this exercise?

About: **This scale is a self-report measure of anxiety.**
Items: **21**
Reliability: Internal consistency for the BAI = (Cronbach's α=0.92)
Test-retest reliability (1 week) for the BAI = 0.75 (Beck, Epstein, Brown, & Steer, 1988).

Validity: The BAI was moderately correlated with the revised Hamilton Anxiety Rating Scale (.51), and mildly correlated with the Hamilton Depression Rating Scale (.25) (Beck et al., 1988)

Scoring:

TABLE A2.1 Scoring

	Not at all	Mildly but it didn't bother me much	Moderately—it wasn't pleasant at times	Severely—it bothered me a lot
All questions	0	1	2	3

The total score is calculated by finding the sum of the 21 items.
Score of 0 – 21 = low anxiety
Score of 22 – 35 = moderate anxiety
Score of 36 and above = potentially concerning levels of anxiety

Reference

Beck, A.T., Epstein, N., Brown, G., Steer, R.A. (1988). An inventory for measuring clinical anxiety: Psychometric properties. *Journal of Consulting and Clinical Psychology, 56*, 893–7.

Beck Anxiety Inventory (BAI)

Below is a list of common symptoms of anxiety. Please carefully read each item in the list. Indicate how much you have been bothered by that symptom during the past month, including today, by circling the number in the corresponding space in the column next to each symptom.

TABLE A2.2 Beck Anxiety Inventory

	Not at all	Mildly but it didn't bother me much	Moderately—it wasn't pleasant at times	Severely—it bothered me a lot
Numbness or tingling				
Feeling hot				
Wobbliness in legs				
Unable to relax				
Fear of the worst happening				
Dizzy or lightheaded				
Heart pounding/racing				
Unsteady				
Terrified or afraid				
Nervous				
Feeling of choking				
Hands trembling				
Shaky/unsteady				
Fear of losing control				
Difficulty in breathing				
Fear of dying				
Scared				
Indigestion				
Faint/lightheaded				
Face flushed				
Hot/cold sweats				

Source: Beck, A. T., Epstein, N., Brown, G., Steer, R. A. (1988). An inventory for measuring clinical anxiety: Psychometric properties. *Journal of Consulting and Clinical Psychology*, 56, 893–7.

Glossary

active listening All the verbal and non-verbal skills that affirm another person's conversation and provide a clear message that you are listening and understanding. The *skills* of active listening include the *verbal skills* of questioning, responding, *reflecting*, and *summarizing*, and the *non-verbal skills* of physically and psychologically attending to that person.

adversity Events or conditions of personal, family, or community difficulty or distress.

anomie The absence of established social norms or standards in a relationship or group of people. It often leads to a sense of anxiety and disorientation as people are unsure as to how to behave.

assertiveness To put forward a particular point of view with the conviction that it will at least be heard, if not acted upon.

assessment A very broad term that means different things to different professions. Assessment focuses on how people are functioning and how optimal functioning and well-being can be enhanced through the provision of specific resources for their inner and outer worlds. The type of assessment required varies according to your agency context.

attachment The relational bond established with primary caregivers in infancy, which enables a sense of a secure base to be established within an individual's inner world. A secure attachment relationship is different from other relationships in that it provides a secure base for the infant and enables the development of a sense of basic trust; an infant seeks this relationship particularly in times of high stress.

authenticity The quality of being real or genuine in relating to another person.

biopsychosocial-spiritual dimensions All the significant facets of an individual that may be taken into account in a multi-dimensional approach, including the biological, psychological, social, and spiritual.

challenging In counselling work, the process of calling into question a particular view, behaviour, or feeling; for example, challenging a self-defeating belief that someone may hold about himself or herself.

client A person who is using human services in some way, either voluntarily or involuntarily (e.g., court-mandated).

closed questions Questions that seek confirmation or disconfirmation of information by requiring a simple response such as "yes," "no," "maybe," or "never."

cognitive behavioural therapy (CBT) Therapy based on the understanding that a person's difficulties emerge as a result of the interaction of thoughts, feelings, and behaviours. This therapeutic approach focuses on creating change in any of these domains, particularly cognitions, so that change in the other domains will follow.

compassion fatigue The experience of "a sense of helplessness and confusion, and a sense of isolation from supporters" (Figley, 1995). It is understood as a trauma reaction that *human service workers* may develop in response to their work with *clients* who experience grief, stress, or trauma. Unlike burnout, however, compassion fatigue can happen following a single incident.

consciousness-raising The process of bringing to people's awareness an understanding of experiences of *oppression* and/or *discrimination*. This is the first step in liberation or emancipatory processes.

constructivist perspective A *paradigm*, in contrast to *positivism*, that does not consider that there is one objective truth or reality, but subjective positions only. The construction of the individual, family, or community is what shapes and informs "reality." At the extreme end of this view is the idea that "reality" does not exist outside of these subjective perceptions.

consumer A term frequently used to describe a user of a service. As it emphasizes the notion that the *client* is making choices about services used, this term is more frequently used self-referentially and is seen to be more empowering.

continuing bonds A term coined by grief theorists to refer to the ways in which bonds can be maintained with a person who has died. This is in contrast to other grief theories, which saw the work of grief counselling to be about breaking any sense of connection with a person who has died.

conversational style The unique verbal and non-verbal communication skills we use in very particular ways depending on context, for example, under the influence of familial, peer, gender, ethnic, and regional expectations.

counter-transference Generally speaking, the reaction (conscious and unconscious) provoked in the *human service worker* by the *client*'s story and presence. Some theorists argue that this may then "result in a distorted perception of a client's behaviour" (Corey & Corey, 2012).

crisis An upset to a steady state of being.

critical incident An unexpected, stressful occurrence in which a person experiences unusually strong emotional reactions that have the potential to interfere with her or his ability to function.

critical incident stress management (CISM) A range of specific interventions offered in the aftermath of a *critical incident*, which includes *debriefing*, incident management, *psycho-education*, and counselling support.

critical perspective A *paradigm* based on an explicit ideological or value base and in which change is central. It is critical of the status quo, seeing *power*, conflict, and *oppression* as dominant concerns to be addressed.

cross-cultural communication Communication among people of different cultural groups that is sensitive to others' ways of living and norms as much as language differences. In some situations, this involves working with an interpreter where there are language barriers. In other situations, it involves working with a cultural consultant, who can advise on social norms and expectations.

cultural screening According to Hall, the process by which information is taken in by an individual and translated to fit the context of the individual's cultural group. If information becomes overwhelming or threatens the individual's cultural identity a cultural screen can interrupt the process as a personal safety mechanism.

debriefing A strategy that aims to reduce distress, educate, and provide support around reactions to *critical incidents*, and, if appropriate, to review workforce strategies. Debriefing provides an opportunity to emotionally *ventilate* and psychologically process what has occurred. It can occur in dyads or in larger groups.

decision making A process of coming to a decision about a particular course of action. In counselling work, this involves a series of steps: brainstorming all the options, considering the pros and cons of each course of action, and deciding on the most manageable, realistic, and achievable option.

decoding The process of translating, analyzing, or interpreting a message.

defence mechanisms According to psychoanalytic thought, the unconscious patterns of response adopted when a person experiences anxiety.

denial According to psychoanalytic thought, a *defence mechanism* that enables the individual to dismiss a particular thought or observation as untrue.

differential use of self The ways in which you vary your *engagement* with, responses to, and focuses of your work according to the particular situation in which you are working.

discrimination The process of recognizing differences between people or things, which then can lead to differential treatment based on these observations.

ego strengths The strengths within a person's mental structure. The ego is seen as "a mental structure of the personality that is responsible for negotiating between the internal needs of the individual and the outside world" (Goldstein, 1995, p. xi; Walsh, 2006, p. 32). Thus, ego strengths enable a person to cope with demands and stressors by mediating the inner and outer worlds successfully.

emotional intelligence The conscious and careful self-management of feelings in social relationships, as distinguished from academic intelligence.

empathic highlights The *verbal skill* of *reflecting* back to the *client* what you have heard in terms of how she or he feels and in relation to what, to convey that you have understood.

empathy The "power of mentally identifying oneself with (and so fully comprehending) a person or object of contemplation" (Brown, 1993, p. 808). Empathy is an active *skill*, through which "components of affective sharing, self-other awareness, and emotional regulation/metal flexibility will enhance empathy (Gerdes & Segal, 2011). Many argue that empathy must be expressed verbally as well as non-verbally, to demonstrate to the *client* that she or he has been heard and understood.

encoding The process of converting information into another form. In relation to communication, it is the conversion of a thought into words and feelings into non-verbal messages.

engagement When you as a *human service worker* enter into a positive, trusting relationship with your *client* so that your work together can occur.

evaluation The action of assessing the process and the outcome of a client–worker relationship.

externalizing A strategy within narrative approaches that understands the "problem" as residing externally to the person. That is, the person is not the problem. The person is invited to explore the problem as she or he relates to it and as it influences that person's life.

feminist theory Theoretical approach that aims to create structural change, redressing the continuing *oppression* of women within male-dominated *power* structures. Feminism locates the focus of its attention beyond the inner world of an individual, arguing that these inner worlds are influenced profoundly by the wider social and political context (Remer, 2014).

goal setting Setting particular actions as aims to achieve, such as changing behaviours or actions.

human service worker Someone who provides targeted services, typically within a government, non-profit agency, or community setting, to alleviate human *adversity* and bring about constructive social and individual change.

invitation A statement or a question that invites someone to talk more about their situation. Examples include the question "Can you tell me about that?" and the statement "Go on . . ."

microskills The building blocks of human communication, i.e., the non-verbal (nodding, smiling, etc.) and verbal (questions, reflections, etc.) *skills* we use to influence a communication process.

minimal encouragers The verbal and non-verbal cues we use to encourage the person to continue talking. They are minimal in the sense of not being major statements, questions, or reactions—they include smiling or nodding as non-verbal minimal encouragers, or "aha," "oh," "hmmm" as verbal cues.

mutual clarity When a *human service worker* and *client* have established a shared understanding and clarity regarding a situation or issue.

narrative theory A *theory* that places a major emphasis on how an individual constructs and relates the stories, and particularly the problem stories, of his or her life. This approach is grounded in the belief that meaning-making, through the formulation of narrative, is integral to well-being because it leads to an integrated inner state.

non-verbal skills The cues or *skills* that emanate from our physical reactions and presence, rather than through our speech. Non-verbal skills include facial expressions, body *posture* and movements, and the use of touch.

normalizing A *skill* of affirmation; typically, it draws on a wider pool of knowledge or experience to place a person's experience in context. Normalizing provides a useful reflection and reminder that people are not alone in their distress and difficulty.

open-ended questions Questions that are open in the sense that they invite the *client* to provide further narrative detail. Questions beginning with the words "how," "what," "why," "when," "who," and "where" are all typically open-ended in that they invite some kind of descriptive, expansive response, not merely confirmation of information that has been provided by the person asking the question.

oppression The negative and often overwhelming experience of being weighed down by circumstances or being overpowered by the influence and control of other people or institutions.

organizational context The agency in which you are located and its wider context of operation (influenced by considerations such as size, staff composition, management structures, auspice, policy, geography, and agency interconnections).

paradigm A view often dominant among a group of people at a particular period of time that both determines and explains aspects of human society, including science, and the appropriate responses to problems.

paraphrasing A term that describes the process of relating back in your own words what you think you have heard the other person say. Paraphrasing is seen by some to reflect cognitive aspects of messages rather than feelings (Hepworth, Rooney, Rooney, & Strom-Gottfried, 2017).

positivism A world view that understands social reality as based on "stable, pre-existing patterns" (Neuman, 2006, p. 105). A positivist *paradigm* is based on assumptions of cause and effect (Morris, 2006, p. 3), whereby it is possible to identify the cause of problems or difficulties and intervene to alter them.

posture The positioning of your body as a whole, which can indicate to another person varying degrees of interest and attentiveness.

power "The possession of control or authority over others" (Brown, 1993, p. 2315); dominance or influence.

practice wisdom "The accumulation of information, assumptions, ideologies and judgements that have seemed practically useful in fulfilling the expectations of the job" (De Roos, 1990, p. 282, cited in Osmond, 2005, p. 891).

probes Questions, prompts, statements, even single words used by the worker to "examine or look into closely, especially in order to discover something" (Brown, 1993, p. 2362).

psychodynamic theory A *theory* primarily concerned with the inner worlds of individuals, and how difficulties arise in functioning because of these past and present inner-world preoccupations. Thus, psychodynamic theories are concerned with human drives or motivations in relation to pleasure, *power*, conflict, and anxiety. These experiences are thought to develop across the lifespan, through various psychosocial or *psychosexual* phases.

psycho-education Education related to psychological process; for example, in the aftermath of a *crisis*, people affected are often provided with psycho-education about what to expect by way of psychological responses in the aftermath experience.

psychosexual development An approach that understands human development to involve an interconnected series of psychological and sexual development across the lifespan.

purpose An intention or aim of doing something. In the context of human service work, purpose relates to the overall aim of an intervention or the reason for your professional involvement with a particular person at a particular time.

rational and irrational thoughts The focus of *cognitive behavioural therapy*. Rational thoughts are considered helpful in that they are reality-based and enable appropriate behaviour and feelings to follow; irrational thoughts are considered unhealthy or unhelpful because they distort reality or focus on irrelevant dimensions of experience.

referral The process of identifying another person who can be of assistance to the person and ensuring that this linkage occurs.

reflecting A distinction sometimes made between the two types of responses—reflecting and *paraphrasing*—"while paraphrases are restricted to what is actually said, reflections concentrate upon less obvious information frequently revealed in more subtle ways" (Dickson, 2006, p. 171).

reflexivity or critical reflection A process of reflection that involves a further step of turning back on oneself in a reflective process to see how your own actions perpetuate or contribute to a particular situation, and to attempt therefore to critically appraise and adjust as necessary your own positioning within a client–worker relationship. Through a process of reflexive awareness, one of the questions we begin to ask is, "What do I (we) do in the agency on a day-to-day basis that might contribute to the structuring of unequal outcomes?" (Kondrat, 1999, p. 468).

repetition A psychoanalytic term referring to a person's tendency to remain stuck, repeating particular ways of behaving, thinking, or feeling, because these behaviours, thoughts, or feelings have not been understood and resolved.

resistance In psychoanalytic terms, the opposition to the emergence of particular insights, memories, or repressed desires; in narrative terms, the process of withstanding particular stories being perpetuated about a person that maintain their *oppression* or particular status.

respect Social workers respect the unique worth and inherent dignity of all people and uphold human rights (CASW, 2005).

risk assessment An *assessment* of the likelihood that certain things will or may happen, based on the currently available evidence.

self-care Strategies about taking care of yourself, in relation to all your *biopsychosocial-spiritual dimensions* and in relation to the impact of your work.

self-disclosure While we are always revealing things about ourselves through both our verbal and non-verbal interactions, we mediate these decisions and provide some boundary around some information. Self-disclosure can be thought of as your explicit use of your own circumstances, either past or present, within your conversations with your *clients*.

skill An ability to do something well. In the context of practice, this means having the ability to communicate or intervene successfully.

smoothing skill A communication *skill* designed to smooth over difficulties and conflict, rather than escalate a disagreement currently being expressed.

social intelligence The conscious self-management of relationships and social interactions; distinguished from academic and *emotional intelligence*.

social justice The maintenance of social rights, integrity, and fairness for individuals, families, and communities within the wider social order.

stages of change A model that understands the change process as occurring in a series of stages, within which someone can "relapse" at any point. Developed from research in relation to addictions, the model proposes people move from a pre-contemplation to a contemplation stage, then to preparation and on to action. When change is achieved, a maintenance phase begins.

structural context The wider context of systems that influence our daily lives, such as legal, political, educational, health, and welfare systems.

summarizing The drawing together in conversation the various issues that have been discussed.

supervision The time focused on discussion of your work, your learning, and your support needs with a supervisor. For *human service workers*, a supervisor takes responsibility, typically within the context of the agency, for the workers, their learning, and their practice. A supervisor assists the workers in developing their practice and *practice wisdom* through direct modelling, support, and intervention as an experienced worker.

survival Continuing to live after some event.

task-centred A practice that has emerged from a pragmatic approach to human service delivery. It is a time-limited, contracted, and highly structured approach. Interventions focus on "doing"—on activities either within the context of the contact itself or outside as homework (Marsh & Doel, 2005, p. 38).

termination The process of finishing the work and the relationship with a *client*.

theory A system of ideas that provides an explanation of a phenomenon.

therapeutic A healing influence.

transference A part of every relationship in which we engage, referring to the unconscious motivations and desires, conflicts, and anxieties that we experience in our relationships. These patterns of relationship are thought to have emerged in infancy in the context of parent–infant relationships. In *therapeutic* work, the intention is to understand these conscious and unconscious experiences and expectations in the context of the client–worker relationship, enabling the working through of earlier and current significant relationships. By developing insight into the transference, change can occur as these needs and desires come under more conscious control.

transformative action Action that creates change, often more at broader social, structural, and cultural levels than just the individual level of experience.

unique outcomes In narrative approaches, the situations when the problem under analysis has not been a problem. Exploring unique outcomes enables a focus on what helps to understand what changes the imagined problem's influence in a person's life.

validation In counselling work, the process of confirming the story or emotions of another person, so that she or he feels that subjective experience has been affirmed and understood.

values Values can be regarded as particular types of belief that people hold about what is regarded as worthy or valuable (Banks, 2012). Professions will often define a set of values that they regard as core to the practice of their work.

ventilation The expression and, therefore, the release of feelings, often referred to as a process of catharsis.

verbal skills Specific verbal communication processes that influence a communication in a positive and/or directed way.

vicarious traumatization A worker's reaction in response to hearing or witnessing the traumatic experiences of *clients*; similar to *compassion fatigue*, and also referred to as secondary traumatization.

violence The use of force to cause injury or harm to another person. Violence is usually thought about in its physical, sexual, and emotional forms, but others such as Mullaly and West (2018) have suggested that the wider social context can be responsible for structural violence—that is, the abuse of people through the failure to eliminate poverty and *oppression*.

Bibliography

Preface

Chenowith, L., & McAuliffe, D. (2005). *The road to social work and human service practice: An introductory text.* Southbank: Thomson.

Chapter 1

Allen, M. (2013). *Social work and intimate partner violence.* New York, NY: Routledge.

Banks, S. (2012). *Ethics and values in social work* (4th edn). Basingstoke: Palgrave Macmillan.

Brown, L. (Ed.). (1993). *The new shorter Oxford English dictionary.* Oxford: Clarendon Press.

Brun, C., & Rapp, R. (2001). Strengths-based case management: Individuals' perspectives on strengths and the case manager relationship. *Social Work, 46*(3), 278–88.

Canadian Association of Social Workers (CASW). (2005). *Code of Ethics.* Ottawa, ON: CASW.

Canadian Association of Social Workers (CASW). (2005). *Practice Guidelines.* Ottawa, ON: CASW.

Canadian Association of Social Workers (CASW). (n.d.). *What is social work?* Retrieved from https://www.casw-acts.ca/en/what-social-work

Coates, J., & Hetherington, T. (2016). *Decolonizing social work: Contemporary social work studies.* New York, NY: Routledge Publishing.

Coggins, K. (2016). *The practice of social work in North America: Culture, context, and competency development.* New York, NY: Oxford University Press.

Connolly, M. (Ed.). (2001). *New Zealand social work: Contexts and practice.* South Melbourne: Oxford University Press.

Corey, M., & Corey, G. (2007). *Becoming a helper* (5th edn). Belmont, CA: Thomson.

Division for the Advancement of Women. (2003, June). *Women2000 and beyond: Women, nationality and citizenship.* Geneva: World Health Organization.

Dowrick, C. (1983). Strange meeting: Marxism, psychoanalysis and social work. *British Journal of Social Work, 13*, 1–18.

Duffy, S., Jackson, F., Schim, S., Ronis, D., & Fowler, K. (2006). Cultural concepts at the end of life: How do culture, race, gender and ethnicity influence nursing interventions in end-of-life care? *Nursing Older People, 18*(8), 10–15.

Dwairy, M. (2006). *Counselling and psychotherapy with Arabs and Muslims.* New York, NY: Teachers College Press.

Egan, G. (2007). *The skilled helper: A problem-management and opportunity-development approach to helping* (8th edn). Pacific Grove, CA: Brooks/Cole.

Esteva, G., & Prakash, M. (1998). Human rights: The Trojan horse of recolonization? In G. Esteva & M. Prakash (Eds), *Grassroots post-modernism: Remaking the soil of cultures* (pp. 110–52). London: Zed Books.

Fisher, D. (1991). *An introduction to constructivism for social workers.* New York, NY: Praeger.

Fook, J. (2000). Critical perspectives on social work practice. In I. O'Connor, P. Smyth, & J. Warburton (Eds), *Contemporary perspectives on social work & the human services: Challenges and change.* Frenchs Forest: Addison-Wesley Longman Australia.

Fook, J. (2016). *Social work: A critical approach to practice.* Thousand Oaks, CA: Sage Publications.

Furlong, M., & Ata, A. (2006). Observing different faiths, learning about ourselves: Practice with inter-married Muslims and Christians. *Australian Social Work, 59*(3), 250–64.

Gaita, R. (1999). *A common humanity: Thinking about love and truth and justice.* Melbourne: Text Publishing.

Haebich, A. (2006). *Broken circles: Fragmenting Indigenous families, 1800–2000.* Fremantle: Fremantle Arts Centre Press.

Hall, E. (1976). *Beyond culture.* New York, NY: Anchor Press.

Harms, L. (2005). *Understanding human development: A multidimensional approach.* South Melbourne: Oxford University Press.

Hepworth, D.R., Rooney, R.H., Dewberry-Rooney, G., Strom-Gottfried, K., & Larsen, J.A. (2017). *Direct social work practice: Theory and skills* (10th edn). Boston, MA: Cengage Learning.

Hick, S. (2005). *Social work in Canada: An introduction* (2nd edn). Toronto, ON: Thompson Educational.

Hick, S., & Stokes, J. (2017). *Social work in Canada: An introduction* (4th edn). Toronto, ON: Thompson.

Hobfoll, S., Ennis, N. & Kay, J. (2000). Loss, resources and resiliency in close interpersonal relationships. In J. Harvey & E. Miller (Eds), *Loss and trauma: General and close relationship perspectives* (pp. 267–85). Philadelphia: Brunner-Routledge.

Howard, S. (2006). *Psychodynamic counselling in a nutshell.* London: Sage.

Howe, D. (1994). Modernity, post-modernity and social work. *British Journal of Social Work, 24*(5), 513–32.

Howe, D. (2008). *The emotionally intelligent social worker.* Basingstock: Palgrave Macmillan.

Ife, J. & Tesoriero, F. (2006). *Community development: Community-based alternatives in an Age of globalisation.* Frenchs Forest: Pearson Education.

John Howard Society of Canada. (2019). *Our role.* Retrieved from http://johnhoward.ca/about-us/our-role

Knott, C., & Scragg, T. (2016). *Transforming social work practice: Reflective practice in social work* (4th edn). Los Angeles, CA: Sage.

Laming, C. (2005). *A constructivist approach to challenging men's violence against women* (Unpublished doctoral dissertation). University of Melbourne, Melbourne.

Levesque, D., Cummins, C., Prochaska, J., & Prochaska, J. (2006). Stage of change for making an informed decision about Medicare health plans. *Health Services Research, 41*(4), 1372–92.

Martin, J.N., & Nakayama, T.K. (2012). *Intercultural communication in contexts* (6th edn). New York, NY: McGraw-Hill Education.

Mullaly, B. (2007). *The new structural social work.* Toronto, ON: Oxford University Press.

Mullaly, B., & West, J. (2018). *Challenging oppression and confronting privilege: A critical approach to anti-oppressive and anti-privilege theory and practice* (3rd edn). Toronto, ON: Oxford University Press.

O'Hagan, K. (2001). *Cultural competence in the caring profession.* London: Jessica Kingsley.

O'Hara, A. (2006). The practitioner's use of self in the professional relationship. In A. O'Hara and Z. Weber (Eds), *Skills for human service practice: Working with individuals, groups and communities* (pp. 46–57). South Melbourne: Oxford University Press.

Payne, M. (2006). *What is professional social work?* (2nd edn). Bristol, UK: Policy Press.

Payne, M. (2014). *Modern social work theory* (4th edn). New York, NY: Oxford University Press.

Pierce, J. (2007). *Cross-cultural communication in social work practice: An interpretive descriptive approach to cross-cultural communication difficulties* (Unpublished MSW thesis). University of Northern British Columbia, Prince George, BC.

Prochaska, J., & DiClemente, C. (1983). Stages and processes of self change of smoking: Toward an integrative model of change. *Journal of Consulting and Clinical Psychology, 51*, 390–5.

Shebib, B. (2017). *Choices: Interviewing and counselling skills for Canadians* (6th edn). Toronto, ON: Pearson.

Shulman, L. (1999). *The skills of helping individuals, families, groups and communities* (4th edn). Itasca, IL: F.E. Peacock.

Sommers-Flanagan, J., & Sommers-Flanagan, R. (2004). *Counseling and psychotherapy theories in context and practice: Skills, strategies and techniques.* Hoboken, NJ: John Wiley and Sons.

Trevithick, P. (2005). *Social work skills: A practice handbook* (2nd edn) Maidenhead, UK: Open University Press.

United Nations General Assembly. (1948). *Universal declaration of human rights.* Retrieved from www.un.org

Weber, Z. (2006). Professional values and ethical practice. In A. O'Hara and Z. Weber (Eds), *Skills for human service practice: Working with individuals, groups and communities* (pp. 17–33). South Melbourne: Oxford University Press.

World Health Organization (WHO). (2018). *Constitution of the World Health Organization.* Geneva: United Nations.

Chapter 2

Atkinson, J. (2002). *Trauma trails, recreating song lines: The transgenerational effects of trauma in Indigenous Australia.* North Melbourne: Spinifex.

Bishop, A. (2015). *Becoming an ally: Breaking the cycle of oppression.* Halifax, NS: Fernwood Publishing.

Bull, P. (2002). *Communication under the microscope: The theory and practice of microanalysis.* New York, NY: Routledge.

Cartney, P. (2006). Using video interviewing in the assessment of social work communication skills. *British Journal of Social Work, 36*, 827–44.

Cech, M. (2010). *Interventions with children and youth in Canada.* Toronto, ON: Oxford University Press.

Coates, J., & Hetherington, T. (2016). *Decolonizing social work: Contemporary social work studies.* New York, NY: Routledge.

Coggins, K. (2016). *The practice of social work in North America: Culture, context, and competency development.* New York, NY: Oxford University Press.

Dean, R. (2001). The myth of cross-cultural competence. *Families in Society: The Journal of Contemporary Human Services, 82*(6), 623–30.

Deveson, A. (1991). *Tell me I'm here.* Ringwood, Victoria: Penguin.

Egan, G. (2002). *The skilled helper: A problem-management and opportunity-development approach to helping* (7th edn). Pacific Grove, CA: Brooks/Cole.

Egan, G. (2007). *The skilled helper: A problem-management and opportunity-development approach to helping* (8th edn). Pacific Grove, CA: Brooks/Cole.

Evans, W., Tulsky, J., Back, A., & Arnold, R. (2006). Communication at times of transitions: How to help patients cope with loss and re-define hope. *Cancer Journal, 12*, 417–24.

First Nations Health Authority. (n.d.). Cultural humility. Retrieved from http://www.fnha.ca/wellness/cultural-humility

Glintborg, B., Andersen, S.E., & Dalhoff, K. (2007). Insufficient communication about medication use at the interface between hospital and primary care. *Quality and Safety in Health Care, 16*(1), 34–9.

Goleman, D. (2006). *Social intelligence: The new science of human relationships.* London: Hutchinson.

Hargie, O. (2006). Training in communication skills. In O. Hargie (Ed.), *The handbook of communication skills* (3rd edn, pp. 553–65). New York, NY: Routledge.

Harris, J. (1995). Where is the child's environment? A group socialization theory of development. *Psychological Review, 102*(3), 458–89.

Heath, R., & Bryant, J. (2000). *Human communication theory and research: Concepts, contexts and challenges.* Mahwah, NJ: Lawrence Erlbaum.

Hudson, C. (2000). At the edge of chaos: A new paradigm for social work? *Journal of Social Work Education, 36*(2), 215–30.

Jaworski, A. (1993). *The power of silence: Social and pragmatic perspectives.* London: Sage.

Jung, C. (1963). *Memories, dreams, reflections.* Glasgow: Collins Fount.

Kadushin, A. (1972). *The social work interview.* New York, NY: Columbia University Press.

Kinloch, P., & Metge, J. (2014). *Talking past each other: Problems of cross cultural communication.* Wellington, New Zealand: Victoria University Press.

Koprowska, J. (2005). *Communication and interpersonal skills in social work.* Exeter: Learning Matters.

Miller, J., Donner, S., & Fraser, E. (2004). Talking when talking is tough: Taking on conversations about race, sexual orientation, gender, class and other aspects of social identity. *Smith College Studies in Social Work, 74*(2), 377–93.

Morris, T. (2006). *Social work research methods: Four alternative paradigms*. Thousand Oaks, CA: Sage.

Morrissette, V., McKenzie, B., & Morrissette, L. (1993). Towards an Aboriginal model of social work practice: Cultural knowledge and traditional practices. *Canadian Social Work Review, 10*(1), 91–108.

Moore, J., & Purton, C. (Eds). (2006). *Spirituality and counselling: Experiential and theoretical perspectives*. Ross-on-Wye: PCCS Books.

Osmond, J. (2005). The knowledge spectrum: A framework for teaching knowledge and its use in social work practice. *British Journal of Social Work, 35*, 881–900.

Rider, E., & Keefer, C. (2006). Communication skills competencies: Definitions and a teaching toolbox. *Medical Education, 40*, 624–9.

Schacter, D. (1996). *Searching for memory: The brain, the mind and the past*. New York, NY: Basic Books.

Schmidt, G. (2017). *Social work practice in remote communities*. New York, NY: Linus Learning.

Sciarra, D. (1999). *Multiculturalism in counselling*. Itasca, IL: F.E. Peacock.

Selye, H. (1987). *Stress without distress*. London: Corgi.

Smith, L.T. (2001). *Decolonizing methodologies: Research and Indigenous Peoples*. Dunedin: Otago University Press.

Sullivan, H. (1953). *Conceptions of modern psychiatry*. New York, NY: Norton.

Tannen, D. (2000). "Don't just sit there—interrupt!" Pacing and pausing in conversational style. *American Speech, 75*(4), 393–5.

Tao, J., Kang, Y., & Li, A. 2006. Prosody conversion from neutral speech to emotional speech. *IEEE Transactions on Audio, Speech and Language Processing*, 14(4), 1145–50.

Thompson, B.J., & Ladany, N. (2003). Therapist use of silence in therapy: A survey. *Journal of Clinical Psychology, 59*: 513–24.

Trevithick, P. (2005). *Social work skills: A practice handbook* (2nd edn). Maidenhead, UK: Open University Press.

Victorian Interpreting and Translating Service (VITS). (2017). *We speak your language: A guide to cross-cultural communication*. Melbourne: VITS LanguageLink.

Vogel, D., Wester, S., Heesacker, M. Boysen, G., & Seeman, J. (2006). Gender differences in emotional expression: Do mental health trainees overestimate the magnitude? *Journal of Social and Clinical Psychology, 25*(3), 305–32.

Walter, C.A, & McCoyd, J.L.M. (2009). *Grief and loss across the lifespan: A biopsychosocial perspective*. New York, NY: Springer.

Whitaker, R. (2010). *Anatomy of an epidemic: Magic bullets, psychiatric drugs, and the astonishing rise of mental illness in America*. New York, NY: Crown.

Whyte, J. (2005). Contesting paradigms: Indigenous worldviews, western science and professional social work (Unpublished PhD dissertation). University of Melbourne, Melbourne.

Yedidia, M.J. (2007). Transforming doctor–patient relationships to promote patient-centered care: Lessons from palliative care. *Journal of Pain and Symptom Management, 33*(1), 40–57.

Yoo, S., Matsumoto, D., & LeRoux, J. (2006). The influence of emotion recognition and emotion regulation on intercultural adjustment. *International Journal of Intercultural Relations, 30*(3), 345–63.

Zapf, M.K. (2001). Notions of rurality. *Rural Social Work, 6*(3), 12–26.

Chapter 3

Banks, S. (2012). *Ethics and values in social work* (4th edn). Basingstoke: Palgrave Macmillan.

Baskin, C. (2016). *Strong helpers' teachings: The value of Indigenous knowledges in the helping professions* (Vol. 2). Toronto, ON: Canadian Scholars' Press.

Benvenuto, J., & Woolford, A. (2015). Canada and colonial genocide. *Journal of Genocide Research, 17*(4), 373–90.

Blackstock, C. (2011). The emergence of the breath of life theory. *Journal of Social Work Values and Ethics, 8*(1). Retrieved from https://www.researchgate.net/publication/264889109_The_Emergence_of_the_Breath_of_Life_Theory

Bishop, A. 2015. *Becoming an ally: Breaking the cycle of oppression*. Halifax, NS: Fernwood Publishing.

Butchart, A., & T. Kahane. (2006). *Preventing child maltreatment: A guide to taking action and generating evidence*. Geneva: World Health Organization and International Society for Prevention of Child Abuse and Neglect.

Chui, W.H., & J. Wilson (Eds). (2006). *Social work and human services best practice*. Leichhardt: Federation Press.

Coggins, K. (2016). *The practice of social work in North America: Culture, context, and competency development*. New York, NY: Oxford University Press.

de Boer, C., & Coady, N. (2007). Good helping relationships in child welfare: Learning from stories of success. *Child and Family Social Work, 12*, 32–42.

Duncan, B., & Miller, S. (2005). The manual is not the territory: Treatment manuals do not improve outcomes. In J. Norcross, R. Levant, and L. Beutler (Eds), *Evidence-based practices in mental health: Debate and dialogue on the fundamental questions*. Washington, DC: American Psychological Association.

Evans, J., & Benefield, P. (2001). Systematic reviews of educational research: Does the medical model fit? *British Educational Research Journal, 27*(5), 527–41.

Gambrill, E. (1999). Evidence-based practice: An alternative to authority-based practice. *Families in Society, 80*(4), 341–50.

Germain, C., & Bloom, M. (1999). *Human behavior in the social environment: An ecological view*. New York, NY: Columbia University Press.

Harms, L. (2007). *Working with people: Communication skills for reflective practice*. South Melbourne: Oxford University Press.

Hick, S. (2010). *Social work in Canada: An introduction* (3rd edn). Toronto, ON: Thompson Educational.

Hobfoll, S., Ennis, N., & Kay, J. (2000). Loss, resources and resiliency in close interpersonal relationships. In J. Harvey & E. Miller (Eds), *Loss and trauma: General and close relationship perspectives* (pp. 267–85). Philadelphia, PA: Brunner-Routledge.

Howe, D. (2002). Relating theory to practice. In M. Davies (Ed.), *The Blackwell companion to social work* (2nd edn, pp. 81–7). Oxford: Blackwell Publishing.

Hutchison, E. (2003). *Dimensions of human behavior: The changing life course*. Thousand Oaks, CA: Sage.

Jeffrey, D. (2015). Meeting here and now: Reflections on racial and cultural differences in social work encounters. In J. Carrier & S. Strega, *Walking this path together: Anti-racist and anti-oppressive child welfare practice*. Winnipeg, MB: Fernwood Publishing

Kessler, M., Gira, E., & Poertner, J. (2005). Moving best practice to evidence-based practice in child welfare. *Families in Society, 86*(2), 244–50.

Lewis, J. (2002). The contribution of research findings to practice change. *MCC: Building Knowledge for Integrated Care, 10*(1), 9–12.

Macdonald, D. (2007). First Nations, residential schools, and the Americanization of the Holocaust: Rewriting Indigenous history in the United States and Canada. *Journal of Political Science, 40*(4), 995–1015.

Mattsson, T. (2013). Intersectionality as a useful tool: Anti-oppressive social work and critical reflection. *Journal of Women and Social Work, 29*(1), 8–17.

Miller, J., Donner, S., & Fraser, E. (2004). Talking when talking is tough: Taking on conversations about race, sexual orientation, gender, class and other aspects of social identity. *Smith College Studies in Social Work, 74*(2), 377–93.

Mullaly, B., & West, J. (2018). *Challenging oppression and confronting privilege: A critical approach to anti-oppressive and anti-privilege theory and practice* (3rd edn). Toronto, ON: Oxford University Press.

Nelson, S., & Wilson, K. (2017). The mental health of Indigenous Peoples in Canada: A critical review of research. *Social Science & Medicine, 176*, 93–112.

Nelson-Jones, R. 2006. *Theory and practice of counselling and therapy* (4th edn). Thousand Oaks, CA: Sage.

Neuman, W. (2006). *Social research methods: Qualitative and qualitative approaches*. Needham Heights, MA: Pearson Education.

Osmond, J. (2005). The knowledge spectrum: A framework for teaching knowledge and its use in social work practice. *British Journal of Social Work, 35*, 881–900.

Ribner, D., & Knei-Paz, C. (2002). Client's view of a successful helping relationship. *Social Work, 47*(4), 379–87.

Scott, D. (1990). Practice wisdom: The neglected source of practice research. *Social Work, 35*(6): 564–8.

Sheafor, B.W., & Horejsi, C.R. (2008). *Techniques and guidelines for social work practice* (8th edn). Boston, MA: Allyn & Bacon.

Sinclair, R. (2007). Identity lost and found: Lessons from the Sixties Scoop. *First Peoples Child & Family Review, 3*(1), 65–82.

Smith, L.T. (2001). *Decolonizing methodologies: Research and Indigenous Peoples*. Dunedin: Otago University Press.

Sommers-Flanagan, J., & Sommers-Flanagan, R. (2004). *Counseling and psychotherapy theories in context and practice: Skills, strategies and techniques*. Hoboken, NJ: John Wiley and Sons.

Swain, P. (Ed.). (2002). *In the shadow of the law: The legal context of social work practice*. Annandale: Federation Press.

Thompson, N. (2002). *People skills* (2nd edn). Basingstoke: Palgrave Macmillan.

Truth and Reconciliation Commission of Canada. (2015a). *Canada's Residential Schools: Missing Children and Unmarked Burials*. Vol. 4 of *The Final Report of the Truth and Reconciliation Commission of Canada*. Montreal and Kingston: McGill-Queen's University Press.

Truth and Reconciliation Commission of Canada. (2015b). *Honouring the Truth, Reconciling for the Future: Summary of the Final Report of the Truth and Reconciliation Commission of Canada*. Winnipeg, MB: Truth and Reconciliation Commission of Canada.

Walsh, J. (2006). *Theories of direct social work practice*. Southbank: Thomson Brooks/Cole.

Webb, S. (2006). *Social work in a risk society: Social and political perspectives*. Basingstoke: Palgrave Macmillan.

Yan, M., & Anucha, U. (Eds). (2017). *Working with immigrants and refugees: Issues, theories, and approaches for social work and human service practice*. Toronto, ON: Oxford University Press.

Chapter 4

Coates, J., Graham, J.R., Swartzentruber, B., & Ouellette, B. (2007). *Spirituality and social work: Selected Canadian readings*. Toronto, ON: Canadian Scholars' Press.

Coggins, K. (2016). *The practice of social work in North America: Culture, context, and competency development*. New York, NY: Oxford University Press.

Egan, G. (2007). *The skilled helper: A problem-management and opportunity-development approach to helping* (8th edn). Pacific Grove, CA: Brooks/Cole.

Egan, G., & Schroeder, W. (2009). *The skilled helper: A problem-management and opportunity-development approach to helping* (1st Cdn edn). Toronto, ON: Nelson Education.

Elkhuizen, K., Kelleher, R., Gibson, L., & Attoe, R. (2006). "Sitting on the mourning bench": Mental health workers and an elderly client. *Australian Social Work, 59*(3), 281–7.

Freedberg, S. (2007). Re-examining empathy: A relational-feminist point of view. *Journal of Social Work, 52*(3), 251–9.

Green, R. (2003). Social work in rural areas: A personal and professional challenge. *Australian Social Work, 56*(3), 209–19.

Harms, L. (2005). *Understanding human development: A multidimensional approach*. South Melbourne: Oxford University Press.

Koltko-Rivera, M. (2006). Rediscovering the later version of Maslow's hierarchy of needs: Self-transcendence and opportunities for theory, research, and unification. *Review of General Psychology, 10*(4), 302–17.

Rogers, C. (1987). Comments on the issue of equality in psychotherapy. *Journal of Humanistic Psychology, 27*(1), 38–9.

Schmidt, G. (2017). *Social work practice in remote* communities. New York, NY: Linus Learning.

Smith, R., Marshall-Dorsey, A., Osborn, G., Shebroe, V., Lyles, J., Stoffelmayr, B., Van Egeren, L. Mettler, J., Maduschke, K., Stanley, J., & Gardiner, J. (2000). Evidence-based guidelines for teaching patient-centered interviewing. *Patient Education and Counseling, 39*, 27–36.

Taylor, S. (2004). Public secrets/private pain: Difficulties encountered by victims/survivors of sexual abuse in rural communities. *Women against Violence, 15*, 12–21.

Trotter, C. 2006. *Working with involuntary clients: A guide to practice*. Thousand Oaks, CA: Sage.

Wolterstorff, N. 1987. *Lament for a Son*. Grand Rapids, Mich: Eerdman.

Zapf, M.K. (1991). Ideology and geography: The Canadian north. In B. Kirwin (Ed.), *Ideology, development and social welfare: Canadian perspectives* (2nd edn, 656–99). Toronto, ON: Canadian Scholars' Press.

Zapf, M.K. (2001). Notions of rurality. *Rural Social Work, 6*(3), 12–26.

Chapter 5

Bucknell, D. (2006). Outcome focused supervision. In H. Reid & J. Westergaard (Eds), *Providing support and supervision: An introduction for professionals working with young people* (pp. 41–56). London: Routledge.

Canfield. J. (2016). Secondary traumatization, burnout, and vicarious traumatization: A review of the literature as it relates to therapists who treat trauma. *Smith College Studies in Social Work, 75*(2), 81–101. doi.org/10.1300/J497v75n02_06

Cleak, H., & Wilson, J. (2004). *Making the most of field placement.* Southbank: Thomson.

Coggins, K. (2016). *The practice of social work in North America: Culture, context, and competency development.* New York, NY: Oxford University Press.

Deahl, M., Srinivasan, M., Jones, N., Neblett, C., & Jolly, A. (2001). Evaluating psychological debriefing: Are we measuring the right outcomes? *Journal of Traumatic Stress, 14*(3), 527–9.

Dyregrov, A. (1997). The process in psychological debriefings. *Journal of Traumatic Stress, 10*(4), 589–605.

Everly, G., Flannery, R., & Mitchell, J. (2000). Critical Incident Stress Management (CISM): A review of the literature. *Aggression and Violent Behavior, 5*(1), 23–40.

Figley, C. (Ed.). (1995). *Compassion fatigue: Coping with secondary traumatic stress disorder in those who treat the traumatized.* New York, NY: Brunner/Mazel.

Fook, J. (2002). *Social work: Critical theory and practice.* Thousand Oaks, CA: Sage.

Fook, J. (2016). *Social work: A critical approach to practice.* Thousand Oaks, CA: Sage Publications.

Furlong, M., & Ata, A. (2006). Observing different faiths, learning about ourselves: Practice with inter-married Muslims and Christians. *Australian Social Work, 59*(3), 250–64.

Jenaro, C., Flores, N., & Arias, B. (2007). Burnout and coping in human service practitioners. *Professional Psychology: Research and Practice, 38*(1), 80–7.

Kondrat, M.E. (1999). Who is the "self" in self-aware: Professional self-awareness from a critical theory perspective. *Social Service Review, 73*(4), 451–77.

McNally, R., Bryant, R., & Ehlers, A. (2003). Does early psychological intervention promote recovery from posttraumatic stress? *Psychological Sciences in the Public Interest, 4*(2), 45–80.

McNamara, M. (2006). Protectors need protecting too. *The Age*, 1 July, 9.

Margolin, I., Pierce, J. & Wiley, A. (2011). Wellness through a creative lens: meditation and visualization. *Journal of Religion & Spirituality in Social Work: Social Thought, 30*(3), 234–52. doi: 10.1080/15426432.2011.587385

Mitchell, J. (1983). When disaster strikes: The Critical Incident Stress Debriefing process. *Journal of Emergency Medical Services, 8*, 36–9.

Mitchell, J. (2004). *Crisis intervention and Critical Incident Stress Management: A defense of the field.* Ellicott City, MD: International Critical Incident Stress Foundation Inc.

Payne, M. (2006). *What is professional social work?* (2nd edn). Bristol, UK: Policy Press.

Payne, M. (2014). *Modern social work theory* (4th edn) New York, NY: Oxford University Press.

Reid, H., & Westergaard, J. (2006). *Providing support and supervision: An introduction for professionals working with young people.* London: Routledge.

Renzenbrink, I. (2005). Staff support: Whose responsibility? *Grief Matters, 8*(1), 13–17.

Rose, S., Bisson, J., & Wessely, S. (2003). Counselling and psychotherapy: Media distortion. *British Journal of Psychiatry, 183*, 263–4.

Steier, F. (1995). Reflexivity, interpersonal communication and interpersonal communication research. In W. Leeds-Hurwitz (Ed.), *Social approaches to communication* (pp. 63–87). New York, NY: Guilford Press.

White, M. (2004). Working with people who are suffering the consequences of multiple trauma: A narrative perspective. *International Journal of Narrative Therapy and Community Work, 1*, 45–76.

Chapter 6

Al-Krenawi, A., & Graham, J.R. (2003). *Multicultural social work in Canada: Working with diverse ethno-racial communities.* Toronto, ON: Oxford University Press.

Bitter, J.R. (2009). *Theory and practice of family therapy and counseling.* Belmont, CA: Brooks/Cole.

Bond, T. (2000). *Standards and ethics for therapy in action* (2nd edn). London: Sage.

Brownlee, K., & Graham, J.R. (Eds). (2005). *Violence in the family: Social work readings and research from northern and rural Canada.* Toronto, ON: Canadian Scholars' Press.

Canadian Association of Social Workers (CASW). (2005). *Guidelines for ethical practice.* Ottawa, ON: CASW.

Coggins, K. (2016). *The practice of social work in North America: Culture, context, and competency development.* New York, NY: Oxford University Press.

Daines, B., Gask, L., & Usherwood, T. (1997). *Medical and psychiatric issues for therapists.* London: Sage.

Davis, S. (2006). *Community mental health in Canada.* Vancouver, BC: University of British Columbia Press.

Egan, G., & Schroeder, W. (2009). *The skilled helper: A problem-management and opportunity-development approach to helping* (1st Cdn edn). Toronto, ON: Nelson Education.

Egan, G., & Schroeder, W. (2012). *The skilled helper: A problem-management and opportunity-development approach to helping* (11th edn). Toronto, ON: Brooks/Cole, Cengage Learning.

Gibney, P. (2003). *The pragmatics of therapeutic practice.* Melbourne: PsychOz.

Jenkins, R. (2002). *Legal issues in therapy and psychotherapy.* London: Sage.

Koprowska, J. (2005). *Communication and interpersonal skills in social work.* Exeter: Learning Matters.

Petrakis, M. (2004). Keeping the client safe: Complexities and clinician risk in working with the suicidal client. Paper presented at the RISK (Faculty of Arts Research Student Colloquium: antiTHESIS Forum), University of Melbourne.

Reeves, A., & Seber, P. (2004). Working with the suicidal client. *Counselling and Psychotherapy, 15*(4), 45–50.

Sharry, J., Darmody, M., & Madden, B. (2002). A solution-focused approach to working with clients who are suicidal. *British Journal of Guidance & Counselling, 30*(4), 383–99.

Thompson, N. (2003). *Promoting equality: Challenging discrimination and oppression* (2nd edn). Basingstoke: Palgrave Macmillan.

Thompson, N. (2006). *Anti-discriminatory practice.* Basingstoke: Palgrave Macmillan.

Trevithick, P. (2005). *Social work skills: A practice handbook* (2nd edn). Maidenhead: Open University Press.

Trotter, C. 2006. *Working with involuntary clients: A guide to practice.* Thousand Oaks, CA: Sage.

Victorian Foundation for Survivors of Torture Inc. (2016). Integrated trauma recovery service model. Retrieved from www.foundationhouse.org.au/wp-content/uploads/2018/08/INTEGRATED-TRAUMA-SERVICE-RECOVERY-MODEL_cr.pdf

Chapter 7

Armstrong, J. (2006). *Love, life, Goethe: How to be happy in an imperfect world.* London: Allan Lane.

Black, D., &. Trickey, D. (2005). Children bereaved by murder and manslaughter. Paper presented at Seventh International Conference on Grief and Bereavement in Contemporary Society, 12 July, London.

Brown, L. (Ed.). (1993). *The new shorter Oxford English dictionary.* Oxford: Clarendon Press.

Corey, G. (2008). *Theory and practice of counseling and psychotherapy* (8th edn). Toronto, ON: Thomson Learning.

Dickson, D., & Hargie, O. (2006). Questioning. In O. Hargie (Ed.), *The handbook of communication skills* (3rd edn, pp. 121–45). New York, NY: Routledge.

Egan, G. (2009). *The skilled helper: A problem-management and opportunity-development approach to helping* (9th edn). Belmont, CA: Brooks/Cole Cengage Learning.

Egan, G. (2013). *The skilled helper: a problem-management and opportunity-development approach to helping* (10th edn). Belmont, CA: Brooks/Cole Cengage Learning.

Egan, G., & Schroeder, W. (2009). *The skilled helper: A problem-management and opportunity-development approach to helping* (1st Cdn edn). Toronto, ON: Nelson Education.

Evans, W., Tulsky, J. Back, A., & Arnold, R. (2006). Communication at times of transitions: How to help patients cope with loss and re-define hope. *Cancer Journal, 12*, 417–24.

Geldard, D., & Geldard, K. (2005). *Basic personal counselling: A training manual for counsellors* (5th edn). Frenchs Forest: Pearson Education Australia.

Hepworth, D.R., Rooney, R.H., Dewberry-Rooney, G., Strom-Gottfried, K., & Larsen, J.A. (2017). *Direct social work practice: Theory and skills* (10th edn). Boston, MA: Cengage Learning.

James, R.K., & Gilliland, B.E. (2017). *Crisis intervention strategies* (7th edn). Pacific Grove, CA: Brooks/Cole Cengage Learning.

Kiselica, M.S. (1998). Preparing Anglos for the challenges and joys of multiculturalism. *The Counseling Psychologist, 26*(1), 5–21.

Kohli, H.K., Huber, R., & Faul, A.C. (2010). Historical and theoretical development of culturally competent social work practice. *Journal of Teaching in Social Work, 30*(3), 252–71.

Koprowska, J. (2005). *Communication and interpersonal skills in social work.* Exeter: Learning Matters.

Martin, P. (1997). *The sickening mind: Brain, behaviour, immunity and disease.* London: HarperCollins.

Payne, M. (2006). *What is professional social work?* (2nd edn). Bristol, UK: Policy Press.

Rogers, C., Ellis, A., & Perls, F. (1977). *Three approaches to psychotherapy* [Film]. Orange County, CA: Psychological Films.

Saleebey, D. (2017). *The strengths perspective in social work practice.* Boston, MA: Allyn & Bacon.

Shulman, L. (2009). *The skills of helping individuals, families, groups and communities.* Belmont, CA: Brooks/Cole, Cengage Learning.

Sinason, V. (1992). *Mental handicap and the human condition.* London: Free Association Books.

Trevithick, P. (2005). *Social work skills: A practice handbook* (2nd edn). Maidenhead: Open University Press.

Youssef, J., & Deane, F. (2006). Barriers to mental health care and opportunities to facilitate utilisation of services in Arabic-speaking communities. *Synergy, 1*, 5–16.

Chapter 8

Bitter, J.R. (2009). *Theory and practice of family therapy and counseling.* Belmont, CA: Brooks/Cole.

Dickson, D. (2006). Reflecting. In O. Hargie (Ed.), *The handbook of communication skills* (3rd edn, pp. 165–94). New York, NY: Routledge.

Egan, G. (2013). *The skilled helper: A problem-management and opportunity-development approach to helping* (10th edn). Belmont, CA: Brooks/Cole Cengage Learning.

Egan, G., & Schroeder, W. (2009). *The skilled helper: A problem-management and opportunity-development approach to helping* (1st Cdn edn). Toronto, ON: Nelson Education.

Hargie, O. (2006). Training in communication skills. In O. Hargie (Ed.), *The handbook of communication skills* (3rd edn, pp. 553–65). New York, NY: Routledge.

Hepworth, D., Rooney, R., & Larson, J.A. (2002). *Direct social work practice: Theory and skills* (6th edn). Pacific Grove, CA: Brooks/Cole.

Ingram, R. (2012). Locating emotional intelligence at the heart of social work practice. *British Journal of Social Work, 43*(5), 987–1004.

James, R.K., & Gilliland, B.E. (2017). *Crisis intervention strategies* (7th edn). Pacific Grove, CA: Brooks/Cole Cengage Learning.

Raphael, B. (1983). *The anatomy of bereavement.* New York, NY: Basic Books.

Scott, N.E., & Borodovsky, L.G. (1990). Effective use of cultural role-taking. *Professional Psychology: Research and Practice, 21*, 167–70.

Trevithick, P. (2005). *Social work skills: A practice handbook* (2nd edn). Maidenhead: Open University Press.

Chapter 9

American Psychiatric Association (APA). (2013). *The diagnostic and statistical manual of mental disorders* (5th edn). Washington, DC: American Psychiatric Association.

Anglem, J., & Maidment, J. (2004). Introduction to assessment. In J. Maidment & R. Egan (Eds), *Practice skills in social work and welfare: More than just common sense* (pp. 112–26). Crows Nest: Allen & Unwin.

Bitter, J.R. (2009). *Theory and practice of family therapy and counseling*. Belmont, CA: Brooks/Cole.

Bloch, S., & Singh, B. (Eds). (2007). *Foundations of clinical psychiatry*. Carlton: Melbourne University Press.

Bronfenbrenner, U. (1979). *The ecology of human development: Experiments by nature and design*. Cambridge, MA: Harvard University Press.

Burstow, B. (1987). Humanistic psychotherapy and the issue of equality. Journal of *Humanistic Psycology, 27*(1), 9–25.

Cech, M. (2015). *Interventions with children and youth in Canada* (2nd edn). Toronto, ON: Oxford University Press.

Coggins, K. (2016). *The practice of social work in North America: Culture, context, and competency development*. New York, NY: Oxford University Press.

Corey, G. (1996). *Theory and practice of counseling and psychotherapy*. Pacific Grove, CA: Brooks/Cole.

Corey, G. (2008). *Theory and practice of counselling and psychotherapy* (8th edn). Pacific Grove, CA: Brooks/Cole.

Coulehan, J., & Block, M. (2006). *The medical interview: Mastering skills for clinical practice*. Philadelphia, PA: F.A. Davis Co.

Davis, S. (2006). *Community mental health in Canada*. Vancouver, BC: University of British Columbia Press.

Egan, G. (2002). *The skilled helper: A problem-management and opportunity-development approach to helping* (7th edn). Pacific Grove, CA: Brooks/Cole.

Egan, G. (2007). *The skilled helper: A problem-management and opportunity-development approach to helping* (8th edn). Pacific Grove, CA: Brooks/Cole.

Falicov, C.J. (1995). Training to think culturally: A multidimensional comparative framework. *Family Process, 34*, 373–88.

Fook, J. (1993). *Radical casework: A theory of practice*. St Leonards: Allen & Unwin.

Germain, C. (1991). *Human behavior in the social environment: An ecological view* (2nd edn). New York, NY: Columbia University Press.

Giddens, A. (2002). *Runaway world: How globalization is reshaping our lives* (2nd edn). London: Profile Books.

Goldberg, D. (1978). *Manual of the general health questionnaire*. Windsor, UK: NFER Publishing.

Goodman, D. (2001). *Promoting diversity and social justice: Educating people from privileged groups*. Thousand Oaks, CA: Sage.

Harms, L. (2005). *Understanding human development: A multidimensional approach*. South Melbourne: Oxford University Press.

Harms, L., & McDermott, F. (2003). Trauma: A concept and a practice across borders. *Psychotherapy in Australia, 10*(1), 32–7.

Hepworth, D.R., Rooney, R.H., Dewberry-Rooney, G., Strom-Gottfried, K., & Larsen, J.A. (2017). *Direct social work practice: Theory and skills* (10th edn). Boston, MA: Cengage Learning.

Hobfoll, S., Ennis, N. & Kay, J. (2000). Loss, resources and resiliency in close interpersonal relationships. In J. Harvey & E. Miller (Eds), *Loss and trauma: General and close relationship perspectives* (pp. 267–85). Philadelphia, PA: Brunner-Routledge.

Howatt, W. (2000). *The human services counselling toolbox: Theory, development, technique and resources*. Pacific Grove, CA: Brooks/Cole. Initial interview, page 170.

Ife, J. (2001). *Human rights and social work: Towards rights-based practice*. Melbourne: Cambridge University Press.

James, R.K., & Gilliland, B.E. (2017). *Crisis intervention strategies* (7th edn). Pacific Grove, CA: Brooks/Cole Cengage Learning.

Lloyd, M., & Taylor, C. (1995). From Hollis to the Orange Book: Developing a holistic model of assessment in the 1990s. *British Journal of Social Work, 25*, 691–710.

Lupton, D. (1999). *Risk*. London: Routledge.

Marsh, P., & Doel, M. (2005). *The task-centred book*. London: Routledge.

Miller, J., Donner, S., & Fraser, E. (2004). Talking when talking is tough: Taking on conversations about race, sexual orientation, gender, class and other aspects of social identity. *Smith College Studies in Social Work, 74*(2), 377–93.

Morley, C. (2004). Conducting risk assessments. In J. Maidment & R. Egan (Eds), *Practice skills in social work and welfare: More than just common sense* (pp. 127–45). Crows Nest: Allen & Unwin.

Mussel, B., Cardiff, K., & White, J. (2004). *The mental health and wellbeing of Aboriginal children and youth: Guidance for new approaches and services*. Report prepared for the British Columbia Ministry for Children and Family Development, Victoria, BC.

Parker, S. (2006). Measuring faith development. *Journal of Psychology and Theology, 34*(4), 337–48.

Rigney, D., & Cooper, L. (2004). Preparing for practice. In J. Maidment & R. Egan (Eds), *Practice skills in social work and welfare: More than just common sense* (pp. 51–68). Crows Nest: Allen & Unwin.

Room, G., & Britton, N. (2006). The dynamics of social exclusion. *International Journal of Social Welfare, 15*, 280–9.

Saleebey, D. (2017). *The strengths perspective in social work practice*. Boston, MA: Allyn & Bacon.

Smith, L.T. (2001). *Decolonizing methodologies: Research and Indigenous Peoples*. Dunedin: Otago University Press.

Tobin, M. (2005). *Lost opportunity or lifeline? Women with substance use issues and their perceptions of the barriers to pregnancy care* (Unpublished MSW thesis). University of Melbourne, Melbourne.

Trevithick, P. (2005). *Social work skills: A practice handbook* (2nd edn). Maidenhead: Open University Press.

Trotter, C. (2006). *Working with involuntary clients: A guide to practice*. Thousand Oaks, CA: Sage.

Webb, S. (2006). *Social work in a risk society: Social and political perspectives*. Basingstoke: Palgrave Macmillan.

Chapter 10

Brownlee, K., & Graham, J.R. (Eds). (2005). *Violence in the family: Social work readings and research from northern and rural Canada*. Toronto, ON: Canadian Scholars' Press.

Canadian Association of Social Workers (CASW). (2005). *Guidelines for ethical practice*. Ottawa, ON: CASW.

Canadian Centre for Occupational Health and Safety (CCOHS). (2009). Violence in the workplace [Factsheet]. Retrieved from https://www.ccohs.ca/oshanswers/psychosocial/violence.html

Cutcliffe, J. (2005). Toward an understanding of suicide in First Nation Canadians. *Journal of Crisis Intervention and Suicide Prevention, 26*(3), 141–5.

James, R.K., & Gilliland, B.E. (2017). *Crisis intervention strategies* (7th edn). Pacific Grove, CA: Brooks/Cole Cengage Learning.

Kotzman, A. (1995). *Listen to me, listen to you*. Camberwell: ACER.

Ogloff, J. (2006). Advances in violence risk assessment. *InPsych, 28*(5), 12–16.

Rakos, R. (2006). Asserting and confronting. In O. Hargie (Ed.), *The handbook of communication skills* (3rd edn, pp. 345–81). New York, NY: Routledge.

Regehr, C., & Glancy, G. (2014). *Mental health social work practice in Canada* (2nd edn). Toronto, ON: Oxford University Press.

Shebib, B. (2000). *Choices: Practical interviewing and counselling skills*. Don Mills, ON: Allyn & Bacon.

Warren, L. (2006). Managing the client who threatens violence. *InPsych, 28*(5): 20–1.

Chapter 11

Bandura, A., Caprara, G., Barbaranelli, C., Gerbino, M., & Pastorelli, C. (2003). Role of affective self-regulatory efficacy in diverse spheres of psychosocial functioning. *Child Development, 74*(3), 769–82.

Baskin, C. (2005). Mino-yaa-daa: Healing together. In K. Brownlee & J.R. Graham (Eds). *Violence in the family: Social work readings and research from northern and rural Canada* (pp. 170–81). Toronto, ON: Canadian Scholars' Press.

Brown, F., & Rainer, J. (2006). Too much to bear: An introduction to crisis intervention and therapy. *Journal of Clinical Psychology, 62*(8), 953–7.

Caplan, G. (1990). Loss, stress and mental health. *Community Mental Health Journal, 26*(1), 27–48.

Crumpton-Cook, R. (1996). But we have the expertise. *Psychotherapy in Australia, 3*(1), 16–17.

Davis, S. (2006). *Community mental health in Canada*. Vancouver, BC: University of British Columbia Press.

Davis, S. (2013). *Community mental health in Canada, revised and expanded edition: Theory, policy, and practice*. Vancouver, BC: University of British Columbia Press.

Doel, M., & Marsh, P. (2017). *Task-centered social work*. New York, NY: Routledge.

Flannery, R., & Everly, G. (2000). Crisis intervention: A review. *International Journal of Emergency Mental Health, 2*(2), 119–25.

Gelman, C.R., & Mirabito, D. (2005). Practicing what we teach: Using case studies from 9/11 to teach crisis intervention from a generalist perspective. *Journal of Social Work Education, 41*(3), 479–94.

Granot, H. (1996, May). The impact of disaster on mental health. *Counselling*, 140–3.

Harms, L. (2005). *Understanding human development: A multidimensional approach*. South Melbourne: Oxford University Press.

Harms, L., Rowe, C., & Suss, S. (2006). *Family adaptation following trauma*. Paper presented at the Fifth International Conference on Social Work in Health and Mental Health, Hong Kong.

Healy, K. (2005). *Social work theories in context: Creating frameworks for practice*. Basingstoke: Palgrave Macmillan.

Hobfoll, S., Ennis, N., & Kay, J. (2000). Loss, resources and resiliency in close interpersonal relationships. In J. Harvey & E. Miller (Eds), *Loss and trauma: General and close relationship perspectives* (pp. 267–85). Philadelphia, PA: Brunner-Routledge.

Herman, J. (1992). *Trauma and recovery: The aftermath of violence—from domestic abuse to political terror*. New York, NY: Basic Books.

Hoff, L.A, Hallisey, B.J., & Hoff, M. (2009). *People in crisis: Clinical and diversity perspectives* (6th edn). London: Routledge.

James, R.K., & Gilliland, B.E. (2017). *Crisis intervention strategies* (7th edn). Pacific Grove, CA: Brooks/Cole Cengage Learning.

Lindemann, E. (1944). Symptomatology and management of acute grief. *American Journal of Psychiatry, 101*, 141–9.

Marsh, P., & Doel, M. (2005). *The task-centred book*. London: Routledge.

Maslow, A.H. (2013). *Toward a psychology of being*. New York, NY: Start Publishing LLC.

Myer, R., & Conte, C. (2006). Assessment for crisis intervention. *Journal of Clinical Psychology, 62*(8), 959–70.

Poindexter, C. (1997). In the aftermath: Serial crisis intervention for people with HIV. *Health and Social Work, 22*(2), 125–32.

Tolson, E., Reid, W., & Garvin, C. (2003). *Generalist practice: A task-centered approach*. New York, NY: Columbia University Press.

Trevithick, P. (2005). *Social work skills: A practice handbook* (2nd edn). Maidenhead: Open University Press.

Walsh, J. (2006). *Theories of direct social work practice*. Southbank: Thomson Brooks/Cole.

Webb, S. (2006). *Social work in a risk society: Social and political perspectives*. Basingstoke: Palgrave Macmillan.

Chapter 12

Beck, A., Freeman, A., & Davis, D. (2004). *Cognitive therapy of personality disorders*. New York, NY: Guilford Press.

Bowlby, J. (1984). *Attachment*. London: Penguin.

Brandell, J. (2004). *Psychodynamic social work*. New York, NY: Columbia University Press.

Corey, M., & Corey, G., (2007). *Becoming a helper* (5th edn). Belmont, CA: Brooks/Cole/Thomson Learning.

Dean, R. (2002). Teaching contemporary psychodynamic theory for contemporary social work practice. *Smith College Studies in Social Work, 7*(1), 11–27.

Egan, G. (2007). *The skilled helper: A problem-management and opportunity-development approach to helping* (8th edn). Pacific Grove, CA: Brooks/Cole.

Ellis, A. (1974). *Humanistic psychotherapy: The rational emotive approach*. San Francisco, CA: McGraw-Hill.

Ellis, A. (1995). *Better, deeper, and more enduring brief therapy: The rational emotive behavior therapy approach*. Bristol, PA: Brunner/Mazel.

Fook, J. (1993). *Radical casework: A theory of practice*. St Leonards: Allen & Unwin.

Gibney, P. (2003). *The pragmatics of therapeutic practice*. Melbourne: PsychOz.

Goldstein, E. (1995). *Ego psychology and social work practice*. New York, NY: Free Press.

Healy, K. (2005). *Social work theories in context: Creating frameworks for practice*. Basingstoke: Palgrave Macmillan.

Howard, S. (2006). *Psychodynamic counselling in a nutshell*. London: Sage.

Jacoby, M. (1984). *The analytic encounter: Transference and human relationship*. Toronto, ON: Inner City Books.

Klein, M. (1962). *Love, hate and reparation.* London: Hogarth Press and Institute of Psychoanalysis.

McCluskey, U. (2002). The dynamics of attachment and system-centered group psychotherapy. *Group Dynamics, 6*(2), 131–42.

Macnab, F. (1989). *Traumas of life and their treatment.* Melbourne: Spectrum Publications.

Miller, L. (2012). *Counselling skills for social work* (2nd edn). Thousand Oaks, CA: Sage.

Miller, W.R., & Rollnick, S. (2014). *Motivational interviewing: Helping people change* (3rd edn). New York, NY: Guilford Press.

Nelson-Jones, R. (2002). *Basic counselling skills: A helpers' manual.* Thousand Oaks, CA: Sage.

Payne, M. (2005). *Modern social work theory* (3rd edn). Chicago, IL: Lyceum Books.

Reber, A. (1985). *The Penguin dictionary of psychology.* Ringwood: Penguin Books.

Rutter, J.G., & Friedberg, R.D. (1999). Guidelines for the effective use of Socratic dialogue in cognitive therapy. In L. VandeCreek & T.L. Jackson (Eds), *Innovations in clinical practice: A source book,* vol. 17 (pp. 481–90). Sarasota, FL: Professional Resource Press.

Shulman, L. (2016). *The skills of helping individuals, families, groups and communities* (8th edn). Boston, MA: Cengage Learning.

Simmons, J. (2012).

Simmons, J. and R. Griffiths (2014). *CBT for Beginners* (2nd edn). London: Sage.

Smith, L.T. (2001). *Decolonizing methodologies: Research and indigenous peoples.* Dunedin: Otago University Press.

Sommers-Flanagan, J., & Sommers-Flanagan, R. (2004). *Counseling and psychotherapy theories in context and practice: Skills, strategies and techniques.* Hoboken, NJ: John Wiley & Sons.

Thompson, N. (2002). *People skills* (2nd ed). Basingstoke: Palgrave Macmillan.

Trevithick, P. (2005). *Social work skills: A practice handbook* (2nd edn). Maidenhead: Open University Press.

Walsh, J. (2006). *Theories of direct social work practice.* Southbank: Thomson Brooks/Cole.

Winnicott, D. (1987). *Babies and their mothers.* Reading, MA: Addison-Wesley.

Chapter 13

Bitter, J.R. (2009). *Theory and practice of family therapy and counseling.* Belmont, CA: Brooks/Cole.

Brown, C., & Augusta-Scott, T. (2007). *Narrative therapy: Making meaning, making lives.* Thousand Oaks, CA: Sage.

Canadian Association of Social Workers (CASW). 2005. *Code of ethics.* Ottawa, ON: CASW.

de Shazer, S. (1985). *Keys to solutions in brief therapy.* New York: W.W. Norton.

de Shazer, S. (1994). *Words were originally magic.* New York, NY: Norton.

Dowrick, S. (2006). The heart of the story. *The Age,* 10 June, 57.

Egan, G., & Schroeder, W. (2012). *The skilled helper: A problem-management and opportunity-development approach to helping* (11th edn). Toronto: Brooks/Cole, Cengage Learning.

Hoffman, L. (2002). *Family therapy: An intimate history.* New York: W.W. Norton

Laub, D., & Auerhahn, N. (1993). Knowing and not knowing massive psychic trauma: Forms of traumatic memory. International *Journal of Psycho-Analysis, 74,* 287–302.

Manthei, R. (1997). *Counselling: The skills of finding solutions to problems.* New York, NY: Routledge.

Miller, L. (2012). *Counselling skills for social work* (2nd ed). Thousand Oaks, CA: Sage.

Moore, T. (2004). *Dark nights of the soul: A guide to finding your way through life's ordeals.* London: Piatkus Books.

O'Connell, B. (1998). *Solution-focused therapy.* London: Sage.

Payne, M. (2014). *Modern social work theory* (4th edn). New York, NY: Oxford University Press.

Reiter, A. (2000). *Narrating the Holocaust.* London: Continuum.

Russell, S., & Carey, M. (2003). Feminism, therapy and narrative ideas: Exploring some not so commonly asked questions. *International Journal of Narrative Therapy and Community Work, 3*(1), 76–84.

Sharp, C. (2006). Towards a phenomenology of the divine. In J. Moore & C. Purton (Eds), *Spirituality and counselling: Experiential and theoretical perspectives* (pp. 65–80). Ross-on-Wye: PCCS Books.

Smith, L.T. (2001). *Decolonizing methodologies: Research and indigenous peoples.* Dunedin: Otago University Press.

Tamasese, K. (2000). Talking about culture and gender. In D. Centre (Ed.), *Working with the stories of women's lives.* Adelaide: Dulwich Centre.

Walsh, J. (2006). *Theories of direct social work practice.* Southbank: Thomson Brooks/Cole.

White, M. (2004). Working with people who are suffering the consequences of multiple trauma: A narrative perspective. *International Journal of Narrative Therapy and Community Work,* 1, 45–76.

White, M., & Epston, D. (2005). Externalising the problem. In C. Malone, L. Forbat, M. Robb, & J. Seden (Eds), *Relating experience: Stories from health and social care.* Oxon: Routledge.

Wingard, B. (2001). *Telling our stories in ways that make us stronger.* Adelaide: Dulwich Centre.

Chapter 14

Bishop, A. (2015). *Becoming an ally: Breaking the cycle of oppression.* Halifax, NS: Fernwood.

Bricker-Jenkins, M., Hooyman, N., & Gottlieb, N. (Eds). (1991). *Feminist social work practice in clinical settings.* London: Sage.

Brown, L. (Ed.) (1993). *The new shorter Oxford English dictionary.* Oxford: Clarendon Press.

Canadian Association of Social Workers (CASW). 2005. *Guidelines for ethical practice. Ottawa*: CASW.

Corey, G. (2001). *Theory and practice of counseling and psychotherapy* (6th edn). Wadsworth: Brooks Cole, Thomson Learning.

Corey, G. (2008). *Theory and practice of counseling and psychotherapy* (8th edn). Toronto, ON: Thomson Learning.

Dominelli, L. (2002). *Feminist social work theory and practice.* Basingstoke: Palgrave Macmillan.

Healy, K. (2005). *Social work theories in context: Creating frameworks for practice.* Basingstoke: Palgrave Macmillan.

Herman, J. (1992). *Trauma and recovery: The aftermath of violence—from domestic abuse to political terror.* New York, NY: Basic Books.

Ife, J. (1997). *Rethinking social work: Towards critical practice.* South Melbourne: Longman.

Maidment, J., & Egan, R. (Eds). (2004). *Practice skills in social work and welfare: More than just common sense.* Crows Nest: Allen & Unwin.

Mullaly, B., & Dupre, M. (2019). *The new structural social work: Ideology, theory, and practice* (4th edn). Toronto, ON: Oxford University Press.

Mullaly, B., & West, J. (2018). *Challenging oppression: A critical approach to anti-oppressive and anti-privilege theory and practice.* Toronto, ON: Oxford University Press.

Payne, M. (2005). *Modern social work theory* (3rd edn). Chicago, IL: Lyceum Books.

Pease, B., & Fook, J. (Eds). (1999). *Transforming social work practice: Postmodern critical perspectives.* St Leonards: Allen & Unwin.

Shin, R.Q. (2015). The application of critical consciousness and intersectionality as tools for decolonizing racial/ethnic identity development models in the fields of counseling and psychology. In R.D. Goodman & P C. Gorski (Eds), *Decolonizing "multicultural" counseling through social justice* (pp. 11–22). New York, NY: Springer.

Tong, R. (1998). *Feminist thought: A more comprehensive introduction* (2nd edn). St Leonards: Allen & Unwin.

Trevithick, P. (1998). *Feminism and psychotherapy: Reflections on contemporary theories and practices.* London: Sage.

Wakefield, S. (2017). *Transformative and feminist leadership for women's rights.* Oxfam Research Backgrounder. Retrieved from https://www.oxfamamerica.org/static/media/files/Transformative_and_Feminist_Leadership_for_Womens_Rights_1.24.17.pdf

Chapter 15

Bitter, J.R. (2009). *Theory and practice of family therapy and counseling.* Belmont, CA: Brooks/Cole.

Canadian Association of Social Workers (CASW). (2005). *Code of ethics.* Ottawa, ON: CASW.

Crossley, R., & McDonald, A. (1984). *Annie's coming out.* Ringwood: Penguin Books.

Green, R. (2003). Social work in rural areas: A personal and professional challenge. *Australian Social Work, 56*(3), 209–19.

Green, R., Gregory, R., & Mason, R. (2006). Professional distance and social work: Stretching the elastic? *Australian Social Work, 59*(4), 449–61.

Herman, J. (1992). *Trauma and recovery: The aftermath of violence—from domestic abuse to political terror.* New York, NY: Basic Books.

Klass, D.P., Silverman, P.R., & Nickman, S. (1996). *Continuing bonds: New understandings of grief.* Washington, DC: Taylor & Francis.

Lewis, J. (2002). The contribution of research findings to practice change. *MCC: Building Knowledge for Integrated Care, 10*(1), 9–12.

Loader, R. (1995). A personal statement about counselling and an exploration of the person as counselor. *Australian Social Work, 48*(2), 35–8.

Mancini, A., & Bonanno, G. (2006). Resilience in the face of potential trauma: Clinical practices and illustrations. *Journal of Clinical Psychology, 62*(8), 971–85.

Marsh, P., & Doel, M. (2005). *The task-centred book.* London: Routledge.

Miller, P. (2007). *Ethical decision-making in social work and counseling: A problem/inquiry-based approach.* Toronto: Thompson/Nelson.

Morris, T. (2006). *Social work research methods: Four alternative paradigms.* Thousand Oaks, CA: Sage.

Sheafor, B.W., & Horejsi, C.R. (2008). *Techniques and guidelines for social work practice* (8th edn). Boston, MA: Alyn & Bacon.

Shulman, L. (1999). *The skills of helping individuals, families, groups and communities.* Itasca, IL: F.E. Peacock.

Shulman, L. (2009). *The skills of helping individuals, families, groups and communities* (6th edn). Belmont, CA: Brooks/Cole.

Stansfield, C. (2006, 23 September). The two of us. *The Age, 16.*

Taylor, S. (2004). Public secrets/private pain: Difficulties encountered by victims/survivors of sexual abuse in rural communities. *Women against Violence, 15,* 12–21.

Trotter, C. (2006). *Working with involuntary clients: A guide to practice.* Thousand Oaks, CA: Sage.

Turner, F.J. (2002). *Social work practice: A Canadian perspective* (2nd edn). Toronto, ON: Prentice-Hall.

Turner, F.J. (2017). *Social work treatment: Interlocking theoretical approaches.* New York, NY: Oxford University Press.

Walsh, J. (2006). *Theories of direct social work practice.* Southbank: Thomson Brooks/Cole.

Yalom, I. (2005). *The Schopenhauer cure.* Melbourne: Scribe.

Appendix 2

Miller, P. 2007. *Ethical decision-making in social work and counseling: A problem/inquiry-based approach.* Toronto: Thompson/Nelson.

Index